Prentice Hall **LITERATURE**

PENGUIN EDITION

Reader's Notebook

Adapted Version

Grade Twelve

PEARSON

Upper Saddle River, New Jersey
Boston, Massachusetts
Chandler, Arizona
Glenview, Illinois

PEARSON

ISBN: 978-0-13-366716-5

4 5 6 7 8 9 10   V001   17 16 15 14 13 12 11 10

ACKNOWLEDGMENTS

Grateful acknowledgment is made to the following for copyrighted material:

Arthur C. Clarke
"Extra-Terrestrial Relays" by Arthur C. Clarke from *Wireless World*, October 1945, pp 305–308 © 1945.

Jonathan Clowes Ltd.
"No Witchcraft for Sale," from *African Short Stories* by Doris Lessing. Copyright © 1981 Doris Lessing.

Cumbria County Council
Table of Traffic Flow at Waterhead, Ambleside. A591 from *Transport and Policies 1999/2000, and Local Transport Plan 2001/2–2005/6*. Copyright © Cumbria County Council.

The Charles Dickens Museum
Charles Dickens Museum in London Homepage & Online Tour retrieved from *http://www. dickensmuseum.com*. Copyright © 2005 Charles Dickens Museum.

Dutton Signet
From *Beowulf* by Burton Raffel, translator. Translation copyright © 1963, renewed © 1991 by Burton Raffel.

Encyclopædia Britannica
Search results: Anglo-Saxon Poetry from *http:// search.eb.com/search?query=anglo+saxon+ poetry&x=0&y=0*. "English Literature: The Old English Period: Poetry: The major manuscripts" Copyright © 2007 by Encyclopædia Britannica.

Faber and Faber Limited
"Journey of the Magi" from *Collected Poems 1909–1962* by T. S. Eliot, copyright 1936, copyright © 1964, 1963 by T. S. Eliot.

Greater London Authority
From *The Mayor's Annual Report 2004* from *http://www.london.gov.uk/mayor/annual_report/ docs/ann_rpt_2004.pdf*. Copyright April 2004, Greater London Authority.

Harcourt, Inc.
"Journey of the Magi" from *Collected Poems 1909–1962* by T. S. Eliot, copyright 1936 by Harcourt Brace & Company, copyright © 1964, 1963 by T. S. Eliot.

A.M. Heath & Company Limited
"Shooting an Elephant" from *Shooting an Elephant and Other Essays* by George Orwell. Copyright © George Orwell, 1936.

Lake District National Park Authority
Education Service Tracking Management from *Education Service Traffic Management*. Copyright © Lake District National Park Authority.

Michelin Travel Publications
"Tintern Abbey" by Staff from *The Green Guide*. Copyright © Michelin et Cie, proprietaires-editeurs.

(Acknowledgments continue on page V68)

CONTENTS

CONTENTS

CONTENTS

CONTENTS

UNIT 3 A Turbulent Time: The Seventeenth and Eighteenth Centuries (1625–1798)

© Pearson Education

CONTENTS

CONTENTS

UNIT 4 Rebels and Dreamers:
The Romantic Period (1798–1832)

CONTENTS

CONTENTS

UNIT 5 Progress and Decline: The Victorian Period (1833–1901)

© Pearson Education

CONTENTS

UNIT 6 A Time of Rapid Change: The Modern and Postmodern Periods (1901–Present)

CONTENTS

CONTENTS

© Pearson Education

CONTENTS

CONTENTS

CONTENTS

PART 2 Turbo Vocabulary

INTERACTING WITH THE TEXT

As you read your hardcover student edition of *Prentice Hall Literature*, use the **Reader's Notebook,** Adapted Version, to guide you in learning and practicing the skills presented. In addition, many selections in your student edition are presented here in an interactive format. The notes and instruction will guide you in applying reading and literary skills and in thinking about the selection. The examples on these pages show you how to use the notes as a companion when you read.

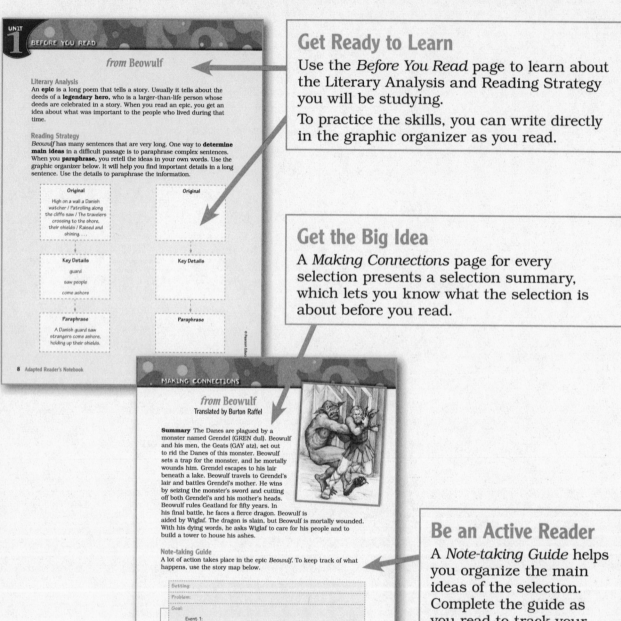

Get Ready to Learn

Use the *Before You Read* page to learn about the Literary Analysis and Reading Strategy you will be studying.

To practice the skills, you can write directly in the graphic organizer as you read.

Get the Big Idea

A *Making Connections* page for every selection presents a selection summary, which lets you know what the selection is about before you read.

Be an Active Reader

A *Note-taking Guide* helps you organize the main ideas of the selection. Complete the guide as you read to track your understanding.

Take Notes

Side-column questions accompany the selections that appear in the Reader's Notebooks. These questions are a built-in tutor to help you practice the skills and understand what you read.

Mark the Text

Use write-on lines to answer questions in the side column. You may also want to use the lines for your own notes.

When you see a pencil, you should underline, circle, or mark the text as indicated.

TAKE NOTES

Stop to Reflect
Circle the words in the bracketed section that stress how unexpected Grendel's attack will be. What do you think Grendel will do to the warriors?

_____

_____

Reading Check
Circle at least one detail that shows that Grendel is evil.

from Beowulf
Translated by Burton Raffel

Beowulf is a legend that comes out of the early Anglo-Saxon tradition. The story takes place in what today are the nations of Denmark and Sweden. As the selection opens, the Danes are celebrating at Herot, the banquet hall of the Danish king Hrothgar.¹ They eat, drink, and listen to poets singing of great heroes. Little do they know that outside in the dark is an evil monster named Grendel. Disturbed by the Danes' singing and jealous of their joy, he wishes to put an end to them.

✦ ✦ ✦

Then, when darkness had dropped, Grendel
Went up to Herot, wondering what the warriors
Would do in that hall when their drinking was done.
He found them sprawled in sleep, suspecting
Nothing, their dreams undisturbed. The monster's
Thoughts were as quick as his greed or his claws:
He slipped through the door and there in the silence
Snatched up thirty men, smashed them
Unknowing in their beds and ran out with their bodies,
The blood dripping behind him, back
To his lair, delighted with his night's slaughter.
    At daybreak, with the sun's first light, they saw
How well he had worked, and in that gray morning

Vocabulary Development
lair (LAYR) n. den; hangout

1. **Hrothgar** (RUHTH guhr).

12 Adapted Reader's Notebook

AFTER YOU READ

from Beowulf

1. **Analyze:** Epics usually tell about a battle between good and evil. Who is the "good" in this epic? Who is the "evil"? Explain how you know.

_____

_____

2. **Literary Analysis:** An **epic** shows us what people long ago thought was important. The chart below lists a feature in _Beowulf_ that people valued and tells why it pleased them. Complete the row to explain what this tells us about the Anglo-Saxons. Then, add another feature, and complete the chart.

Feature	Why It Is Pleasing	What It Tells About the Anglo-Saxons
boastful speeches	makes hero seem superhuman	

3. **Reading Strategy:** Read the last section of _Beowulf_, starting with the line "Wiglaf, lead my people" (p. 18). **Paraphrase** the lines. In your own words, tell what the lines mean.

_____

_____

Writing About the Essential Question
How does literature shape or reflect society? What does _Beowulf_ reveal about the way in which Anglo-Saxons defined evil and good?

_____

_____

from Beowulf 19

Check Your Understanding

Questions after every selection help you think about the selection. You can use the write-on lines and charts to answer the questions. Then, share your ideas in class discussions.

Essential Question

Write a short paragraph in which you connect the selection to the Essential Question.

Selections and Skills Support

The pages in your **Reader's Notebook** go with the pages in the hardcover student edition. The pages in the **Reader's Notebook** allow you to participate in class instruction and take notes on the concepts and selections.

Before You Read

Before You Read Follow along in your **Reader's Notebook** as your teacher introduces the **Vocabulary** from the selection. You can complete the **Vocabulary Practice** sentences by writing in your **Reader's Notebook.** Use the question in **Getting Ready to Read** to discuss your ideas with classmates.

Making Connections Use this page for a preview of the selection you are about to read.

- The **Summary** gives you essential points of the selection.
- Use **Writing About the Essential Question** to understand an important theme of the selection.
- Use the **Note-taking Guide** while you read the selection. Doing so will help you organize and remember information you will need later in thinking about what you have read.

While You Read

Selection Text and Sidenotes You can read the text of one selection in each pair in your **Reader's Notebook.**

- You can write in the **Reader's Notebook.** Underline important details to help you find them later.
- Use the **Take Notes** column to jot down your reactions, ideas, and answers to questions about the text. If your assigned selection is not the one that is included in the **Reader's Notebook,** use sticky notes to make your own **Take Notes** section in the side column as you read the selection in the hardcover student edition. Alternatively, you may work on a **Reader's Notebook**-styled page, available to your teacher at **www.PHLitOnline.com.**

After You Read

After You Read Use this page to answer questions about the selection right in your **Reader's Notebook.** You can complete the graphic organizer right on the page in your **Reader's Notebook.**

Vocabulary Skill Review Use this page to help you develop important vocabulary skills that will be useful to you.

Other Features in the Reader's Notebook You will also find note-taking opportunities for these features:

- Support for reading Informational Texts

The Seafarer • The Wanderer • The Wife's Lament

Literary Analysis

A lyric poem tells the thoughts and feelings of one person. **Anglo-Saxon lyrics** were written so they could be easily memorized and recited. They have these elements:

- Lines with regular rhythms, usually four strong beats.
- Caesura: rhythmic breaks in the middle of the lines. These breaks let the person saying the poem pause to take a breath.
- Kennings: two-word poetic renamings of people, places, and things. For example, *whale's home* means the sea.
- Assonance: repeated vowel sounds in unrhymed, stressed syllables (for example, "batter these ramparts")
- Alliteration: the repetition of beginning consonant sounds in words (for example, "smashing surf")

Each lyric poem in this grouping is an **elegy,** or a lyric poem that tells about the loss of someone or something.

Reading Strategy

The social and political attitudes and the cultural values during the period in which a poem was written is its **historical context.** Think about historical context as you read the poems in this grouping. Use this diagram for "The Wanderer."

Event/Idea	Event/Idea	Event/Idea
The speaker is exiled when his lord dies.		

↑ ↑ ↑

Historical Context	Historical Context	Historical Context
Anglo-Saxon warriors depended on the protection of a powerful lord.		

Word List A

Study these words from the selections. Then, complete the activities.

perched [PURCHT] *v.* seated on a high or insecure resting place
The falcon's nest was perched *on the edge of the cliff.*

whirled [WHURLD] *v.* moved rapidly in a circular manner
The couple whirled *around the dance floor as they waltzed.*

terns [TURNZ] *n.* any birds of the seagull family
Hundreds of terns *flew over the garbage dump.*

unfurl [un FUHRL] *v.* to unfold or unroll
The cabin boy learned to unfurl *the sails on the ship.*

scorch [SKAWRCH] *v.* to shrivel or parch with heat
The sun can scorch *fresh paint, causing it to blister.*

billowing [BIL oh ing] *adj.* rising and rolling in large waves
The smoke was billowing *from the chimney.*

smitten [SMITN] *v.* fascinated with someone or something; in love
The young man was smitten *with love when he read the girl's poetry.*

strive [STRYV] *v.* try very hard
Always strive *to do your best.*

Exercise A

Fill in each blank in the paragraph with the appropriate word from Word List A. Use each word only once.

The first ship builders developed the sail and the oar by trial and error. Their creations were refined as the need for larger, stronger, and faster vessels increased. At first, sailors would [1] _____ only one sail per vessel. But over the centuries, a variety of arrangements and sizes of sails were seen [2] _____ in the wind. With greater wind power, explorers did [3] _____ to go further into uncharted waters. Frightened sailors, [4] _____ on top of masts, kept a lookout for the currents that [5] _____ dangerously, threatening to sink ships. Although their skin would [6] _____ in the sun, and rations were meager, those [7] _____ by the ocean were not discouraged. Like the [8] _____ that accompanied even the earliest vessels, these seamen built their homes and thrived near the coastlines.

1. Circle the words that tell what many ancient cultures strive to do. Then, explain what *strive* means.

2. Circle the word that tells what was billowing. Then, rewrite the sentence, using a synonym for *billowing*.

3. Circle the words that explain what had the Europeans smitten. Then, describe how someone who is *smitten* might behave.

4. Circle the words that describe where the sailors perched. Explain what *perched* means.

5. Underline the word that is a clue to the meaning of scorch. Describe something that might *scorch*.

6. Circle the words that tell what the winds unfurl. Then, describe something you have seen *unfurl*.

7. Circle the phrase that describes what the terns did. Then, tell where you might find *terns*.

8. Describe how something that whirled might look.

Read the following passage. Pay special attention to the underlined words. Then, read it again and complete the activities. Use a separate sheet of paper for your written answers.

Many cultures strive to extend their knowledge of the world. The Vikings, the Arabs, and the Polynesians are noteworthy for mapping the world's oceans. These peoples were the earliest and most successful navigators. From the end of the eighth century, Scandinavians used the tides, currents, and stars to explore the rivers of Russia and the Black Sea. The billowing sails on their longships also permitted voyages across the freezing Atlantic to Iceland and North America. Once they arrived, they attempted early settlements, which quickly failed. The Norsemen were more successful in the British Isles and Northern France, where they built thriving kingdoms.

During the same period, the Arabs discovered a sea route to China, via the Strait of Malacca. This allowed more goods to be transported to Europeans who were smitten by the riches of the east.

Meanwhile, the Polynesians colonized the islands of the Pacific. Perched on their canoes and braving the hot sun that might scorch them, they trusted the winds to unfurl their sails and carry them great distances across empty oceans. Once they were closer to land, oars were essential. Without them, it was hard to avoid the reefs that destroyed larger European sailing ships centuries later.

No matter when they lived, or what part of the world they explored, these sailors had one thing in common: the companionship of the terns that hovered and whirled over their vessels.

The Seafarer
Translated by Burton Raffel

The Wanderer
Translated by Charles W. Kennedy

Summaries In **"The Seafarer,"** a sailor returns again and again to the sea. He describes the fear and loneliness of such a life. He concludes that the only home he has is the "heavenly home." **"The Wanderer"** tells of the sad journeying of a man who no longer has a lord. He wants the comforts and companionship of the mead-hall, the place where the men feast and talk. He concludes that the earth is a horrible place.

Note-taking Guide

Use this chart to recall things lost or missed by the speaker of the poem. Record examples of people, things, or experiences lost. Write the line number in parentheses after each example you find.

The Seafarer	The Wanderer
shelter and quiet of land (line 13)	his lord (line 21)

The Wife's Lament
Translated by Ann Stanford

Summary In **"The Wife's Lament,"** a woman talks about her life in the dark, overgrown place where her husband has sent her to live. She is all alone and friendless. She wishes he would experience the same grief.

Note-taking Guide
Use this chart to recall things lost or missed by the speaker of the poem. Record examples of people, things, or experiences lost. Write the line number in parentheses after each example you find.

The Wife's Lament
her husband's love and friendship (lines 21–25)

The Seafarer • The Wanderer • The Wife's Lament

1. **Literary Analysis:** An **elegy** reveals the sorrow of loss. What does the speaker feel is lost in "The Wife's Lament"?

_____

_____

2. **Literary Analysis:** What suffering is described in each poem, and what causes it? Use the graphic organizer below to record examples of suffering. Write the lesson or insight you learn about suffering from each example. Follow the example given for "The Seafarer."

Poem	Cause of Suffering	Insight Gained
The Seafarer	He feels like an outcast at home and at sea.	We are exiles on earth. Heaven is home.

3. **Reading Strategy:** Anglo-Saxon women did not have many rights. How does understanding the position of Anglo-Saxon women help you understand "A Wife's Lament"?

_____

_____

_____

? Writing About the Essential Question

What is the relationship between place and literature? How does the Anglo-Saxon sense of home compare with ours?

_____

_____

_____

_____

from Beowulf

Literary Analysis

An **epic** is a long poem that tells a story. Usually it tells about the deeds of a **legendary hero,** who is a larger-than-life person whose deeds are celebrated in a story. When you read an epic, you get an idea about what was important to the people who lived during that time.

Reading Strategy

Beowulf has many sentences that are very long. One way to **determine main ideas** in a difficult passage is to paraphrase complex sentences. When you **paraphrase,** you retell the ideas in your own words. Use the graphic organizer below. It will help you find important details in a long sentence. Use the details to paraphrase the information.

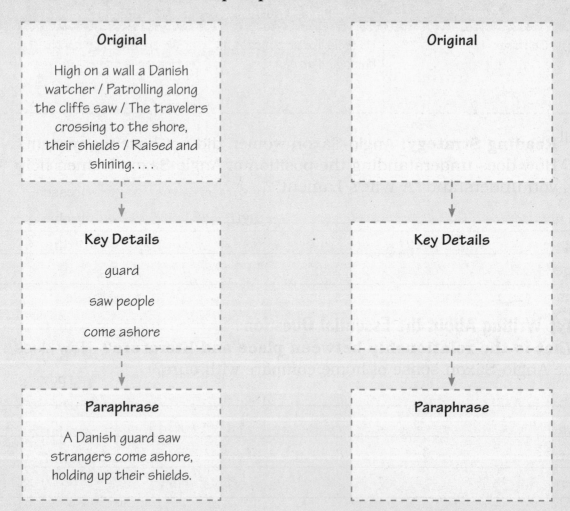

Original

High on a wall a Danish watcher / Patrolling along the cliffs saw / The travelers crossing to the shore, their shields / Raised and shining. . . .

Original

Key Details

guard

saw people

come ashore

Key Details

Paraphrase

A Danish guard saw strangers come ashore, holding up their shields.

Paraphrase

Word List A

Study these words from the selection. Then, complete the activities.

mail [MAYL] *n.* armor made of connected metal rings, or loops of chain
  The museum displayed chain mail that was designed to protect a horse.

fleeing [FLEE ing] *adj.* running away; vanishing
  When it rained on the baseball field, the fleeing players ran to the dugouts.

boast [BOHST] *v.* speak with excessive pride; brag
  The team captain told his players not to boast even though they were undefeated.

inherited [in HER i tid] *v.* received property from a person by a will
  Mary inherited an antique silver tea service from her grandmother.

feud [FYOOD] *n.* a long, bitter quarrel, especially between families
  The man refused to enter the store because his family was in a feud with the owner's family.

protector [proh TEK ter] *n.* someone or something who guards others from harm
  Joe never got into any fights at school because his older brother was his protector.

truce [TROOS] *n.* an agreement to stop fighting
  The two countries signed a truce agreeing not to fight during the holiday.

swayed [SWAYD] *v.* shifted from side to side; rocked back and forth
  The dancers swayed with the music, moving back and forth.

Exercise A

Fill in each blank in the paragraph with the appropriate word from Word List A.

Many illustrations depict dragons as green, scaly reptiles with wings and claws. Typically, they are shown battling medieval knights that are dressed in chain [1] _____. Sometimes these mythological creatures perched on top of a priceless, stolen treasure, acting as its [2] _____. According to legend, attacking the dragon was tricky, since it moved quickly. You can imagine its hypnotic movements as it [3] _____ from side to side. Dragons liked to [4] _____ about their incredible strength, hoping to frighten the hero. Once angered, the creature sought revenge, breathing fire and chasing after [5] _____ villagers. If the dragon could not be overpowered, it had to be outsmarted. However, negotiating a [6] _____ with the dragon was almost impossible. Defeating the dragon could be part of a larger battle or an ongoing [7] _____ that has raged for centuries. Often, the hero had [8] _____ his mission from previous generations.

1. Circle the words that describe what <u>mail</u> is made of. Then, explain why *mail* offered a good defense.

2. Rewrite the sentence using a phrase that means the same as <u>swayed</u>. Then, tell what *swayed* means.

3. What is a likely reason mail did not serve as a <u>protector</u> from a bullet? Explain what *protector* means.

4. Circle the words that tell why knights would <u>boast</u> about their ornate armor. Then, tell what *boast* means.

5. Circle the words that tell from whom a knight <u>inherited</u> mail. Why might it be helpful to have *inherited* mail?

6. Underline the phrase that is a clue to the meaning of <u>truce</u>. Why might some battles end with a *truce* instead of a victory?

7. Circle the word that is a clue to the meaning of <u>feud</u>. Explain how a *feud* might differ from a war.

8. Rewrite the sentence using a synonym for <u>fleeing</u>. Describe something you have seen *fleeing*.

Read the following passage. Pay special attention to the underlined words. Then, read it again, and complete the activities. Use a separate sheet of paper for your written answers.

<u>Mail</u> is body armor made from chain links woven together to form a metal fabric. It is then fashioned into gloves, hoods, shirts, and leggings that cover the entire body from head to toe. From the time of the Roman conquest until the mid-fourteenth century, mail was the best available defense against the sword and lance that dominated hand-to-hand combat.

The metal mesh allowed the warrior flexibility as he lifted his weapon or <u>swayed</u> to avoid an enemy's blade. However, mail was not a <u>protector</u> from the piercing power of a crossbow bolt or a bullet. By the end of the 1600s, mail was no longer used for protection.

Because it was so expensive, mail was worn only by the wealthiest warriors. The cost did not come from the material, but from the time required to assemble it. Tiny rings made from short lengths of iron or steel wire were fastened together with a small rivet. Next, the clusters of rings were attached together to form a seamless garment. The typical knight also wore a solid helmet and a breastplate, and carried a shield.

Knights would <u>boast</u> about ornate armor since it indicated wealth and position. Mail might be something a knight <u>inherited</u> from his father and then passed on to his own offspring. However, armor was also taken as bounty or offered as part of a <u>truce</u> when a battle or <u>feud</u> ended.

The knights of the Crusades wore chain mail armor. Although it wasn't as heavy as plate armor, it still weighed more than the leather armor worn by the Moors. The lighter leather gave the Moors and their horses much greater mobility on the battlefield. Even when <u>fleeing</u>, they had an advantage.

from Beowulf
Translated by Burton Raffel

Summary The Danes are plagued by a monster named Grendel (GREN dul). Beowulf and his men, the Geats (GAY atz), set out to rid the Danes of this monster. Beowulf sets a trap for the monster, and he mortally wounds him. Grendel escapes to his lair beneath a lake. Beowulf travels to Grendel's lair and battles Grendel's mother. He wins by seizing the monster's sword and cutting off both Grendel's and his mother's heads. Beowulf rules Geatland for fifty years. In his final battle, he faces a fierce dragon. Beowulf is aided by Wiglaf. The dragon is slain, but Beowulf is mortally wounded. With his dying words, he asks Wiglaf to care for his people and to build a tower to house his ashes.

Note-taking Guide

A lot of action takes place in the epic *Beowulf.* To keep track of what happens, use the story map below.

Setting:

Problem:

Goal:

Event 1:

Event 2:

Event 3:

Event 4:

Climax:

Resolution:

Stop to Reflect

Circle the words in the bracketed section that stress how unexpected Grendel's attack will be. What do you think Grendel will do to the warriors?

_____

_____

_____

Reading Check ✎

Circle at least one detail that shows that Grendel is evil.

from Beowulf
Translated by Burton Raffel

Beowulf is a legend that comes out of the early Anglo-Saxon tradition. The story takes place in what today are the nations of Denmark and Sweden. As the selection opens, the Danes are celebrating at Herot, the banquet hall of the Danish king Hrothgar.[1] They eat, drink, and listen to poets singing of great heroes. Little do they know that outside in the dark is an evil monster named Grendel. Disturbed by the Danes' singing and jealous of their joy, he wishes to put an end to them.

◆ ◆ ◆

Then, when darkness had dropped, Grendel
Went up to Herot, wondering what the
    warriors
Would do in that hall when their drinking was
    done.
He found them sprawled in sleep, suspecting
Nothing, their dreams undisturbed. The
    monster's
Thoughts were as quick as his greed or his
    claws:
He slipped through the door and there in the
    silence
Snatched up thirty men, smashed them
Unknowing in their beds and ran out with
    their bodies,
The blood dripping behind him, back
To his lair, delighted with his night's slaughter.
  At daybreak, with the sun's first light, they saw
How well he had worked, and in that gray
    morning

Vocabulary Development
lair (LAYR) *n.* den; hangout

1. **Hrothgar** (RUHTH guhr).

Broke their long feast with tears and laments
For the dead. Hrothgar, their lord, sat joyless
In Herot, a mighty prince mourning
The fate of his lost friends and companions,
Knowing by its tracks that some demon had
 torn
His followers apart. He wept, fearing
The beginning might not be the end. And that
 night
Grendel came again. . . .

⬧   ⬧   ⬧

For twelve long years, Grendel continues to attack the Danes. Stories of their sorrow reach across the sea to the land of the Geats,[2] where Beowulf, nephew of the Geat king, hears of the horror. Beowulf has already won fame and glory for his powerful fighting skills. Hoping to win more, he sails to the land of the Danes to help Hrothgar and his people. That night, Grendel attacks Herot again.

⬧   ⬧   ⬧

Grendel snatched at the first Geat
He came to, ripped him apart, cut
His body to bits with powerful jaws,
Drank the blood from his veins and bolted
Him down, hands and feet; death
And Grendel's great teeth came together,
Snapping life shut. Then he stepped to another
Still body, clutched at Beowulf with his claws,
Grasped at a strong-hearted wakeful sleeper
—And was instantly seized himself, claws
Bent back as Beowulf leaned up on one arm.

© Pearson Education

Vocabulary Development
bolted (BOHL ted) *v.* swallowed

2. **Geats** (GAY atz) a people living in what today is the northern European nation of Sweden.

TAKE NOTES

Reading Strategy

Circle the letter of the choice below that best **paraphrases** the underlined lines.

a. He cried because he has missed the start of the attack and could do little at the end.
b. He cried because he was afraid there might be more attacks.
c. He cried because he feared a different monster would come.
d. He cried because his rule of Denmark was beginning to end.

Reading Check

What do you think will happen when Grendel attacks this second man? Write your prediction on these lines.

_____

_____

_____

Stop to Reflect

Who is the "shepherd of evil" and "guardian of crime"? Write this character's name:

_____

What do the phrases "shepherd of evil" and "guardian of crime" stress about this character? Circle the letter of the best answer below.

a. He is powerful but bad.

b. He is cowardly but good.

c. He lives in a rural area.

d. He will not live much longer.

Reading Check

What has happened here? Circle the letter of the best answer below.

a. Beowulf failed to kill Grendel, who crawls off to fight another day.

b. Having received a fatal wound, Grendel crawls off to die.

c. Beowulf killed Grendel on the spot and now goes to Grendel's den.

d. Beowulf and Grendel fought to a draw and will now make peace.

That shepherd of evil, guardian of crime,
Knew at once that nowhere on earth
Had he met a man whose hands were harder;
His mind was flooded with fear—but nothing
Could take his <u>talons</u> and himself from that
     tight
Hard grip. . . .
The monster's hatred rose higher,
But his power had gone. He twisted in pain,
And the bleeding <u>sinews</u> deep in his shoulder
Snapped, muscle and bone split
And broke. The battle was over, Beowulf
Had been granted new glory: Grendel
     escaped,
But wounded as he was could flee to his den,
His miserable hole at the bottom of the
     marsh
Only to die. . . .

◆ ◆ ◆

The Danes are delighted by Grendel's death and honor Beowulf that night in celebrations. But another monster still threatens them—Grendel's mother. Outraged by her son's death, she attacks Herot that very night. She kills Hrothgar's friend and then returns to her lair at the bottom of the lake. Beowulf bravely follows.

◆ ◆ ◆

     Then he saw
The mighty water witch and swung his sword,
His ring-marked blade, straight at her
     head; . . .
     But her guest

Vocabulary Development

talons (TA luhnz) *n.* claws

sinews (SIN yooz) *n.* tendons; cords that connect muscles to bones and other body parts

Discovered that no sword could slice her evil
Skin, that Hrunting[3] could not hurt her, was useless
Now when he needed it. They wrestled, she
　　ripped
And tore and clawed at him, bit holes in his
　　helmet,
And that too failed him; for the first time in
　　years
Of being worn to war it would earn no glory;
It was the last time anyone would wear it.
　　　　But Beowulf
Longed only for fame, leaped back
Into battle. He tossed his sword aside,
Angry; the steel-edged blade lay where
He'd dropped it. If weapons were useless he'd
　　use
His hands, the strength in his fingers. So fame
Comes to men who mean to win it
And care about nothing else! . . .
　　　　Then he saw, hanging on the wall, a heavy
Sword, hammered by giants, strong
And blessed with their magic, the best of all
　　weapons
But so massive that no ordinary man could
　　lift
Its carved and decorated length. He drew it
From its scabbard, broke the chain on its hilt,
And then, savage, now, angry
And desperate, lifted it high over his head

Vocabulary Development

massive (MAS iv) *adj.* big and solid

hilt (HILT) *n.* the top section of a sword, where there is a handle to grip

---

3. **Hrunting** (RUHNT ing) the name of Beowulf's sword. Valuable swords were often given names.

TAKE NOTES

Literary Analysis

Circle two details in the first bracketed passage that show that Beowulf wants to win glory as a **legendary hero**. Which qualities below does Beowulf display in the passage? Circle the letter of the best answer.

a. courage and strength
b. skill and modesty
c. anger and jealousy
d. kindness and honesty

Reading Strategy

Analyzing details can lead you to the **main idea**. Circle three or four details that you would include in a **paraphrase** of the second bracketed passage. Then, write the passage in your own words on the lines below.

_____

_____

_____

_____

_____

_____

_____

_____

TAKE NOTES

Stop to Reflect ✎

Why is this sword able to kill Grendel's mother when Beowulf's own sword, Hrunting, could not? Circle an earlier detail in the second bracketed passage on page 9 that helps you answer.

_____

_____

_____

Literary Analysis 🔍

List two ways in which Beowulf's behavior here displays qualities of a **legendary hero**.

1. _____

_____

2. _____

_____

And struck with all the strength he had left,
Caught her in the neck and cut it through,
Broke bones and all. Her body fell
To the floor, lifeless, the sword was wet
With her blood, and Beowulf <u>rejoiced</u> at the
      sight.

◆　◆　◆

After being honored by Hrothgar, Beowulf and the other Geats return home. There Beowulf eventually becomes king. He rules with success for fifty years. Then a Geat man steals a drinking cup from a treasure in a tower guarded by a fire-breathing dragon. When the angry dragon attacks his kingdom, Beowulf, despite old age, goes to battle the creature.

◆　◆　◆

Then Beowulf rose, still brave, still strong,
And with his shield at his side, and a mail
      shirt[4] on his breast,
<u>Strode</u> calmly, confidently, toward the tower,
      under
The rocky cliffs; no coward could have walked
      there! . . .
      The beast rose, angry,
Knowing a man had come—and then nothing
But war could have followed. Its breath came
      first,
A steaming cloud pouring from the stone,
Then the earth itself shook. Beowulf
Swung his shield into place. . . .

Vocabulary Development
rejoiced (re JOYST) _v._ took joy in; was happy
strode (STROHD) _v._ walked

4. **mail shirt** a shirt made out of metal links that give protection in battle.

The Geats'
Great prince stood firm, unmoving, prepared
Behind his high shield, waiting in his
        shining
Armor. The monster came quickly toward
        him,
Pouring out fire and smoke, hurrying
To its fate. Flames beat at the iron
Shield, and for a time it held, protected
Beowulf as he'd planned; then it began to melt,
And for the first time in his life that famous
        prince
Fought with fate against him, with glory
Denied him. He knew it, but he raised his
        sword
And struck at the dragon's scaly hide.
The ancient blade broke, bit into
The monster's skin, drew blood, but
        cracked
And failed him before it went deep enough,
        helped him
Less than he needed. The dragon leaped
With pain, thrashed and beat at him,
        spouting
Murderous flames, spreading them
        everywhere.

◆ ◆ ◆

   All of Beowulf's subjects have fled in
terror except Wiglaf, who fights at Beowulf's
side. But though Beowulf manages to kill the
dragon, he receives a fatal wound himself.
Gasping, he reminds Wiglaf to claim the
dragon's treasure for the Geats. He then
gives his final instructions.

◆ ◆ ◆

Reading Check

What happens to Beowulf's shield? What causes it to happen? Circle the cause, and label it *cause*. Then, circle what happens, and label it *effect*.

Literary Analysis

Circle the detail in the bracketed passage that shows the early Anglo-Saxon belief in fate guiding human affairs. Based on this passage, what other values does this **epic** reflect?

_____

_____

_____

Reading Strategy

Paraphrase the underlined sentence. Write it on these lines in your own words.

_____

_____

_____

_____

Vocabulary Development
thrashed (THRASHT) *v.* moved wildly

© Pearson Education

TAKE NOTES

Read Fluently

Read Beowulf's speech here aloud. Practice any words that are difficult to pronounce. Make sure you understand all of the words.

Stop to Reflect

What did Beowulf expect to happen to the dragon's treasure? Circle the words in the last paragraph on page 17 that tell you. Then, explain why you think the treasure is buried with Beowulf.

_____

_____

_____

Literary Analysis 🔍

Based on this closing portion of the **epic**, what do the early Anglo-Saxons seem to admire in their leaders?

_____

_____

_____

"... Wiglaf, lead my people,
Help them; my time is gone. Have
The brave Geats build me a tomb,
When the funeral flames have burned me, and
    build it
Here, at the water's edge, high
On this <u>spit</u> of land, so sailors can see
This tower, and remember my name, and
    call it
Beowulf's tower. . . ."
    Then the Geats built the tower, as Beowulf
Had asked, strong and tall, so sailors
Could find it from far and wide; working
For ten long days they made his monument,
Sealed his ashes in walls as straight
And high as wise and willing hands
Could raise them. And the riches he and Wiglaf
Had won from the dragon, rings, necklaces,
Ancient, hammered armor—all
The treasures they'd taken were left there, too,
Silver and jewels buried in the sandy
Ground, back in the earth, again
And forever hidden and useless to men.
And then twelve of the bravest Geats
Rode their horses around the tower,
Telling their sorrow, telling stories
Of their dead king and his greatness, his glory,
Praising him for heroic deeds, for a life
As noble as his name, . . .
Crying that no better king had ever
Lived, no prince so mild, no man
So open to his people, so deserving of praise.

Vocabulary Development
spit (SPIT) *n.* a narrow point of land

18 Adapted Reader's Notebook

© Pearson Education

from Beowulf

1. **Analyze:** Epics usually tell about a battle between good and evil. Who is the "good" in this epic? Who is the "evil"? Explain how you know.

_____

_____

2. **Literary Analysis:** An **epic** shows us what people long ago thought was important. The chart below lists a feature in *Beowulf* that people valued and tells why it pleased them. Complete the row to explain what this tells us about the Anglo-Saxons. Then, add another feature, and complete the chart.

Feature	Why It Is Pleasing	What It Tells About the Anglo-Saxons
boastful speeches	makes hero seem superhuman	

3. **Reading Strategy:** Read the last section of *Beowulf*, starting with the line "Wiglaf, lead my people" (p. 18). **Paraphrase** the lines. In your own words, tell what the lines mean.

_____

_____

_____

_____

Writing About the Essential Question

How does literature shape or reflect society? What does *Beowulf* reveal about the way in which Anglo-Saxons defined evil and good?

_____

_____

_____

© Pearson Education

Web Site Search Tools

About Web Site Search Tools

A **Web site search tool** helps you find information in a Web site. Many Web sites, such as encyclopedia Web sites, include search programs that allow you to use keywords to search for information. Keywords are important terms related to a subject. When you use a general keyword, the search program returns many pages of results. Specific keywords are more useful because they result in fewer pages that are more closely related to your topic.

For example, suppose you are looking for information on Anglo Saxon poetry. The search term *poetry* will call up many pages, or hits, about all kinds of poetry. A search using the keywords *anglo saxon poetry* will locate information about only poetry fitting that category.

In addition to text articles, many Web sites have search programs that will provide links to other media or other Web sites.

Reading Skill

Certain sources of information work best for certain research topics. For example, articles are probably the most useful source for a research paper on Anglo Saxon poetry. Keep in mind the best sources for your topic as you **evaluate the appropriateness of a search result.**

For a focused search, avoid Web sites that do not reflect the topic or the type of information you need. In addition, avoid sites that are not recognized by experts or sponsored by noteworthy institutions. You may need to modify your keywords to broaden or narrow the focus of your search.

Complete the chart below to illustrate how you would organize a search.

Research Topic	Search Keywords	Useful Types of Information	Information to Avoid
• Anglo Saxon poetry	•	•	•
	•	•	•
	•	•	•

Jump to: navigation, search

🔍 Old English poetry

ENCYCLOPEDIA
BRITANNICA › **online**

Home | Blog | Board | Newsletters | International | Store

English Literature — The Major Manuscripts

The Old English period > Poetry > The major manuscripts

Most Old English poetry is preserved in four manuscripts of the late 10th and early 11th centuries. The Beowulf manuscript (British Library) contains *Beowulf, Judith*, and three prose tracts; the Exeter Book (Exeter Cathedral) is a miscellaneous gathering of lyrics, riddles, didactic poems, and religious narratives; the Junius Manuscript (Bodleian Library, Oxford)—also called the Caedmon Manuscript, even though its contents are no longer attributed to Caedmon—contains biblical paraphrases; and the Vercelli Book (found in the cathedral library in Vercelli, Italy) contains saints' lives, several short religious poems, and prose homilies. In addition to the poems in these books are historical poems in the Anglo-Saxon Chronicle; poetic renderings of Psalms 51–150; the 31 Metres included in King Alfred the Great's translation of Boethius's *De consolatione philosophiae (Consolation of Philosophy)*; magical, didactic, elegiac, and heroic poems; and others, miscellaneously interspersed with prose, jotted in margins, and even worked in stone or metal.

Words in blue are hyperlinks or connections to other sources.

Related Topics

Poetry

from the English literature *article*

The Norman Conquest worked no immediate transformation on either the language or the literature of the English. Older poetry continued to be copied during the last half of the 11th century; two poems . . .

Development as a poet

from the Pound, Ezra *article*

Unsettled by the slaughter of World War I and the spirit of hopelessness he felt was pervading England after its conclusion, Pound decided to move to Paris, publishing before he left two of his most . . .

lament

a nonnarrative poem expressing deep grief or sorrow over a personal loss. The form developed as part of the oral tradition along with heroic poetry and exists in most languages. Examples include . . .

Chadwick, H. Munro

English philologist and historian, professor of Anglo-Saxon at the University of Cambridge (1912–41), who helped develop an integral approach to Old English studies.

The major manuscripts

from the English literature *article*

Most Old English poetry is preserved in four manuscripts of the late 10th and early 11th centuries. The Beowulf manuscript (British Library) contains Beowulf, Judith, and three prose tracts; the . . .

The Eddaic verse forms

from the Scandinavian literature *article*

Three metres are commonly distinguished in Eddaic poetry: the epic measure, the speech measure, and the song measure. Most narrative poems were in the first measure, which consisted of short lines of . . .

Alliterative verse

from the English literature *article*

Virtually all Old English poetry is written in a single metre, a four-stress line with a syntactical break, or caesura, between the second and third stresses, and with alliteration linking the two . . .

Lattimore, Richmond

American poet and translator renowned for his disciplined yet poetic translations of Greek classics.

> Each source listed provides clarification and additional information.

Caedmon

first Old English Christian poet, whose fragmentary hymn to the creation remains a symbol of the adaptation of the aristocratic-heroic Anglo-Saxon verse tradition to the expression of Christian . . .

The golden age of Bede

from the United Kingdom *article*

Within a century of Augustine's landing, England was in the forefront of scholarship. This high standard arose from a combination of influences: that from Ireland, which had escaped the decay caused . . .

Exeter Book

the largest extant collection of Old English poetry. Copied c. 975, the manuscript was given to Exeter Cathedral by Bishop Leofric (died 1072). It begins with some long religious poems: the Christ, . . .

Thinking About Web Site Search Tools

1. How many hits, or results, did the Web site's search program find for anglo saxon poetry?

   _____

2. Examine the links in the paragraph about the Old English period. Which link would you use to learn more about Old English riddles and didactic poems?

   _____

TALK ABOUT IT Reading Skill

3. Which hit would you use if you decided to learn more about preserved copies of Beowulf? How do you know?

   _____

4. Other than an encyclopedia Web site, what other types of Web sites might provide useful information about anglo saxon poetry?

   _____

WRITE ABOUT IT Timed Writing: Explanation (25 minutes)

Create a chart for a new research topic related to British literature. Use the chart from the Informational Texts page as a model. Explain why you chose each search keyword. Also explain which types of Web sites and information would be best for your topic.

To help you get started, think about stories, poems, or plays you have read in class. Then, list three possible research topics below.

_____

_____

_____

Circle the topic you would most like to research. Choose three keywords for the search. Be as specific as possible. Use these notes as you complete the chart and finish your written response.

from A History of the English Church and People

Literary Analysis

Historical writing tells the story of past events using research evidence. A historical writer checks the research to make sure it is accurate. Checking research helps a writer take a step back in time from the beliefs of people around them. You can see this historical "step back" in a sentence from Bede's *History:* "Britain, formerly known as Albion, is an island in the ocean. . . ." Bede left behind his tiny corner of England when he wrote this sentence. He wrote for a wider world that did not know much about Britain.

Reading Strategy

Nonfiction texts tell about real places and events. Writers of nonfiction use these **characteristics** to achieve their **purposes,** or goals.

- suitable **language,** or word choice
- an appropriate **style,** or way of writing, including clear **syntax,** or sentence structure
- effective **rhetorical strategies,** such as examples, descriptions, comparisons, and narration

Use a chart like this one to note other characteristics of nonfiction that Bede uses to achieve his purpose.

Purpose:	
Language	
Style	
Rhetorical Strategy	

Word List A

Study these words from the selection. Then, complete the activities.

amber [AM ber] *n.* hard, semiclear yellow or orange natural resin
   Her yellow bracelet is made of amber, not plastic.

breadth [BREDTH] *n.* width
   The breadth of many doorways is 30 inches.

climate [KLY muht] *n.* ordinary or average weather conditions of a place
   The mild, rainy climate in England is perfect for growing roses.

extracted [ek STRAK tid] *v.* drew out; pulled out
   He extracted a confession from the criminal.

fortified [FAWRT uh fyd] *adj.* strengthened against military attack
   The fortified walls of the castle were three feet thick.

horizon [huh RY zuhn] *n.* the line where the earth and sky seem to meet
   At sunset, the sun appears to move below the horizon.

lingers [LIN guhrz] *v.* continues to stay
   Sometimes a customer lingers and must be asked to leave when a shop is closing.

twilight [TWY lyt] *n.* early evening; the soft light at the end of the day
   After sunset, I could barely see my friend's face in the dim twilight.

Exercise A

Fill in the blanks, using each word from Word List A only once.

   The Age of the Vikings began in the late 700s when raiding Norwegians began attacking Scotland and Ireland. During these raids, the Vikings looted monasteries and [1] _____ valuable objects from them, including some decorated with pearls, [2] _____, and other precious stones. It was the custom to bury a Viking with his possessions, so evidence of these long-ago thefts [3] _____ in Viking burial sites. Successful Viking attacks required fast ships and a favorable [4] _____. The eighth century had mild winters that made long sea voyages possible. Vikings found their way across the [5] _____ of the ocean by using a few different techniques, such as observing the point where the sun rose and set on the [6] _____. As soon as [7] _____ came, they would land, leaving their boats. After conquering an area, the Vikings established their own [8] _____ settlements.

© Pearson Education

1. Circle the word that tells what was made of amber. Then, describe *amber*.

2. Underline the words that tell what was extracted. Write a sentence using the word *extracted*.

3. Underline the words that give a clue to the meaning of the word fortified. What is the opposite of *fortified*?

4. Circle the word that tells what crosses the horizon. Then, tell what *horizon* means.

5. Underline the words that describe twilight. Then, explain what *twilight* is.

6. Circle the words that tell what lingers. Then, underline the words that tell why it *lingers*.

7. Circle the words that describe the breadth of many stones. Give a synonym for *breadth*.

8. Circle the word that is a clue to the meaning of the word climate. What word could be substituted for the word *climate* in this sentence?

Read the following passage. Then, complete the activities.

Early British peoples have left behind relics of their communities, including tools, silver, gold, and amber jewelry, pottery, and other objects. But perhaps the most famous remainder of Britain's early peoples is the remarkable Stonehenge.

Stonehenge is a combination of manmade mounds and a circle of huge stones. It was built in stages between 3000 B.C. and 1600 B.C. on Salisbury Plain in southern England.

No explanation of the original purpose served by Stonehenge has been conclusively verified. But scholars have extracted a lot of information about Stonehenge, drawing out their facts from studying the position of its stones. It is clear this was not intended to be a fortified place, strengthened against attack from a warring people. Instead, the stones were arranged to mark events in the sky. On the summer solstice, one stone lines up with the rising sun just as the sun crosses the horizon and becomes visible over the rim of the Earth. The stones also line up with the moon and the stars at various times. Stonehenge may also have been used as a temple for ceremonies held in the dim light of twilight. However, the mystery of Stonehenge has not yet been solved and lingers still, continuing to puzzle scientists.

What is certain is that the construction process required great labor, time, and skill. Stones had to be transported for miles across the land, an incredible feat. Many of the stones were more than thirteen feet in height, seven feet in breadth, and more than three feet thick.

Over time, some stones have been stolen and put to other uses. The rainy climate and the thousands of visitors have caused additional damage. Access to the site is now regulated. Stonehenge has been designated a World Heritage Site by the United Nations.

from A History of the English Church and People

Bede
Translated by
Leo Sherley-Price

Summary Bede describes Britain's geography and natural resources. He then focuses on its four different nations. Each nation speaks its own language. He tells why each group settled in the area it did. Bede also describes Ireland.

Note-taking Guide

Use the chart below to compare and contrast England and Ireland. In the outer circles, record how England and Ireland are different. In the center, where the circles overlap, note how they are the same.

England   Ireland

Both

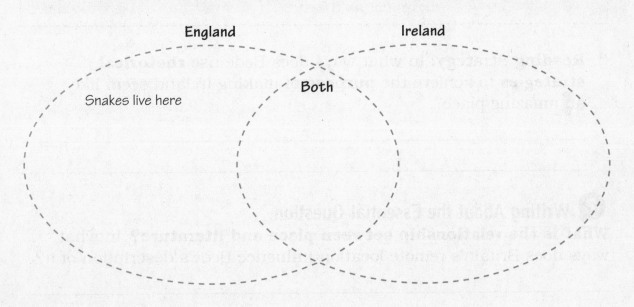

Snakes live here

from A History of the English Church and People

1. **Interpret:** What factors are important in uniting a people and giving them a common identity?

_____

_____

2. **Literary Analysis:** Evaluate Bade's *History* as **historical writing.** Use the chart below. Give examples of where you thought the author provided too little information or evidence. List examples of where the organization helped or did not help understanding. Follow the example given.

Necessary Background	Evidence	Clear Organization
"Five languages and four nations"	"English, British, Scots, Picts, & Latin"	The organization makes it easier to understand.

3. **Reading Strategy:** In what ways does Bede use **rhetorical strategies** to achieve the **purpose** of making Ireland seem like an amazing place?

_____

_____

Writing About the Essential Question

What is the relationship between place and literature? In what ways does Britain's remote location influence Bede's description of it?

_____

_____

_____

_____

_____

from The Canterbury Tales: The Prologue

Literary Analysis

As you read the Prologue, look for the following types of **characterization,** or ways of describing character:

- **Direct characterization** uses direct statements made about a character.
- **Indirect characterization** uses actions, thoughts, and speech to show a character's personality.

Each character in *The Canterbury Tales* is from a different part of society in Chaucer's time. By showing the strengths and weaknesses of each, Chaucer gives **social commentary,** writing that makes a point about society, its values, and its customs.

Reading Strategy

One way to repair your comprehension when you encounter challenging passages is to **analyze difficult sentences.** Ask the questions *when, who, where, what, why,* and *how* to figure out the main information in the sentence. Complete a chart like the one below to analyze difficult sentences.

When?	
Who?	
Where?	
What?	
Why?	
How?	

Word List A

Study these words from the selection. Then, complete the activities.

adversity [ad VER si tee] *n.* great hardship; misfortune
   Forest fires, droughts, and mudslides can cause adversity for people.

courteous [KUR tee us] *adj.* considerate of others; polite
   It is important for a receptionist to be courteous to visitors.

devout [di VOWT] *adj.* extremely religious; pious
   The devout woman could be seen going to church every day.

dispense [di SPENS] *v.* administer; distribute in portions
   It was the head nurse's responsibility to dispense the medicine.

distinguished [di STING gwisht] *adj.* marked by excellence; well-known
   All the world leaders respected the distinguished diplomat.

pilgrimages [PIL gruhm ij iz] *n.* journeys to shrines or sacred places
   The man has made pilgrimages to Mecca and other religious cities.

prudent [PROOD uhnt] *adj.* using good judgment; acting wisely
   The prudent shopper spends less than he or she earns.

repented [ree PENT id] *v.* felt remorse or regret; resolved to reform
   The thief repented and returned the stolen items.

Exercise A

Fill in each blank in the paragraph with the appropriate word from Word List A.
Use each word only once.

During the eleventh and twelfth centuries, kings often commissioned the construction of cathedrals—they thought it would be [1] _____ to be seenas supporters of the church. The builders were not generally important or [2] _____ people. Instead, they were ordinary people who contributed their labor and skill. Often progress was slowed by hardships, but despite the [3] _____, the workers dedicated themselves to these stone masterpieces.

In cathedrals, [4] _____ Christians prayed piously and [5] _____ their sins. Some cathedrals were not just places of worship but also the destination of [6] _____. In addition, they were centers of learning. They explored subjects from serious philosophy to the rules of [7] _____ behavior. To students who met the requirements, they would [8] _____ degrees. In many ways, then, the cathedral was the center of medieval society.

Read the following passage. Pay special attention to the underlined words. Then, read it again, and complete the activities. Use a separate sheet of paper for your written answers.

Travel in the Middle Ages was slow and difficult, and travelers were subject to <u>adversity</u>. People who were well-known and excellent in their field—<u>distinguished</u> scholars, for example—as well as pilgrims and actors moved freely through Europe. Most people, however, never wandered more than a few miles from their birthplace. If they did go on journeys or <u>pilgrimages</u>, they were guided by the advice of other travelers. This advice was not reliable, however, because travel conditions changed constantly. Maps did not offer much help either, because they were often inaccurate.

Medieval travelers usually set off on foot or by oxcart, since horses were a luxury reserved for the wealthy. If conditions were favorable, a traveler could walk about twenty miles a day. Conditions were rarely favorable, however. Even the main roads were little more than paths that became impassable during snowstorms and rainstorms. Dense woods hid thieves and bandits who preyed on passersby. Inns offered meals and beds, but they were not pleasant places. Sometimes guests were not <u>courteous</u>—they might treat a fellow traveler rudely. Not infrequently, too, guests might be dishonest. Therefore, <u>prudent</u> travelers set forth in groups, hoping to find protection in numbers.

A ship or riverboat was a quicker, less expensive option for traveling a long distance. Travel by water had its own perils, however. Storms and pirates made it just as dangerous as travel by land. Still, many <u>devout</u> Christians, who valued religious acts more than personal safety, undertook journeys to the Holy Land or to shrines closer to home. There, wishing to cleanse themselves of remorse, they <u>repented</u> their sins. They believed that the church would <u>dispense</u> spiritual pardons, granting forgiveness because of the severe hardships they endured.

1. Circle the words that hint at the meaning of <u>adversity</u>. Write a sentence about overcoming *adversity*.

2. Underline the words that explain what might make a person <u>distinguished</u>. Describe someone who is *distinguished*.

3. Underline the words that tell what travelers relied on when they went on <u>pilgrimages</u>. Define *pilgrimages* in your own words.

4. Underline the words that describe the opposite of <u>courteous</u> behavior. Describe a *courteous* person.

5. Circle the words that explain why <u>prudent</u> travelers set forth in groups. Then, tell what *prudent* means.

6. Circle the words that suggest the meaning of <u>devout</u>. Use *devout* in a sentence of your own.

7. Underline the words that are a clue to the meaning of <u>repented</u>. Tell what *repented* means.

8. Circle the word that suggests the meaning of <u>dispense</u>. What is a synonym for *dispense*?

© Pearson Education

from The Canterbury Tales: The Prologue

Geoffrey Chaucer
Translated by Nevill Coghill

Summary The author joins a group of pilgrims traveling toward the shrine at Canterbury. He describes in detail the people making the trip with him. The characters represent a cross-section of society. Among them are a knight and his son, who is a squire or knight's helper; a yeoman, who is a servant to the squire; a nun, accompanied by another nun and three priests; a well-dressed monk; a jolly friar, a member of a religious order; a merchant; a clergyman who is an impoverished student; and a number of others. They all agree to tell stories on the trip.

Note-taking Guide

Use this chart to list details about the characters.

Characters	Traits and Appearance
1. Knight	
2. Squire	
3. Yeoman	
4. Nun	
5. Monk	
6. Friar	
7. Merchant	
8. Oxford Cleric	

from The Canterbury Tales: The Prologue

Geoffrey Chaucer

People in the Middle Ages often made holy journeys, or pilgrimages, to the city of Canterbury to honor Archbishop Thomas à Becket, killed in 1170. One April in the 1300s, a group of pilgrims, or travelers making this pilgrimage, met at the Tabard Inn just outside London. Chaucer describes each pilgrim, starting with a Knight.

♦ ♦ ♦

There was a Knight, a most distinguished man,
Who from the day on which he first began
To ride abroad had followed chivalry,[1]
Truth, honor, generousness and courtesy.
He had done nobly in his sovereign's[2] war
And ridden into battle, no man more . . .

♦ ♦ ♦

The Knight has fought in the Crusades, the Christian holy wars to gain control of Jerusalem. He makes his pilgrimage to give thanks for surviving. With him is his son, a knight-in-training, or Squire, of about twenty. The Squire likes to joust, or fight in tournaments, but he also likes music, poetry, and showy clothes.

♦ ♦ ♦

He was embroidered like a meadow bright
And full of freshest flowers, red and white.
Singing he was, or fluting all the day;
He was as fresh as is the month of May.
Short was his gown, the sleeves were long and
   wide;
He knew the way to sit a horse and ride.

Literary Analysis

1. In the bracketed passage, circle an example of **direct characterization,** or a direct statement about a character. Label it *direct.*
2. Circle an example of **indirect characterization,** or personality revealed through actions. Label it *indirect.*
3. Then complete the sentence below by listing four words that describe the Knight's personality.

The characterization shows that the Knight is

_____

_____

_____

Reading Check

What is embroidered, or sewn, on the Squire's outfit?

_____

_____

_____

1. **chivalry** (SHIV uhl ree) *n.* the code of behavior for knights, which stressed truth, honor, generosity, and courtesy.
2. **sovereign's** (SOV ruhnz) ruler's; king's.

He could make songs and poems and recite,
Knew how to joust and dance, to draw and write.

◆ ◆ ◆

    The Knight also travels with a Yeoman (YOH man) dressed like a forest hunter. The Yeoman serves as the Knight's attendant. Next Chaucer describes a Nun who is Prioress (PRY uhr uhs), or assistant head, of the nunnery where she lives.

◆ ◆ ◆

And she was known as Madam Eglantyne.
And well she sang a service,[3] with a fine
<u>Intoning</u> through her nose, as was most <u>seemly</u>,
And she spoke daintily in French, extremely,
After the school of Stratford-atte-Bowe;[4]
French in the Paris style she did not know.
At meat[5] her manners were well taught withal;[6]
No <u>morsel</u> from her lips did she let fall,
Nor dipped her fingers in the sauce too deep;
But she could carry a morsel up and keep
The smallest drop from falling on her breast.
For <u>courtliness</u> she had a special zest,
And she would wipe her upper lip so clean
That not a trace of grease was to be seen.

◆ ◆ ◆

    The Nun's group includes another Nun and several Priests. There are also other members of the clergy going to Canterbury.

◆ ◆ ◆

Reading Check

List three of the Squire's talents.

1. _____

2. _____

3. _____

Stop to Reflect

The French spoken in Paris was considered the most proper.

1. What can you assume about the French that the Nun speaks?

_____

_____

_____

2. Why do you think the Nun tries to speak French at all?

_____

_____

_____

Vocabulary Development

intoning (in TOHN ing) *n.* chanting; humming
seemly (SEEM lee) *adv.* proper; fitting
morsel (MOHR suhl) *n.* small bite or piece
courtliness (KORT lee nuhs) *n.* elegant manners

3. **service** daily prayer.
4. **Stratford-atte-Bowe** a nunnery near London.
5. **At meat** at meals.
6. **withal** (with AWL) *adv.* in addition; nevertheless; besides.

A Monk there was, one of the finest sort
Who rode the country; hunting was his sport.
A manly man, to be an Abbot[7] able;
Many a dainty horse he had in stable.
His bridle, when he rode, a man might hear
Jingling in a whistling wind as clear,
Aye, and as loud as does the chapel bell
Where my lord Monk was Prior of the cell.[8]
The Rule of good St. Benet or St. Maur[9]
As old and strict he tended to ignore;
He let go by the things of yesterday
And took the modern world's more spacious way.

♦ ♦ ♦

Next there is a Friar, or begging Monk,
who likes the company of innkeepers and
barmaids far more than that of the poor. And
there is a Merchant who seems so successful
that no one knows he is in debt. In contrast
is the Oxford Cleric, a student of religion at
Oxford University. He cares only about his
study and his faith.

♦ ♦ ♦

Whatever money from his friends he took
He spent on learning or another book
And prayed for them most earnestly, returning
Thanks to them thus for paying for his learning.
His only care was study, and indeed
He never spoke a word more than was need,
Formal at that, respectful in the extreme,
Short, to the point, and lofty in his theme.

© Pearson Education

Vocabulary Development

earnestly (ER nuhst lee) *adv.* in a sincere way

lofty (LAWF tee) *adj.* elevated; high minded; idealistic

7. **Abbot** (AB uht) *n.* a monk in charge of a monastery, or community of monks.

8. **Prior** (PRY uhr) **of the cell** head of a smaller monastery that is part of a larger one.

9. **St. Benet** (buh NAY) **and St. Maur** (MAWR) the French names for St. Benedict, who established the rules for monks, and St. Maurice, one of his followers.

TAKE NOTES

Reading Strategy

Repair your comprehension
by analyzing the long bracketed
sentence. Ask these questions to
determine the main points. Circle
the details that answer each
question, and label your circled
answers *What? When?*
and *Who?*

- *What* might you hear jingling?
- *When* might you hear it?
- *Who* is Prior of the cell?

Reading Check

The Monk embraces the modern
world's more spacious, or open,
way. What does he abandon as
old fashioned?

_____

_____

_____

Literary Analysis

Study the **indirect
characterization**, or personality
revealed through actions, in the
second bracketed passage. Then,
put a check in front of the three
words below that best describe
the Oxford Cleric.

____ scholarly   ____ greedy

____ worldly   ____ single-minded

____ religious   ____ self-reliant

The thought of moral virtue filled his speech
And he would gladly learn, and gladly teach.

◆ ◆ ◆

There is also a Sergeant at the Law, a lawyer for the king's courts; a Franklin, or wealthy landowner; a Skipper, or ship's captain; a Cook; and several tradesmen—a Weaver, a Carpenter, a Carpet Maker, and others. Then there is a Doctor skilled in the medical practices of the day.

◆ ◆ ◆

In his own diet he observed some measure;
There were no superfluities[10] for pleasure,
Only digestives, nutritives[11] and such.
He did not read the Bible very much.
In blood-red garments, slashed with
    bluish-gray
And lined with taffeta,[12] he rode his way;
Yet he was rather close as to expenses
And kept the gold he won in pestilences.
Gold stimulates the heart, or so we're told.
He therefore had a special love of gold.

◆ ◆ ◆

Also traveling to Canterbury is a woman from the English city of Bath, and a Parson, or village priest. The woman, known as the Wife of Bath, has been married and widowed five times. She now spends her days making pilgrimages all over Europe and the Middle East.

◆ ◆ ◆

Literary Analysis

The bracketed passage helps in the **characterization** of the Oxford Cleric. Circle the **direct characterization,** or direct statement by the author about the character's personality, in this passage.

Read Fluently

Read the underlined lines aloud. What is funny about them?

_____

_____

_____

Vocabulary Development

close (KLOHS) *adj.* stingy
pestilences (PES tuh luhn siz) *n.* contagious diseases; plagues

10. **superfluities** (soo puhr FLOO uh teez) *n.* things that are not necessities.

11. **digestives** (duh JES tivs), **nutritives** (NOO truh tivs) foods eaten because they are healthy.

12. **taffeta** (TAF uh tuh) *n.* a fine silk fabric.

Easily on an <u>ambling</u> horse she sat
Well wimpled up,[13] and on her head a hat
As broad as is a buckler[14] or a shield;
She had a flowing mantle[15] that concealed
Large hips, her heels spurred sharply under that.
In company she liked to laugh and chat
And knew the remedies for love's <u>mischances</u>,
An art in which she knew the oldest dances.

   A holy-minded man of good <u>renown</u>
There was, and poor, the Parson to a town,
Yet he was rich in holy thought and work.
He also was a learned man, a clerk,
Who truly knew Christ's gospel[16] and would
   preach it
<u>Devoutly</u> to <u>parishioners</u>, and teach it.

◆   ◆   ◆

   Traveling with the Parson is his honest,
   hard-working brother, a farmer, or Plowman.
   A bit less honest is the Miller, a jolly fellow
   with a red beard and a wart at the end of his
   nose.

◆   ◆   ◆

His nostrils were as black as they were wide.
He had a sword and buckler at his side,
His mighty mouth was like a furnace door.

Reading Check

Because of her great experience with love, what does the Wife of Bath know?

_____

_____

_____

Literary Analysis

Circle at least two examples of **direct characterization** in which Chaucer directly states something about the type of person the Parson is.

Vocabulary Development

ambling (AM bling) *adj.* moving at a slow, easy speed
mischances (mis CHAN siz) *n.* unlucky accidents; misfortunes
renown (ree NOWN) *n.* fame
devoutly (duh VOWT lee) *adv.* in a religious way
parishioners (puh RISH uhn uhrz) *n.* churchgoers in the priest's district

13. **wimpled** (WIM puhld) **up** wearing a scarf covering the head, neck, and chin, as was customary for married women.

14. **buckler** (BUCK luhr) n. small round shield.

15. **mantle** (MAN tuhl) n. cloak.

16. **gospel** (GAHS puhl) a part of the Bible that tells of Christ's life and teachings.

© Pearson Education

from The Canterbury Tales: The Prologue   **37**

Stop to Reflect

What is the meaning of the "thumb of gold"? Circle the letter of the best answer below.

a. the Miller's thumb, used to cheat customers of their gold

b. the Miller's thumb, playing lovely music on the bagpipes

c. gold valve the Miller pushes with his thumb when playing bagpipes

d. thumb-shaped golden grain

Reading Check

What musical instrument does the Miller play as the pilgrims leave the town?

_____

A wrangler and buffoon,[17] he had a store
Of tavern stories, filthy in the main.[18]
His was a master-hand at stealing grain.
He felt it with his thumb and thus he knew
Its quality and took three times his due—
A thumb of gold, by God, to gauge an oat!
He wore a hood of blue and a white coat.
He liked to play his bagpipes up and down
And that was how he brought us out of town.

♦ ♦ ♦

The Manciple, or caterer, works at one of the London law schools. Though not a learned man, he manages to cheat all the clever law students. The Reeve, or estate manager, is skilled at managing his master's wealth. He has also managed to stash away quite a bit for himself. The Summoner, who summons people to appear in Church court, is a heavy drinker with a bad complexion. His companion is a Pardoner, an official who sells papal pardons to those summoned to the court. The Pardoner also claims to own several holy relics, or items associated with Jesus, Mary, and the saints.

♦ ♦ ♦

For in his trunk he had a pillowcase
Which he asserted was Our Lady's veil.[19]
He said he had a gobbet[20] of the sail
Saint Peter had the time when he made bold
To walk the waves, till Jesu Christ took hold.
He had a cross of metal set with stones
And, in a glass, a rubble of pigs' bones.

Vocabulary Development
gauge (GAYJ) v. measure; weigh

---

17. **wrangler** (RANG luhr) **and buffoon** (buh FOON) someone who often argues or clowns around.

18. **in the main** mainly; for the most part.

19. **Our Lady's veil** (VAYL) a veil worn by Mary, mother of Jesus.

20. **gobbet** (GAHB it) n. piece.

And with these relics, any time he found
Some poor up-country parson to astound,
On one short day, in money down, he drew
More than the parson in a month or two,
And by his flatteries and <u>prevarication</u>
Made monkeys of the priest and congregation.

        ◆   ◆   ◆

      Having now described everyone,
Chaucer tells of the merry meal at the Tabard
Inn before the group leaves for Canterbury.
The Innkeeper joins the fun and makes an
interesting offer.

        ◆   ◆   ◆

<u>"My lords," he said, "now listen for your good,
And please don't treat my notion with disdain.</u>
This is the point. I'll make it short and plain.
Each one of you shall help to make things slip[21]
By telling two stories on the outward trip
To Canterbury, that's what I intend,
And, on the homeward way to journey's end
Another two, tales from the days of old;
And then the man whose story is best told,
That is to say who gives the fullest measure
Of good morality and general pleasure,
He shall be given a supper, paid by all,
Here in this tavern, in this very hall,
When we come back again from Canterbury.
And in the hope to keep you bright and merry
I'll go along with you myself and ride
All at my own expense and serve as guide.
I'll be the judge, and those who won't obey
Shall pay for what we spend upon the way."

        ◆   ◆   ◆

      Everyone is happy to agree to the
Innkeeper's offer. The stories the pilgrims tell
become the individual stories of the rest of
The Canterbury Tales.

© Pearson Education

Vocabulary Development

prevarication (pree var uh KAY shuhn) *n.* avoiding the truth
disdain (dis DAYN) *n.* scorn; contempt

21. **make things slip** make the time go faster.

TAKE NOTES

Read Fluently

Read the underlined sentence
aloud. In what sort of tone do
you think the Innkeeper said it?
Circle the letter of the best
answer below.

a. angry   c. puzzled
b. sad   d. polite

Reading Strategy

Analyze the bracketed **sentence**
by answering the questions
below to determine its main
points.

1. *What* does the Innkeeper
propose the pilgrims do in a
contest?

_____

_____

2. *When* will the pilgrims do it?

_____

_____

3. *Why* should the pilgrims do it?

_____

_____

from The Canterbury Tales: The Prologue

1. **Literary Analysis:** Choose one **character.** Explain what the appearance or actions of the character tell the reader.

_____

_____

_____

2. **Literary Analysis:** Use the chart to reflect on the **social commentary** in the Prologue. What social comment does Chaucer make in his sketch of the Pardoner? What does the sketch of the Knight suggest were some of the excellences promoted by medieval society? Include the details that support the social comment.

Character	Detail	Comment About Society
Pardoner		
Knight		

3. **Reading Strategy: Analyze** the first two sentences that describes the Knight on page 33, answering the questions _who, what, where,_ and _how._

_____

_____

_____

? Writing About the Essential Question

How does literature shape or reflect society? Explain what a description of clothing reveals about a character and about medieval society.

_____

_____

_____

_____

from The Canterbury Tales: The Pardoner's Tale

Literary Analysis

An **allegory** is a type of story. An allegory has both a literal meaning and a deeper, more symbolic meaning. "The Pardoner's Tale" is a type of allegory called an **exemplum.** That is Latin for *example*. This tale is an exemplum about greed.

This story contains some storytelling patterns known as **archetypal narrative elements.** These elements include the following:

- characters or events that come in threes
- a character who must undergo a test
- a mysterious guide
- an ending that rewards good and punishes evil

Reading Strategy

Rereading passages can help you understand the story. It can help you

- understand the characters and events.
- figure out the meaning of unfamiliar words.

As you read "The Pardoner's Tale," you might come to a line that you do not understand. Reread the lines that come before. They may have clues to meaning. Read the following sample diagram. Create a diagram like this on another sheet of paper to help you clarify a difficult passage.

Passage	Reread Earlier Passage	Clarification
"He gathered **lots** and hid them in his hand. . . ."	"'We draw for **lots** and see the way it goes; / The one who draws the longest, lucky man, . . .'"	"Drawing lots" must be like drawing straws: The one who draws the longest is "it."

Word List A

Study these words from the selection. Then, complete the activities.

congregation [kahn gre GAY shun] *n.* people gathered for religious worship
The rabbi asked his congregation to hold a fundraiser for homeless people.

discourse [DIS kawrs] *n.* a complete or thorough discussion of a topic
The professor gave a long discourse explaining the reasons for the Civil War.

dignity [DIG ni tee] *n.* honor; self-respect; the quality of deserving esteem or respect
The singer ignored the boos and walked off the stage with dignity, holding his head high.

pulpit [PUHL pit] *n.* a platform from which a religious leader speaks to worshipers
The preacher spoke to the crowd from the pulpit at the front of the church.

sermon [SUR muhn] *n.* a lecture on right and wrong, often by a religious leader
The preacher spoke for half an hour; his sermon was about forgiveness.

vanity [VAHN i tee] *n.* too much pride in your appearance or accomplishments
Out of vanity, the ninety-year-old movie star had surgery to remove his wrinkles.

vice [VYS] *n.* bad or evil habit
I think lying is a vice worse than laziness.

wary [WAYR ee] *adj.* on guard; watchful
They told me their dog was friendly, but I was still wary of it and kept my distance.

Exercise A

Fill in each blank in the paragraph using the appropriate word from Word List A. Use each word only once.

When giving a speech, a public speaker often stands on a raised platform before a desk of some kind. A religious leader, for example, may speak from a [1] _____ when he or she addresses the [2] _____ of worshipers. Speaking from a formal platform adds to the speaker's [3] _____ and helps ensure that the audience listens with respect. Whether the speech is a humorous toast to an honored guest or a religious [4] _____ on a bad habit or [5] _____, the best speeches are short and simple. Listeners are [6] _____ of long speeches and will avoid a speaker who always gives a lengthy [7] _____ explaining his or her topic. If nothing else, a speaker's pride and [8] _____ should make the speaker take care not to be boring!

Read the following passage. Pay special attention to the underlined words. Then, read it again, and complete the activities. Use a separate sheet of paper for your written answers.

The parish priest was a central figure in the lives of medieval Christian Europeans. He was obliged to set a moral example for his parishioners by working hard and leading his life with <u>dignity</u> and self-respect.

By most accounts, the priest's life was not an easy one. His duties included presiding at weddings, funerals, baptisms (name-giving ceremonies), as well as giving the Sunday <u>sermon</u> from the <u>pulpit</u> at the front of the church. Many of his parishioners relied on this weekly speech for inspiration and guidance. The priest also celebrated mass, a daily Catholic ceremony, and heard people's confessions of their sins. In addition, the priest was responsible for running the local school, tending the sick, and providing hospitality to travelers. He also collected taxes called *tithes*.

Tithing was a system in which every member of the <u>congregation</u> was expected to give a tithe, or one-tenth of yearly earnings, to support the church. Parishioners could pay either in cash or in grain. The tithe income was shared among the parish priest, the church maintenance fund, the poor, and the bishop (the church official who oversaw the priest). Tithes could be a burden on the people, but village folk may have been <u>wary</u> of complaining too freely about them for fear of the authorities. Tithing was considered part of leading a moral life and could even be required by law.

Since most of the population could not read, people relied upon the priest for religious instruction. They also learned lessons from miracle and morality plays. These were short dramas that were acted out in the churchyards, usually on feast days. Miracle plays were based on biblical stories. A morality play might present a conflict between a virtue, such as charity, and a <u>vice</u>, such as <u>vanity</u>, or excessive pride. Instead of explaining religious ideas in a lengthy <u>discourse</u>, a play told a story—it entertained listeners even as it taught them.

1. Circle the word that is a clue to the meaning of <u>dignity</u>. Explain what a person needs to do to live with *dignity*.

2. Underline the phrase in the next sentence that helps explain what a <u>sermon</u> is. What might be the topic of a medieval *sermon*?

3. Circle the words that tell where you are likely to find a <u>pulpit</u>. Then, explain what a *pulpit* is.

4. Underline the words that show that a <u>congregation</u> is made up of more than one person. Rewrite the sentence using a phrase that means the same as *congregation*.

5. Underline the phrase that tells what folk were <u>wary</u> of. Explain whether people today are *wary* of similar things.

6. Circle the word that means the opposite of <u>vice</u>. Then, explain what *vice* means.

7. Underline the words that define <u>vanity</u>. Give an example that demonstrates *vanity*.

8. Circle the word that tells what a <u>discourse</u> is meant to do. Explain why simple folk might prefer a play to a *discourse*.

from The Canterbury Tales: The Pardoner's Tale

Geoffrey Chaucer
Translated by Nevill Coghill

Summary The Pardoner tells a tale about "Greed is the root of all evil." Three young people search for Death. An old man directs them to look under a tree. They find a lot of money. The three men try to cheat each other to get more money. Their greed brings a bad result for all of them.

Note-taking Guide

Use this diagram to recall the events of the tale.

Beginning Event

Three men are looking for Death.

↓

↓

↓

↓

Final Event

from The Canterbury Tales: The Pardoner's Tale

1. **Literary Analysis:** Explain how the **allegory** proves that greed is the root of all evil.

_____

_____

2. **Literary Analysis:** This story contains some patterns known as **archetypal narrative elements.** For example, the three rioters represent things that come in threes. How is the rioters' search for Death an archetypal element?

_____

_____

3. **Reading Strategy:** In line 319, the Pardoner speaks of "blackguardly excess" and goes on to refer to people killing each other. Use the following chart to help you clarify the meaning of this passage.

Passage	Reread Earlier Passage	Meaning
"Blackguardly excess"		

Writing About the Essential Question

How does literature shape or reflect society? What can you learn about life in the Middle Ages from "The Pardoner's Tale"?

_____

_____

_____

_____

from The Canterbury Tales:
The Wife of Bath's Tale

Literary Analysis

Sometimes you might read a story *within* a story. The main story serves as a **frame** around the "inner" story. For example:

- In *The Canterbury Tales*, the frame (or main story) is the characters' journey to Canterbury Cathedral.

- Within the frame lie the "inner" tales. These tales are told by the characters on their way to the cathedral.

"The Wife of Bath's Tale" is an inner story of *The Canterbury Tales*, but it also serves as a frame for another story.

Notice how the **setting** in this story is different from the setting in "the Prologue." The setting is the time and place in which a story happens. Look for ways in which the setting relates to plot, mood, and theme.

Reading Strategy

Context clues are words and phrases in a text that help show what an unfamiliar word means. Common context clues are synonyms and antonyms. The chart below shows an example.

Passage	Passage
Hundreds of years ago, in days of yore	

Unfamiliar Word	Unfamiliar Word
yore	

Context Clue	Context Clue
hundreds of years ago	

Conclusion	Conclusion
If days of yore took place hundreds of years ago, yore must mean "time long past."	

Word List A

Study these words from the selection. Then, complete the activities.

bottled [BAHT uhld] *v.* (with up) held in; restrained; contained
  The mourner kept her grief and sadness bottled up.

crone [KROHN] *n.* an ugly old woman; hag
  Fairy tales often feature a crone who later becomes a beautiful maiden.

extort [ek STOHRT] *v.* obtain by using violence or threats
  Blackmailers extort money by threatening to reveal damaging secrets.

forlorn [fohr LOHRN] *adj.* abandoned or forsaken; sad and lonely
  The stray dog looked hungry and forlorn when the children found her.

matrons [MAY truhns] *n.* married women or widows; mature women
  The matrons in the garden club have exchanged advice for years.

purged [PERJD] *v.* removed; cleansed; to have gotten rid of
  The exterminator purged the house of unwanted insects.

reprove [ri PROOV] *v.* admonish; find fault with; rebuke
  The coach had to reprove his players for not following the game plan.

void [VOYD] *adj.* empty; containing no matter
  The manager discovered that the safe was mysteriously void of cash.

Exercise A

Fill in each blank in the paragraph with the appropriate word from Word List A. Use each word only once.

  Grooming was important to people in the Middle Ages. They bathed openly in lakes and rivers without fear that someone might [1] _____ them for being indecent. Hot baths were popular, but because woodcutters had [2] _____ the forests of trees and the landscape became [3] _____ of firewood, the cost of heating water became too great for most people. However, people did not keep their dismay about this lack of hygiene [4] _____ up. They spoke about it openly and used perfumes to mask body odors. To avoid looking like a [5] _____ as they aged, wealthy [6] _____ painted their faces with cosmetics and sun-bleached their hair. Those who could not keep up appearances were often avoided and became desperately [7] _____. An easy way to [8] _____ money from them was to sell miracle elixirs promising the appearance of youth.

1. Underline the sentence that explains why <u>matrons</u> often took new vows quickly. Explain what *matrons* are.

2. Underline the words that tell what some writers wanted to <u>reprove</u> widows for. Then, tell what *reprove* means.

3. Underline the words that suggest what <u>forlorn</u> means. Then, describe something that might make a person *forlorn*.

4. Explain what marriages in the Middle Ages were not <u>void</u> of. Then, give a synonym for *void*.

5. Underline the words that tell why spouses did not keep negative feelings <u>bottled</u> up. Then give a synonym for "*bottled* up."

6. Circle the words that tell what a groom's family might <u>extort</u>. Then, explain what *extort* means.

7. Rewrite the sentence using a synonym for <u>purged</u>. Then, tell what *purged* means.

8. Circle the words that tell what a young woman did so she would not end up a lonely, unmarried <u>crone</u>. Then, describe a *crone*.

Read the following passage. Pay special attention to the underlined words. Then, read it again, and complete the activities. Use a separate sheet of paper for your written answers.

It was not unusual for widows in fifteenth-century England to wed again after the deaths of their husbands. <u>Matrons</u> in the lower classes often took new vows only weeks or months after burying their spouses. Some writers wanted to <u>reprove</u> widows for remarrying. However, the reasons for remarriage were compelling and strictly practical. It was difficult for a woman to raise a family, manage assets, and maintain her reputation on her own.

Instead of being <u>forlorn</u>, having no one to turn to, some widows used their chance of remarriage to find a man who could increase their fortunes. This was not frowned upon since medieval marriage was mostly seen as an economic arrangement, not the fulfillment of romantic love.

Of course, the survival of a family depended upon good alliances, and matrimonial partners were usually chosen for social or political reasons. If a husband and wife were fond of each other, that was considered fortunate. In many cases, these marriages were not <u>void</u> of the kind of love and affection one might find today. However, these were not requirements for a successful marriage. Because there were no illusions about this type of arrangement, spouses did not keep hostile feelings <u>bottled</u> up. As a result, sometimes the relationships were challenging, oppressive, and violent.

Girls were raised primarily to be wives, but they had little say about whom they would marry. Sometimes a groom's family would <u>extort</u> an extravagant dowry from the bride's parents. If a woman didn't want to marry, she could join a convent, but this required considerable wealth. To a degree, individual desires and preferences were <u>purged</u> from the minds of young girls. No young woman wanted to end up a lonely, unmarried <u>crone</u>, so she deferred to her parents' choice.

from The Canterbury Tales: The Wife of Bath's Tale

Geoffrey Chaucer
Translated by Nevill Coghill

Summary A knight goes on a quest to find an answer to the question of what women most want. He meets an old woman. She will give him the answer if the knight promises to marry her. The old woman lectures the knight about all his objections to her as a wife. A surprise ending happens after the knight agrees to do what his wife says.

Note-taking Guide

In this tale, men sometimes dominate women, and the women react. What happens? Explain in the first diagram. Also, in this tale, women sometimes dominate, and the men react. What happens then? Explain in the second diagram.

Man's Action	Woman's Reaction	Outcome

Woman's Action	Man's Reaction	Outcome

from The Canterbury Tales: The Wife of Bath's Tale

1. **Compare and Contrast:** Compare the Wife of Bath described in the Prologue to the old woman in the tale. How are they the same? How are they different?

   _____

   _____

   _____

2. **Literary Analysis:** In the **frame**, the Host says he will judge the pilgrims' tales on their ability to teach a moral lesson and on their entertainment value. If you were the Host, how would you respond to the Wife's tale? Use the chart to note details from the tale. Use the details to make a final judgment. One detail has been given to you.

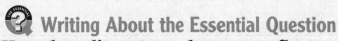

Good Morality/ Lesson	General Pleasure/ Entertainment Value	Final Judgement
The knight is forced to marry the old woman.		

3. **Reading Strategy:** What **context clues** help you understand the word *dejected* in line 135?

   _____

   _____

? Writing About the Essential Question

How does literature shape or reflect society? By discussing self-same sovereignty, was Chaucer reflecting or trying to influence social trends?

   _____

   _____

   _____

   _____

from Sir Gawain and the Green Knight
• from Morte d'Arthur

Literary Analysis

Medieval romances are adventure stories. The characters are kings, knights, and damsels in distress. They tell of quests, battles, and love. The stories of King Arthur and his Knights are examples of medieval romances. As you read these stories, look for ideas of love and honor in a mix of realism and fantasy.

The stories in this grouping are based on the same **legend,** or anonymous traditional story about the past. Legends usually have some basis in fact and often feature these elements:

- heroic figures who perform great deeds
- quests, contests, or challenges
- patterns, such as events occurring in threes

Reading Strategy

When you read unfamiliar material written long ago, it helps to record **main ideas** and key **details** in order to create a summary. When you **summarize** a story, you

- retell the main parts of a story.
- explain the main ideas.
- include only important details.

Create a chart like the following to summarize the main ideas and details in a passage.

Passage	Summary
"Ah, traitor unto me and untrue," said King Arthur, "now hast thou betrayed me twice. Who would have weened that thou that has been to me so loved and dear . . . , and would betray me for the riches of this sword."	King Arthur charges his knight with betraying him twice out of greed.

Word List A

Study these words the selections. Then, complete the activities.

slumbering [SLUHM ber ing] *v.* sleeping; dozing
The child was slumbering during the entire concert, in spite of the loud music.

fused [FYOOZD] *v.* mixed together; united together to become inseparable
The electrician fused the separate strands of wire together.

marvel [MAHR vuhl] *v.* to become filled with astonishment and wonder; be in awe
We marvel at the tricks performed by a skilled magician.

swooned [SWOOND] *v.* fainted; collapsed
The starstruck fan swooned when she finally shook hands with her idol.

puny [PYOO nee] *adj.* of inferior size, strength, or significance; weak
The tomatoes in the garden looked puny and needed water and fertilizer.

almighty [AWL my tee] *adj.* great; extreme; all-powerful
Most religions teach that their god is almighty.

hermit [HUR mit] *n.* person living alone away from society; a recluse
Sometimes a medieval monk would leave his monastery to live as a hermit.

accorded [uh KORD id] *v.* granted; given what is due or appropriate
The audience accorded the star respect and stood when he entered.

Exercise A

Fill in each blank in the paragraph with the appropriate word from Word List A. Use each word only once.

People in the Dark Ages were very superstitious. They believed that while naughty children were [1] _____ fairies could steal them out of their beds. Although legends [2] _____ fairies some magical powers, they were by no means [3] _____. People would [4] _____ at natural wonders, such as icicles, spider webs, and dewdrops, convinced that fairies made them. Fairies were physically [5] _____, but used their small size to travel unnoticed. They also developed spells as a means of self-protection. Anyone who came in contact with a fairy promptly [6] _____. When the person awoke, he or she would believe that seeing the fairy had been just a dream. Artists' drawings show fairies as tiny people with dragonfly wings [7] _____ on their backs. Of course, no one ever really saw fairies, not even a [8] _____ living alone in the forest.

Read the following passage. Pay special attention to the underlined words. Then, read it again, and complete the activities. Use a separate sheet of paper for your written answers.

When "courtly love" emerged during the 1100s, it consisted of a code of noble behavior called chivalry that <u>fused</u> loyalty, honor, self-sacrifice, and defense of the weak. It was made popular through tales of brave knights, and maidens who <u>swooned</u> when battles were fought in their name. Ideal love for one pure woman was supposed to inspire a knight to magnificent deeds. It was also expected to make the knight's beloved <u>marvel</u> at his attempts to be worthy of her. Because of her virtue, the lady was put on a pedestal. For the first time, the woman was considered superior to her male suitor.

This attitude was a dramatic change in the way noble women were viewed. Although they received more respect, being adored didn't give women more freedom, and they still had little choice when it came to a mate. Romantic love rarely led to a marriage, since matrimonial decisions were <u>accorded</u> to the parents of the bride and groom. Often wedding plans were made while the future husband and wife were still <u>slumbering</u> in their cradles.

The social classes and assets of both families had to be taken into account when marriages were arranged. A wealthy <u>father would never promise his daughter to a hermit</u>, or expect her to marry someone whose prospects were <u>puny</u>. It was understood that a man who married the daughter of a wealthy merchant would receive a generous dowry. Finances, not love, continued to determine most marriages. Money was still <u>almighty</u>, in spite of the poets, and the longing for true love that they created.

1. Circle the part of the sentence that tells what chivalry <u>fused</u> together to create a code of behavior. Then, give an antonym for *fused*.

2. Circle the words that explain when maidens <u>swooned</u>. Then, give a synonym for *swooned*.

3. Circle the words that tell who was expected to <u>marvel</u> at a knight's attempts to be worthy. Then, rewrite the sentence using a synonym for *marvel*.

4. Circle the word that says what was <u>accorded</u> to parents. Define *accorded*.

5. Circle the words that tell who was <u>slumbering</u>. Describe *slumbering*.

6. Circle the part of the sentence that tells who would never promise his daughter to a <u>hermit</u>. Where might you find a *hermit*?

7. Underline the words that say what a father wouldn't expect his daughter to do if a groom's prospects were <u>puny</u>. What would you consider a *puny* sum?

8. Circle the word that tells what was <u>almighty</u>. Explain what *almighty* means.

from Sir Gawain and the Green Knight
Translated by Marie Borroff

Summary A huge green knight dares Arthur's knights to cut off his head. The knight who beheads him must then have his own head cut off in a year. Sir Gawain accepts the Green Knight's challenge. He cuts off the Green Knight's head. The headless knight survives. A year later, Gawain sets off to find the knight and fulfill his promise. His loyalty and honesty undergo different tests.

Note-taking Guide
Use this diagram to summarize the key events in the story of *Sir Gawain and the Green Knight*.

King Arthur and his knights are celebrating New Year's Eve.

from Morte d'Arthur

Sir Thomas Malory

Summary King Arthur has a dream. In his dream, Gawain warns him not to fight Mordred. Arthur does fight Mordred, and he receives a mortal wound. He knows he is going to die. He asks his knight Bedivere to throw his magic sword into a lake. Bedivere places Arthur on a mysterious barge. The barge sails away. The next day Bedivere finds a new grave. No one knows if Arthur will return to be king.

Note-Taking Guide

Use this chart to write down the key events in the story of King Arthur's death.

In a dream, Gawain warns Arthur not to fight with Mordred.

Circle a remark in the bracketed paragraph that shows how King Arthur feels about Mordred.

Stop to Reflect

Based on the bracketed passage, what do you predict will happen when the two sides meet? Why?

Prediction:

_____

_____

_____

Explanation:

_____

_____

_____

from Morte d'Arthur

Sir Thomas Malory

King Arthur creates an ideal kingdom called Camelot where talented knights sit at a Round Table and all feel equal. But jealousy and other human weaknesses eventually destroy Camelot. Arthur is forced to fight his friend Sir Lancelot in France. While he is away, his illegitimate son Mordred tries to steal the English throne. When Arthur races home to fight Mordred, Arthur's nephew Sir Gawain is killed almost immediately. Gawain returns to Arthur in a dream, surrounded by lovely ladies Gawain has helped in life. He warns Arthur not to fight Mordred the next day. If he does, both sides will take huge losses, and Arthur will die. So Arthur arranges a one-month treaty. The two sides each bring fourteen men to the place where the treaty will be signed.

◆ ◆ ◆

And when King Arthur should depart, he warned all his host that, and[1] they see any sword drawn, "Look ye come on fiercely and slay that traitor Sir Mordred, for I in no wise[2] trust him." In like wise Sir Mordred warned his host that "And ye see any manner of sword drawn, look that ye come on fiercely, and so slay all that ever before you standeth, for in no wise I will not trust for this treaty." And in the same wise said Sir Mordred unto his host, "For I know well my father will be avenged upon me."

Vocabulary Development

host (HOHST) *n.* army; troops
slay (SLAY) *v.* kill
be avenged (uh VENJD) *v.* get revenge

1. **and** if.
2. **wis:** way.

And so they met as their pointment[3] was and were agreed and accorded thoroughly. And wine was fetched and they drank together. Right so came an adder out of a little heathbush, and it stung a knight in the foot. And so when the knight felt him so stung, he looked down and saw the adder. And anon[4] he drew his sword to slay the adder, and thought none other harm. And when the host on both parties saw that sword drawn, then they blew beams,[5] trumpets, horns, and shouted grimly. And so both hosts dressed them[6] together. And King Arthur took his horse and said, "Alas, this unhappy day!" and so rode to his party, and Sir Mordred in like wise.

♦   ♦   ♦

The battle that breaks out is a horrible one. A hundred thousand soldiers are killed. Arthur is horrified to see so many of his noble knights fall.

♦   ♦   ♦

Then King Arthur looked about and was ware[7] where stood Sir Mordred leaning upon his sword among a great heap of dead men.

"Now give me my spear," said King Arthur unto Sir Lucan, "for yonder I have espied the traitor that all this woe hath wrought."[8]

♦   ♦   ♦

Reading Strategy

Circle **main ideas** and details in the bracketed passage. Then, **summarize** how the fighting begins.

_____

_____

_____

_____

_____

Literary Analysis

Arthur keeps calling Mordred a traitor. To which of these themes of **medieval romances** is Mordred's behavior most related? Circle the letter of your answer below. Then, explain how his behavior is related to this theme.

a. love   c. faith
b. loyalty   d. courage

Explanation:

_____

_____

_____

_____

_____

Vocabulary Development

accorded (uh KAWR did) *v.* brought into harmony or agreement

adder (AD uhr) *n.* poisonous snake

espied (es PYD) *v.* spotted; seen

3. **pointment** arrangement.

4. **anon** soon after; immediately.

5. **beams** a type of trumpet.

6. **dressed** them prepared to come.

7. **ware** aware.

8. **hath wrought** (RAWT): has made.

Read Fluently

Read Arthur's underlined words aloud. How do you think he said these words? Circle the letter of the best answer below.

a. in a loud, angry voice

b. in a tired, weary voice

c. in a frightened, trembling voice

d. in a dangerously quiet voice

Reading Check

Put a *T* in front of the statements below that are true. Put an *F* in front of the false statements. Circle details in the bracketed passage that help you answer.

_____ Arthur gets his sword past Mordred's shield.

_____ Arthur gives Mordred a shallow wound that still kills him.

_____ Before he dies, Mordred gives Arthur a serious head injury.

_____ Mordred uses only one hand to wound Arthur.

Stop to Reflect

Consider the behavior and attitudes of Sir Lucan and Sir Bedivere toward their king. How are they different from Mordred's?

_____

_____

Sir Lucan, one of Arthur's knights, advises him not to fight. He points out that Arthur has already won the day and reminds the king of his dream. But Arthur insists on fighting Mordred.

◆　　◆　　◆

Then the King got his spear in both his hands and ran toward Sir Mordred, crying and saying, "Traitor, now is thy deathday come!"

And when Sir Mordred saw King Arthur he ran until him with his sword drawn in his hand, and there King Arthur smote Sir Mordred under the shield, with a thrust of his spear, throughout the body more than a fathom.[9] And when Sir Mordred felt that he had his death's wound, he thrust himself with the might that he had up to the burr[10] of King Arthur's spear, and right so he smote his father King Arthur with his sword holden in both his hands, upon the side of the head, that the sword pierced the helmet and the casing of the brain. And therewith Sir Mordred dashed down stark dead to the earth.

And noble King Arthur fell in a swough[11] to the earth, and there he swooned oftentimes, and Sir Lucan and Sir Bedivere ofttimes heaved him up. And so, weakly betwixt[12] them, they led him to a little chapel not far from the seaside. . . .

◆　　◆　　◆

Vocabulary Development

smote (SMOHT) *v.* struck down or killed; past tense of smite

swooned (SWOOND) *v.* fainted

---

9. **fathom** (FATH uhm) *n.* six feet.

10. **burr** hand guard.

11. **swough** (SWOH) *n.* faint or swoon.

12. **betwixt** (buh TWIXT) *prep.* between.

Sir Lucan and his brother Sir Bedivere decide to bring the wounded Arthur to the safety of a town. They try to lift him up again. But Lucan, who was wounded in battle, collapses and dies. Bedivere weeps at the death of his brother and the likely death of his king.

◆ ◆ ◆

"Now leave this mourning and weeping gentle knight," said the King, "for all this will not avail me.[13] For wit thou[14] well, and might I live myself, the death of Sir Lucan would grieve me evermore. But my time passeth on fast," said the King. "Therefore," said King Arthur unto Sir Bedivere, "take thou here Excalibur my good sword and go with it to yonder water's side; and when thou comest there I charge thee throw my sword in that water and come again and tell me what thou sawest there."

"My lord," said Sir Bedivere, "your commandment shall be done, and I shall lightly[15] bring you word again."

◆ ◆ ◆

Sir Bedivere takes the sword to the lake. But he cannot bring himself to throw it in. It simply seems too valuable. There are even jewels in the hilt, or handle. So Bedivere hides the sword under a tree and returns to Arthur.

◆ ◆ ◆

"What saw thou there?" said the King.

"Sir," he said, "I saw nothing but waves and winds."

"That is untruly said of thee," said the King. "And therefore go thou lightly again and do my commandment; as thou art to me loved and dear, spare not, but throw it in."

◆ ◆ ◆

© Pearson Education

Vocabulary Development

commandment (kuh MAND muhnt) *n.* order; command

13. avail (uh VAYL) me help me; do me any good.

14. wit thou know you.

15. lightly quickly.

Reading Check

What does Arthur ask Sir Bedivere to do?

_____

_____

_____

_____

Reading Check

Why is Bedivere unable to throw the sword in the lake? Circle the reason.

Stop to Reflect

How do you think Arthur knows that Bedivere is lying?

_____

_____

_____

Literary Analysis

Which element of **medieval romances** does the underlined passage illustrate? Circle the letter of the best answer below.

a. unusual settings
b. supernatural events
c. beautiful ladies in need of help
d. battles or contests

Reading Strategy

Summarize, or retell briefly in your own words, what happens in the bracketed passage.

_____

_____

_____

_____

_____

Sir Bedivere goes again to the lake. He still cannot throw the sword in. Again he returns to Arthur and pretends he has thrown it in. Again Arthur knows he is lying. Arthur begs Bedivere to obey him.

◆　◆　◆

Then Sir Bedivere departed and went to the sword and lightly took it up, and so he went to the water's side; and there he bound the girdle[16] about the hilts, and threw the sword as far into the water as he might. And there came an arm and an hand above the water and took it and clutched it, and shook it thrice[17] and brandished; and then vanished away the hand with the sword into the water. So Sir Bedivere came again to the King and told him what he saw.

"Alas," said the King, "help me hence,[18] for I dread me[19] I have tarried overlong."

Then Sir Bedivere took the King upon his back and so went with him to that water's side. And when they were at the water's side, even fast[20] by the bank floated a little barge with many fair ladies in it; and among them all was a queen; and all they had black hoods, and all they wept and shrieked when they saw King Arthur.

Vocabulary Development

brandished (BRAN disht) *v.* waved in a threatening way
tarried (TAR eed) *v.* waited; lingered
bank (BANK) *n.* the land alongside a lake or river
barge (BAHRJ) *n.* a flat-bottomed boat
fair (FAYR) *adj.* pretty; nice looking

16. **girdle** (GER duhl) *n.* the sash or belt used to strap the sword around the hips of the person wearing it.
17. **thrice** (THRYS) *adv.* three times.
18. **hence** from here.
19. **dread** (DRED) *me* fear.
20. **fast** close.

"Now put me into that barge," said the King; and so he did softly. And there received him three ladies with great mourning, and so they set them down. And in one of their laps King Arthur laid his head. . . .

◆　◆　◆

Sir Bedivere weeps as Arthur explains that he must leave him and go to the legendary island of Avilion. He asks Bedivere to pray for him. The next morning, Bedivere meets a hermit who was once the Archbishop of Canterbury. The hermit explains that some women brought him a dead body. They asked him to bury it. So the hermit buried it in the little chapel.

◆　◆　◆

Now more of the death of King Arthur could I never find, but that these ladies brought him to his grave, and such one was <u>interred</u> there which the hermit bare witness that was once Bishop of Canterbury. But yet the hermit knew not in certain that he was verily[21] the body of King Arthur; for this tale Sir Bedivere, a knight of the Table Round, made it to be written.

Yet some men say in many parts of England that King Arthur is not dead, but carried by the will of our Lord Jesu into another place; and men say that he shall come again, and he shall win the Holy Cross. Yet I will not say that it shall be so, but rather I would say: here in this world he changed his life. And many men say that there is written upon the tomb this:

HIC IACET ARTHURUS, REX QUONDAM, REXQUE FUTURUS[22]

© Pearson Education

Vocabulary Development
interred (in TURD) *n.* buried

21. **verily** (VER uh lee) *adv.* truly.
22. **HIC . . . FUTURUS** Here lies Arthur, who was once king and will be king again.

TAKE NOTES

Reading Check

According to the ending, what has happened or will happen to Arthur? Answer by completing the sentence below.

Either he

_____

_____

_____

or he

_____

_____

_____

from Sir Gawain and the Green Knight
• *from* Morte d'Arthur

1. **Interpret:** Mordred is Arthur's son. How does the conflict between the two emphasize the theme of betrayal in *Morte d'Arthur?*

   _____

   _____

   _____

2. **Literary Analysis:** Compare Sir Gawain and Sir Bedivere. Read the way Sir Gawain reacts to the Green Knight's questioning of his honor in lines 459–477. Then, read about Bedivere's reaction to King Arthur's request to throw the sword in the water. Write details in the chart.

	Gawain's Reactions	Bedivere's Reactions
What He Says	He confesses to having lied.	
What He Does		
What He Feels		

3. **Reading Strategy:** Pretend you are Sir Bedivere and a curious traveler comes to visit you. **Summarize** the main events leading up to Arthur's death.

   _____

   _____

   _____

Writing About the Essential Question

What is the relationship of the writer to tradition? Do the authors of these selections accept or question the code of chivalry?

   _____

   _____

   _____

Sonnet 1 • Sonnet 35 • Sonnet 75 • Sonnet 31 • Sonnet 39

Literary Analysis

These are the elements of the literary form known as a **sonnet:**

- lyric poem • fourteen lines • single theme
- each line written in iambic pentameter, which means there are five groups of two syllables, with the stress falling on the second syllable

Two types of sonnets are as follows:

Petrarchan (pi TRAHR kuhn)

- First eight lines ("octave")
  - rhyme *abba abba*
  - often present a problem
- Last six lines ("sestet")
  - rhyme *cdecde*
  - often give solution

Spenserian (spen SIR ee uhn)

- First 12 lines are three groups of four lines each
  - rhyme *abab bcbc cdcd*
- Last two lines (called a "couplet")
  - rhyme *ee*

A **sonnet sequence** is a group of sonnets. They are linked by theme or addressed to the same person. As you read these sonnets, notice their form and how they are linked.

Reading Strategy

One way to **determine** a poet's **main message** is to paraphrase challenging lines. To **paraphrase** a poem, read until you find a complete thought. Then, restate important ideas in your own words. Use this chart to help.

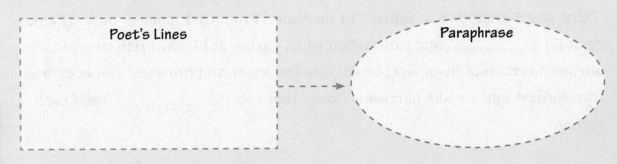

Poet's Lines

Paraphrase

Word List A

Study these words from the selections. Then, complete the activities.

chamber [CHAYM ber] *n.* a room in a house, especially a bedroom
The fireplace was the only source of heat in the chamber.

contentment [kuhn TENT ment] *n.* peaceful satisfaction
Once he retired, the general found contentment.

decay [dee KAY] *v.* to decline in health or vigor; to spoil
If you do not brush your teeth, they will decay.

garland [GAHR lind] *n.* a wreath of flowers or leaves
The bride wore a garland of roses in her hair.

renew [ri NOO] *v.* to repeat so as to reaffirm
The couple decided to renew their wedding vows after 25 years.

vain [VAYN] *adj.* excessively proud of one's self; conceited
The vain young man would not stop looking in the mirror.

virtues [VUR chooz] *n.* moral excellence and righteousness; goodness
The plan had three virtues: it was simple, practical, and inexpensive.

weary [WEER ee] *adj.* physically or mentally fatigued
After driving all night, the weary trucker finally slept.

Exercise A

Fill in each blank in the paragraph below with an appropriate word from Word List A. Use each word only once.

In Greek myths, transformation was sometimes a substitute for death and

[1] _____. Once changed, the human often lived on as a flower in a

[2] _____ or a hillside in bloom. That is the case with Narcissus, who

was a handsome youth who preferred the woods to the confinement of a house

or [3] _____. Narcissus thought very highly himself and was considered

[4] _____. Although he lacked many [5] _____, such as

compassion and humility, the nymph Echo fell in love with him. Despite her

persistence, Echo finally grew [6] _____ of rejection, and died of grief.

One day, Narcissus saw himself in the water. From that moment on, he found

great [7] _____ and satisfaction when gazing at his own reflection. In an

attempt to embrace his image, he fell into the water and drowned. His body was

transformed into a white narcissus flower that can [8] _____ itself each

spring.

Read the following passage. Pay special attention to the underlined words. Then, read it again, and complete the activities. Use a separate sheet of paper for your written answers.

One of the most famous symbols of romance is the winged infant Cupid. Armed with a bow and arrows, he inspires love wherever his darts strike. Rosy-cheeked and chubby, Cupid is the picture of contentment. Artists constantly renew his image, allowing Cupid to reflect the popular taste of the day. But no matter how he appears, no one seems to grow tired or weary of his charms.

Both the Romans and the Greeks regarded Cupid as the god of love, although there were some differences between their views. The Romans usually depicted him as a mischievous baby boy. He was often blindfolded to symbolize that love is blind. Sometimes he was pictured as a cherub, draped in a garland of decorative flowers. Other times he was depicted sleeping peacefully in his mother's chamber. The Greeks called him Eros and described him as a fickle teenage god with flaws as well as virtues. He had a second type of arrow which destroyed love, making even the deepest affection decay when it struck.

Eros performed pranks for his vain mother, Aphrodite, who was consumed with her own beauty. When Aphrodite decided that the beautiful mortal Psyche was her rival, she ordered Eros to make Psyche fall in love with the ugliest man on earth. Instead, Eros accidentally struck himself with his own arrow, and fell in love with Psyche himself. Their happiness was ruined by Psyche's jealous sisters, and Psyche was forced to descend into the underworld in order to prove her love and be reunited with Eros. Eventually, she was made a goddess herself, and resided in Olympus with Eros.

1. Circle the words that describe why Cupid is the "picture of contentment." Explain what *contentment* means.

2. Underline the phrase that describes why an artist might renew Cupid's image. Use *renew* in a sentence.

3. Circle the synonym for weary. Give an example something that has made you *weary*.

4. Underline the words that provide a hint to the meaning of garland. Explain how a *garland* is used.

5. Underline the words that describe what Cupid did in the chamber. What is a *chamber*?

6. Circle the antonym for virtues. Then, give one *virtue* that Cupid might possess.

7. Circle the word that means about the same as decay. What is an antonym of *decay*?

8. Underline the words that describe how Aphrodite was vain. Give an example of something a *vain* person might do.

Sonnets 1, 35, 75
Edmund Spenser

Sonnets 31 and 39
Sir Philip Sidney

Summaries In **Sonnet 1,** Spenser asks his pages, lines, and rhymes to please his beloved. In **Sonnet 35,** he says that he cannot gaze upon his beloved without feeling the pain of hopeless desire. In **Sonnet 75,** he writes his beloved's name in the sand. However, the waves wash it away.

In **Sonnet 31,** Sidney sees the pale moon. He asks if the moon is pale because, like him, it is unhappy in love. Sidney asks for the peace and healing of sleep in **Sonnet 39.** Asleep, he may dream of Stella, his beloved.

Note-Taking Guide
One way an author tries to describe something for a reader is to compare it to something else. As you read these sonnets, use this chart explain the comparison that the poet is making in each of the listed phrases.

Sonnet	The Comparison, in the Poet's Words	What Two Items Are Being Compared?
1	"lily hands"	The beloved's hands are being compared to
35	"hungry eyes"	The yearning of the poet's eyes is being compared to
75	"My verse . . . shall . . . in the heavens write your glorious name."	The poet's verse is being compared to
31	"With how sad steps, O Moon, thou climb'st . . ."	The moon is being compared to
39	"sleep, the certain knot of peace"	Sleep is being compared to

Sonnet 1 • Sonnet 35 • Sonnet 75 • Sonnet 31 • Sonnet 39

1. **Literary Analysis:** Use this chart to compare and contrast one of Sidney's **sonnets** with one of Spenser's. Some information has been filled in.

Petrarchan/ Spenserian?	Speaker's Situation	Addressed to...	Types of Images	Speaker's Conclusion
Spenser, Sonnet 1		Leaves, lines, and rhymes		
Sidney, Sonnet 31		the moon		

2. **Literary Analysis:** Do Sidney's Sonnets 31 and 39 more closely follow the **Spenserian** or the **Petrarchan** form? Explain.

_____

_____

3. **Reading Strategy:** Write a **paraphrase** of lines 1–8 of Sidney's Sonnet 39.

_____

_____

_____

Writing About the Essential Question

What is the relationship of the writer to tradition? What, if anything, do the regular rhymes and briefness of the sonnet form add to these poets' expressions of love? Explain.

_____

_____

The Passionate Shepherd to His Love
• The Nymph's Reply to the Shepherd

Literary Analysis

A **pastoral** poem celebrates life in the country. In many pastoral poems, the speaker is a shepherd. The shepherd usually writes to someone he loves about how beautiful nature is.

Pastoral poems were written for people who lived in the city. The poems let people experience what a simple country life was like. When you read these pastoral poems, look for:

- details in "The Passionate Shepherd to His Love" that describe how beautiful nature in the country is;

- details in "The Nymph's Reply to the Shepherd" that point out what is wrong with the shepherd's ideas about nature.

Look for **common themes** in these poems. Common themes occur so often that they are considered universal. One common theme is love and its connection to youth and nature.

Reading Strategy

Before reading, it is important to **establish a purpose for reading,** such as identifying with the speaker of a poem. When you **identify with the speaker of a poem,** you try to understand the speaker's feelings and goals. Recognizing these feelings and goals can help you figure out a poem's theme. Fill in this chart. It will help you identify with each speaker.

Character	Feelings	Goals	Themes
Me			

Word List A

Study these words from the selections. Then, complete the activities.

passionate [PA shuhn it] *adj.* capable of, having, or dominated by powerful emotions
Everyone in the actor's family had a passionate personality.

shepherd [SHEP erd] *n.* one who herds, guards, and tends sheep
The shepherd had a dog that stopped the sheep from straying.

groves [GROHVZ] *n.* A small stand of trees lacking dense undergrowth
The scouts pitched their tents in the palm groves.

flocks [FLOKZ] *n.* groups of animals that live, travel, or feed together
When the television crew flew over Scotland, they filmed flocks of sheep on the hillsides.

shallow [SHAL loh] *adj.* lacking physical depth
The toddler's swimming pool was very shallow.

melodious [muh LOH dee uhs] *adj.* agreeable to hear
When played well, the clarinet has a melodious sound.

fragrant [FRAY gruhnt] *adj.* having a pleasant odor
The florist used roses and lavender to make a fragrant sachet.

nymph [NIMF] *n.* a beautiful maiden
The director of the opera put an extra nymph in the forest scene.

Exercise A

Fill in each blank in the paragraph below with an appropriate word from Word List A. Use each word only once.

At the end of the sixteenth century, people in England believed that moon and all the planets traveled around the earth, in [1] _____ harmony, creating the "music of the spheres." Planets were believed to influence a person's fate and personality. Both melancholy and [2] _____ tempers were thought to occur when a person was out of tune with the universe. The planets controlled everything from luck to weather. To keep his [3] _____ safe, a [4] _____ might consult an astrologer to learn if a storm was coming. The sound of wind rustling leaves through [5] _____ of trees might be attributed to an enchanted wood [6] _____. Similarly, the babbling sounds of a [7] _____ brook might be credited to a water sprite. Sweetly [8] _____ fennel was stuffed into door locks to prevent evil spirits from entering the house.

1. Circle the words that tell what symbolizes <u>passionate</u> true love. Then, tell what *passionate* means.

2. Underline the words that tell what kinds of <u>groves</u> the leaves came from. Write a sentence using the word *groves*.

3. Circle the word that describes the kind of <u>flocks</u> that were grazing. Name a *flock* of something you have seen.

4. Underline the words that gives a clue as to what a <u>shepherd</u> does. Describe what you think the duties of a *shepherd* were.

5. Circle the words that help to define <u>melodious</u>. Give a synonym for *melodious*.

6. Circle the word that describes the <u>nymph</u>. Tell what a *nymph* is.

7. Underline the nearby word that is a synonym for <u>fragrant</u>. Then, write a sentence using the word *fragrant*.

8. Circle the words that help to explain the meaning of <u>shallow</u>. Describe something that is *shallow*.

Read the following passage. Pay special attention to the underlined words. Then, read it again, and complete the activities. Use a separate sheet of paper for your written answers.

While almost everyone knows that a red rose symbolizes <u>passionate</u> love, few people realize that flowers have been used for centuries to convey a range of emotions. The Victorians specialized in this subtle form of communication and even published books on what they called the "language of flowers." Using various blossoms and floral arrangements, they expressed feelings which otherwise might not be spoken.

In addition to flowers, plants and herbs were used to send messages. For example, rue meant disdain, mint implied wisdom, rosemary was a sign of remembrance, and parsley was connected with celebrations. Leaves from <u>groves</u> of laurel trees were woven into wreaths to symbolize victory, a custom that began in ancient Greece.

Ancient Greece—sometimes idealized by the Victorians as a landscape dotted with <u>flocks</u> of gently grazing sheep, the contented <u>shepherd</u> watching nearby, playing a <u>melodious</u> tune on his pipes, and perhaps a lovely <u>nymph</u> hiding in the woods—was where the pastoral tradition had its beginnings. Flowers are one of nature's simple joys that are celebrated in the pastoral tradition, and the "language of flowers" certainly has some connection to the classical world.

For years, this form of sweet-smelling, <u>fragrant</u> communication was full of nuances: the type of flower, its color, and especially the way it was given, all held special meaning. A rosebud presented upright would convey the message: "I fear, but I hope." The same rosebud presented upside down would signal there was no reason to hope. The nuances of this "language" are now mostly forgotten, but some remain. White roses still signify virtue, yellow roses stand for friendship, pansies mean "thoughts of you," and lilies imply purity. So, though we may not be fluent in the "language of flowers," and our gestures may be <u>shallow</u> rather than deep, we still use flowers to express our feelings.

The Passionate Shepherd to His Love
Christopher Marlowe

The Nymph's Reply to the Shepherd
Sir Walter Raleigh

Summaries In **"The Passionate Shepherd to His Love,"** a shepherd invites his love to live with him. They will live in nature, surrounded by valleys and hills. The shepherd describes all the beauties they will see and enjoy.

In **"The Nymph's Reply to the Shepherd,"** the shepherd's love answers his passionate request. She turns him down because everything changes and ages. All the beauties he describes will fade. Neither youth nor love will last.

Note-taking Guide

As you read these two poems, record the shepherd's promises and the nymph's replies on this chart. Also, explain who you think is more convincing.

What Does the Shepherd Promise?	What Does the Nymph Respond?	Who Is More Convincing? Why?

The Passionate Shepherd to His Love
• The Nymph's Reply to the Shepherd

1. **Literary Analysis:** Both poems are examples of **pastoral** poetry. Each poem expresses a different idea. Use the chart to record details that express the shepherd's idealistic version of nature and the nymph's less idealistic view. One item has been filled in for you.

Shepherd's Idealism	Nymph's Realism
We will enjoy the beauty of valley's groves, hills, and fields.	

2. **Literary Analysis:** Both poems present some **common themes.** How does each speaker present the common theme of the beauty of life in nature?

_____

_____

3. **Reading Strategy:** Do you **sympathize** with the speaker's feelings and goals in "The Passionate Shepherd to His Love"? Why or why not?

_____

_____

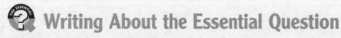 Writing About the Essential Question

What is the relationship between place and literature? What is the good, if any, of using literature to imagine an ideal setting?

_____

_____

_____

Sonnet 29 • Sonnet 106 • Sonnet 116 • Sonnet 130

Literary Analysis

A **Shakespearean** (shayk SPIR ee uhn) sonnet has fourteen lines, as do all sonnets. However, unlike Petrarchan and Spenserian sonnets, a Shakespearean sonnet follows this rhyme scheme: *abab cdcd efef gg.* Shakespearean sonnets contain the following elements:

- three **quatrains,** or four-line stanzas
- a rhyming **couplet,** which often resolves the central problem of the sonnet

Shakespeare was free with his **syntax,** or sentence structure. He includes different sentence types and lengths. His changes often result in unusual and dramatic effects.

Reading Strategy

As you read, **relate structure to meaning.** In each sonnet, Shakespeare builds on his meaning from quatrain to quatrain. Notice how he uses the couplet to deliver a dramatic final statement. As you read, fill in this chart. Record the main idea in the second quatrain of Sonnet 29. Then, in the third box, explain how the ideas in the first two quatrains are related.

Quatrain 1		Quatrain 2		Relation of 1 and 2
Content: Speaker has bad luck, which causes him to feel isolated. He pities himself and bemoans his condition. **Theme:** bad fortune; self-pity	+		=	**Change in Theme:**

Word List A

Study these words from the selections. Then, complete the activities.

disgrace [dis GRAYS] *n.* loss of honor or respect
The mayor was found to be corrupt, and resigned in <u>disgrace</u>.

fortune [FOR chun] *n.* a person's standing in life determined by money or possessions
His <u>fortune</u> *improved after he won cash and prizes on the game show.*

contented [kon TENT id] *adj.* satisfied; desiring nothing more
After eating his favorite lunch, the <u>contented</u> *child fell asleep.*

scorn [SKORN] *v.* to reject
Teachers <u>scorn</u> *disruptive behavior in class.*

prophecies [PRAHF i seez] *n.* predictions
The palm-reader's <u>prophecies</u> *hardly ever came true.*

divining [di VYN ing] *v.* to know by intuition or reflection
The Hollywood insider was famous for <u>divining</u> *each year's Oscar winners.*

tempests [TEM pists] *n.* violent wind and rain storms
Violent <u>tempests</u> *wrecked many ships that tried to sail around the Cape of Good Hope.*

despising [dis PYZ ing] *v.* to dislike intensely
<u>Despising</u> the bitter taste, the boy refused to eat his spinach.

Exercise A

Fill in each blank below with the appropriate word from Word List A.

If you are considering a career as a television or movie actor, do not expect a glamorous life. First, you will need a professional agent who will help your career by arranging auditions, giving advice, and [1] _____ mysterious knowledge about the industry. Using inside knowledge and experience, good agents often can make accurate [2] _____ about who will be successful. But even a great agent can't guarantee you a [3] _____. Most actors take extra jobs as waiters, bartenders, or caterers to pay the bills. Actors usually do not [4] _____ their poverty, they just try to hold their heads high through the [5] _____ that unemployment can bring. Most actors know their chances are slim, and enter the profession [6] _____ the fact that they will never be wealthy. They deal with disappointment and the raging, emotional [7] _____ that rejection creates, feeling they will never live [8] _____ lives if they ignore their passion for the theater.

Read the following passage. Pay special attention to the underlined words. Then, read it again, and complete the activities. Use a separate sheet of paper for your written answers.

Ted Smitty was the meteorologist for WUCG's evening news broadcast, and he was best in the business because his <u>prophecies</u> were almost always accurate. If he predicted a rainstorm, the entire metro area would retrieve their umbrellas. He didn't make a <u>fortune</u>, but he earned enough to live comfortably. Ted had gained a reputation as being the most reliable weatherman on television, a mixed blessing considering what he was about to do.

"We'll see gathering clouds, followed by showers and heavy precipitation throughout the week," he reported, <u>despising</u> the fact that viewers would be distressed by the inclement weather. He reminded himself that his job required an honest assessment of meteorological patterns and sudden climate changes. Still, it was difficult to say what nobody wanted to hear, especially for a <u>contented</u> weatherman who was happiest standing in front of maps and charts, <u>divining</u> crucial information.

"By Saturday we will experience monsoon-like cloudbursts," he continued, indicating threatening swirls on the screen. "<u>Tempests</u> will blow in from the Northeast, so batten down the lawn furniture and heed small craft warnings." Ruining weekends for his audience was hard, but listening to the jokes from his co-workers was even worse.

"<u>Tempests</u> are the best you can do? Gosh, thanks, Ted, I'll have to forego my weekend plans!" said Katie, the cheery news anchor, in a fake tone of annoyance. Ted felt himself blush. It wasn't his fault that the weather was a <u>disgrace</u> to his profession. He just reported it!

Ted shrugged off the insensitive remark, but his <u>scorn</u> seeped through as he continued his report. "Actually, Katie," he quipped, "by Sunday the deluge will be over and the storm system will have lifted, so you can spend the day on your sailboat while I'm in the office reading pressure charts. Now let's turn to Bob with sports."

© Pearson Education

1. Circle the part of the sentence that describes Ted's prophecies. Then, explain what a *prophecy* is.

2. Circle the part of the sentence that describes how Ted lived without making a fortune. In what jobs do people make *fortunes*?

3. Rewrite the sentence using a synonym for <u>despising</u>. What is Ted *despising*?

4. Circle the words that tell why Ted was a <u>contented</u> weatherman. Then, tell what *contented* means.

5. Circle the words that tell what Ted uses when he is <u>divining</u>. Then, explain what *divining* means.

6. Circle the part of the sentence that tells how people should prepare for the <u>tempests</u>. What are *tempests*?

7. Rewrite the sentence using a synonym for <u>disgrace</u>. Is Ted over-reacting? Would bad weather really be a *disgrace* to a weatherman?

8. Circle how Ted expressed his <u>scorn</u> for Katie. Why did he *scorn* her?

Sonnet 29 • Sonnet 106 • Sonnet 116 • Sonnet 130

William Shakespeare

Summaries The speaker in **Sonnet 29** wallows in his own misfortune and wishes he were someone else. However, thinking about his loved one brings him such joy that he is happy to be himself. In **Sonnet 106,** the speaker says that even the best writers of the past lacked the words and skill to praise his love. **Sonnet 116** is about true love and how it never changes. In **Sonnet 130,** the speaker says that his beloved is not the typical beauty described in many poems.

Note-taking Guide

In some of the sonnets, the speaker seems to be addressing a specific person. In others, the speaker appears to address the general public. For each sonnet, use the chart to record whom the speaker addresses and the main idea of the couplet at the end of the poem.

	Whom the speaker addresses	Main idea of the couplet
Sonnet 29		
Sonnet 106		
Sonnet 116		
Sonnet 130		

Sonnet 29 • Sonnet 106 • Sonnet 116 • Sonnet 130

1. **Literary Analysis:** Shakespeare uses different **syntax** in different poems. Contrast the syntax of Sonnet 106 and Sonnet 116. Explain how they are different.

_____

_____

2. **Literary Analysis:** Use the chart below to explain Shakespeare's message in Sonnet 106. One box is filled in for you.

Theme:		
Message of Quatrain 1: When in historical records and old poems I see descriptions of lovely women and handsome knights.	Message of Quatrain 2:	Message of Quatrain 3:
Connection to Theme:	Connection to Theme:	Connection to Theme:
Message of Couplet:		

3. **Reading Strategy:** Does each idea in Sonnet 116 correspond to a quatrain or couplet? Explain.

_____

_____

Writing About the Essential Question

What is the relationship of the writer to tradition? What advantages or disadvantages does the Shakespearean sonnet have compared with the Petrarchan sonnet? Explain.

_____

_____

from The King James Bible

Literary Analysis

Faith is a theme that appears in the Bible. It appears in literary forms such as these:

- **Psalms**—sacred songs or lyric poems that praise God. The Old Testament's Book of Psalms contains 150 such pieces.

- **Sermons**—speeches that give religious or moral instruction. The Sermon on the Mount contains the basic teachings of Christianity.

- **Parables**—simple stories from which a moral or religious lesson can be drawn. The most famous are in the New Testament.

Notice that each type of writing communicates in its own way. As songs, psalms use vivid **metaphors,** comparisons in which one thing is spoken of as if it were another. Sermons may use **analogies,** explanations that compare abstract things to familiar ones. Parables use **narratives,** or stories, to illustrate a message.

Reading Strategy

Some parts of the Bible do not include a direct explanation of their meaning. To find the main idea or **essential message,** a reader must **make inferences,** or uncover meaning that is not stated directly. To make inferences, find key details in the text. Then, examine the relation of one detail to another. Use the chart below.

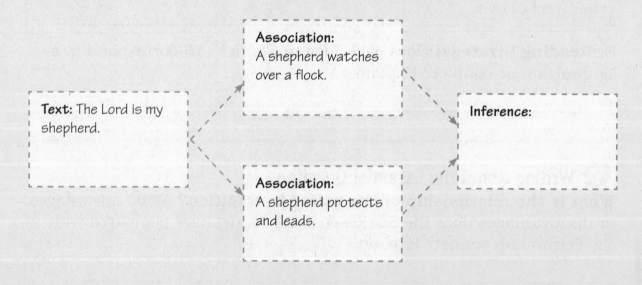

Association:
A shepherd watches over a flock.

Text: The Lord is my shepherd.

Inference:

Association:
A shepherd protects and leads.

Word List A

Study these words from the selection. Then, complete the activities.

consider [kuhn SID uhr] *v.* think about in order to understand or decide
If you like working with computers, consider taking a course in programming.

devoured [di VOWRD] *v.* ate or otherwise consumed with great hunger
After completing the marathon, the runner devoured two bowls of pasta.

famine [FAM uhn] *n.* a severe shortage of food
During the famine, the government sent food to the people suffering from starvation.

mercy [MUR see] *n.* kindness; forgiveness; kind or forgiving actions
The animal shelter takes mercy on abandoned dogs and finds them homes.

pastures [PAS chuhrz] *n.* grassy, open fields
Wild flowers grew in the pastures where the cows grazed.

perish [PER ish] *v.* die; become spoiled; be destroyed
Forgetting to water the tomato plants could cause them to perish.

portion [PAWR shuhn] *n.* a section or part of a whole; a share
My portion of ice cream is bigger than his.

presence [PREZ uhns] *n.* fact of being in a particular place
The critic's presence at the performance made the actors nervous.

Exercise A

Fill in each blank in the paragraph below with an appropriate word from Word List A. Use each word only once.

Starvation was a widespread problem in ancient history, a fact shown by

the frequent mention of [1] _____ in the Bible. Changes in weather, crop

diseases, plagues, insects, drought, and other natural disasters could easily

provoke a food shortage. Drawings on walls in ancient Rome show farmers

fighting locusts that have [2] _____ their crops. Drought turned the

growing fields to dust and dried up [3] _____ where animals grazed.

Unless governments or individuals had stored a [4] _____ of their

harvest, there was no available relief. An extended famine meant many would

[5] _____, especially the poor. Those who did survive were vulnerable to

disease and attack. [6] _____ how a population weak from hunger might

react to the [7] _____ of an enemy. Rather than mounting a defense, they

could do little but beg for [8] _____.

1. Circle the phrase in the next sentence that is a clue to the meaning of <u>presence</u>. Describe something that is a *presence* in most homes today.

2. Underline the phrase that hints at the meaning of <u>devoured</u>. If a person *devoured* a meal, how did he or she feel before eating?

3. Circle the words that tell who completed each <u>portion</u> of the work. Then, tell what *portion* means.

4. Underline the words that name an action the scribes <u>consider</u>. Then, rewrite the sentence using a phrase that means the same as *consider*.

5. Circle the phrase that gives an example of a work of <u>mercy</u>. Then, tell what *mercy* means.

6. Underline the words that are clues to the meaning of <u>famine</u>. Tell what a *famine* might be like.

7. Circle the words that tell what the monks' <u>pastures</u> were used for. Explain what *pastures* look like.

8. Underline the phrase that is a clue to the meaning of <u>perish</u>. Tell why a work might *perish*.

Read the following passage. Pay special attention to the underlined words. Then, read it again, and complete the activities. Use a separate sheet of paper for your written answers.

Before the invention of printing press, books were made by hand and treated as works of art. Often, they were heavily illustrated and bound with jeweled and enameled covers that increased their worth. Most of these elaborate volumes were bibles. They featured vivid lettering and colorful drawings that depicted incidents from the Old and New Testaments.

Some ornate books contained classic works by Latin and Greek philosophers. Others were mathematical or scientific texts. Books were too valuable to be a <u>presence</u> in the homes of ordinary people, most of whom could not read anyway. Instead, books were found in religious institutions, such as monasteries, and in palaces. Since books were almost irreplaceable, they had to be kept where they would not be chewed up and <u>devoured</u> by rodents or insects.

The creation of a book was usually a collaborative effort. Individual craftsmen each completed a <u>portion</u> of the work. For example, dried hides of animals were needed to make parchment pages. One group of craftsmen sized, cut, lined, and sewed these together. Another group created and mixed the inks and dyes used. Still another was responsible for pens and brushes. These had to be ready for use before scribes could <u>consider</u> copying the text and passing the pages to illustrators.

Most bookmakers in the Middle Ages were monks, usually the best educated members of a largely illiterate society. Medieval monks dedicated their lives to prayer and scholarship. They also performed works of <u>mercy</u>. For example, they shared their food with the hungry, not just in times of <u>famine</u>, but whenever they were asked.

The monks sustained themselves by raising their own crops, by grazing animals in <u>pastures</u>, and by copying ancient and sacred texts, especially bibles. This work gave them an income, and also ensured that the contents of these works did not <u>perish</u> when their original manuscripts turned to dust.

Psalms 23, 137

Summaries Psalm 23 is a sacred song or lyric poem that praises God. The speaker compares God to a shepherd who cares for his flock both during and after life. Some of the words do not address God directly. However, this psalm is often used as a prayer asking God to continue providing loving care for the person praying.

Psalm 137
In this Psalm, the narrator is sitting on a riverbank remembering Zion, a sacred city in the Bible. When asked to sing a song of the city, the narrator shares his uncertainty about singing.

Note-taking Guide

Psalm 23 praises God for acting as a shepherd to his people. As you read, use this chart to record what God does in the left column. Then, in the right column, restate these actions in your own words. One item has already been filled in.

Deeds Listed in Text	How God Is Comforting and Protecting
He maketh me lie down in green pastures; he leadeth me beside the still waters.	He provides a place to rest and drink.

from The Sermon on the Mount

Summary The Sermon on the Mount is a speech thought to have been made by Jesus. The sermon includes many basic principles of the Christian religion. This section of the longer speech teaches that people cannot serve both God and money. Also, no one should worry about physical needs because God will provide everything, just as He does for birds and plants.

Note-taking Guide

Use the chart below to record important details from The Sermon on the Mount.

Title: The Sermon on the Mount

Audience:

Purpose:

Advice Given:

The Parable of the Prodigal Son

Summary The Parable of the Prodigal Son is the story of a man with two sons. One son stays home and works. The other son leaves home, lives wildly, and spends everything. He is the prodigal (PRAH di GUHL), a person who is recklessly wasteful. When that son becomes hungry, he returns home and apologizes. His father is delighted and holds a feast. This angers the brother who stayed home and worked. The father explains that it is worth celebrating when someone who goes astray is found again.

Note-taking Guide

As you read, fill in the chart below with information about the two sons in the story. Then, write the overall message in the box at the bottom.

Young Son	Older Son
How he lives his life:	How he lives his life:
What he does at the end:	How he feels at the end:
Message of the story:	

from The King James Bible

1. **Literary Analysis:** Why is the form of a **sermon** suited to the message taught by the Sermon on the Mount?

_____

_____

2. **Literary Analysis:** Explain how the **metaphor** of the shepherd in Psalm 23, the **analogy** of the birds in the Sermon on the Mount, and the **narrative** in the Parable of the Prodigal Son are all suited to an audience of simple, rural folk. Enter your reasons in the following chart. Some entries have been filled in for you.

Images: Familiar/Unfamiliar	Simple/Difficult?	Memorable? Why?
Psalm 23: shepherd metaphor	Simple image, familiar to rural folk	Memorable because it expresses God's care in a vivid way

3. **Reading Strategy: Make inferences** about the meaning of this quotation from Psalm 23: "I will dwell in the house of the Lord forever."

_____

_____

Writing About the Essential Question

How does literature shape or reflect society? What made the King James Bible so influential?

_____

_____

_____

The Tragedy of Macbeth, Act I

Literary Analysis

Elizabethan drama came into full bloom during the late 1500s. Playwrights stopped writing about religion. They began writing more complicated plays about human nature. Playwrights reintroduced plays called **tragedies.** These plays tell about a hero to whom something terrible happens.

A **soliloquy** (suh LIL uh KWEE) is a long speech. It is usually made by a character alone on stage. A soliloquy reveals a character's private thoughts and feelings to the audience. However, other characters do not hear it. In Shakespeare's tragedies, characters reveal secret desires or fears through their soliloquies. As you read Lady Macbeth's soliloquy in Act I, use the chart below to note the inner struggles she reveals.

```
┌─────────────────────────┐
│ Detail:                 │
│                         │                    ┌───────────────────────────┐
│ Reveals:                │ ⟍                  │ Likely Outcome:           │
│                         │   ⟍                │                           │
└─────────────────────────┘     ↘              │                           │
                                  →             │                           │
┌─────────────────────────┐     ↗              │                           │
│ Detail:                 │   ⟋                │                           │
│                         │ ⟋                  │                           │
│ Reveals:                │                    └───────────────────────────┘
│                         │
└─────────────────────────┘
```

Reading Strategy

Shakepeare's plays were meant to be performed, not read. Playwrights and editors often add **text features** to printed versions of the plays. These features explain how to interpret the play. They include stage directions in brackets and notes on the side of the text. Analyze and evaluate these features when you read the play.

Word List A

Study these words from the selection. Then, complete the activities.

ambition [am BISH uhn] *n.* strong desire to achieve something
　The pitcher's ambition was to play baseball in a major league.

assault [uh SAWLT] *n.* an attack
　The soldiers began an assault on the enemies' fort.

plight [PLYT] *n.* bad condition or situation that someone is in
　As the scared kitten climbed further up the tree, her plight grew worse.

rebel [REB uhl] *n.* one who opposes a government or other authority
　The rebel refused to obey the laws of his country and fought its government.

revolt [ree VOHLT] *n.* actions taken to overthrow an authority
　In revolt against the babysitter, the twins locked themselves in their room.

swarm [SWAWRM] *n.* a large, moving group of people, animals, or insects
　A swarm of flies landed on the picnic sandwiches.

traitor [TRAYT uhr] *n.* disloyal person; someone who turns against his or her country
　The traitor gave his own government's secrets to the enemy.

vanished [VAN ishd] *v.* disappeared
　The box is still on the table, but the cookies inside have all vanished.

Exercise A

Fill in each blank below using the appropriate word from Word List A.

　Many tourists who visit England explore the historic Tower of London. The landmark is an eighteen-acre complex of buildings entirely surrounded by thick walls designed to protect against an enemy [1] _____. Today, the Tower serves as a museum where the crown jewels are stored. But for many hundreds of years, it was a prison and a place of execution, where people would come in a [2] _____ to witness the terrible [3] _____ of doomed prisoners. These public displays reminded nobles with political [4] _____ and common people tempted to [5] _____ that challenging the king could be fatal.

　Anyone who spoke out against a ruling monarch was considered either a [6] _____ or a [7] _____ and risked being convicted of treason. Many of those who suffered that fate are buried in a chapel on the site. Still others lived and died there, but the records of their lives have [8] _____.

© Pearson Education

Read the following passage. Pay special attention to the underlined words. Then, read it again, and complete the activities. Use a separate sheet of paper for your written answers.

Everything most people know about the historical Scottish leader Macbeth they learned from William Shakespeare's play *The Tragedy of Macbeth*. In the play, Macbeth and his queen are ruthless murderers eager for power and driven by ambition. The fictional Macbeth is introduced as a hero, but he soon becomes a desperate character. He listens to witches and plots to take the Scottish crown. His first victim is King Duncan. Many others follow, as Macbeth uses murder to clear a path to the throne. Macbeth's descent into evil and his plight as one crime forces him to commit another make great drama. However, most of the story is not historically accurate.

Records kept by eleventh-century monks report that the real King Duncan died in battle with Macbeth. Macbeth may have been a rebel, challenging the king's authority, but he certainly was not a secretly scheming traitor who murdered his sleeping king. In addition, Macbeth's loyal wife was innocent of any wrongdoing.

Macbeth became king after Duncan, but there are no reports of King Macbeth wiping out families who might challenge his claim to the crown. By all accounts, he ruled a united Scotland for seventeen years. In fact, his kingdom was so stable, he left the country to visit Rome without fear of an uprising or a revolt.

Any assault against Macbeth came from without, not from within. During his reign, a swarm of invaders attacked Scotland, making it the center of an ongoing battle for control of Britain. Norse, Danes, Romans, English Saxons, and others struggled to take over the country, but their campaigns were not successful.

Macbeth was hailed as a great king at the time of his death, but his reputation for peace and prosperity has almost completely vanished. Thanks to the vivid portrait created by Shakespeare, Macbeth is remembered not as a popular monarch, but as a warrior corrupted by his desire for power.

1. Underline the phrase that is a clue to the meaning of ambition. Tell what the word *ambition* means.

2. Circle the words that describe Macbeth's plight. Then, use *plight* in a sentence of your own.

3. Underline the words that help define the word rebel. Explain what a *rebel* is.

4. Circle the words that describe the way a traitor might act. Why might Macbeth seem like a *traitor* in the play?

5. Circle the phrase that suggests the opposite of revolt. Then, give an example of a *revolt*.

6. Circle the word that is a clue to the meaning of assault. Rewrite the sentence using a synonym for *assault*.

7. Underline the words that name the peoples making up the swarm. Explain what the word *swarm* means.

8. Circle the words that tell what vanished means. Then, give a synonym for *vanished*.

The Tragedy of Macbeth, Act I
William Shakespeare

Summary Macbeth and Banquo (BANK wo), a fellow noble, have helped win an important battle for King Duncan of Scotland. Returning from the battle, they encounter three witches. The witches hail Macbeth as the Thane of Glamis, the Thane of Cawdor, and King. At the time, however, Macbeth is only Thane of Glamis. The witches also say that Banquo shall father a long line of kings.

Then, King Duncan honors Macbeth by making him Thane of Cawdor. Macbeth imagines he will be king as well. However, Duncan also names his own son, Malcolm, as his successor. Macbeth begins to think of murdering the king. Lady Macbeth fears Macbeth will not carry out their plot. She urges him on.

Note-taking Guide
As you read, use this chart to record important information in Act I.

Background Information:

Witches' Prediction:

Macbeth's Plan:

The Tragedy of Macbeth, Act I

1. **Literary Analysis:** How does Macbeth's meeting with the witches show that this **Elizabethan drama** will probably be a **tragedy?**

   _____

   _____

2. **Literary Analysis:** What does Lady Macbeth's **soliloquy** in Act I, Scene v, lines 1–30, reveal about her thoughts and plans?

   _____

   _____

3. **Reading Strategy:** Using text features, analyze the details of setting in the lines shown on the chart. Then, in the boxes on the right, indicate how modern sets and lighting could produce such a setting. One box has been filled in for you.

Shakespeare's Words	Modern Sets and Lighting
Act I, Scene i, lines 1–11	To show thunder and lightning, flashing lights and recordings of thunder and lightning
Act I, Scene vi, lines 3–10	

? Writing About the Essential Question

What is the relationship of the writer to tradition? Unlike classical tragedies, Macbeth includes comedy in its portrayal of a noble character's downfall. Explain.

_____

_____

_____

The Tragedy of Macbeth, Act II

Literary Analysis

Lines written in **blank verse** are lines that have a strict meter but do not rhyme. This meter is called iambic (i AM bik) pentameter. Each line is made up of pairs of syllables called iambs. An **iamb** (I am) consists of an unstressed syllable followed by a stressed syllable (indicated by the accent marks ˘ ´). In iambic pentameter, there are five iambs in each line. *Macbeth* is written mainly in blank verse:

Me thought I heard a voice cry, "Sleep no more!" (II, ii, 34)

Shakespeare often changes his meter to make his verse more interesting. Sometimes, he begins lines with a stressed syllable followed by an unstressed syllable. This pair of syllables is called a **trochaic** (troh KAY ik) **foot.** He also sometimes uses an **anapestic** (an uh PES tik) **foot.** This foot has two unstressed syllables followed by a stressed syllable.

Sometimes Shakespeare uses prose. **Prose** is writing that is not divided into poetic lines. Also, prose lacks a regular rhythm. Characters such as servants often speak in prose. These lower-ranking characters often provide comic relief.

Reading Strategy

The way in which a passage is organized can affect its meaning. This play is organized in blank verse. To **read blank verse for meaning,** follow sentences past line endings. Use the chart to distinguish between lines and sentences. Count the sentences and lines. Then, write the meaning.

Passage: II, i, 33–39	
Begins: "Is this a dagger which I see before me…"	
Number of Lines	**Number of Sentences**
Meaning	

Word List A

Study these words from the selection. Then, complete the activities.

clutch [KLUCH] *v.* hold onto something tightly
The man tried to clutch the railing when he slipped on the stairs.

conclusion [kuhn KLOO zhuhn] *n.* ending; the finish of something
At the conclusion of her speech, the mayor received loud applause.

contradict [KAHN truh dikt] *v.* say or prove the opposite of
I said, "It's green," and just to contradict me, she said, "No, it's blue."

repose [ri POHZ] *n.* rest; sleep
The children were so noisy that they disturbed their grandmother's repose.

resembled [ri ZEM buhld] *v.* had a similarity to someone or something
The new car resembled their old car; it was the same model and color.

restrain [ri STRAYN] *v.* stop; hold back; prevent from acting
The cowboy had to restrain the horse, which was bucking wildly.

seize [SEEZ] *v.* take possession by force; grab and hold
*When playing capture the flag, the winning team must seize their
opponents' flag.*

suspicion [suh SPISH uhn] *n.* unproven idea that something is wrong
*I have a suspicion that he took the cookies, but I have no evidence to
prove it.*

Exercise A

Fill in each blank below using the appropriate word from Word List A.

Sometimes it is impossible to prevent snakebites. When a person

accidentally steps on a snake in the woods, disturbing its [1] _____,

the snake's first reaction will be to strike. Snakes are predators with jaws

designed to [2] _____ prey. Once poisonous snakes [3] _____

a creature in their jaws, their fangs quickly deliver venom into the victim's

body. You must reduce your chances of being a target. Remain on hiking

paths. Regard loose rocks and firewood with [4] _____. Do not move

either without checking for snakes first. If fellow hikers say you are being

too cautious, do not hesitate to [5] _____ them! By the [6] _____

of your hike, they may thank you. Once you see a snake, [7] _____

yourself from touching it, even if it looks harmless. People have picked up

poisonous snakes because they [8] _____ nonpoisonous ones. If you

are bitten, seek help immediately.

1. Circle the word that means nearly the same as repose. Then, explain why *repose* might be important to health.

2. Circle the word that tells what people will not have to restrain themselves from. Then, tell what the word *restrain* means.

3. Circle the phrase that tells what seems to contradict common sense. Tell of another idea that seems to *contradict* common sense.

4. Underline the phrase that is a clue to the meaning of conclusion. Then, describe the *conclusion* of some event.

5. Circle the word that suggests the opposite of suspicion. Then, explain when it might be a good idea to view something with *suspicion*.

6. Circle the word that is a clue to the meaning of seize. Then, tell what *seize* means.

7. Circle the words that describe what a person might clutch. Then, use *clutch* in a sentence of your own.

8. Underline the words telling what two things resembled one another. Then, explain why the fact that they *resembled* one another does not mean they are the same.

Read the following passage. Pay special attention to the underlined words. Then, read it again, and complete the activities. Use a separate sheet of paper for your written answers.

For people who wish to be their healthiest, many experts recommend proper eating and exercise. Government guidelines include suggestions such as starting the day with a healthy breakfast and consuming five to seven servings of fruit and vegetables daily. Experts also recommend reducing stress and increasing time for repose and relaxation.

Unfortunately, not everyone follows these recommendations. For example, people who wish to lose weight may decide to follow a popular diet. Some of these diets gain popularity by promising people that they will not have to restrain themselves from eating as long as they stick to the recommended foods. That logic seems to contradict common sense and can even lead to excessive eating.

At the conclusion of a diet, when the careful calorie counting comes to an end, the result is often weight gain, not weight loss. That is because keeping weight off requires persistence and discipline. People should regard any "miracle" diet with suspicion. They should trust instead the advice of their doctor.

People who are not trying to follow a diet may also develop poor eating habits. A person may skip meals, for instance, and later seize whatever snack is most convenient, grabbing it on the way to the living room. The person may clutch a bag of chips and a soda, flop on the couch, and munch away. Even if the chips are low-fat and the soda is sugar-free, though, the person is not eating properly. These foods do not provide the body with necessary nutrients. Just after eating such a "meal," a person may have had a feeling that resembled the satisfaction of eating a good dinner. In the long run, though, the person is missing out on important nutrition.

The key to good health is not a miracle or a quick fix. Most experts agree that good health means regular, reasonable habits and a healthy variety of foods.

The Tragedy of Macbeth, Act II
William Shakespeare

Summary Macbeth wants to murder King Duncan. He imagines that he sees a dagger before him, yet he cannot seize it. Then, Macbeth kills Duncan while the king sleeps. Lady Macbeth has helped by drugging Duncan's servants so Macbeth will not wake them. Then, she covers the servants with Duncan's blood to make it seem as if they have killed him. Macduff, a nobleman, discovers the king's body. Afraid that they will be murdered next, Duncan's sons flee Scotland. With the king dead and his sons gone, Macbeth is free to seize the throne.

Note-taking Guide
Use the chart below to record important information in Act II.

Macbeth's vision:

Who is murdered:

How Malcolm and Donalbain react:

The Tragedy of Macbeth, Act II

1. **Literary Analysis:** Analyze Shakespeare's use of **blank verse.** Complete this chart by identifying the rhythm of each of the lines indicated. The first row has been filled in for you.

Line	Iambic Feet	Trochaic or Anapestic Feet
"It is the bloody business which informs. . ."	the BLOO dy BUS / iness WHICH / in FORMS	IT is (trochaic)
"'Macbeth does murder sleep'—the innocent sleep,. . ."		

2. **Literary Analysis:** How does the Porter's speech in **prose,** Act II, Scene iii, lines 1–21, offer **comic relief?**

_____

_____

3. **Reading Strategy:** The organization of text can affect its meaning. In your own words, express the meaning of the sentences in Act II, Scene i, lines 62–64.

_____

_____

 Writing About the Essential Question

How does literature shape or reflect society? Whom do you blame more for the murder of King Duncan—Macbeth or Lady Macbeth? Explain.

_____

_____

_____

_____

The Tragedy of Macbeth, Act III

Literary Analysis

Conflict is a struggle between two people or forces. Conflict creates drama.

- An **external conflict** is a struggle between two characters.
- An **internal conflict** is a struggle within a character.

The **climax** of a play is the moment when the internal and external conflicts are greatest. The action rises to the climax. This is the moment of highest tension. After the climax, the action falls as the conflicts are resolved.

Dramatic irony happens when a character's words or actions have a meaning that is different from the meaning that the character intends. In Act III, Macbeth invites Banquo to a feast. Later the audience will see how Macbeth's invitation is answered by a different guest.

Reading Strategy

Meaning is not always explained directly. As a reader, you need to **draw and support inferences** by reading "between the lines." Reading *line by line* tells you *what* happens. Reading *between the lines* tells you *why*.

Use this chart to help you read between the lines of Act III. Enter details from the play in the first two boxes. Then, in the third box, show how the link between them suggests future action.

Link to Act I, Scene iii, lines 65–69	Act III, Scene i, line 35	Future Actions?

Word List A

Study these words from the selection. Then, complete the activities.

absence [AB sens] *n.* the condition of being away
   His absence from school is due to a bad cold, and he will be back soon.

affliction [uh FLIK shuhn] *n.* suffering; a cause of suffering, such as an illness
   His illness had no cure and was a constant affliction.

confined [kuhn FYND] *adj.* kept from moving out of a place; restricted
   The power went out, and I was confined in the elevator for an hour.

custom [KUHS tuhm] *n.* habit; tradition
   It is their custom to have dinner at six o'clock.

eternal [ee TER nuhl] *adj.* without beginning or end; everlasting
   The fireman earned the mother's eternal gratitude when he saved her child.

patience [PAY shuntz] *n.* ability to wait or to suffer without complaint
   The critic needed patience to sit through the boring movie.

remedy [REM uh dee] *n.* cure; medicine; something that solves a problem
   There was no remedy for her broken heart.

summons [SUHM muhnz] *n.* order to appear at a particular place
   She received a summons for jury duty, so she went to the court the next day.

Exercise A

Fill in each blank below using the appropriate word from Word List A.

The kids loved to play hide and seek. It was their [1] _____ to gather in the park as soon as the sun went down. They would squeeze into small spaces, keeping themselves [2] _____ between rocks or under benches, hoping not to be seen or heard. Staying still and quiet required [3] _____. It also meant they could not cry out of they got a mosquito bite or were suffering from some other minor [4] _____. If the waiting was unbearable, the only [5] _____ was to make a run for home base. There was one child who could outlast everyone else. The game could not end until Elizabeth was found, and sometimes the search went on for so long that it felt [6] _____. If it lasted too long, Elizabeth's mother would notice her daughter's [7] _____ at dinner and would call out a stern [8] _____ to "Come home this instant!"

Read the following passage. Pay special attention to the underlined words. Then, read it again, and complete the activities. Use a separate sheet of paper for your written answers.

A doctor on the American frontier during the nineteenth century had to perform minor surgeries, ease many a common <u>affliction</u>, such as stomach problems, bandage wounds, mend broken bones, deliver babies, and relieve pain. He was expected to be available for these tasks at any time of day or night. When a <u>summons</u> came from a patient, he had to rush to the sick person's bedside. Once he made the journey, he had to work in whatever conditions he encountered.

Imagine traveling through a snowstorm to set a broken bone, amputate a limb, or deliver a baby by gaslight. Then, imagine performing these procedures in the <u>absence</u> of clean sheets, heat, and running water.

In return for these services, the doctor was paid very little. He did charge fees, but it was the <u>custom</u> to accept payment however it arrived. A chicken or a bushel of beans might be used to pay a debt instead of cash.

There were times when the only thing physicians could do for a patient was to offer a pain <u>remedy</u>. These doctors also served as apothecaries, preparing and dispensing medicines.

Very few of the physicians on the Western frontier had gone to school for medicine. Most learned what they knew by assisting experienced doctors. Medical knowledge was important when they came upon signs of smallpox or other contagious diseases. The doctor had to identify such illnesses and make sure the sick person was <u>confined</u> to his or her home. If the doctor failed, the illness could spread.

Besides trying to make a patient comfortable, the doctor provided compassion. A doctor's visit was not a brief, impersonal examination. He was expected to show <u>patience</u> while listening to complaints. One of his most important jobs may have been giving compassion to the dying as they prepared for their everlasting, <u>eternal</u> rest.

1. Circle the phrase that describes an example of an <u>affliction</u>. Then, give your own example of an *affliction*.

2. Underline the words that tell who gave the <u>summons</u>. Then, tell what a *summons* is.

3. Underline the words that explain what the <u>absence</u> is of. Why might the *absence* of these things be important?

4. Circle the words that are a clue to the meaning of the word <u>custom</u>. What is one *custom* people follow when going to a modern doctor?

5. Circle the word that tells what kind of <u>remedy</u> the doctors offered. Then, tell what *remedy* means.

6. Circle the words that explain where the sick person was <u>confined</u>. Explain why a *confined* smallpox patient was less of a risk to people.

7. Underline the words that tell when a doctor would need to show <u>patience</u>. Explain why *patience* might be needed.

8. Circle the word that means nearly the same as <u>eternal</u>. Then, explain what the writer means by the phrase *"eternal rest."*

The Tragedy of Macbeth, Act III

William Shakespeare

Summary Fearing the witches' prediction that Banquo will be the father of kings, Macbeth plots to have Banquo and his son, Fleance, killed. Banquo is killed, but Fleance escapes. At a banquet, Banquo's ghost appears, sitting at Macbeth's place. The ghost is visible only to Macbeth, who becomes very upset. Macbeth pledges to kill anyone who stands in his way. Also, he wants to visit the witches again. Meanwhile, Duncan's son Malcolm is living at the English court. Malcolm is raising an army to fight against Macbeth. Macduff has gone to England in order to help Malcolm.

Note-taking Guide

The action comes to a climax in Act III. Use this chart to summarize what happens in Act III and to make predictions about what will happen as the play continues.

Event	Cause	Effect	Prediction
Macbeth arranges Banquo's murder.			
Macbeth vows to keep killing until his place on the throne is secure.			
Macduff goes to England to help raise an army against Macbeth.			

The Tragedy of Macbeth, Act III

1. **Literary Analysis:** Why is Macbeth involved in an **external conflict** with Banquo?

   _____

   _____

2. **Literary Analysis:** Complete this chart to show how the **conflict** increases and moves toward a **climax.**

Action	Result	Internal Conflict	Result	Proposed Actions
Murder of Banquo: Fleance escapes	→	Macbeth struggles with fear of threat posed by Fleance	→	

3. **Reading Strategy:** Some critics say that the third murderer is Macbeth himself. By drawing inferences and reading between the lines, support or refute this claim.

   _____

   _____

Writing About the Essential Question

How does literature shape or reflect society? What does the murder of Banquo suggest about the effects of evil on evildoers? Explain.

   _____

   _____

   _____

   _____

   _____

   _____

The Tragedy of Macbeth, Act IV

Literary Analysis

Imagery is the language writers use to appeal to your senses. Imagery helps you see, hear, feel, smell, and taste what writers describe. Vivid imagery also stirs emotions. Shakespeare often uses related groups of images. In *Macbeth*, he uses these images throughout the play:

- Blood
- Ill-fitting clothes
- Babies and children, sometimes killed by Macbeth, sometimes threatening him

These images relate to important themes in the play. As you read, link these groups of images to the play's central ideas.

Some images are powerful because they are **archetypal.** This means that they relate to ideas and emotions expressed by people in many cultures. For example, in Act IV, there are **images of a fallen world**—shrieking, groaning, and bleeding. These images indicate that Macbeth's Scotland is like an underworld region where the dead are punished. Look for archetypal images as you read.

Reading Strategy

People **read for a variety of purposes.** One common purpose is to be entertained, or to enjoy the experience. You will enjoy a work of literature more if you **use your senses** to experience the imagery it contains. In the chart below, note the images in the lines listed. Then, identify which senses the images appeal to. One image has been filled in for you.

Line	Images	Appeals to which sense?
Scene i, 52	"untie the winds"	
Scene i, 53		

© Pearson Education

Word List A

Study these words from the selection. Then, complete the activities.

boasting [BOHST ing] *n.* bragging; talk that shows excessive pride
The tennis player was famous for his loud boasting about his own talent.

caldron [KAWL druhn] *n.* large pot used for boiling liquid
In the cafeteria, they keep the soup boiling in a huge caldron.

mortal [MORT uhl] *adj.* fatal; deadly
The two lions fought, and the one who received mortal injuries died.

motives [MOHT ivz] *n.* reasons for an action
He has two motives for taking this job: He needs money, and he loves the work.

rumor [ROO muhr] *n.* gossip; unproven claim spread from one person to another
The false rumor about the movie star's secret was published in a magazine.

scruples [SKROO puhlz] *n.* doubts that keep you from doing something
I was about to take the last donut, but my scruples stopped me.

trifle [TRY fuhl] *n.* something of little importance or value
I do not care that you lost my plastic bracelet, since it was just a trifle.

vanquished [VANG kwisht] *v.* defeated; conquered
The large army quickly vanquished the small army.

Exercise A

Fill in each blank below using the appropriate word from Word List A.

The girls' soccer team expected to be [1] _____ by their opponents. Their goalie had the flu, and their best player was sidelined. She had broken her leg on a field trip, when she tripped on a large [2] _____ in the kitchen of the colonial museum. The injury was not [3] _____, but the loss of their best player hurt the team's spirit. In addition, they had heard a [4] _____ that the opposing team had no [5] _____ about breaking rules. Seeing morale was low, the coach stepped in. He showered the team with praise, calling these setbacks a small [6] _____. His [7] _____ for the speech were obvious. He did not want his team to be discouraged. Listening to his [8] _____ about their playing skills, the girls felt their confidence returning. They were ready to play to win!

1. Circle the phrase that suggests how a caldron was used. Then, explain what a *caldron* might look like.

2. Circle the word that suggests the opposite of a trifle. Then, give your own example of a *trifle*.

3. Underline the phrase that is a clue to the meaning of mortal. Tell what *mortal* means.

4. Circle the word that means the opposite of vanquished. Then, rewrite the sentence using a synonym for *vanquished*.

5. Underline the phrase that is a clue to the meaning of scruples. Then, use *scruples* in a sentence of your own.

6. Underline the phrase that tells what motives these hunters had. Then, give an example of what these *motives* lead modern people to do.

7. Circle the word in the paragraph that is a clue to the meaning of boasting. What is people's *boasting* usually about?

8. Circle the word that means nearly the same as rumor. Then, give an example of a *rumor*.

Read the following passage. Pay special attention to the underlined words. Then, read it again, and complete the activities. Use a separate sheet of paper for your written answers.

Jill took her students on a tour of the natural history museum. There, she hoped they would recognize that there are connections between all people, no matter when or how they lived.

In the first gallery, the children studied old pottery, cooking utensils, and an iron caldron hung over a fire. They noticed a lot of items that were similar to the cups, plates, and spoons we use today. Next, they stopped at the cases of ancient jewelry, which included everyday objects made of pure gold and covered in gems. It surprised them that something we might consider a trifle, such as a comb, clasp, or a buckle, was so precious to our ancestors.

A model of a medieval castle was next. Tiny soldiers were locked in battle, as archers inflicted mortal wounds on the enemy, causing widespread death. It was hard to tell which army was winning and which would be vanquished. The students wondered if the people of the day had scruples about causing so much harm, or whether their ideas of right and wrong led them to accept war.

Another room contained re-creations of hunts in which primitive men captured fierce-looking wild boars. Jill explained that these hunters had good motives for putting themselves at risk. Just like modern people, they needed to feed and clothe their families.

In the next scene, the hunters had gathered around a cooking fire. The primitive men seemed to be engaged in boasting about their conquest. One had his arms stretched wide. Two women, sitting close to the coals, appeared to be whispering. Jill asked her students to imagine what gossip or rumor those women might be sharing. One girl was sure the women were telling each other that the hunter making the big gestures always exaggerated.

When everyone laughed, Jill felt she had accomplished her mission. These ancient people had become real to her students.

The Tragedy of Macbeth, Act IV

William Shakespeare

Summary Macbeth visits the witches, and they show him three spirits. The first warns him to beware of Macduff. The second says that no man "of woman born/Shall harm Macbeth." The third says that Macbeth will not be defeated until the woods themselves come to Dunsinane Hill to fight against him. When Macbeth asks about Banquo's descendants, he is shown "eight Kings and Banquo." This vision disturbs Macbeth. However, the witches vanish before Macbeth can find out what the vision means. Macbeth learns that Macduff has gone to England to join Malcolm. In revenge, Macbeth has Macduff's family killed. In England, Malcolm and Macduff discuss Macbeth. Malcolm agrees to lead a force against Macbeth.

Note-taking Guide

In Act IV, Macbeth sees four images when he visits the witches. Each image gives Macbeth a message. Describe each vision below, and note both its message and how Macbeth reacts to the message.

Description of Image	Message	Macbeth's Reaction

The Tragedy of Macbeth, Act IV

1. **Literary Analysis:** Use this chart to indicate the emotions that vivid **imagery** expresses. One passage is suggested for you. Write down the imagery it contains. Then, explain the emotions that this imagery expresses.

Passage	Vivid Imagery		Emotions Expressed
Act IV, Scene iii, lines 164–173		→	

2. **Literary Analysis:** In Act IV, Scene iii, identify two **archetypal images of a fallen world** that describe Scotland in terms of weeping, bleeding, or both.

_____

_____

3. **Reading Strategy:** How does Malcolm's description of Scotland in Act IV, Scene iii, lines 39-41 appeal to the senses of touch, sight, and sound?

_____

_____

_____

Writing About the Essential Question

How does literature shape or reflect society? If Shakespeare were alive today, would he argue that evildoers are primarily influenced by genetics, upbringing, or their own free choice?

_____

_____

_____

_____

The Tragedy of Macbeth, Act V

Literary Analysis

Shakespearean tragedy usually has these elements:

- A main character of high rank and personal quality—a tragic hero; the main character also has a **tragic flaw** or weakness
- Closely linked events that lead this character to disaster, partly through his or her flaw
- Lively action and comic scenes

   Viewing a Shakespearean tragedy is a positive experience. One source of the positive experience is the **tragic impulse.** This impulse celebrates the way in which the hero meets his or her fate in a noble way.

Reading Strategy

Literary works are products of the time period in which they were written. They reflect beliefs held by many people at that time. When you consider these beliefs, you are **relating works to the historical period.** Readers can infer, or make educated guesses about, those beliefs by focusing on the ideas the characters express. Then, readers can compare these ideas with modern ideas on the same subject.

   Use this chart to compare the ideas of the doctor in Act V, Scene i, with those of a modern doctor.

> **Doctor in *Macbeth***
>
> Mental problems may produce nighttime disturbances.

> **Modern Psychiatrist**

Word List A

Study these words from the selection. Then, complete the activities.

confirm [kuhn FERM] *v.* prove; show to be true
All the witnesses confirm his statement that he stopped at the light.

exiled [EG zyld] *adj.* banned from your country; forced to live elsewhere
The wicked prince was forced from his country and exiled to a tiny island.

frets [FRETZ] *v.* worries
Before every concert, the violinist frets and bites his nails.

hew [HYOO] *v.* cut down or chop with an ax
The woodcutter was about to hew down the tree with his hatchet.

murky [MUR kee] *adj.* dark; dim; gloomy
It was hard to see in the murky basement because there were no lights.

perceive [per SEEV] *v.* see; sense; understand
Her hands were shaking, so it was easy to perceive her nervousness.

petty [PET ee] *adj.* of small importance; caring about unimportant things
To work together, ignore petty differences and focus on a common goal.

snares [SNAYRZ] *n.* trapping devices, often consisting of a noose
When the hunter returned, he found several rabbits caught in his snares.

Exercise A

Fill in each blank below using the appropriate word from Word List A.

   People who have had work done on their apartment or house will

[1] _____ that it is a stressful process. Even if you are not someone

who [2] _____ about the mess and dust, you may find it difficult

being [3] _____ from the parts of your home where builders

are working. If the pipes are being replaced, your water may turn

[4] _____ for a while. Other problems range from [5] _____

arguments over paint colors to serious delays. Sometimes sections

of a house are left open and animals may get in, requiring you to set

[6] _____ to trap pests. A poorly worded note might lead a worker to

[7] _____ down the wrong tree in your yard. If you [8] _____

too many mistakes on your project, you might decide not to pay until the

job is done right.

Read the following passage. Pay special attention to the underlined words. Then, read it again, and complete the activities. Use a separate sheet of paper for your written answers.

There are traditions that all actors observe. They never wish each other "good luck" before a performance; instead they say "break a leg." Inside a theater, they do not whistle, nor do they utter the word Macbeth.

During a production of Shakespeare's play *The Tragedy of Macbeth,* everyone in the cast and crew refers to the work as the "Scottish play," or just "the play." They call Macbeth "the king," and Lady Macbeth is always "the queen." Quoting from the play is avoided, as is using any sets, costumes, or props that were part of a previous production of *Macbeth.* Anyone who breaks these rules is exiled from the theater.

Outsiders may perceive this behavior as ridiculous, seeing it as childish or petty, but actors believe that strange accidents confirm that it is best not to violate the custom. The fact that documented disasters are associated with the Scottish play makes some performers nervous.

For example, after *Macbeth* premiered on August 7, 1606, the boy actor who played the queen died backstage. Since then, many an actor frets about problems that could be brought on by a slip of the tongue. Stories of illness, fires, bad reviews, falling lights, people caught in snares created by tangled ropes, broken props, and stage weapons that inflict wounds are legendary. These mishaps are all said to have occurred because someone disregarded tradition.

Naturally, there are other explanations for an ill-fated production. Some of the action in *Macbeth* is set on a murky heath, forcing actors to navigate a dark stage. Lady Macbeth sleepwalks around scenery. Malcolm's army has to hew and carry branches, creating opportunities for injuries. There is also plenty of sword fighting. With all of these elements, it is likely that something could go wrong during *Macbeth,* no matter what anyone says or does not say.

1. Underline the words that tell who would be exiled. Explain what it would mean for an actor to be *exiled* from the theater.

2. Circle the word that is a clue to the meaning of perceive. Then, explain how you *perceive* the behavior that is described.

3. Underline the word that is a clue to the meaning of petty. Then, describe something you would call *petty.*

4. Circle the words telling what the accidents seem to confirm. Then, tell what might *confirm* the opposite.

5. Circle the words that tell what the actor frets about. Explain what *frets* means.

6. Underline the word that suggests what snares do. Then, describe what *snares* are usually used to do.

7. Circle the word that is a clue to the meaning of murky. Then, describe a place or thing that is *murky.*

8. Underline the word that tells what the army has to hew. Then, name or describe some people who often *hew* such things.

© Pearson Education

The Tragedy of Macbeth, Act V

William Shakespeare

Summary Macbeth prepares for battle with the forces of Malcolm and Macduff. Because of the witches' predictions, he feels confident. Meanwhile, Lady Macbeth has been sleepwalking. She feels guilty about the murders. Just before the battle, she dies. Malcolm's soldiers cut down branches of trees to hide their numbers. Disguised in this way, they approach Dunsinane. Malcolm's army defeats Macbeth's army. Then, Macduff kills Macbeth. Malcolm becomes the new king of Scotland.

Note-taking Guide

The play ends, or resolves, in Act V. In the chart below, note the outcome for each character.

Character	Outcome
Macbeth	
Lady Macbeth	
Macduff	
Malcolm	

from The Tragedy of Macbeth
William Shakespeare

Act V, Scene i takes place late at night in Macbeth's castle.

A doctor speaks with one of Lady Macbeth's attendants. She reports that the queen has been walking in her sleep lately. Lady Macbeth enters, sleepwalking and carrying a candle. Her eyes are open, and she moves her hands as if washing them.

◆　◆　◆

LADY MACBETH. Yet here's a spot.

DOCTOR. Hark! She speaks. I will set down what
5　　comes from her, to satisfy my remembrance
　　the more strongly.

LADY MACBETH. Out, damned spot! Out, I say!
　　One: two: why, then 'tis time to do 't. Hell
　　is murky. Fie, my lord, fie! A soldier, and
10　afeard? What need we fear who knows it,
　　when none can call our pow'r to accompt? Yet
　　who would have thought the old man to have
　　had so much blood in him?

DOCTOR. Do you mark that?

15　**LADY MACBETH.** The Thane of Fife had a wife.
　　Where is she now? What, will these hands
　　ne'er be clean? No more o' that, my lord, no
　　more o' that! You mar all with this starting.

DOCTOR. Go to, go to! You have known what you
20　should not.

GENTLEWOMAN. She has spoke what she should
　　not, I am sure of that. Heaven knows what
　　she has known.

LADY MACBETH. Here's the smell of the blood still.
25　All the perfumes of Arabia will sweeten this
　　little hand. Oh, oh, oh!

◆　◆　◆

The doctor says he cannot help. Lady Macbeth exits.

◆　◆　◆

DOCTOR. Foul whisp'rings are abroad. Unnatural
　　deeds

Reading Check

What does the doctor see Lady Macbeth doing as she walks in her sleep?

_____

_____

_____

Read Fluently

With a partner, read aloud with expression the dialogue between Lady Macbeth and the doctor. Note the question marks as you read. Take turns reading the parts of Lady Macbeth and the doctor.

Reading Strategy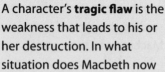

Based on lines 27–35, what does the doctor believe about Lady Macbeth? How does his assessment that she needs divine help reflect the beliefs of the **historical period**?

_____

_____

_____

_____

Literary Analysis

A character's **tragic flaw** is the weakness that leads to his or her destruction. In what situation does Macbeth now find himself as a result of his tragic flaw?

_____

_____

_____

_____

Do breed unnatural troubles. Infected minds
To their deaf pillows will discharge their secrets.
30 More needs she the divine than the physician.
God, God forgive us all! Look after her;
Remove from her the means of all annoyance,
And still keep eyes upon her. So good night.
My mind she has mated and amazed my sight:
35 I think, but dare not speak.

GENTLEWOMAN.   Good night, good doctor.

◆ ◆ ◆

Act V, Scene ii takes place in the countryside near the castle.

The Scottish nobles wait with their soldiers. They are preparing to fight Macbeth. One reports that Malcolm and Macduff are nearby with Siward, general of the English forces, and his troops. They will all meet near Birnam Wood.

Another noble says Macbeth has prepared his castle for attack. The men all march on to meet Malcolm at Birnam wood.

Act V, Scene iii takes place in Macbeth's castle.

Macbeth is meeting with several people, including Seyton and Lady Macbeth's doctor. Macbeth discusses the upcoming battle.

◆ ◆ ◆

MACBETH. Bring me no more reports; let them fly all!
Till Birnam Wood remove to Dunsinane.
I cannot taint with fear. What's the boy Malcolm?
Was he not born of woman? The spirits that
5   know
All mortal consequences have pronounced me thus:
"Fear not, Macbeth; no man that's born of woman
Shall e'er have power upon thee." Then fly, false thanes,
And mingle with the English epicures.
10 The mind I sway by and the heart I bear
Shall never sag with doubt nor shake with fear.

♦ ♦ ♦

A frightened servant tells him that the enemy has 10,000 troops. Macbeth swears he will fight to the end. Macbeth then asks the doctor about his wife's illness. The doctor says that she is not sick but troubled with imaginings. Macbeth is angry.

♦ ♦ ♦

MACBETH. Cure her of that.
Canst thou not minister to a mind diseased,
Pluck from the memory a rooted sorrow,
15 Raze out the written troubles of the brain,
And with some sweet oblivious antidote
Cleanse the stuffed bosom of that perilous stuff
Which weights upon my heart?
DOCTOR. Therein the patient
Must minister to himself.
20 **MACBETH.** Throw physic to the dogs, I'll none of it.
Come, put mine armor on. Give me my staff.

♦ ♦ ♦

Act V, Scene iv takes place at Birnam Wood soon after.

Malcolm is with Macduff and the English and Scottish troops. Malcolm orders the men to cut tree branches to use as camouflage. They march toward Dunsinane castle.

Act V, Scene v takes place within the castle.

♦ ♦ ♦

MACBETH. Hang out our banners on the outward walls.
The cry is still "They come!" Our castle's strength
Will laugh a <u>siege</u> to scorn.

♦ ♦ ♦

Macbeth says that the enemy army will die of famine and disease during the siege.

♦ ♦ ♦

© Pearson Education

Vocabulary Development
siege (SEEJ) *n.* attack or blockade against a fortified place

Reading Check

Why is Macbeth angry with Lady Macbeth's doctor? Underline the sentence that tells you.

Reading Check

What does Malcolm tell the English and Scottish troops to do to hide their advance?

_____

_____

_____

Reading Check

What is Macbeth's attitude toward the attack?

_____

_____

_____

_____

Reading Check

What has happened to Lady Macbeth?

_____

_____

_____

_____

Reading Check

What have "all our yesterdays" done, according to Macbeth? Underline the words that give the answer.

Reading Strategy

In a **Shakespearean tragedy,** a **tragic flaw** or weakness leads the hero to destruction. Read the bracketed text. How does Macbeth's view of life here foreshadow his own downfall?

_____

_____

_____

[A cry within of women.]

5 **MACBETH.** What is that noise?
SEYTON. It is the cry of women, my good lord.

♦ ♦ ♦

Macbeth reflects that, after so much horror in his life, nothing can terrify him.

♦ ♦ ♦

MACBETH. Wherefore¹ was that cry?
SEYTON. The queen, my lord, is dead.
MACBETH. She should² have died hereafter;
10 There would have been a time for such a word.³
Tomorrow, and tomorrow, and tomorrow
Creeps in this petty pace from day to day,
To the last syllable of recorded time;
And all our yesterdays have lighted fools
15 The way to dusty death. Out, out, brief candle!
Life's but a walking shadow, a poor player
That struts and frets his hour upon the stage
And then is heard no more. It is a tale
Told by an idiot, full of sound and fury
20 Signifying nothing.

♦ ♦ ♦

Act V, Scene vi takes place on the battlefield, immediately after.

Malcolm, Macduff, Siward, and their troops gather near Macbeth's castle. Malcolm tells his men to drop the branches for the battle, and Macduff orders the trumpets to sound.

Act V, Scene vii takes place on another part of the battlefield, a little while later.

Macbeth meets up with General Siward's son. Young Siward asks him who he is; upon which Macbeth reveals his identity.

♦ ♦ ♦

MACBETH. My name's Macbeth.
YOUNG SIWARD. The devil himself could not pronounce a title

1. **Wherefore** for what reason; why
2. **should** inevitably would
3. **word** message

5   More hateful to mine ear.

MACBETH.   No, nor more fearful.

YOUNG SIWARD. Thou liest, abhorred tyrant; with
   my sword
I'll prove the lie thou speak'st.

[Fight, and YOUNG SIWARD *slain.]*

MACBETH.   Thou wast born of woman.
10 But swords I smile at, weapons laugh to scorn,
Brandished by man that's of a woman born.

◆ ◆ ◆

Macbeth exits. Macduff enters soon after.

◆ ◆ ◆

MACDUFF. That way the noise is. Tyrant, show
   thy face!

◆ ◆ ◆

Macduff is determined to kill Macbeth.
General Siward reports that their side is winning.
Siward tells Malcolm he can now enter the castle.

Act V, Scene viii takes place on the battlefield

◆ ◆ ◆

MACDUFF.   Turn, hell-hound, turn!

MACBETH. Of all men else I have avoided thee.
But get thee back! My soul is too much charged
5 With blood of thine already.[4]

MACDUFF.   I have no words:
My voice is in my sword, though bloodier villain
Than terms can give thee out!

[Fight. Alarum.]

MACBETH.   Thou losest labor:
10 As easy mayst thou the intrenchant air
With thy keen sword impress as make me
   bleed:
Let fall they blade on <u>vulnerable</u> crests;
I bear a charmèd life, which must not yield
To one of woman born.
15 **MACDUFF.**   Despair thy charm,
And let the angel whom thou still hast served
Tell thee, Macduff was from his mother's womb
Untimely ripped.[5]

Reading Check

Why does Macbeth tell
Macduff to get back?

_____

_____

_____

_____

Stop to Reflect

What does Macduff mean
when he says, "my voice is in
my sword"?

_____

_____

_____

_____

4. **blood...already** Macbeth had ordered the murders of Macduff's wife and children.

5. **his...ripped** Macduff's mother gave birth to him by Caesarean section.

Reading Strategy 📖

Reread the underlined section. These lines explain Macbeth's regret at listening to the witches' prophesies. Think about what these lines reveal about the time period. What do these lines suggest about the **beliefs of the time** about prophecy and predicting the future?

_____

_____

_____

_____

Literary Analysis 🔍

What positive or heroic qualities does Macbeth as tragic hero display here?

_____

_____

_____

Literary Analysis 🔍

How does the conclusion of this scene in lines 38–43 illustrate the lively action and vivid spectacle of **Shakespearean tragedy?**

_____

_____

_____

_____

MACBETH. Accursèd be that tongue that tells me so.

20 For it hath cowed my better part of man!
And be these juggling fiends no more believed,
That palter with us in a double sense;
That keep the word of promise to our ear,
And break it to our hope. I'll not fight with thee.

25 **MACDUFF.** Then yield thee, coward.
And live to be the show and gaze o' th' time;
We'll have thee, as our rarer monsters are,
Painted upon a pole, and underwrit,
"Here you may see the tyrant."

30 **MACBETH.**   I will not yield,
To kiss the ground before young Malcolm's feet,
And to be baited with the rabble's curse.
Though Birnam Wood be come to Dunsinane⁶,
And thou opposed, being of no woman born,

35 Yet I will try the last. Before my body
I throw my warlike shield. Lay on, Macduff;
And damned be him that first cries, "Hold,
enough!"

◆ ◆ ◆

Macduff slays Macbeth. In front of the
soldiers, Macduff hails Duncan's son Malcolm
as the new king of Scotland.

◆ ◆ ◆

[Enter MACDUFF, *with* MACBETH's *head.]*

MACDUFF. Hail, King! For so thou art: behold,
where stands
Th' usurper's cursèd head. The time is free.⁷

40 I see thee compassed with thy kingdom's pearl,
That speak my salutation in their minds,
Whose voices I desire aloud with mine:
Hail, King of Scotland!

ALL.   Hail, King of Scotland!

◆ ◆ ◆

Promising to reward his supporters,
Malcolm invites the army to his coronation.

6. **Birnam . . . Dunsinane** Malcolm's soldiers held tree branches in front of themselves when they marched on Dunsinane, Macbeth's castle.

7. **The . . free** Our country is liberated.

The Tragedy of Macbeth, Act V

1. **Respond:** What evidence from the play suggests that Lady Macbeth's doctor suspects that Lady Macbeth had a role in Duncan's murder?

   _____

   _____

2. **Literary Analysis:** Use examples from Act V to show each element of **Shakespearean Tragedy:** a tragic hero with a flaw; events that lead the tragic hero to disaster; and lively action scenes. Complete the following chart with your responses.

Flaw:

Events that Lead to Disaster	Lively Action

3. **Reading Strategy:** What do the doctor's remarks lead you to **infer,** or figure out, about Elizabethan concepts of mental illness?

   _____

   _____

Writing About the Essential Question

What is the relationship of the writer to tradition? How do Shakespeare's use of comic relief and his revealing of Macbeth's inner turmoil add new dimensions to tragedy?

_____

_____

_____

Feature Articles

About Feature Articles

Feature articles provide information about topics of general interest. Although they are not news articles, feature articles answer the questions *who, what, when, where,* and *why.* They may also include direct quotations from people interviewed. However, the purpose of feature articles is both to inform and to entertain. Feature writers often describe their personal experience with a topic, and they may also share their opinions. Feature articles appear in newspapers and magazines and on Web sites.

Reading Skill

The author's purpose and perspective is his or her reason for writing and point of view on a particular subject. In a feature, these factors shape the story by affecting the information the author includes. As you read, evaluate the author's purpose and perspective as it appears in the following elements:

- the title
- the tone of the article, especially in the first paragraph, or lead
- the use of anecdotes and direct quotes, as well as facts and interesting details.

Use a chart like the one shown to evaluate the author's purpose.

Text Structures	Example	Affect on Meaning
Title		
Lead		
Positive/Negative Adjectives		
Direct Quotes		
Facts and details		

Smithsonian
MAGAZINE

Designing a Globe Theatre for the 21ˢᵗ century

By Eric Jaffe

The tractor-trailer planted firmly in the Wal-Mart parking lot did not seem out of place, but the actors who performed *Merchant of Venice* right beside it sure did. When the vehicle arrived it deployed into a full-size stage. Behind the set, pneumatic pods inflated to become ticket-windows and dressing rooms. Sunlight powered the spotlights and speakers. And when the play-house folded up and drove off, a screen mounted on the side of the trailer replayed the show for all to see.

This is the Globe Theatre—not the one that housed Shakespeare's best dramas, but one conceived by Jennifer Siegal for a modern audience. Siegal's Globe is part homage to the Elizabethan era's itinerant theatre troupe, part shout-out to today's compact, on-the-go gizmos. The Los Angeles-based architect was one of five designers asked to create a 21st-century Shakespearean theatre for "Reinventing the Globe," a new exhibit at the National Building Museum in Washington, D.C., that opens January 13 and runs through August 2007.

Illustration of Jennifer Siegal's "Globetrotter"—a portable Shakespeare theater

Given only brief guidance and a few months to finish, these architects created modern Globes that challenge conventional thoughts about dramatic performances and the spaces that accommodate them, says Martin Moeller, the exhibition's curator. "When the words stay the same but all else changes, you realize how much power the words have," he says.

Theatre designer John Coyne delivered a truly virtual Globe. To reflect today's cross-cultural world, Coyne's performances would occur simultaneously in several locations. Gigantic screens with live streaming would hang above the stages, and characters would interact in real time. So, speaking in Russian from Moscow, Polonius offers advice to Laertes in New York; standing oceans away, Hamlet pierces Claudius with a venom-tipped sword.

Michele (pronounced *Mi-keleh*) Saee, who did not have theatre design experience, modeled a Globe that would capture an actor's fluidity in the structure itself. He proposed tracing the movements of an actor throughout a performance

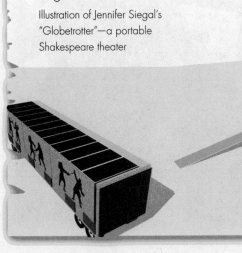

using electronic monitors then, with the help of a computer, turning these motions into a three-dimensional image that would become the building. "It's like those photos at night where you see red and white lights streaking down the road," Moeller says. "It's almost like you have a history built into one image."

David Rockwell's transparent Globe is intended to erase the barrier between outdoor and indoor settings. H3, the architectural firm guided by Hugh Hardy, created a floating Globe that could bounce around to various New York City boroughs, like so many bar-hopping hipsters, as a way to increase public access.

Siegel, who is the founder of the Office of Mobile Design, says her portable Globe, dubbed the "Globetrotter," is ready to go into production with the right client.

"We're a mobile society that deals with communication devices in a compact way, and theatre can be represented in a similar take," she says. "It doesn't have to be going to this old, stodgy building. It could be much more accessible, transient and lighter."

In some ways, conceptualizing a Globe Theatre for the future requires as much imagination as re-creating the one that stood in Shakespeare's day. Despite the playhouse's prominence, historians still argue over many aspects of the theatre, says Franklin J. Hildy of the University of Maryland, an advisor to the London Globe reconstruction that opened in 1997.

Notable uncertainties include the shape of the stage (some say it was rectangular, others square); how many sides the structure had (with ranges from 16 to 24); even the size of the building itself (some call the diameter 100 feet across, others 90).

Globe reconstructions work off evidence from seven maps of London in that day, texts from Shakespeare's plays and a site excavation (the original theatre, built in 1599, burned down in 1613 and was restored in the same place). Perhaps the most crucial historical document is a contract to build the Fortune theatre, a contemporaneous playhouse, which instructs builders to copy many of the Globe's dimensions.

Of the Globe's certainties, the stage that jutted out into the crowd was one of its most impressive attributes, says Hildy. "Everywhere you looked there was life, audience, energy." Standing patrons, known as groundlings, surrounded the stage, often shouting at the actors, cracking hazelnut shells—even sitting on stage.

Though Shakespeare's work also appeared at the Rose and Curtain theatres, the Globe hosted most of his famous dramas—including *Hamlet*, *King Lear* and *Macbeth*—which explains part of its lasting allure, Hildy says.

"The sense has always been that you could feel a closer connection to Shakespeare if you could understand how he saw theatre, how he saw his plays staged," he says. "Shakespeare was working during one of the most successful periods that theatre has ever had. There seems to be a relationship between buildings and that success."

> The writer gives the reader historical background to put the current project in context.

The restored Globe Theatre in London

Thinking About the Feature Article

1. Why were architects and theater designers asked to create modern versions of the Globe Theatre?

   _____

2. What part of the original Globe Theatre can historians describe with certainty?

   _____

   _____

TALK ABOUT IT **Reading Skill**

3. Which direct quote supports the point of view that Shakespeare's plays do not need to be performed in traditional theater buildings?

   _____

   _____

4. What details does the author include to demonstrate the appeal of the historic Globe Theatre?

   _____

   _____

WRITE ABOUT IT **Timed Writing: Persuasive Essay (25 minutes)**

Make a case for or against the modernizing of classic works such as Shakespeare's plays. Give reasons why you think either updated versions or traditional productions are better, drawing ideas and examples from the Feature Article. Allow five minutes for prewriting to plan your essay. Spend fifteen minutes drafting, and save five minutes for reviewing and revising.

The Works of John Donne

Literary Analysis

John Donne and his followers wrote **metaphysical** (MET uh FIZ i kuhl) **poetry**. This type of poetry uses **conceits** (kuhn SEETS) and **paradoxes** (PAR uh DAHKS ez).

- **Conceits** are extended comparisons. They compare objects or ideas not usually connected. In his poem "A Valediction: Forbidding Mourning," for example, Donne compares two parting lovers to the legs of a drawing compass. The one who stays behind is like the leg of the compass that stays fixed. The one who travels is like the leg of the compass that draws the circle.

- **Paradoxes** are images or descriptions that seem to contradict themselves. For example, in Donne's "Holy Sonnet 10," he writes, "Death, thou shalt die." At first, such a statement seems impossible. However, paradoxes often reveal a deeper truth. Donne is addressing Death as if it were a person. He is saying that Death itself will die. He says this because he believes that when people die and go to heaven, they will live forever.

Look for the conceits and paradoxes in Donne's work. Then, see what they mean.

Reading Strategy

One way to **establish a purpose for reading** is to imagine the **speaker's situation**. Ask yourself what the speaker is doing and what the speaker wants. Also, try to figure out his **motivation,** or reason, for speaking to another person. As you read "Song," use this chart to note the speaker's words, his situation, and his motivation.

Speaker's Words	Situation	Motivation
"Sweetest love, I do not go, For weariness of thee, . . ."		

Word List A

Study these words from the selections. Then, complete the activities.

bind [BYND] *v.* tie together; tie down or secure; fasten
To make a book, you must bind all the pages together using glue or thread.

defray [di FRAY] *v.* pay the money needed for
If you travel on business, your company will defray your expenses.

dreadful [DRED fuhl] *adj.* inspiring terror; alarming; awful
The tropical storm was dreadful and left many people homeless.

desperate [DES puhr it] *adj.* without hope; in extreme need
As night fell, the lost hiker began to grow desperate, but just then the rescuers arrived.

jest [JEST] *n.* a joke; a prank; a witty remark
As a jest, the clown sprayed the volunteer from the audience with water.

reckon [REK uhn] *v.* judge; count; calculate
Counting them one by one, it took ten minutes to reckon how many pennies were in the jar.

roam [ROHM] *v.* travel; move about without a definite plan; wander
When some people travel, they make a list of places to visit, but I like to roam around.

tolls [TOHLZ] *v.* rings slowly and steadily
The bell in the church tower tolls before the ceremony begins.

Exercise A

Fill in each blank in the paragraphs below with the appropriate word from Word List A.

Some churches employ a person to ring the church bells. Contributions to the church may help [1] _____ the cost of the person's wages. The bells ring at a volume loud enough so that they may be heard by anyone who may happen to [2] _____ into the vicinity. Because of their volume, the person who regularly [3] _____ the bells may develop a hearing problem. To prevent the [4] _____ damage loud bells can do to sensitive eardrums, a ringer should wear earplugs. Having an ordinary conversation depends on hearing, so no one can [5] _____ the true cost of hearing loss.

Bells can be played by traditional ropes and wheels or by a keyboard connected electronically to the bells. Unlike movie characters, real bell ringers do not actually [6] _____ themselves to the bell ropes or swing inside the tower in a [7] _____ attempt to build momentum and volume. It is worth noting that not all of the music performed with church bells is solemn; popular music is sometimes played in the spirit of a [8] _____.

1. Circle the word that hints at the meaning of dreadful. Then, describe something you think is *dreadful*.

2. Circle the word that is a clue to the meaning of reckon. Then, describe a situation in which you would need to *reckon*.

3. Circle the synonym for tolls in the next sentence. Then, using the word *tolls*, describe a scene from the plague.

4. Underline the phrase that explains how rats were able to roam the world. Give two examples of animals that *roam* in the wild.

5. Circle the words that tell what was used to bind wounds. What is used to *bind* wounds now?

6. Underline the word that is a clue to the meaning of "grow desperate." Then, explain why people with symptoms of the plague grew *desperate*.

7. Circle the word that means the opposite of "as a jest." Why might people turn something horrible like the plague into a *jest*?

8. Underline the phrase that tells what an insurance company would have helped to defray.

Read the following passage. Pay special attention to the underlined words. Then, read it again, and complete the activities. Use a separate sheet of paper for your written answers.

Among the most dreadful catastrophes in European history were the awful outbreaks of bubonic plague, also called the black death. Historians reckon that between the years 1347 and 1352, the plague killed about 25 million Europeans; according to their calculations, this fact means that about one third of the population died.

Later outbreaks were smaller, but the plague brought death wherever it struck. Understanding these facts can help readers appreciate John Donne's statement, "Ask not for whom the bell tolls, it tolls for thee." In times of plague, the church bell that rings to announce one man's death may soon be ringing for another's.

Had medieval people understood the causes of the disease, they might have been able to control it. Bubonic plague is spread by fleas, which infect the rats on which they live. Rats can survive on ships, and so they can roam almost anywhere in the world. Ship-borne rats brought the plague to Europe from China.

Some habits of medieval people helped spread the disease. For example, it was common to reuse clothing and sheets that belonged to the dead; people also would bind wounds with any available fabric. These practices spread both bacteria and fleas.

Symptoms of the plague include swellings in the groin and armpits, as well as rose-colored blotches on the skin that eventually turned black. People might panic and grow desperate when they saw the first symptoms appear. Yet the rose-colored blotches that sufferers took so seriously gave rise to a nursery rhyme sung as a jest, "Ring Around the Rosy."

The plague struck rich and poor people alike; a person who could not afford treatment did not suffer more from the plague than a person with money. Even if there had been insurance companies to help defray a poor person's medical costs, there simply was no treatment worth paying for.

Song • A Valediction: Forbidding Mourning • Holy Sonnet 10

John Donne

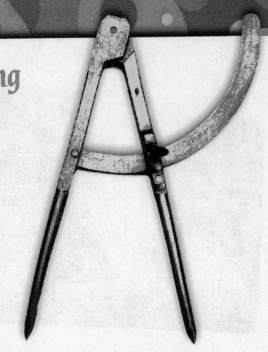

Summaries In "**Song**," the speaker is going away. He asks his beloved not to mourn his absence. In "**A Valediction: Forbidding Mourning**," the speaker also asks a loved one not to mourn his absence. He compares himself and his beloved to the two legs of a drawing compass. Like the legs of a compass, the lovers will be linked even when they are separated.

The speaker talks to Death in "**Holy Sonnet 10**" as if Death were a person. He tells Death not to be so proud. Once people have died and gone to heaven, there will be no more death.

Note-taking Guide

As you read, use this chart. For each poem, fill in the person the speaker is addressing. Also indicate the main idea the speaker is expressing.

Poem	To Whom it is Addressed	Main Idea
Song		
A Valediction		
Holy Sonnet 10		

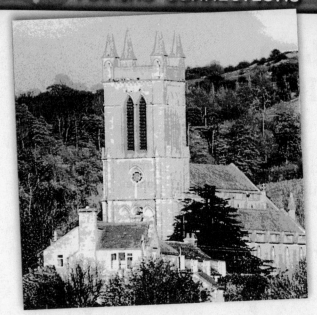

Meditation 17
John Donne

Summary The speaker hears a church bell ringing. The ringing bell means that someone has died. The speaker realizes that someday he will die, too. Every person adds something to this world. One person's death affects everyone. The death bell rings, then, for everyone.

Note-taking Guide

Read the basic arguments from "Meditation 17" in the chart below. Find the comparisons in the poem that support these arguments. Write the comparisons in the ovals to the right.

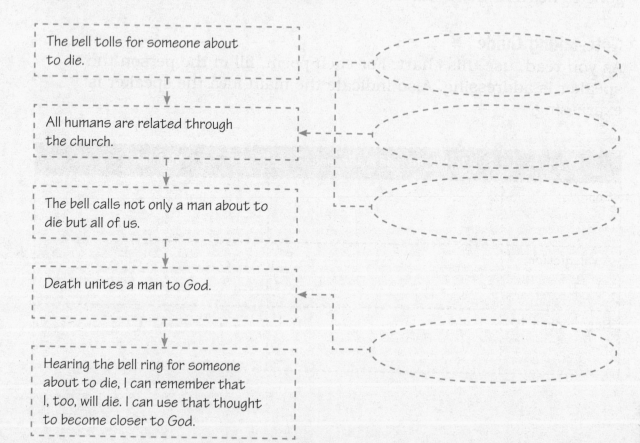

The bell tolls for someone about to die.

All humans are related through the church.

The bell calls not only a man about to die but all of us.

Death unites a man to God.

Hearing the bell ring for someone about to die, I can remember that I, too, will die. I can use that thought to become closer to God.

Meditation 17

John Donne

Donne talks about a bell that is tolling, or ringing. It is announcing someone's death or coming death. He says that maybe the person doesn't know that the bell is tolling for him. He says it might even be for Donne himself, and he doesn't know it. The church that rings the bell is for all people. So are all the things that the church does.

◆ ◆ ◆

When she baptizes a child, that action concerns me; for that child is thereby connected to that head which is my head too,[1] . . . . And when she buries a man, that action concerns me: all mankind is of one author and is one volume; when one man dies, one chapter is not torn out of the book, but translated into a better language; and every chapter must be so translated. God employs several translators; some pieces are translated by age, some by sickness, some by war, some by justice; but God's hand is in every translation, and his hand shall bind up all our scattered leaves again for that library where every book shall lie open to one another.

◆ ◆ ◆

He goes on to say that the bell is not just for the preacher. It is for the people of the church. It is also for Donne, who is suffering from a sickness. . . . The bell tolls for the person who thinks it is tolling for him. If the bell stops for a time, it doesn't matter. The person who thought it was tolling for him is united to God from that moment.

◆ ◆ ◆

© Pearson Education

1. **that head which is my head too** In the Bible, St. Paul calls Jesus the head (spiritual leader) of all the faithful.

TAKE NOTES

Literary Analysis 🔍

Here, Donne presents a feature of **metaphysical poetry** when he makes an extended comparison between one thing and another, seemingly unrelated thing. This is called a **conceit**. Read the bracketed passage, and then circle the letter of the correct answer.

In this conceit, Donne compares a person to _____.

a. a foreign language
b. a chapter in a book
c. God
d. a translator

Reading Strategy

Based on Donne's **situation**, what can you guess about his **motivation**?

_____

_____

_____

Read aloud the bracketed paragraph. Then circle the part that tells how Donne feels about any other person's death.

Stop to Reflect

Do you agree with Donne that troubles are good for us? Why, or why not?

_____

_____

_____

No man is an island, entire of itself; every man is a piece of the continent, a part of the main.[2] If a clod be washed away by the sea, Europe is the less, as well as if a <u>promontory</u> were, as well as if a <u>manor</u> of thy friend's or of thine own were. Any man's death <u>diminishes</u> me because I am involved in mankind, and therefore never send to know for whom the bell tolls; it tolls for thee.

◆ ◆ ◆

Donne goes on to say that our troubles are good for us. No one has enough of them. Troubles help us mature. They make us fit for God. We might listen to a bell that tolls for someone else and apply its meaning to ourselves. If we do this, we become closer to God, our only security.

Vocabulary Development

promontory (PRAH muhn tor ee) *n.* a high point of land or rock jutting out into a body of water

manor (MAN uhr) *n.* the house of an estate

diminishes (di MIN ish uhs) *v.* lessens, reduces

2. **main** (MAYN) *n.* the mainland.

The Works of John Donne

1. **Literary Analysis:** In "Meditation 17," Donne uses a **conceit**, or extended comparison, to compare suffering and treasure. Think about the forms of treasure he discusses. Then, fill in the chart below. One kind of treasure, for example, is gold. Something else that Donne calls treasure is very surprising.

Main Idea: There are two forms of suffering, just as there are two forms of treasure.		
First Form of Treasure:	Second Form of Treasure:	Relationship Between Forms of Treasure:

2. **Literary Analysis:** What is the **paradox**, or apparent contradiction, that Donne uses in the fourth stanza of "Song"?

_____

_____

3. **Reading Strategy:** To establish a purpose for reading, **recognize a speaker's situation and motivation**. Picture the speaker's circumstances and determine his or her reasons for speaking or acting. Choose one of John Donne's poems. Who is the speaker, what is the **speaker's situation**, and what is the speaker's **motivation?**

_____

_____

 Writing About the Essential Question

What is the relationship between the writer and tradition? Does the statement "No man is an island" still apply today? Why or why not?

_____

_____

On My First Son • Still to Be Neat • Song: To Celia

Literary Analysis

A **lyric** is a poem in which a single speaker expresses the way that he or she feels or what he or she observes. The earliest lyric poems were verses sung by the ancient Greeks to the accompaniment of a stringed instrument called a lyre. The lyric poems written by the ancient Greeks influenced the poetry written during the Renaissance. Lyric poems do not follow a particular form. They may be rhymed, unrhymed, metered, or free verse. Lyric poetry contains the following elements:

- figurative language, such as simile, metaphor, personification, and oxymoron
- repetition of sounds, words, phrases, or sentences, including alliteration, consonance, assonance, and rhyme
- imagery, or language that appeals to the five senses

Look for these elements as you read Jonson's poems.

Reading Strategy

To **draw inferences** means to reach logical conclusions about what is not stated in a piece of writing. When you draw inferences, you

- use text evidence to make a logical conclusion about the people, events, or ideas in a work.
- use your own experiences to help you reach a conclusion.

Use this chart to help you draw inferences.

Inference	Text Evidence
	Experience

Word List A

Study these words from the selections. Then, complete the activities.

envy [EN vee] *v.* feel unhappy because someone else has something you want
I only have a three-speed bicycle, and I envy my neighbor's fifteen-speed.

lament [luh MENT] *v.* mourn; express sorrow or regret
In this song, the two singers lament their separation.

loosely [LOOS lee] *adv.* not tightly; without strong ties
The dress fit too loosely, and I asked the tailor to make it tighter.

pledge [PLEJ] *v.* solemnly promise, often to give something to someone
The knights pledge their loyalty to the king and promise never to betray him.

rage [RAYJ] *n.* furious anger; great force, as in a fire or storm
In his rage, he shouted and slammed the door.

sound [SOWND] *adj.* free from damage; in good condition; healthy
The boat was sound and needed no repairs.

state [STAYT] *n.* condition; way of existence
After I found my cat, my state of mind improved greatly.

vows [VOWZ] *n.* solemn promises or commitments
In their marriage vows, the couple promised to support each other in sickness and in health.

Exercise A

Fill in each blank below using the appropriate word from Word List A.

It was only in the seventeenth century that nations formed large, permanent armies. Before that time, an army consisted of men called up for a specific war. When the war was over, the army would cease to exist. Some soldiers fought out of loyalty to a cause or country, and they were glad to [1] _____ their allegiance to their leaders. Other soldiers, though, were mercenaries willing to turn their battle [2] _____ against anyone's enemy for a price. They gave their loyalty [3] _____, without making lasting [4] _____, and might fight on one side in one war and the other side in the next.

Whatever the [5] _____ of the army a mercenary temporarily joined, he made sure he was well prepared. He had his own supplies and weapons, which he kept in [6] _____ condition. A mercenary might [7] _____ the losses on his side, and he might [8] _____ the enemy if the enemy won. Yet his loyalty stopped short of true patriotism.

1. Circle the words that give a clue to the meaning of "state of the world." Then, explain what you think the *state* of the world is today.

2. Underline the phrase that tells what patrons might go into a *rage* about. Then, describe what people look like when they are in a *rage*.

3. Circle the word that hints at why the customers might *lament* a court decision. What else might a person *lament*?

4. Underline the word that means about the same as *pledge*. Name something to which people *pledge* themselves today.

5. Circle the word that is a clue to the meaning of *sound*. Explain what makes a decision *sound*.

6. Underline the word that is a clue to the meaning of *vows*. Explain whether you think people should always live up to their *vows*.

7. Circle the phrase that means the opposite of "loosely interconnected." Then, explain what *loosely* means.

8. Underline the words that tell why it seems that some had grown to *envy* coffee houses' prosperity. Name something people today often *envy*.

Read the following passage. Pay special attention to the underlined words. Then, read it again, and complete the activities. Use a separate sheet of paper for your written answers.

In seventeenth-century London, a coffee house was the place to go for gossip, trading prices, book reviews, and updates on the state of the world, especially the political and economic conditions that concerned businessmen. For the price of a cup of coffee, anyone could go into a rage about high taxes, read the latest pamphlets, lament a harmful court decision, or make a business deal. Some cafes were centers for literary discussion. Others specialized in political dissent and allowed customers to pledge themselves to a movement or promise their loyalty to a cause.

The coffee house was the gathering place of choice for the growing middle class of society. Coffee was the ideal drink for the clerks, merchants, and businessmen who made up this middle class. They believed that coffee sharpened their mental faculties and helped them make solid, sound decisions.

While the new middle class gathered in coffee houses, the working classes continued to gather in taverns. Taverns were dirty and dark, the scene of brawls and angry vows promising revenge for insults. By contrast, coffee houses were lined with bookshelves, mirrors, framed pictures, and good furniture. Quarrels were not permitted inside.

Rumors and news were carried between coffee houses by their patrons and by runners sent to report major events, such as the outbreak of a war. Europe's coffee houses were only loosely interconnected, not tightly bound together by a common owner or organization. Still, the web of coffee houses formed the equivalent of the Internet for the period.

By 1663, a total of 82 coffee houses had been set up in London. Seventeen years later, there were more than 500 in business. Some people may have grown to envy their prosperity or fear their influence, since the government attempted to close them. Coffee houses were too popular, however, and the effort failed miserably.

On My First Son
• Still to Be Neat
• Song: To Celia
Ben Jonson

Summaries In "**On My First Son**," Jonson says farewell to his young son. The boy died at the age of seven.

In "**Still to Be Neat**," Jonson says that he does not admire women who dress up too much. He prefers beauty that looks more natural.

In "**Song: To Celia**," he expresses his love for a woman. He asks her to give him loving looks, rather than drinks of wine. She has returned a wreath of flowers he sent to her. Now, the wreath grows. It also carries her lovely scent.

Note-taking Guide
Choose a line or two from each poem that tells the main idea. Write the lines on this chart. Then explain the main idea in your own words.

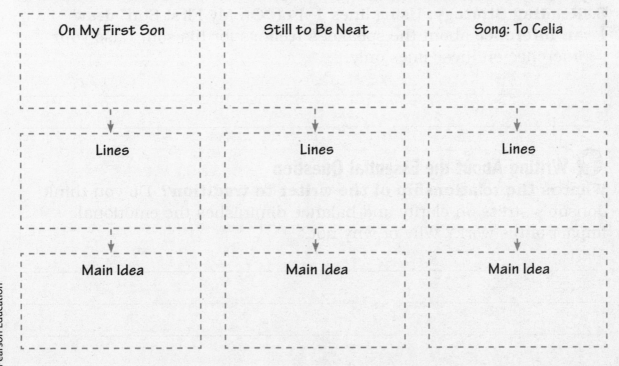

On My First Son	Still to Be Neat	Song: To Celia
↓	↓	↓
Lines	Lines	Lines
↓	↓	↓
Main Idea	Main Idea	Main Idea

On My First Son • Still to Be Neat • Song: To Celia

1. **Evaluate:** Review Jonson's "Still to Be Neat." Does it seem artificial or false by today's standards, or does it capture true feelings?

_____

_____

2. **Literary Analysis:** A **lyric** has these elements: figurative language, repetition, and imagery. Using this chart, note such features in "Song: To Celia."

Figurative Language	Repetition	Imagery

3. **Reading Strategy:** Using lines 1-4 of "On My First Son" **draw an inference** about the speaker's feelings for his son. Base your inference on these lines only.

_____

_____

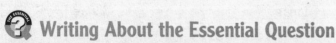 **Writing About the Essential Question**

What is the relationship of the writer to tradition? Do you think Jonson's stress on clarity and balance diminishes the emotional impact of his work? Why or why not?

_____

_____

_____

To His Coy Mistress • To the Virgins, to Make Much of Time • Song

Literary Analysis

Theme is a universal view or comment on life. The theme of the poems in this grouping is *carpe diem,* which was also a theme in classical literature. **Carpe diem** (KAR pay DEE em) is Latin for "seize the day." These poems tell the reader that time is rushing by. Therefore, it is important to enjoy love in the present moment. Herrick expresses this theme in a traditional way. Marvell expresses this theme in an extended way.

Suckling's poem gives the *carpe diem* theme a twist. He does not tell a friend to seize love. Instead, he tells the friend to abandon a lover who is not responding to him.

Look for the *carpe diem* theme as you read these selections.

Reading Strategy

To understand a poem, you must **infer the speaker's attitude**. This means you must figure out how the speaker feels about the subject of the poem. You must also figure out how the speaker feels about the person he or she is addressing. To recognize the speaker's attitude, you should do the following:

- Focus on evidence from the text, such as the connotations, or emotional associations, of the speaker's words.

- Decide which associations are positive and which are negative.

- Use those emotional associations and your own experience to figure out the speaker's attitude.

Use this chart to note details that convey the speaker's attitude.

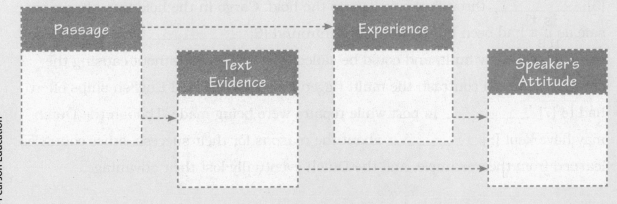

© Pearson Education

Word List A

Study these words from the selections. Then, complete the activities.

echoing [EK oh ing] *adj.* repeating a sound or idea
I shouted in the mountains, and I could hear my shout echoing again and again.

mute [MYOOT] *adj.* silent; unable to speak; choosing not to speak
They yelled "Surprise!" and I stood mute, unable to speak because of the shock.

prime [PRYM] *n.* peak condition; the best period or stage of a thing
The runner reached his prime at the age of 24 and was past it at age 30.

strife [STRYF] *n.* fighting; conflict; arguments
There was a good deal of strife between the two friends, but then they made up.

tarry [TAR ee] *v.* delay while going, coming, or doing; wait; linger
If you tarry at the mall after the movie, you'll miss your bus.

transpires [tran SPYRZ] *v.* breathes out; leaks out and becomes known
A plant breathes as air transpires through tiny holes in its leaves.

vast [VAST] *adj.* enormous; of great size or number
The ocean is so vast that parts of it have not yet been explored.

vault [VAHLT] *n.* a burial chamber, especially when underground
Scientists found the king's mummy buried in an underground vault.

Exercise A

Fill in each blank below using the appropriate word from Word List A.

Dutch merchants were in their [1] _____ during the 1600s. In the
[2] _____ among nations over world trade, the Dutch easily won dominance
over the East India trade route. They owed their victory to their superior ships,
which were built in sleek shapes with only three masts and a single deck. This
straightforward arrangement created a [3] _____ storage space, or hold,
below deck, where [4] _____ sounds could be heard when the hold was
empty. The Dutch ships were well waterproofed to make sure that little moisture
[5] _____ through the walls into the hold. Cargo in the hold was almost as
safe as if it had been buried in an underground [6] _____. These ships were
easily and cheaply built, and could be sailed long distances without causing the
crew hardship. In contrast, the multi-rigged and multi-masted English ships often
had to [7] _____ in port while repairs were being made. Though the Dutch
may have kept [8] _____ about the reasons for their success, other countries
learned from their example, and the Dutch eventually lost their advantage.

Read the following passage. Pay special attention to the underlined words. Then, read it again, and complete the activities. Use a separate sheet of paper for your written answers.

Charles I was born in 1600, the second son of James I and Anne of Denmark. In his childhood he was sickly and stammering child, but in his prime he was an excellent horseman and a strong-willed king.

Upon becoming king of England in 1625, Charles I immediately found himself in great trouble—his father had left the kingdom with vast financial and political problems. Charles's own marriage to the French Roman Catholic princess Henrietta Maria alarmed Protestant England.

At first, Charles was cold to his wife. For example, he would not let her French servants tarry forever in England but sent them home. Later, however, he grew close to his queen. Echoing the French fashions that pleased her, he spent huge sums on the arts and his court, causing further concern among his people.

Charles faced a Parliament hostile to his concept of absolute rule—a subject he was never mute about—and King and Parliament quarreled on numerous occasions. Tired of the ongoing strife, Charles dissolved Parliament three times and ruled eleven years without it. In 1642, Charles's financial and political troubles led to a civil war pitting English King against English Parliament.

In 1647, Charles was taken prisoner by the forces of Parliament. Tried for treason and found guilty, he was beheaded on January 30, 1649 and buried in a vault beneath Windsor Castle. A week after Charles's death, the office of king was abolished.

For some, the lack of an English monarch was a unique disaster. A true royalist believes that the soul of a nation lives in its king, and that this soul transpires from his body with his last breath; the nation's soul can only find a home in the new monarch. For Charles's opponents, however, the soul of the nation was in its people. For them, the end of English monarchy was an astonishing opportunity for democracy.

1. Circle the phrase that means something opposite to "in his prime." Explain whether you are in your *prime*.

2. Underline the synonym for vast. Then, name something else that is *vast*.

3. Underline the phrase that shows that the servants did not tarry. Then, tell what *tarry* means.

4. Circle the words that tell what Charles spent huge sums echoing. Would you be annoyed by someone *echoing* your ideas? Explain.

5. Circle the words that tell what Charles was never mute about. Then, explain what *mute* means.

6. Underline the word that is a clue to the meaning of strife. Then, describe a situation in which there is *strife*.

7. Underline the word that indicates the location of a vault. Then, describe what a *vault* might look like inside.

8. Circle the word that is a clue to the meaning of transpires. When an animal *transpires*, what part of its body does it use?

To His Coy Mistress
Andrew Marvell

To the Virgins, to Make Much of Time
Robert Herrick

Song
Sir John Suckling

Summaries The speaker in **"To His Coy Mistress"** explains that time is not limitless. His beloved should return his love now. The speaker in **"To the Virgins, to Make Much of Time"** also urges young women to look for love now. **"Song"** tells a young man to forget his beloved if she does not love him.

Note-taking Guide
Use these diagrams to answer questions about each poem.

To His Coy Mistress	To the Virgins, to Make Much of Time	Song
↓	↓	↓
To Whom is the Speaker Talking?	To Whom is the Speaker Talking?	To Whom is the Speaker Talking?
↓	↓	↓
What is the Speaker's Message?	What is the Speaker's Message?	What is the Speaker's Message?

To His Coy Mistress
• To the Virgins, to Make Much of Time • Song

1. **Compare and Contrast:** Compare the attitudes toward time at the beginning and end of "To His Coy Mistress."

_____

_____

2. **Literary Analysis:** Contrast the *carpe diem* **theme** in the three poems. Write your ideas in this chart. Find images that express the theme. Explain whether the theme is expressed simply or not. Also, explain whether it is expressed humorously, passionately, or reasonably.

Title	Carpe Diem Images	Qualities: Fanciful? Simple?	Humorous? Passionate? Reasonable?
To His Coy Mistress			
To the Virgins, to Make Much of Time			
Song			

3. **Reading Strategy:** Read lines 1–20 of "To His Coy Mistress." The images in these lines are exaggerated. What can you **infer** about the **speaker's attitude** toward his beloved from these lines?

_____

_____

② Writing About the Essential Question

What is the relationship between the writer and tradition? Do these poets mechanically repeat the classical *carpe diem* theme, or do they manage to give it new life? Explain.

_____

_____

Sonnet VII • Sonnet XIX • *from* Paradise Lost

Literary Analysis

An **Italian sonnet** is a fourteen-line lyric poem. It is also called a **Petrarchan** (pi TRAHR kuhn) sonnet. The first eight lines are called the octave (AHK tiv). They present a problem or a question. The next six lines are called the sestet (ses TET). They solve the problem or answer the question that appears in the octave.

An **epic poem** is a long narrative poem about a hero. Milton uses the following features of ancient epics in *Paradise Lost:*

- The story begins in the middle of the action.
- The opening has an invocation (IN voh KAY shuhn). This is a passage in which the poet calls for divine aid in writing.
- The poet uses extended similes. These are long comparisons of unlike things using the words *like* or *as.*

Milton wrote sonnets as well as epics. In his sonnets, he reflects on his ambition to achieve poetic greatness.

Reading Strategy

To help you repair comprehension when understanding breaks down, you can reread text and **break down sentences** into smaller parts to clarify meaning. First, identify the main clause, which states the main idea of the sentence. The main clause can stand on its own as a sentence. Then, identify the supporting clauses. These clauses add thoughts to the main clause. However, they cannot stand on their own. Use the chart below to help you break down long sentences.

Supporting Element		Supporting Element

Main Clause

Supporting Element		Supporting Element

© Pearson Education

Word List A

Study these words from the selections. Then, complete the activities.

bidding [BID ing] *n.* command; order; request
The servant worked loyally for the king and always did his bidding.

chide [CHYD] *v.* scold or criticize gently
His mother would chide him when he forgot to say "please."

hideous [HID ee uhs] *adj.* extremely unpleasant or horrible; repulsive
The movie monster had a twisted and hideous appearance.

invoke [in VOHK] *v.* call upon a greater power; ask solemnly for help
When the customer became rude, the clerk dialed her boss to invoke his help.

lodged [LAHJD] *adj.* given as a power or responsibility
The power to pardon criminals is lodged in the governor of the state.

ordained [awr DAYND] *v.* established formally; appointed
The mayor ordained a community garden on this vacant lot, so no one can build on it.

stench [STENCH] *n.* strong, disgusting smell
The broken sewage pipe created a stench that filled the house.

torments [tawr MENTZ] *v.* tortures; causes great pain or suffering
A cat that has caught a mouse torments it, playing with it before killing it.

Exercise A

Fill in each blank below using the appropriate word from Word List A.

Last summer, I took part in a cultural experiment that placed people from cities in a colonial village. I went at my mother's [1] _____, because I didn't want her to [2] _____ me for being lazy. The villagers dressed, worked, and behaved according to strict rules, and all power was [3] _____ with a governing council. At first, I resented the [4] _____, ugly clothing, but eventually, I got used to wearing long skirts. I despised going to the barn that held the farm animals, since there was a horrible [5] _____ there. The villagers lived simply, and I missed conveniences, such as dental floss. But then I realized that even though I lacked some comforts, I was enjoying the calm and quiet of the village. Without the stress of city living, which sometimes [6] _____ even the toughest person, I could finally unwind. The village even had a building that was officially [7] _____ a place of silence. I had no need to [8] _____ the power of my headphones to escape from life. At the end of the experiment, I decided to adjust my busy lifestyle and work time for relaxation into my schedule.

1. Underline the words that tell in what way the cubicle was hideous. Then, tell what you would do to fix its *hideous* appearance.

2. Circle the word that is a clue to the meaning of <u>stench</u>. What is causing the *stench*?

3. Underline the word that is a clue to the meaning of <u>ordained</u>. Then, give an example of a room that has been *ordained* for a purpose.

4. Circle the word that helps explain what <u>chide</u> means. What phrase might a person use to *chide* someone?

5. Underline the words that tell what type of authority was <u>lodged</u> in the boss. Give an example of someone else in whom this authority might be *lodged*.

6. Circle the phrase that is a clue to the meaning of bidding. Give an example of someone whose *bidding* you might do.

7. Underline the phrase that has a meaning similar to <u>torments</u>. Describe another situation in which an uncooperative machine *torments* someone.

8. Circle the words that tell what the employee decided to <u>invoke</u>. Then, use *invoke* in a sentence of your own.

Read the following passage. Pay special attention to the underlined words. Then, read it again, and complete the activities. Use a separate sheet of paper for your written answers.

I was delighted when I was promoted from receptionist to administrative assistant, and I imagined my new, private office would be well equipped and tidy, but that fantasy was quickly shattered. The room assigned to me was a <u>hideous</u> cubicle with paint splattered on the walls and garbage strewn all over the floor. There was an overwhelming <u>stench</u> coming from one corner, the odor of rotting lunches and stale coffee; apparently, after the previous assistant left, the empty cubicle had been <u>ordained</u> the official dumping space for the office. Trying to remain optimistic, I cleaned up the disgusting mess and went to get my first assignment from my new boss.

When I arrived at his office, I knocked, and he bellowed back, ordering me to come in. I paused before entering, and he criticized me for hesitating: "There's no time to be shy." I thought I was being polite, and I had no idea that he would <u>chide</u> me. The authority to tell me what to do was <u>lodged</u> in him, though, and I did not want to risk further irritating him I just apologized. He handed me a stack of papers and instructed me to copy, collate, and distribute them.

Eager to do his <u>bidding</u>, I followed his instructions and began to photocopy the papers. The machine quickly overheated and refused to cooperate. I turned it off and then on again and repositioned the paper tray. The stubborn machine kept producing blanks, though, and even burned my fingers.

"It seems to enjoy causing people pain," said a coworker, "and it <u>torments</u> one of us at least once a day."

After I arranged for the copier to be serviced, I decided it was time to <u>invoke</u> my sacred right as an employee—I took my lunch break.

Sonnet VII and Sonnet XIX
John Milton

Summaries The speaker in **Sonnet VII** is 24 years old. He feels he has not yet accomplished much. Whether he does or not will depend on the will of Heaven.

The speaker in **Sonnet XIX** wonders why he is blind. He still has much of his life to live. First, he asks how God can expect a blind person like himself to accomplish anything. Then, he decides that he can best serve God by patiently waiting.

Note-taking Guide

Use the diagram below to compare Sonnets VII and XIX. In the middle of the diagram, list what the sonnets have in common. List their differences on either side.

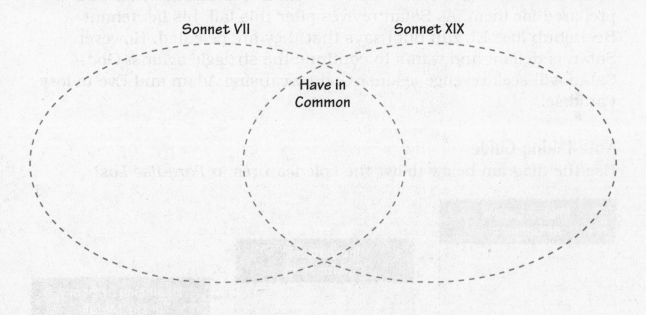

Sonnet VII   Have in Common   Sonnet XIX

from Paradise Lost
John Milton

Summary *Paradise Lost* is a long narrative poem written from a Christian point of view. It tells how Adam and Eve, the first humans according to Jewish and Christian belief, were tempted by the evil angel Satan to disobey God. This disobedience caused them to lose their home in the garden known as Paradise. Instead of living a life of ease forever, they would have to work and, eventually, die.

In this excerpt from the beginning of the poem, Milton explains what his subject will be. He also calls on Urania (yoo RAY nee uh), goddess of astronomy and poetry, to help him write his poem. Then, he tells how Satan, once a great angel, rebelled against God's rule. In punishment, God hurled Satan and the other rebel angels out of heaven. These angels fell to a place of darkness and fire that God prepared for them. As Satan revives after this fall, his lieutenant Beelzebub (bee EL zuh bub) says that they are defeated. However, Satan is defiant and wants to continue the struggle against God. Satan will seek revenge against God by causing Adam and Eve to lose Paradise.

Note-taking Guide
Use the diagram below to list the epic features in *Paradise Lost*.

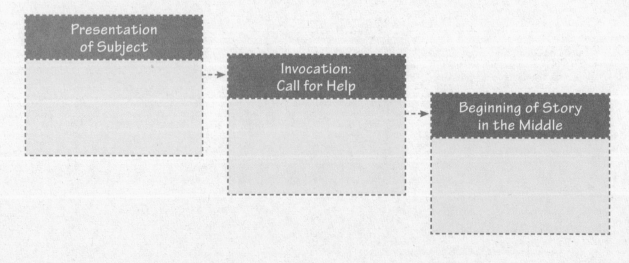

Presentation
of Subject

Invocation:
Call for Help

Beginning of Story
in the Middle

from Paradise Lost

John Milton

Of man's first disobedience, and the fruit
Of that forbidden tree, whose mortal[1] taste
Brought death into the world, and all our woe,
With loss of Eden, till one greater Man[2]
Restore us, and regain the blissful seat,
Sing Heavenly Muse,[3] . . . .

◆ ◆

> The speaker of the poem suggests that the Muse is the same spirit that inspired Moses. The speaker asks the Muse to help him finish the epic he is now writing. Then, the poet asks the Holy Spirit to help him too.

◆ ◆ ◆

. . . what in me is dark
Illumine, what is low raise and support;
That to the height of this great argument[4]
I may assert Eternal Providence,
And justify the ways of God to men.

◆ ◆ ◆

> The speaker then asks the Holy Spirit to tell him what made Adam and Eve disobey God's commandment. They were so happy. They were the lords of the world. All they had to do was obey God and avoid eating the fruit of the tree of knowledge.

◆ ◆ ◆

Vocabulary Development

illumine (i LOO muhn) *v.* light up
assert (uh SERT) *v.* declare firmly
justify (JUS tuh FY) *v.* to prove or show to be right

---

1. **mortal** (MOR tuhl) adj. deadly.
2. **one greater Man** Jesus Christ.
3. **Heavenly Muse** (MYOOZ) Urania, the muse of astronomy and sacred poetry in Greek mythology. Here, Milton associates Urania with the holy spirit that inspired Moses. Moses received the Ten Commandments from God. He also wrote the first five books of the Bible, including Genesis, the book on which *Paradise* Lost is based.
4. **argument** (AR gyoo ment) *n.* theme.

TAKE NOTES

Literary Analysis

In the first paragraph, for whose divine aid does the poet ask in writing his **epic poem?** Circle the answer.

Literary Analysis

What clues tell you that this is an **epic poem?** List two clues.

1. _____

2. _____

Reading Check

What command of God did Adam and Eve disobey?

_____

_____

_____

Read Fluently

Read aloud the bracketed section. Then, circle the phrase Milton uses to refer to Satan. Underline the phrase that refers to Eve.

Reading Strategy

To check **comprehension,** divide the difficult underlined sentence into smaller parts.

1. What is the subject? (Who performs the action?)

_____

2. What is the simple predicate? (What is the main action?)

_____

3. What is the direct object? (Who receives the action?)

_____

Reading Check

To whom is Satan speaking?

_____

_____

Who first seduced them to that foul revolt?
The infernal Serpent; he it was, whose <u>guile</u>
Stirred up with envy and revenge, deceived
The mother of mankind, what time his pride
Had cast him out from Heaven, with all his
   host
Of rebel angels, by whose aid <u>aspiring</u>
To set himself in glory above his peers. . . .

◆ ◆ ◆

The speaker tells more about the fallen angels. Their leader wanted to be equal to God. He waged a war against God. He was very ambitious and fought a brave battle, but he lost. God punished him severely.

◆ ◆ ◆

<u>Him the Almighty Power
Hurled headlong flaming from the ethereal sky
With hideous ruin and combustion down
To bottomless perdition, there to dwell
In adamantine⁵ chains and penal fire</u>. . . .

◆ ◆ ◆

Now Satan is tormented by thoughts of lost happiness and lasting pain. He is in a dungeon full of flames. Yet the flames give off no light. He can never find any peace, rest, or hope. The rebel angels are as far from God and the light of Heaven as possible. Soon Satan sees Beelzebub,⁶ his main helper in the fight against God. He speaks to Beelzebub about how changed Beelzebub is. Once his own brightness outshone that of the other angels. He joined Satan in the fight against God, and now misery has joined them both in equal ruin. Satan then tells Beelzebub that

Vocabulary Development

guile (GYL) *n.* deceitful cunning
aspiring (as PYR ing) *adj.* trying to accomplish a goal
perdition (per DI shun) *n.* complete destruction

5. **adamantine** (ad uh MAN teen) *adj.* not able to be broken.

6. **Beelzebub** (bee EL zuh buhb) Usually, this name refers to the chief devil, or Satan. Here, it refers to Satan's main helper among the fallen angels.

he is not sorry for what they did.

◆ ◆ ◆

          What though the field be lost?
All is not lost; the unconquerable will
And study of revenge, immortal hate,
And courage never to submit or yield:
And what is else not to be overcome?
That glory never shall his wrath or might
<u>Extort</u> from me.

◆ ◆ ◆

      Satan tells Beelzebub that he will never give up in his fight against God. He plans to wage eternal war. Then, Beelzebub calls Satan a prince, a chief, and a leader of the angels. He says that the mind and spirit are still strong, even though their glory and happiness have changed to endless misery. Then, Beelzebub says that it is clear that God is almighty, for how else could he have won against such a mighty force? He wonders what good it is to have eternal life, if all that is in store for them is eternal punishment. Satan answers Beelzebub:

◆ ◆ ◆

"Fallen cherub, to be weak is miserable,
Doing or suffering:[7] but of this be sure,
To do aught[8] good never will be our task,
But ever to do ill our sole delight,
As being the contrary to his high will
Whom we resist. If then his providence
Out of our evil seek to bring forth good,
Our labor must be to pervert that end,
And out of good still[9] to find means of evil;

◆ ◆ ◆

      Satan goes on to say that their activities will cause God grief and trouble. He sees that

© Pearson Education

Vocabulary Development

extort (ex TORT) *v.* to obtain by force

7. **doing or suffering** whether one is active or passive.
8. **aught** (AWT) anything.
9. **still** always.

Literary Analysis 🔍

What details suggest that Satan has the qualities of an **epic hero?** List two.

1. _____

2. _____

Literary Analysis 🔍

Epic poems commonly tell of famous battles. What famous battle is Milton writing about?

_____

_____

Reading Check 📖

What does Satan plan to do in the future?

_____

_____

_____

Reading Strategy

Build comprehension by dividing the bracketed passage into two sentences. Write the sentences below in your own words.

_____

_____

_____

Reading Check

What will Heaven bring out of Satan's evil?

_____

_____

_____

God has called his good angels back to Heaven. It looks as if the war is over, at least for now. Satan sees this as an opportunity to rest and gather together their overthrown armies. He wants to think about how they can most offend their Enemy in the future. As Satan talks to Beelzebub, he lies chained on a burning lake of fire. His huge body is as big as any monster from ancient stories.

◆ ◆ ◆

So stretched out huge in length the Archfiend
    lay
Chained on the burning lake, nor ever thence
Had risen or heaved his head, but that the will
And high permission of all-ruling Heaven
Left him at large to his own dark designs,
That with reiterated crimes he might
Heap on himself damnation, while he sought
Evil to others, and enraged might see
How all his malice served but to bring forth
Infinite goodness, grace and mercy shown
On man by him seduced, but on himself
Treble confusion, wrath and vengeance poured.

◆ ◆ ◆

Suddenly Satan gets up from the fiery pool. He opens his wings and flies to dry land. Beelzebub follows him. They are both happy to have escaped on their own strength, rather than by the permission of heavenly power.

◆ ◆ ◆

Vocabulary Development
designs (duh ZYNZ) *n.* plans
reiterated (ree IT er ay tuhd) *v.* repeated

"Is this the region, this the soil, the clime,"
Said then the lost Archangel, "this the seat
That we must change for Heaven, this
            mournful gloom
For that celestial light? Be it so, since he
Who now is sovereign can dispose and bid
What shall be right: farthest from him is best,
Whom reason hath equaled, force hath made
            supreme
Above his equals. Farewell happy fields,
Where joy forever dwells. Hail horrors! Hail
Infernal world! and thou, profoundest Hell
Receive thy new possessor, one who brings
A mind not to be changed by place or time.
The mind is its own place, and in itself
Can make a Heaven of Hell, a Hell of Heaven.
What matter where, if I be still the same,
And what I should be, all but less than he
Whom thunder hath made greater? Here at
            least
We shall be free; the Almighty hath not built
Here for his envy, will not drive us hence:
Here we may reign secure, and in my choice
To reign is worth ambition though in Hell:
Better to reign in Hell than serve in Heaven."

◆   ◆   ◆

Satan asks why they should let their
fellow fallen angels lie in the fires. Why not
call them together again? Together, they can
find out what they might regain in Heaven,
or what more they might lose in Hell.

© Pearson Education

Reading Strategy 📖

Check your **comprehension** by
dividing the underlined sentence
into smaller parts. Rewrite it
below in your own words.

_____

_____

_____

Literary Analysis 🔍

Reread the bracketed section. In
what way are these ideas fitting
for the hero of an **epic poem**?

_____

_____

_____

Stop to Reflect 📖

What do you think Satan means
by the underlined comment?

_____

_____

_____

Sonnet VII • Sonnet XIX • *from* Paradise Lost

1. **Literary Analysis:** In **Italian sonnets** VII and XIX, Milton reflects on setbacks to his poetic ambition. Use the chart below to compare the two poems.

Title	Speaker's Situation	Effect on Ambition	Solution and How It Helps
Sonnet VII			
Sonnet XIX			

2. **Literary Analysis:** A main character in an **epic** often has a powerful personality. Does Satan have such a personality? Explain.

_____

_____

_____

3. **Reading Strategy:** Build **comprehension** by dividing sentences into smaller parts to identify the main clause in lines 1-8 of Sonnet XIX. Clue: A semicolon separates the main clause from the supporting clauses.

_____

_____

Writing About the Essential Question

What is the relationship between the writer and tradition? Focus on an especially strong passage in *Paradise Lost?* What devices—word choice, rhythms, characterization, description—help Milton re-invent the story of the fallen angels?

_____

_____

_____

_____

from The Pilgrim's Progress

Literary Analysis

An **allegory** is a story that has a symbolic meaning quite different from the story's literal meaning. *The Pilgrim's Progress* tells the story of an adventure-packed journey. However, beneath the surface, it tells the symbolic story of a Christian soul's journey through life to salvation. For example, Christian tries to free himself from the Slough of Despond. His literal struggle in the swamp is a **symbol** of his struggle to free himself from unhappiness and sin. Look for other symbolic meanings as you read this allegory. Bunyan uses names that tell what many of his symbols represent.

Reading Strategy

You **establish a purpose for reading** when you decide why you are reading a selection. One reason for reading *The Pilgrim's Progress* is to **interpret** the meaning of the allegory. To interpret something means to explain its meaning or significance. Use details and your own knowledge and experience to determine what the symbols mean. As you read this story, use this chart to list symbols from the story. Then, write your interpretation of what each symbol represents in the story.

Interpreting an Allegory	
Overall symbolism	Christian's Journey = a Christian's journey through life to salvation
Specific symbols with names that signal their meaning	Christian = a Christian Celestial City = heaven
Main message or lesson	

Word List A

Study these words from the selections. Then, complete the activities.

apprehensions [ap ruh HEN shuhnz] *n.* fears or anxieties felt in advance
   Jacob had apprehensions *about boarding a plane to fly during a storm.*

filth [FILTH] *n.* disgustingly offensive dirt; anything considered foul
   After the basement flooded and mold set in, the room was full of filth.

midst [MIDST] *n.* middle
   Sarah waved to her parents from the midst *of the crowd.*

mire [MY er] *n.* bog; deep, soggy mud
   The wheel of Sandy's car became stuck in the mire.

scum [SKUM] *n.* a thin layer of waste that can form on top of a liquid
   The pond in the forest was covered with a layer of greenish scum.

slough [SLUF] *n.* deep swamp or marsh
   We wore tall rubber boots to walk through the slough.

spew [SPYOO] *v.* to gush
   The actor began to spew *out words too quickly for anyone to understand.*

surveyors [ser VAY ers] *n.* people whose job is to examine, or measure, land
   The surveyors *must measure the road before it can be widened.*

Exercise A

Fill in the blanks, using each word from Word List A only once.

Talia and Frank had some [1] _____ about the new video game
sent to them by their wacky Uncle Zorro. He worked for a company that
invented outrageous new games, and this one was no exception. The name
of the game was "Survive the [2] _____," and it was set in a deep
swamp. Each player belonged to a team of [3] _____ who were
supposed to be examining land in the middle of an enchanted forest to find
the right place to build a bridge over the deepest part of a mysterious, soggy
[4] _____. Of course, the swampy water was covered with a thin film
of [5] _____. Points were lost if a player fell in and became covered
with dirt and [6] _____. Points were also lost if an underwater
volcano was disturbed, which seemed to [7] _____ hot lava at random
moments. In the [8] _____ of the game, Talia and Frank grew bored
and decided to play chess instead.

Read the following passage. Then, complete the activities.

Wetlands can be found near ponds, streams, lakes, rivers, and also near ocean coasts. These are places where the ground is covered with or soaked by water for most of the year. Wetlands are important ecosystems for plants and animals. In the interest of preserving wetlands, surveyors may be assigned to evaluate and map out these areas.

If you happen to be hiking along a trail and suddenly find yourself in the middle of a mire, an area of deep soggy mud, then you may have walked into the midst of a type of wetland area known as a bog.

A spongy substance covers the ground of a typical bog. This is not disgusting dirt or filth; it is a layer of decayed plant material called peat. The soil of a peat bog has a lot of acid in it and few mineral nutrients. Consequently, mosses and carnivorous plants like to grow there.

Another type of wetland, with deeper water, is a swamp, or slough. It can look like a flooded forest. If water has been standing still there for a long time, scum can form on top. This thin, filmy layer is made of waste from plants and other impurities in the water.

Water does not usually spew into a wetland, like a jet of water released suddenly through an opening in a dam. Instead, the water accumulates gradually. Rainfall supplies water to the most famous wetland area in the United States, the Florida Everglades. Some groundwater also seeps in from nearby Lake Okeechobee, which is fed by the Kissimmee River. In parts of the Everglades, you might have a few apprehensions about doing a lot of walking. The Everglades is the only place on Earth where you can find both alligators and crocodiles living together.

1. Circle the words that describe what surveyors do. Write your own sentence telling what *surveyors* do.

2. Underline the words that have the same meaning as mire. Write a synonym for *mire*.

3. Circle the word that has the same meaning as midst. Use the word *midst* in a sentence.

4. Circle the words that have the same meaning as filth. Write another synonym for the word *filth*.

5. Circle the word that has the same meaning as slough. Name a type of environment that has scarce water, making it very different from a *slough*.

6. Underline the words that have the same meaning as the word scum. Use the word *scum* in a sentence.

7. Underline the simile that hints at the meaning of spew. Give a synonym for the word *spew*.

8. Circle the words that tell what might be your apprehensions. Use the word *apprehensions* in a sentence.

from The Pilgrim's Progress
John Bunyan

Summary In this excerpt from
The Pilgrim's Progress, the narrator
describes his dream. Two men, named
Pliable and Christian, fall into a bog.
Pliable frees himself, and walks off.
A man named Help walks by and
helps Christian out of the bog. Help
explains the secrets of the bog to
Christian.

Note-taking Guide
Use the diagram below to summarize the actions of Christian, Pliable,
and Help.

Christian	Pliable	Help

from The Pilgrim's Progress

1. **Compare and Contrast:** This story depicts Christian and Pliable as traveling companions. Describe how the two are alike and how they are different.

   _____

   _____

2. **Literary Analysis:** *The Pilgrim's Progress* is rich with **symbolic** meaning. What does the Slough of Despond represent in this **allegory?**

   _____

   _____

3. **Reading Strategy:** Consider that Christian's journey represents a Christian's life journey to salvation, or heaven. Which places and characters in the selection have names that signal their meaning and help you **interpret the allegory?** On a chart like the following, list three places and characters other than Christian. Then tell what role these symbolic places and characters have during this journey.

Character/Place	Symbolic Role

Writing About the Essential Question

Do writers influence social trends or just reflect them? What does the selection show about the role of faith in Bunyan's society?

_____

_____

_____

from Eve's Apology in Defense of Women
• To Lucasta, on Going to the Wars
• To Althea, from Prison

Literary Analysis

Readers can **analyze the political assumptions** in a work to find out whether it presents a clear and consistent message. Works of literature may present ideas that support tradition or reform.

- **Tradition** refers to society's approved values, beliefs, and customs.
- **Reform** is an attempt to change traditional practices and ideas.

Lanier is a reformer. She fights to change traditional ideas about women. Lovelace supports traditional values. He goes to war and then to prison for his king. He values his honor more than his beloved.

As you read, look for themes of tradition and reform in these poems.

Reading Strategy

As you read a literary work, you should think about how it **connects to a historical context.** The historical context of a work relates to the ideas, customs, and beliefs of its time period. As you read, look for references to these ideas and beliefs. Also, consider which ideas may be responses to events of the period. Complete the chart below to place Lanier's poem and one of Lovelace's poems in their historical context.

Poem	Historical Context	Connection
Eve's Apology	Seventeenth-century women's rights were restricted; the story of Eve was used to justify these restrictions	

Word List A

Study these words from the selections. Then, complete the activities.

breach [BREECH] *n.* failure to obey a law, a trust, or a promise
If the band does not play tonight, that will be a breach of their contract.

excused [ek SKYOOZD] *v.* forgiven; pardoned
Rude behavior simply cannot be excused.

frame [FRAYM] *v.* shape, influence
Each group will work together to frame a plan for the big project.

hover [HUV uhr] *v.* to linger near a place; to float in the air in one spot
The helicopter will hover over the sinking ship until everyone is rescued.

knowledge [NAHL ij] *n.* general awareness and understanding of facts
The doctor used his knowledge of medicine to ease his patient's pain.

soar [SOR] *v.* to fly or rise high in the air
After an airplane takes off, it will soar, reaching great heights.

tangled [TAN guhld] *adj.* twisted together; entwined
Her hair was so tangled that it took her an hour to comb out all the knots.

voice [VOYS] *v.* to express a sentiment or opinion verbally
The unhappy employees decided to voice their complaints to their boss.

Exercise A

Fill in each blank below using the appropriate word from Word List A.

[1] _____ of science and politics was beginning to [2] _____ in England during the 1700s. These advances would [3] _____ and shape developments in literature and art as well. Some texts during this period went against commonly accepted cultural norms. Discussing politics was acceptable, but encouraging treason was a [4] _____ of the law—it simply could not be [5] _____. Society wasn't always comfortable with the way writers would [6] _____ together, getting [7] _____ up in literature and politics. Nevertheless, the daily papers gave [8] _____ to opinions that both supported and opposed the English Civil War. This encouraged people and writers alike to consider their views carefully.

1. Circle the word means about the same as frame. Tell what it means to *frame* a role.

2. Underline the words that tell what Parliament wanted to voice. Explain what it means to *voice* something.

3. Circle the words that tell what was tangled. Then tells what *tangled* means.

4. Circle the words that tell what was considered a breach of law. Then, use *breach* in a sentence.

5. Underline the words that tell why some of those who had executed Charles I were excused. Then, give a synonym for *excused*.

6. Underline the words that tell what caused the monarchy's popularity to soar. What is something else that can *soar*?

7. Circle the words that tell who had to hover in secrecy. Name something else that might *hover*.

8. Underline the words that tell how Charles used his knowledge. Name something about which you have a great deal of *knowledge*.

Read the following passage. Pay special attention to the underlined words. Then, read it again, and complete the activities. Use a separate sheet of paper for your written answers.

When Oliver Cromwell became Lord Protector of England, Ireland and Scotland, he created a military dictatorship that was sustained by his armies. When that power was eroded by foreign wars, Cromwell's death, and the immediate succession of Cromwell's ineffectual son, the crown was restored. Before Cromwell, the King's extensive power caused many problems, so Parliament now made sure to use their power to frame the king's role—they wanted to shape it with less power.

Parliament did not want an absolute monarch again. Charles II was expected to share decision-making powers with Parliament. This was crucial since they wanted to be able to voice opposition to his policies, if necessary. Although he agreed to this, Charles II made secret deals, violating his promise. It soon became obvious that there were tangled agendas on both sides.

Many loyal to the king now sought revenge on those who had executed King Charles I in 1649, considering his execution a massive breach of law. Nine people who had been involved in the trial and death of Charles I were tried and executed. Those who had been part of the execution, but had since come to support the monarchy, were excused and released.

A restoration of other freedoms, such as dancing and playing music in public places, caused the monarchy's popularity to soar. This was a striking change, since before supporters of the king had to hover together in secrecy, rarely venturing out of their hidden meeting places. Unlike Cromwell, King Charles II used his popularity and his knowledge to encourage cultural growth in England. But while art and science flourished, some Protestant sects believed England had returned to a corrupt style of living. This cultural divide eventually led to another civil war and the removal of another king.

from Eve's Apology in Defense of Women
Amelia Lanier

To Lucasta, on Going to the Wars • To Althea, from Prison
Richard Lovelace

Summaries **"Eve's Apology"** suggests that Adam rather than Eve bears the greater blame for disobeying God in Eden. The speaker in **"Lucasta"** asks his beloved not to judge him for leaving to go to war. The speaker in **"Althea"** has been imprisoned. He is being punished because he fought for his king.

Note-taking Guide

For each poem, consider three questions: Who is the speaker? To whom is he or she addressing the poem? What is his or her main idea or purpose? Record your information in the chart below.

Poem	Speaker	Audience	Main Idea/Purpose
Eve's Apology			
Lucasta			
Althea			

from Eve's Apology in Defense of Women
• To Lucasta, on Going to the Wars
• To Althea, from Prison

1. **Interpret:** What is the meaning of lines 25-26 of "To Althea, from Prison"? In other words, how can the speaker feel free even though he is in prison?

_____

_____

2. **Literary Analysis: Analyze the political assumptions** of "Eve's Apology." What tradition is Lanier trying to reform? In the chart, identify the tradition that Lanier opposes. Then, identify Lanier's beliefs about the tradition.

Tradition Lanier Opposes	Lanier's Beliefs About Tradition

3. **Reading Strategy:** Explain how using the **historical context** helps you understand the third stanza of "To Althea." Why, for example, does the speaker refer to the "glories of my King"?

_____

_____

_____

? Writing About the Essential Question

How does literature shape or reflect society? Which of these authors do you think was reflecting dominant social attitudes about women and which was trying to influence or change those attitudes? Explain.

_____

_____

_____

from A Journal of the Plague Year

Literary Analysis

The **point of view** of a work of literature is the perspective from which the work is told. A journal, for example, is told from the first-person point of view. A journal is a daily account of a writer's experiences. The writer of a journal uses first-person pronouns—*I, me, we,* and *us.* The reader knows only what the writer knows or wishes to reveal.

Another commonly used point of view is third person. The third-person narrator uses the pronouns—*he, she, it, they,* and *them.* There are two types of third-person point of view:

- **Third-person omniscient:** The narrator describes everything that happens and reveals the thoughts and feelings of all characters.
- **Third-person limited:** The narrator describes the story through the thoughts, feelings, and experiences of one character.

As you read, notice how Defoe's *Journal of the Plague Year* makes use of the first-person point of view.

Reading Strategy

To better understand a work, **generate and answer questions** as you read it. For example, you may have trouble understanding Defoe's *Journal of the Plague Year.* To clarify what is happening, ask the questions *when, who, where, what, why,* and *how* to identify essential information. Use a chart like the one below to generate and answer questions about Defoe's *Journal of the Plague Year.*

When?	What?
Who?	Why?
Where?	How?

Word List A

Study these words from the selections. Then, complete the activities.

agony [AG uh nee] *n.* enormous mental or physical pain
The painting depicted people ill with the plague, suffering and in agony.

altered [AWL terd] *v.* changed; modified
We altered *the house by removing a wall in the kitchen.*

calamity [kuh LAM uh tee] *n.* disaster
To avoid a calamity, *never stand on a swivel chair.*

dreadful [DRED fuhl] *adj.* very terrible; truly awful
The hurricane blew off our roof, which left our house in dreadful *shape.*

hazard [HAZ erd] *n.* risk; danger
A firefighter could not do her job if she feared every hazard.

mourning [MAWR ning] *n.* the act of expressing grief over the death of someone or something
The country was in mourning *over the death of its president.*

utmost [UT mohst] *adj.* greatest; to the largest possible degree
Pamela expressed her utmost *enthusiasm for Greer's new red dress.*

venture [VEN cher] *v.* to do something that involves some risk
Linh decided to venture *out in the sailboat alone.*

Exercise A

Fill in the blanks, using each word from Word List A only once.

Patrick was assigned to write a report about the [1] _____
disease known as the Black Plague. He was interested in infectious diseases,
so he did his [2] _____ to research the subject well. What
amazed him was the extent of the [3] _____ people suffered,
both mental and physical, and the courage of the healers who overlooked the
[4] _____ of becoming sick themselves in order to [5]
_____ into homes of the ill. In communities devastated by the
Black Plague, people were constantly in [6] _____ and life was
[7] _____ much more than he expected, because so many
people died. Patrick could not imagine experiencing such a [8]
_____ in his own lifetime.

Read the following passage. Then, complete the activities.

Daniel Defoe's first and most famous novel, *Robinson Crusoe*, was hugely successful from the time it was published in 1719. The title character leaves home at age 19, without telling his parents, in order to *venture* to sea. He has many adventures and winds up shipwrecked on a deserted island off the coast of South America, where he spends 28 years. It is there that he begins writing his autobiography, which is the fictional narrative we read.

As a young sailor, Crusoe survives one calamity after another: violent storms, a rescue from a sinking ship, and an attack by pirates who take him prisoner and force him into slavery. He escapes and has another series of adventures. Eventually, he becomes owner of a plantation in Brazil.

In search of laborers to work his land, Crusoe sails off again. A dreadful storm wrecks the ship, killing everyone on board except Crusoe, who is washed up on the island.

After mourning the loss of his shipmates, he sets about doing his utmost to survive by building a strong shelter and a canoe, hunting wild goats, and sowing grain. He decides to keep a journal to describe his life in these greatly altered, constantly changing, circumstances. After 15 years, he discovers a human footprint. This turns out to be a clue to a new hazard. It belongs to a member of a tribe of cannibals who bring prisoners to the island in order to eat them. Crusoe rescues one of these prisoners, saving him from the agony of his captivity. Crusoe names him Friday, simply because he was rescued on a Friday. Crusoe and Friday have more adventures before they are rescued, finally, from the island. Upon returning to Europe, Crusoe learns that his plantation prospered during his absence, and he has become a wealthy man.

1. Circle the words that tell where Crusoe decided to venture. If you could *venture* to any place in the world, where would it be?

2. Underline the words that describe each calamity. Write a synonym for *calamity*.

3. Write a sentence describing a dreadful storm. Write a synonym for *dreadful*.

4. Underline the words that tell what Crusoe was mourning. Write your own definition for *mourning*.

5. Underline the words that describe some ways Crusoe acted in order to do his utmost. Write a synonym for *utmost*.

6. Circle the word that tells what was altered. Use *altered* in a sentence of your own.

7. Underline the words that are a clue to the meaning of hazard. Write a sentence about another type of *hazard* a person might encounter on a deserted island.

8. Write a sentence describing Friday's agony. Write your own definition for the word *agony*.

from A Journal of the Plague Year

Daniel Defoe

Summary The disease known as the plague is killing many people in London. Dead bodies are taken away on carts. Cries of grief are heard on the streets. People are mourning for their loved ones. The narrator sees a terrible pit in Aldgate where bodies are buried daily. He sees a man faint after his dead wife and children are thrown into the pit. What he witnesses is almost too much for him to bear.

Note-taking Guide

Use the chart below to record important details from *A Journal of the Plague Year*.

The Narrator			
What he hears:	Where he goes:	What he sees:	How he feels:

from A Journal of the Plague Year

1. **Literary Analysis: First-person narrators** describe their own experiences and are identified by the pronoun *I*. Find evidence of these two features in Defoe's *Journal*.

_____

_____

2. **Reading Strategy:** List three **questions** that you asked and answered as you read Defoe's *Journal*.

Questions	Answers

3. **Reading Strategy:** Did **questioning** make your reading more active and focused? Explain your answer.

_____

_____

Writing About the Essential Question

What is the relationship between place and literature? Does Defoe use informational language, emotional language, or both to describe London during this crisis?

_____

_____

_____

Reports

About Reports

A report is a document that presents information. Some reports provide information that has been gathered from other sources. Others present the results of research or the conclusions and decisions made by organizations. One specific type of report is an annual report.

An annual report provides information to the public about an organization's finances and activities. These detailed reports also outline the organization's goals and the progress made to reach those goals. Businesses, government organizations, or other special groups publish annual reports. Basic features of annual reports include the following elements:

- chapter or section headings that define specific goals
- bulleted and bold-faced information to draw readers' attention
- photos, charts, or graphs that provide visual information

Reading Skill

Reports contain text features to help readers understand and locate the information they need. Follow these steps to analyze and evaluate **information from text features:**

- Look for headings and subheadings that name the topics.
- Notice bulleted or numbered lists that highlight specific details.
- Look for charts and tables that display information visually.

As you read, use a chart like the one shown to evaluate text features.

Text Features	Description
Title	The name of the report, which gives clues about the topic
Headings and subheadings	Titles of sections that identify the main idea of each section
Photographs, illustrations, captions	Images and their labels that give additional information
Charts, graphs, diagrams	Information that is presented visually
Maps, legends	Images that show information about places

The Mayor's Annual Report 2004

To reduce congestion in London

Congestion—whether on the roads, on the Underground, on the buses or on the trains—is the scourge of London's current transport system. The result of many years of under-investment combined with significant rates of increase in London's population, it will not be cured overnight. Nevertheless, the Mayor is committed to ensuring that anti-congestion measures are combined with the necessary improvement in the capacity and quality of service of London's transport system to alleviate congestion in a systematic manner.

Congestion Charging

The congestion charging scheme commenced in central London in February 2003. The scheme directly tackles four key transport priorities for London:

- reducing congestion
- improving bus services
- improving journey time reliability for car users
- making the distribution of goods and services more reliable, sustainable and efficient.

TfL are monitoring the impacts and operation of the scheme as set out in the first Annual Monitoring Report in June 2003. They have since produced two reports setting out their findings: Congestion Charging:

Six Months On was published in October 2003; Congestion Charging: February 2004 Update was published after one year's operation. A Second Annual Monitoring Report is currently being prepared for publication in the Spring.

Reduced traffic levels and congestion

TfL estimate that 65,000 fewer cars per day are being driven into or through the charging zone, with the majority of occupants switching to public transport or diverting around the zone. As a result only 4,000 fewer people are coming to the charging zone each day because of the scheme.

Congestion in the zone has dropped by around 30 percent and is at the lowest level seen since the mid-1980s. The number of vehicles with four or more wheels entering the zone during charging hours has dropped by18 per cent—making journeys to and from the charging zone quicker and more reliable. Journey times to and from the zone have decreased by an average 14 percent and journey time reliability has improved by an average of 30 percent.

Congestion levels in the charging zone during charging hours

Reduced congestion has also assisted the wider improvements in bus service reliability and journey times; the additional waiting time due to unreliability within the charging zone has reduced by around one third since the beginning of the scheme. Routes serving the congestion zone also experience 60 percent less congestion due to traffic disruption than before the charge was introduced.

Economic Impact

Reduced traffic delays, improved journey time reliability, reduced waiting time at bus stops and lower fuel consumption resulting from congestion charging all have economic benefits which are increasingly being recognised. TfL's cost benefit analysis of the overall impact of congestion charging is that it generates £50 million per annum of net benefits to London, principally through reduced congestion.

> The chart shows the progress and effect of the congestion charging program.

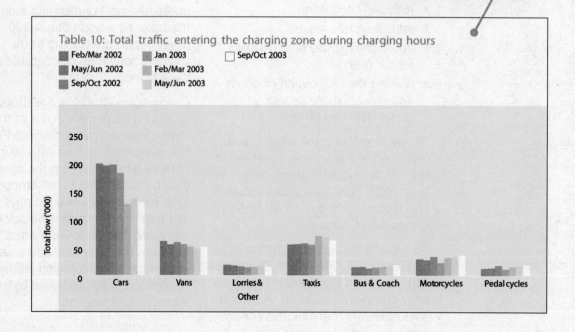

Table 10: Total traffic entering the charging zone during charging hours

- Feb/Mar 2002
- May/Jun 2002
- Sep/Oct 2002
- Jan 2003
- Feb/Mar 2003
- May/Jun 2003
- Sep/Oct 2003

Thinking About Reports

1. According to the annual report, what are the causes of congestion in London?

_____

_____

2. What four results of congestion charging will have economic benefits?

_____

_____

TALK ABOUT IT **Reading Skill**

3. What information does the chart display?

_____

_____

4. What text feature highlights the key transport priorities for London?

_____

WRITE ABOUT IT **Timed Writing: Persuasive Essay (25 minutes)**

Use the Annual Report to argue for or against congestion charging. As you make your case, refer to Table 10 to discuss the advantages or drawbacks of other methods of transportation. Allow about five minutes for prewriting, such as making a pros and cons list of congestion charging and of using public transportation. Use about 15 minutes for writing, and save five minutes for reviewing and revising.

from Gulliver's Travels • A Modest Proposal

Literary Analysis

Satire is writing that uses humor to poke fun at human error and foolishness. Satire can be good-humored, or it can be bitter.

Writers of satire usually do not name their targets. Instead, they make up imaginary characters and situations to mask their targets.

Satirists often use **irony**, a contradiction between the actual meaning of the words and the meaning intended by the writer. As you read, use this chart to record Swift's use of irony.

What Swift Says	What He Means
"Many . . . volumes have been published" about the best way to break an egg.	People often argue too much about unimportant things.

Like other writers, satirists have a **style,** or special way of writing. Many elements contribute to style, such as word choice, tone, and use of imagery and figurative language.

Reading Strategy

You will not get the point a satirist is trying to make if you fail to interpret the masks used to hint at their true targets. To decode Swift's satire, you must **analyze and evaluate information from text features.** Such features as background information, footnotes, and bold and italicized text add crucial information that will help you **interpret** and recognize **author's purpose.**

Word List A

Study these words from the selections. Then, complete the activities.

affirm [uh FERM] *v.* to maintain to be true; to confirm
Serena called the university to affirm her intention to enroll there.

collateral [kuh LAT er uhl] *adj.* related; parallel; corresponding
Sam used the school textbook, plus a collateral book, to teach history.

contemptible [kuhn TEMP tuh buhl] *adj.* despicable; worthless
After what she did, I think she is contemptible.

contrive [kuhn TRYV] *v.* think up; scheme
Alyssa will contrive a way to keep Sue from finding out about the party.

divert [duh VERT] *v.* distract the attention of
Dan will try to divert Sue so the party is a complete surprise.

oppression [uh PRESH uhn] *n.* the infliction of physical or mental hardships;
feeling weighed down by such problems
The villagers suffered from the oppression of the invading army.

laudable [LAWD uh buhl] *adj.* praiseworthy; commendable; deserving
The laudable efforts of the party organizers resulted in a fabulous bash.

prodigious [proh DIJ uhs] *adj.* enormous; of a huge size
The prodigious crowd cheered for the home team.

Exercise A

Fill in the blanks, using each word from Word List A only once.

Diego realized that he had started watching a [1] _____
amount of television, a huge number of hours each day. He decided to
[2] _____ his attention to something more productive. He told his
friend Oskar that he wanted to [3] _____ a way to include some
hours of meaningful community service in his schedule. Oskar replied that this
was a [4] _____ goal and that, by coincidence, he and a bunch of
other kids had started getting together on Saturdays to help rebuild the home of
a family whose house had partially burned down. The man who started the fire
was a [5] _____ person. For the next ten Saturdays, Diego joined
the group at the homesite. The family was there, too, and he could feel their
sense of [6] _____ lifting as the new house took shape. The
project was certainly a way to [7] _____ his belief that it was
important to reach out to people in need in the community. Diego had a
huge amount of fun in the process and, of course, there was an additional
[8] _____ benefit: He learned how to use power tools.

1. Circle the word that is a synonym for <u>prodigious</u>. Give an antonym for the word *prodigious*.

2. Underline the word that has a meaning similar to <u>laudable</u>. Write a sentence about something or someone you find *laudable*.

3. Circle the word that is a synonym for <u>divert</u>. Use the word *divert* in a sentence.

4. Circle the word that is a synonym for the word <u>contemptible</u>. Write a sentence using an antonym for the word *contemptible*.

5. Underline the phrase that explains the meaning of <u>oppression</u>. Write a sentence giving an example of *oppression* in the world today.

6. Circle the word that has a meaning similar to <u>affirm</u>. Give an antonym for the word *affirm*.

7. Underline the words that tell what inventors of stories <u>contrive</u>. Write your own definition for the word *contrive*.

8. Circle the word in a nearby sentence that explains the meaning of <u>collateral</u>. Underline the phrase that explains why fictional places are *collateral* to our own world.

Read the following passage. Then, complete the activities.

Since ancient times, artists have invented a <u>prodigious</u> number of wonderful stories about characters who travel to imaginary places. An enormous amount of the most <u>laudable</u>, terrific works of literature and film are about journeys. Sometimes these trips take place on Earth, as in *Gulliver's Travels*. Other times, the traveling occurs in a galaxy far, far away.

Marvelous, made-up people and places <u>divert</u> and distract us from our own lives. These stories may be pure entertainment. They may make us reflect in a refreshing way upon our lives. Or, like Swift's satire, they may comment about what is wrong with society. Swift's essay, "A Modest Proposal," discussed what he found <u>contemptible</u> and worthless about the affluent classes and their attitudes toward the poor in eighteenth-century Ireland. He described the <u>oppression</u> of the poor through examples of how they are weighted down by hardships and limited opportunities.

Swift used satire to <u>affirm</u> his beliefs, too. For example, Swift confirms his distaste for firearms and the use of force when Gulliver visits the land of Brobdingnag. Out of gratitude to the king, Gulliver offers to share his knowledge about how to make guns and gunpowder. But the king is appalled by the very idea of such a destructive, harmful invention. He commands Gulliver never to mention it again.

Swift and the inventors of other great stories <u>contrive</u> fantastic adventures for their characters. The details they describe may seem outlandish and strange. Yet these far-off places are <u>collateral</u> to our own. They are like parallel worlds, because each story has something to say about life as the author knows it in his own society and time. It is that ability to create amazing new worlds and situations that have earned writers like Swift a permanent spot in the history of the human imagination.

from Gulliver's Travels
Jonathan Swift

Summary The novel *Gulliver's Travels* describes four imaginary voyages of Lemuel Gulliver, the narrator. Swift uses these voyages to satirize, or humorously criticize, the customs and institutions of his time. The first voyage takes Gulliver to Lilliput (LIL uh put), the kingdom of the six-inch-tall Lilliputians (LIL uh PYOO shuhnz).

Note-taking Guide

Read each purpose in the first column of the chart below. As you read *Gulliver's Travels*, find details that achieve these purposes and write them in the second column.

Purpose	Details to Achieve This Purpose
• To criticize and make fun of religious disputes between Protestants and Catholics within England • To criticize and make fun of religious disputes between Protestant England and Catholic France	
• To criticize and make fun of power-hungry rulers in Europe	

from Gulliver's Travels
Jonathan Swift

Reading Strategy

Each footnote at the bottom of the page is a **text feature.** How do the footnotes help you **interpret** Swift's satire?

_____

_____

_____

Literary Analysis

Swift says that Lilliput and Blefuscu cannot agree on the correct way of breaking eggs. Why do you think he makes this the cause of the conflict between the two countries in his **satire?**

_____

_____

_____

Lemuel Gulliver, the narrator, is a doctor on a ship. When he survives a shipwreck, he swims to shore. There, he drifts off to sleep. When he wakes up, he finds that he has been tied down by the Lilliputians. These people are only six inches tall. After a time, Gulliver becomes friendly with the little people. He listens to conversations in the Lilliputian court that remind him of English affairs of state. One day, he talks with the Lilliputian Principal Secretary of Private Affairs. He tells Gulliver that they are at war with the island of Blefuscu.[1] The two countries have been at war for the past three years.

◆　◆　◆

It is allowed on all hands, that the primitive way of breaking eggs before we eat them, was upon the larger end; but his present Majesty's grandfather, while he was a boy, going to eat an egg, and breaking it according to the ancient practice, happened to cut one of his fingers. Whereupon the Emperor, his father, published an edict, commanding all his subjects, upon great penalties, to break the smaller end of their eggs. The people so highly resented this law that our histories tell us there have been six rebellions raised on that account; wherein one emperor lost his life, and another his crown.[2]

◆　◆　◆

Vocabulary Development

allowed (uh LOWD) *v.* thought

edict (EE dikt) *n.* an official public announcement having the force of law

1. **Blefuscu** stands for France.
2. **It is allowed . . . crown** Here, Swift is satirizing the arguments in England between the Catholics (Big-Endians) and the Protestants (Little-Endians). King Henry VIII, who "broke" with the Catholic Church, is referred to. So is King Charles I, who "lost his life." And so is King James, who lost his "crown."

The Secretary tells Gulliver that Blefuscu constantly starts these rebellions. He says that eleven thousand persons have died rather than agree to break their eggs at the smaller end.

♦　♦　♦

Many hundred large volumes have been published upon this controversy; but the books of the Big-Endians have been long forbidden, and the whole party rendered incapable by law of holding employments.[3]

♦　♦　♦

The Secretary then says that the Blefuscudians make accusations against the Lilliputians. They say that the Lilliputians go against an important religious teaching of the great prophet Lustrog. The Secretary then explains the Lilliputians' view.

♦　♦　♦

This, however, is thought to be a mere strain upon the text, for the words are these: That all true believers shall break their eggs at the convenient end; and which is the convenient end, seems, in my humble opinion, to be left to every man's conscience, or at least in the power of the chief magistrate[4] to determine.

♦　♦　♦

The Secretary then says that the Blefuscudians are preparing to attack with a fleet of fifty war ships. Gulliver says that he will defend Lilliput against all invaders.

A channel 800 yards wide separates the two kingdoms. At high tide, it is about six feet deep. Gulliver orders the strongest cable and iron bars available. The cable is about as thick as thread, and the iron bars are like knitting needles. He triples the cable to make it stronger. He twists three iron bars together to make hooks.

© Pearson Education

3. **holding employments** holding office. (The Test Act of 1673 prevented Catholics from holding public office.)
4. **chief magistrate** (CHEEF MAJ uh strayt) ruler.

TAKE NOTES

Stop to Reflect

Do you think the cause of breaking eggs at the smaller end is worth dying for? Write *yes* or *no*, and explain your answer.

_____

_____

_____

Reading Strategy

In this paragraph, Swift is satirizing people who hate other people because of religious differences. Circle two phrases that clearly support this **interpretation.**

Literary Analysis

Here, Gulliver uses his glasses as a shield in a military operation. What is ironic about this **satire?**

_____

_____

_____

Read Fluently

Read aloud the bracketed paragraph. Then, underline the part that tells what the Emperor wanted to do.

Reading Check

What does Gulliver say that causes the Emperor to turn against him?

_____

_____

_____

Gulliver wades into the channel and fastens a hook to each of the fifty ships. He holds them all together with cable. Then, he cuts the cables that hold the anchors. As he does all this, the enemy shoots thousands of tiny arrows at him. Luckily, his eyes are protected by his glasses. Gulliver wades across the channel with the ships. When he gets to shore, he is made a Nardac on the spot. This is the highest title of honor in Lilliput.

◆   ◆   ◆

His Majesty desired I would take some other opportunity of bringing all the rest of his enemy's ships into his ports. And so unmeasurable is the ambition of princes, that he seemed to think of nothing less than reducing the whole empire of Blefuscu into a province and governing it by a viceroy; of destroying the Big-Endian exiles and compelling that people to break the smaller end of their eggs, by which he would remain sole monarch of the whole world.

◆   ◆   ◆

Gulliver thinks this is wrong. He says that he would never help bring free and brave people into slavery. From then on, there is a campaign against Gulliver. Gulliver comments:

◆   ◆   ◆

Of so little weight are the greatest services to princes when put into the balance with a refusal to gratify their passions.

from Gulliver's Travels
Jonathan Swift

Summary In this chapter of *Gulliver's Travels*, Gulliver visits Brobdingnag (BRAHB ding NAG). This is a fictional island located near Alaska that is inhabited by giants. Gulliver describes English politics and society to the king of this country. The king reacts to the description with disgust.

Note-taking Guide

Read each purpose in the first column of the chart below. As you read *Gulliver's Travels*, find details that achieve these purposes and write them in the second column.

Purpose	Details to Achieve This Purpose
• To criticize and make fun of religious disputes between Protestants and Catholics within England • To criticize and make fun of religious disputes between Protestant England and Catholic France	
• To criticize and make fun of power-hungry rulers in Europe	

A Modest Proposal
Jonathan Swift

Summary This essay is a comment on Irish society during the 18th century. Growing numbers of Irish people suffered in poverty every day. Swift scorns the upper classes as selfish and greedy. He feels they do nothing to end this poverty and often contribute to the problem. Using facts about population, unemployment, and social issues, Swift explains a frightening plan to end poverty: kill poor children and use them for food! Were his plan meant to be taken seriously, it would be truly horrifying. However, Swift does not want his plan to be followed. His purpose is to call attention to social ills.

Note-taking Guide
Use this chart to list two examples of each tool of satire that Swift uses.

Understatement	
Exaggeration	
Sarcasm	

from Gulliver's Travels • A Modest Proposal

1. **Literary Analysis:** *Gulliver's Travels* is **satire,** or writing that uses humor to expose human weaknesses. Use the chart below to show three targets of Swift's satire.

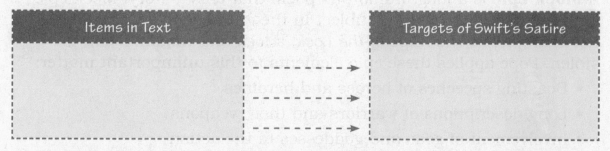

Items in Text		Targets of Swift's Satire
	‑ ‑ ‑ →	
	‑ ‑ ‑ →	
	‑ ‑ ‑ →	

2. **Literary Analysis: Irony** shows the difference between reality and appearance or between what is said and what is meant. Find an example of irony that depends on a difference between appearance and reality. Explain your choice. Clue: The debate about how to break an egg appears to be serious.

_____

_____

_____

3. **Reading Strategy:** In "A Modest Proposal," Swift claims that his **purpose** is to offer a "modest proposal" for preventing poor children from being a burden. Which details in Swift's proposal reveal his deeper purpose for writing it?

_____

_____

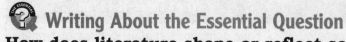 **Writing About the Essential Question**

How does literature shape or reflect society? What do these selections suggest that Swift wanted to change about society?

_____

_____

_____

from An Essay on Man • *from* The Rape of the Lock

Literary Analysis

A **mock epic** is a long, humorous poem that tells a story. Mock epics treat a small, unimportant subject in the grand style of a true epic. For example, in *The Rape of the Lock,* a lock of a woman's hair is stolen. Pope applies these epic elements to this unimportant matter:

- Boasting speeches of heroes and heroines
- Long descriptions of warriors and their weapons
- Involvement of gods and goddesses in the action
- **Epic similes** (SIM uh LEES), or long comparisons in the style of Homer that use the words *like, as,* or *so*

An Essay on Man, by contrast, is a serious work about human nature. However, in both these poems, Pope uses a figure of speech from **rhetoric,** or public speaking, called antithesis (an TI thuh sis). **Antithesis** involves the contrast of opposing words, clauses, sentences, or ideas. Pope organizes his verse in **heroic couplets,** or rhymed pairs of lines in iambic pentameter.

Reading Strategy

The meaning of a work varies with the author's purpose. To understand a work, you must **analyze the effect of the author's purpose** on meaning. For example, an author may tell an outrageous story. However, if you know that his or her purpose is to use that story to make a greater point, then his or her purpose affects the meaning. Use the chart to list examples of how Pope's purposes affect meaning.

Lines	Purpose	What Does It Mean?
33–36	to satirize status-conscious people	Pope compares status-conscious women to Sylphs.

Word List A

Study these words from the selections. Then, complete the activities.

prevails [pree VAYLZ] *v.* to be most common or frequent
  During the winter months in Northern California, rain prevails.

tediousness [TEE dee uhs nuhs] *n.* dullness due to long length or slowness
  Keith didn't enjoy the three-hour movie's tediousness.

intrusion [in TROO zhuhn] *n.* an inappropriate or unwelcome addition
  The loud music is an intrusion on our peace.

languish [LAN gwish] *v.* become weak; lose strength
  Tomato plants need sun, and will languish in cool, rainy weather.

vernal [VER nuhl] *adj.* of or relating to the spring; occurring in the spring
  Tulips and daffodils are vernal blooming flowers.

autumnal [aw TUM nuhl] *adj.* of or relating to the fall; occurring in the fall
  Vermont forests are well known for their autumnal display of color.

transient [TRAN zee uhnt] *adj.* temporary; passing
  A transient feeling doesn't last a long time.

excursion [ek SKER zhuhn] *n.* an outing
  George asked us to join him on an excursion to the beach.

Exercise A

Fill in each blank below using the appropriate word from Word List A.

Gardens are a source of great pleasure for most people. Whether you go on an infrequent [1] _____ to a community park, or enjoy plantings in your yard, spending time with flowers can be a very soothing experience. Most people mix [2] _____ and [3] _____ plants so that they will have flowers blooming in both the spring and the fall. They also grow [4] _____, or short lasting, seasonal flowers for variety, scattering them among recurring perennials, so they don't have to reseed the entire garden every year. However, having a garden isn't for everyone. If you can't stand the [5] _____ of weeding your garden at least twice a week, you will have to deal with a(n) [6] _____ of unwanted plants. If you don't water your garden, your plants will [7] _____, wilt and wither. However, with care, gardens provide pleasure that [8] _____ for many years.

1. Circle the words give clues to the meaning of <u>tediousness</u>. What elements of Renaissance painting represented *tediousness* for the painter?

2. Circle the words that give a clue to the meaning of <u>languish</u>. What is a synonym for *languish*?

3. Underline the phrase that gives a clue to the meaning of <u>transient</u>. What is an antonym for *transient*?

4. Underline the phrase that gives a clue to the meaning of <u>excursion</u>. Use *excursion* in a sentence of your own.

5. Circle the word in the next sentence that gives a clue to the meaning of <u>vernal</u>. What else is *vernal*?

6. Circle the word in the next sentence gives a clue to the meaning of <u>autumnal</u>. Name something else that is *autumnal*.

7. Underline the words that give a clue to the meaning of <u>intrusion</u>. What do you consider an *intrusion* on your time?

8. Circle the words in the next sentence that give a clue to the meaning of <u>prevails</u>. Use *prevails* in an original sentence.

Read the following passage. Pay special attention to the underlined words. Then, read it again, and complete the activities. Use a separate sheet of paper for your written answers.

Thomas Gainsborough was an eighteenth century painter who used nature as a backdrop for his portraits. Gainsborough was weary of the <u>tediousness</u> of Renaissance painting that demanded the same elements in each picture: perfect perspective, calculated composition, stiff postures, and smooth brushstrokes. These were the rules by which the Italian masters painted for most of the fifteenth century, but Gainsborough wished to break away from the limits of that style.

Instead, Gainsborough used quick, visible strokes, and painted an elaborate, fictitious garden behind his subject. He liked to pose people so they were relaxed and comfortable, and they sometimes appeared to <u>languish</u> in plush chairs. The quick strokes and relaxed poses gave the painting a <u>transient</u> appearance, like a temporary moment frozen on the canvas. However, the entire effect was an illusion. Gainsborough would paint the patron in his studio during several sittings. Then, rather than travel to a garden to set up his easel, he would paint the background from his imagination. An <u>excursion</u> to a real garden was entirely unnecessary.

The backgrounds were often featured both <u>vernal</u> and <u>autumnal</u> flowers appearing at the same time. This mix of spring and fall plants was deliberate and created a sense of timelessness. Gainsborough claimed that painting landscapes was his true passion and that painting portraits interrupted his work on them; portraits were merely an <u>intrusion</u> on his time.

However, every artist needs to make money. The wealthy patrons who wanted to him to capture their images on canvas provided him with the income to support himself. Though he considered their portraits to be merely commercial, it is that part of his work that <u>prevails</u>. Gainsborough's portraits are what appear most commonly in museums today.

from An Essay on Man •
from The Rape of the Lock
Alexander Pope

Summaries In the excerpt from *An Essay on Man*, the poet attempts to describe human nature. He claims that human beings exist in a middle state between God and beast. Humans are both wise and confused. They are judges of truth, but they also make endless mistakes. That is why he calls humankind "the glory, jest, and riddle of the world!"

This excerpt from *The Rape of the Lock* tells how the baron cuts a lock of hair from Belinda's head. This silly occurrence is described as if it were a major battle in an epic. First, the baron and Belinda engage in a card game. Then, the baron cuts Belinda's hair. There is a fierce battle over the lock of hair.

Note-taking Guide
Use the diagram below to follow the action in *The Rape of the Lock*. Write the events in the order in which they take place.

Setting	
Events	1.
	2.
	3.
End Result:	

from An Essay on Man •
from The Rape of the Lock

1. **Literary Analysis:** *The Rape of the Lock* is a **mock epic.** It is a humorous poem that uses epic elements to poke fun at silly activities. In the chart below, find lines in which the listed epic element appears. Then, briefly describe the action to which this epic element refers. Review Canto III, 161–162, to find one epic element.

Epic Element	Lines in Poem	Action/Activity
Hero's boasts		
Gods and goddesses		
Description of warriors		

2. **Literary Analysis:** An **epic simile** is an elaborate comparison in the manner of Homer that uses the words *like, as,* or *so.* Why are lines 8–16 in Canto V of *The Rape of the Lock* an example of an *epic simile?*

_____

_____

3. **Reading Strategy:** Show how in Canto III, lines 105–120, of *The Rape of the Lock,* Pope's **purpose** is to poke fun at social customs and to entertain readers. One clue to the custom is that it involves drinking coffee.

_____

_____

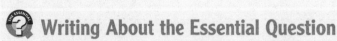 **Writing About the Essential Question**

How does literature shape or reflect society? Was Pope's main goal to change the behavior he mocked or to entertain readers?

_____

_____

from A Dictionary of the English Language
• *from* Life of Samuel Johnson

Literary Analysis

A **dictionary** is a book that defines words. It may also provide information about a word's pronunciation, history, and usage. Samuel Johnson compiled the first standard dictionary of the English language. As you read, look for features he established. Some of them are still in use today.

A **biography** is an account of someone's life written by another person. James Boswell wrote a biography of Samuel Johnson. It was called *Life of Samuel Johnson.* Johnson's *Dictionary* helped set the standard for all future dictionaries. In the same way, Boswell's biography helped set the standard for future biographies. As you read it, note how Boswell uses details from his own knowledge to reveal Johnson's character.

Both these works were products of the Enlightenment. The Enlightenment was an eighteenth-century movement that encouraged the pursuit of knowledge. Note how both these works express a respect for knowledge. Compare their **diction,** or choice of words. Also, notice the **tone,** or attitude, that their word choice reveals.

Reading Strategy

When you **establish a purpose,** you set a goal for reading. For example, two possible goals for reading the *Dictionary* are to learn about Johnson's writing style or to learn about making dictionaries.

To set a purpose, choose a topic related to the selection that you want to know more about. In the chart shown, state what you know about the topic, what you want to know about the topic, and what you learned after reading.

What I Know	What I Want to Know	What I Learned

Word List A

Study these words from the selections. Then, complete the activities.

accumulated [uh KYOOM yoo lay ted] *v.* gathered; piled up
   Over the years, Diane has accumulated *several different instruments.*

console [kuhn SOHL] *v.* to comfort or soothe
   In an effort to console *her, Evan patted Gina on the back.*

convulsive [kuhn VUL siv] *adj.* having involuntary muscle spasms
   She shook with laughter so much that she appeared convulsive.

exuberance [eg ZOO ber uhns] *n.* being extremely excited and joyful
   The home-team fans cheered with exuberance.

harmonious [hahr MOH nee uhs] *adj.* musically pleasing
   Erin liked the piano concerto because it is harmonious.

longevity [lawn JEV i tee] *n.* long life
   You should buy the battery that is known for its longevity.

omitted [oh MIT tid] *v.* left out; failed to include
   The sign is confusing because Isabella accidentally omitted *several words.*

tranquility [trang KWIL i tee] *n.* serenity; a state free from stress
   Grandma was resting with a look of tranquility *on her face.*

Exercise A

Fill in the blanks using each word from Word List A only once.

   Music lovers often feel great [1] _____ when learning to play

a musical instrument. However, many soon discover that practicing is

time consuming, and before long, it is [2] _____ from their schedule.

Although they may still enjoy playing music, without the skills that

are [3] _____ through practice, the musical result is not always

[4] _____. Frustrated musicians may [5] _____ themselves

or create moments of [6] _____ by listening to recordings of their

favorite music. Although parents sometimes joke that the music their

children enjoy makes them feel ill and [7] _____, real devotion to

music has [8] _____, no matter how a person's tastes change over

the years.

Read the following passage. Pay special attention to the underlined words. Then, read it again, and complete the activities. Use a separate sheet of paper for your written answers.

By the eighteenth century, chess was being played with lively <u>exuberance</u> throughout most of Europe, although it had already enjoyed <u>longevity</u> for many years before then. For example, Alexander the Great discovered a version of chess while he was invading India in 327 B.C. An ancient Persian myth describes the origin of chess as a son's attempt to <u>console</u> his mother after his brother died in battle. The surviving son reenacted the movement of the opposing armies on a chessboard. His grieving mother ended her <u>convulsive</u> sobs, which shook her entire body, when she saw how her son had sacrificed himself so their side could be victorious.

In between battles, Christian Crusaders learned chess from the armies of Islam. Apparently, each side enjoyed the <u>tranquility</u> that the matches provided, an escape from the chaos of battle. After the war, the Crusaders brought the game back with them to Europe, where people regarded chess not only as an amusement, but also as a way to strengthen the mind. It was compatible with the soft, <u>harmonious</u> sounds of the lute, a popular musical instrument during that period.

The Game and Play of Chesse, published in 1474, offered <u>accumulated</u> wisdom by gathering multiple perspectives on the practice of playing chess. In it, a philosopher invents chess to teach an evil tyrant how to properly rule his kingdom. The tyrant learns to value patience, knowledge, and strategy. He also abandons his violent butchering of his enemies.

The modern version of the game was developed in the 1400s by Spanish chess players, who wished to speed up the game and <u>omitted</u> a number of rules. They also enhanced the power of certain playing pieces, especially the queen. The result was a quicker, more tactical game that is still played today.

1. Circle the word that provides a clue to the meaning of <u>exuberance</u>. Then, give a synonym for *exuberance.*

2. Circle the words that provide a clue to the meaning of <u>longevity</u>. Then, give an example of something with *longevity.*

3. Rewrite the sentence using a synonym for <u>console</u>. When would you *console* another person?

4. Underline the phrase that describes how the sobs were <u>convulsive</u>. Then, explain what *convulsive* means.

5. Circle an antonym of <u>tranquility</u>. Then, give a synonym for *tranquility.*

6. Underline the words that hint at the meaning of <u>harmonious</u>. Then, give an example of something *harmonious.*

7. Circle the word that has about the same meaning as <u>accumulated</u>. Then, describe what a sports fan may have *accumulated* throughout the years.

8. Underline the words that tell why Spanish chess players <u>omitted</u> a number of rules. Then, use *omitted* in a sentence.

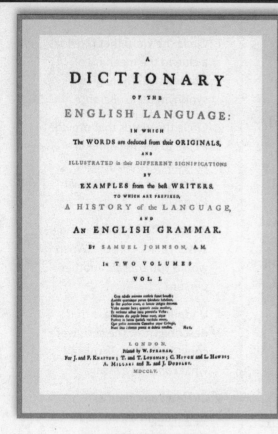

from A Dictionary of the English Language
Samuel Johnson

Summary In the Preface to his dictionary, Johnson explains that writing a dictionary was not an easy task. Johnson faced many problems and challenges. He had to determine the most accurate and thorough definitions of words without relying on any existing dictionaries. Johnson admits that while his dictionary certainly leaves some words out, he has included a great deal of information nonetheless. The sample entries from Johnson's dictionary range from *athletick* to *youth*.

Note-taking Guide

As you read the selections from Johnson's dictionary, note how the author feels about his undertaking. Use this chart to record what you learn.

Johnson's Feelings About Writers of Dictionaries	Johnson's Feelings About the English Language	Johnson's Feelings About His Own Dictionary	Johnson's Feelings About Himself

from Life of Samuel Johnson

James Boswell

Summary Samuel Johnson and James Boswell first met in 1763. Boswell was not sure if their meeting had gone well. As he spent more time with Johnson, he learned more about the writer. Boswell reveals much about this fascinating figure in his biography.

Note-taking Guide

Use this chart to record the different sides of Johnson that Boswell describes.

Contradictory Qualities	Illnesses and Infirmities	Studies and Intellectual Pursuits	Common Conversation

from A Dictionary of the English Language
• *from* Life of Samuel Johnson

1. **Literary Analysis:** Show how both the Preface to the *Dictionary* and *Life of Samuel Johnson* use formal **diction,** or word choice. Consider, Johnson's phrase "those who toil at the lower employments." Then, consider Boswell's phrase, "to obtain the acquaintance of that extraordinary man."

   _____

   _____

2. **Literary Analysis:** Use this chart to compare the definition of a word in Johnson's *Dictionary* with the definition of the same word in a modern **dictionary.** The word *patron*, for example, might reveal an interesting contrast.

Johnson's *Dictionary*	Modern Dictionary	Similarities/Differences

3. **Reading Strategy:** Assume that your **purpose** in reading the Preface to the *Dictionary* is to learn about the history of dictionary-making. What details from the Preface would you record?

   _____

   _____

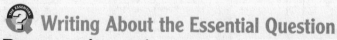 **Writing About the Essential Question**

Does a writer gain more by accepting or by rejecting tradition?
Which label, if any, suits each better, inventor or conservator? Explain.

   _____

   _____

Elegy Written in a Country Churchyard
• A Nocturnal Reverie

Literary Analysis

Eighteenth-century **Pre-Romantic poetry** shares qualities of two different poetic styles. Poetry from this literary period shares styles with the earlier Neoclassical (nee oh KLAS i kuhl) poetry of writers like Pope:

- The polished expression of ideas
- The use of balanced phrases and complicated vocabulary

Pre-Romantic poetry also contains elements that would be used in Romantic poetry:

- A new focus on nature and the life of the common folk
- The expression of feelings

Like the Romantics who come after them, Gray and Finch express strong feelings in their poetry. Gray's stroll through a country churchyard lets him feel the tragedy of life. It also lets him discover life's true value. Finch's nighttime stroll allows her to feel the mind's deep connection with nature.

Reading Strategy

To help you **determine the essential message** in a poem, paraphrase passages in these poems. To **paraphrase** is to restate an idea in your own words. Use this chart to help you paraphrase. Record the poet's line or lines under "Original." Then, record your re-wording of the passage under "Paraphrase."

Original

Paraphrase

Word List A

Study these words from the selections. Then, complete the activities.

annals [AN uhlz] *n.* recorded history; documented research
The annals of history are filled with accounts of war and conquest.

anthem [AN thum] *n.* a song declaring loyalty to something
Every incoming freshman is expected to learn the school's anthem.

celestial [suh LES chuhl] *adj.* relating to the sky or the heavens
In astronomy, we learned about stars, planets, and other celestial bodies.

curfew [KUR fyoo] *n.* a specified time for people to be inside
The teen was grounded for not being home by her eleven o'clock curfew.

drowsy [DROW zee] *adj.* almost asleep; ready to fall asleep
The drowsy man struggled to stay awake during the extremely dull speech.

glimmering [GLIM uhr ing] *adj.* giving off an unsteady light; twinkling
Lizette could see a glimmering bit of sea glass partially buried in the sand.

lull [LUHL] *v.* to soothe or calm someone; to put to rest or sleep
The best way to lull a baby to sleep is to softly sing a lullaby.

rouse [ROWZ] *v.* to wake someone up or stir them to action
Dad was able to rouse Mom from her nap by shaking her shoulder.

Exercise A

Fill in each blank below using the appropriate word from Word List A.

Galileo's innovative telescope changed both his life and the way we view planets
and other [1] _____ bodies in the sky. Before the creation of the telescope,
people could only study the stars with the naked eye. Some stargazers found peace
lying in a field, staring at the heavens long past the [2] _____ at the end of
the day. Inevitably, some would become [3] _____, often falling asleep
beneath the [4] _____ light of the stars.

While his telescope was instantly accepted, Galileo's support of the theory
that the earth revolved around the sun managed to [5] _____ the
anger of religious authorities who were displeased with his scientific findings.
Threatened with lifelong imprisonment, Galileo was able to [6] _____ the
authorities into a lesser punishment by retracting his findings. Galileo stayed
under house arrest for the rest of his life, but his telescope will remain always
in the [7] _____ of scientific accomplishments. Sadly, Galileo was buried
without honors, unlike Darwin, who received a state funeral and a musical
[8] _____ specially composed to celebrate his controversial achievements.

Read the following passage. Pay special attention to the underlined words. Then, read it again, and complete the activities. Use a separate sheet of paper for your written answers.

The award ceremony was drawing to a close as the head counselor at Camp Silver Lake described the final award of the summer. I had not won anything yet, and in all the annals of my ten year camp history, I had always received at least two major awards! I was confident of my merits when we sang the camp anthem, pledging our commitment to enjoying and conserving nature. I was still positive that I had satisfied the requirements for best all-around camper: leadership, sportsmanship, perfect attendance, and especially observance of curfew, since I always returned to the cabins by nine o'clock sharp.

To my dismay, it went to younger recipient who was slumped in a chair, snoring! I nudged him with my elbow to rouse him, so he could rush up to the stage and happily claim his award. The shiny trophy was glimmering in the sunlight as he carried it proudly to his parents.

In the car ride home that night, I closed my eyes, drowsy from sitting in the sun all day. When my father inquired what was wrong, I confessed my disappointment. He assured me that he was proud of me anyway. He promised me that my memories of the summer would be much more valuable than any trophy. Dad pointed out that being too competitive can rob a person of joy, and from feeling satisfied by a job well done. Suddenly, I saw a shooting star, and the celestial sight reminded me of the extraordinary meteor shower that I had watched the week before with my friends. Comforted, I listened to my father whistling the camp anthem, letting the pleasant sound lull me to sleep.

1. Circle the words that indicate the length of the speaker's annals at camp. Then, tell what *annals* means.

2. Underline the words that describe what the campers pledged when they sang the anthem. Tell what else might have an *anthem*.

3. Circle the words that tell what the curfew at camp was. What is the *curfew* of most people your age?

4. Rewrite the sentence using a synonym for rouse. Then, use *rouse* in a sentence.

5. Underline the words that tell what was glimmering in the sunlight. What else might be described as *glimmering*?

6. Circle the words that indicate the camper was drowsy. What usually happens when a person is *drowsy*?

7. Underline the words that describe different celestial sights seen by the camper. Name some other things that are *celestial*.

8. Circle the words that tell what helped lull the boy to sleep. What is a synonym for *lull*?

Elegy Written in a Country Churchyard • A Nocturnal Reverie
Thomas Gray • Anne Finch, Countess of Winchelsea

Summaries In "**Elegy Written in a Country Churchyard**," the speaker walks through a country churchyard as night comes on. He thinks about those who are buried there. They were ordinary village folk, unknown to the outside world. However, they displayed in their daily lives the same traits that famous men and women display. The speaker then imagines that he himself has died. He pictures his own funeral, and he writes his own epitaph.

In "**A Nocturnal Reverie**," the speaker walks through a night landscape. All her senses are alert. She sees passing clouds and the moon reflected in a river. She smells odors from the plants and trees around her. She hears the sound of falling waters and the cry of birds. Feeling a deep connection with nature, her spirit is content.

Note-taking Guide
Use this chart to list details that Pre-Romantic poetry shares with Neoclassical and Romantic poetry. Illustrate each listed quality with a line or lines from the poems.

Poem	Neoclassical	Romantic
Elegy Written in a Country Churchyard	• polished expression • complicated vocabulary	• nature and simple folk • deep feelings
A Nocturnal Reverie	• polished expression • complicated vocabulary	• nature and simple folk • deep feelings

Elegy Written in a Country Churchyard
• A Nocturnal Reverie

1. **Draw Conclusions:** What message about life does the speaker express in The Epitaph at the end of "Elegy Written in a Country Churchyard"? Focus especially on the last two stanzas.

_____

_____

2. **Literary Analysis: Pre-Romantic poetry** anticipates the Romantic emphasis on mystery and emotion. Reread the lines from the poems that are listed in the chart. Then, for each passage, write the ideas, feelings, and message about life it expresses.

Lines	Stated Ideas	Feelings Expressed	Message About Life
Elegy, lines 89–92			
Reverie, lines 39–46			

3. **Reading Strategy:** Paraphrase the wish in lines 47–50 of "A Nocturnal Reverie." Does Finch want to continue walking through the night landscape? Explain.

_____

_____

? Writing About the Essential Question

What is the relationship between place and literature? What qualities of a special place help each author to draw conclusions about life?

_____

_____

The Aims of *The Spectator*

Literary Analysis

An **essay** is a short piece of prose. It explores a topic as if the author were letting you overhear his or her thoughts. The word *essay* means an "attempt" or "test." The term was first applied to writing by the French essayist Michel Montaigne (mee SHEL mahn TAYN).

Addison's essay can be seen as a "test," or an experiment. The writer tries to connect observations and anecdotes in order to form ideas.

It is important to consider the **historical context** when reading this essay. Essays like this one became popular during a time of great change in society. The middle class was growing. This part of society consisted of people like lawyers, shopkeepers, and merchants. As the middle class grew, its members searched for ways to define themselves. The essays of Johnson and Addison helped such readers answer the question, *Who am I?*

Reading Strategy

Writers do not always state everything directly. In some cases, you need to **draw inferences** to figure out what the writer does not say directly. You can draw inferences by using clues from the text and your own experience. Drawing inferences helps you appreciate the writer's attitudes about different topics. Use this chart to make inferences as you read the essays.

Topic	Details	Inference: Author's Attitude

Word List A

Study these words from the selections. Then, complete the activities.

blemishes [BLEM ish iz] *n.* defects or noticeable flaws
A few blemishes greatly reduced the diamond's value.

commiseration [kuh MIZ uh ray shuhn] *n.* a feeling of sympathy for someone in distress
In an act of commiseration, the new champion helped his fallen opponent to his feet.

comprehended [KAHM pree hend ed] *v.* to have grasped mentally; understood
The bus driver comprehended the policeman's signals, as he pulled over immediately.

contrived [kuhn TRYVD] *v.* to have schemed or thought of with cleverness
The youngsters contrived a plan to steal treats from Grandma's cookie jar.

endeavor [en DEV er] *v.* to attempt or try
I recommend her highly for whatever endeavor she wishes to pursue.

folly [FAH lee] *n.* lack of good sense; foolishness
He regretted his folly of hiking in the forest during the rainstorm.

multitudes [MUHL ti toodz] *n.* great numbers of
The multitudes of people at the event caused traffic jams and parking problems outside.

punctually [PUHNK choo wah lee] *adv.* adherence to a schedule
She arrived punctually for her early morning appointment.

Exercise A

Fill in the blanks using each word from Word List A only once.

Nina arrived at her dermatologist appointment [1] _____, as it was

very important for her to be on time. She had been having a lot of breakouts

and was tired of the [2] _____ all over her face. Trying to fix the problem

herself with potions she had [3] _____ wasn't working; the prom

was in five days and Nina needed help! Once she explained to her doctor

her [4] _____ of eating an entire bag of chocolates, thus causing her

breakout, he [5] _____ the situation immediately. While there were

[6] _____ of medicines from which to choose, he quickly narrowed it

down to one. His [7] _____ to clear up Nina's skin before the prom was

genuine, he really wanted to help her. His [8] _____ for her situation

was heartfelt, because he too, had a daughter attending the same prom.

1. Why would Addison want multitudes of readers? Name something that you would want *multitudes* of.

2. Circle the word that <u>punctually</u> describes. Use *punctually* in a sentence.

3. Why was it important that Addison's messages were <u>comprehended</u>? How can you tell if you *comprehended* his essay?

4. What did Addison do about writings that he considered <u>folly</u>? What is a synonym for *folly*?

5. Underline the words in the sentence that offer clues about the meaning of <u>contrived</u>. Why does the word *contrived* have negative associations?

6. Who did Addison consider to be <u>blemishes</u>? Name other things that can be considered *blemishes*.

7. How did Addison handle the people for whom he felt <u>commiseration</u>? When might be a time that a person would feel *commiseration* for others?

8. How did Addison's <u>endeavor</u> pay off in the end? Use *endeavor* in a sentence.

Read the following passage. Pay special attention to the underlined words. Then, read it again, and complete the activities. Use a separate sheet of paper for your written answers.

Joseph Addison wrote about various topics in his periodical *The Spectator.* With the purpose of informing as well as influencing, Addison hoped that <u>multitudes</u> of his countrymen, from all walks of life, would read his essays, although it was the middle-class who comprised the largest portion of his audience. His messages were direct and <u>punctually</u> delivered, each appearing in successive installments of his co-authored periodical. Addison would not miss an opportunity to share his viewpoints; he even co-authored *The Tatler.*

Sending a clear message was important to Addison. Not only did he desire the citizens of Great Britain to read his informative writings, it was also important to him that they <u>comprehended</u> them as well. Addison knew that he might affect a change in society's behavior, but only if they understood his writing. Therefore he kept it succinct and relatively simple. While there were other philosophical and political writings available at the time, Addison considered most of these works <u>folly</u>, and was public about that fact, as it too, became a subject of his writing.

Most of Addison's subject matter dealt with manners, literature, and scientific matter, all of which he deemed important. He carefully crafted his essays from his own beliefs, not from a <u>contrived</u> source; he was more of a philosopher, less of a reporter. For the people who avoided or criticized his messages, he had contempt. Not only did he consider them <u>blemishes</u> to the changing face of England, he thought such people were uneducated. The <u>commiseration</u> that Addison harbored for them was minimal though, as he all but dismissed them totally. Addison need not have worried, as his <u>endeavor</u> to spread his sentiments across the country earned him great notoriety; his ideas are still discussed today, almost 300 years later.

The Aims of *The Spectator*
Joseph Addison

Summary Addison discusses the success of his newspaper, *The Spectator*. About 3,000 copies of the paper are distributed each day. He estimates that 20 people read each paper. So he has an audience of 60,000 readers.

He invites four groups of people to read his paper:

- Families, who can enjoy the paper over breakfast
- Curious men with time on their hands, wealthy or lazy men
- The "blanks" of society, people without ideas
- Women looking for innocent entertainment and, perhaps, knowledge

Note-taking Guide

In this chart, note some of the colorful phrases that Addison uses to describe the four groups of people he addresses in his essay.

Families	Gentlemen, My Good Brothers	The Blanks of Society	The Female World

The Aims of *The Spectator*

1. **Literary Analysis:** Addison uses his **essay** to create a portrait of his four types of readers. Use this chart to record your analysis of the essay. Identify a passage from the essay in the first column. In the second column, note whether the author breaks down ideas or describes social types. In the third column, note whether he generalizes about human nature or describes people of a specific time. In the fourth column, indicate whether he moves logically from idea to idea or writes in a spirit of fun.

Passage	Analytic or Descriptive?	General or Of a Specific Era?	Logical or Humorous?
The Aims of *The Spectator*— Portrait of four types of readers			

2. **Literary Analysis:** What attitude does Addison encourage readers to have toward themselves?

_____

3. **Reading Strategy:** Read Addison's description of the "blanks." **Draw inferences** about Addison's attitude toward these people. Does he look down on them? Does he mock them bitterly or affectionately?

_____

_____

 Writing About the Essential Question

How does literature shape or reflect society? What kinds of things would Addison like to change about society?

_____

_____

To a Mouse • To a Louse • Woo'd and Married and A'

Literary Analysis

Dialect is the way that people of a region, class, or group actually speak. Dialect includes different pronunciations, grammar, and expressions from those that are found in the standard written form of a language. Robert Burns and Joanna Baillie use Scottish dialect in their poems. This is the common language of the people of Scotland. Using dialect helps the poets achieve these goals:

• Establishing character, mood, and setting
• Adding charm for readers who do not speak the dialect

Reading Strategy

When you do not understand a work that is written in dialect, you should **analyze information from text features.** You can do this two ways. First, use the footnotes. Second, look for similarities between English words and the words you read in dialect. Use these similarities together with context clues. For example, in "thou need na start awa," *na* is "not" and *awa* is "away." Use the chart below to help you translate some words of the dialect.

Footnotes		*Sleekit*[3]
	3.	
Context		*saunt an' sinner*
Word Similarities		*dinna*

Word List A

Study these words from the selections. Then, complete the activities that follow.

companion [kuhm PAN yuhn] *n.* one who keeps company with another
  The dog was a companion to the elderly woman.

compared [kuhm PAYRD] *v.* examined to note similarities or differences
  We compared prices in order to find the least expensive product.

impudence [IM pyoo dins] *n.* rudeness; disrespect
  The impudence of the girl's reply startled her mother.

notion [NOH shuhn] *n.* an impulse or whim
  Sarah had a notion to call her grandmother at the last minute.

schemes [SKEEMZ] *n.* plans (especially clever, secret, or devious ones)
  The robbers planned many different schemes to break into the store.

social [SOH shuhl] *adj.* having to do with living in a community
  It is important to achieve a balance between one's work and social life.

trouble [TRUB uhl] *n.* distress; problems
  The thunderstorm created floods that caused much trouble for drivers.

union [YOON yuhn] *n.* a state of being united or in agreement
  The union of the two countries made both of them stronger.

Exercise A

Fill in each blank in the paragraph below with the appropriate word from Word List A. Use each word only once.

Stan suddenly had the [1] _____ that his friend, Joe, was upset

with him. He [2] _____ Joe's recent behavior to the way he acted in

the past. Stan suspected that Joe was jealous of his new [3] _____,

a small dog named Rocky. Stan spent a great deal of time with Rocky in

order to help him deal with the [4] _____ he had in adjusting to his

new surroundings. However, the more time that Stan spent with Rocky,

the more Joe's [5] _____ toward Stan increased. Stan noticed that

in [6] _____ situations, such as parties, Joe would ignore him. Stan

was upset about this situation, and he devised many [7] _____ that he

hoped would solve this problem. He hoped to achieve a [8] _____ of his

old friend and his new one.

Read the following passage. Pay special attention to the underlined words. Then, read it again, and complete the activities. Use a separate sheet of paper for your written answers.

Romanticism was not a fleeting <u>notion</u> in the late-eighteenth and nineteenth centuries. It was a movement that lasted a long time and that rejected the ideas of order, calm, balance, and rejection of nature that were typical of the <u>social</u> ideas of that time.

When Romantic works are <u>compared</u>, it can be seen that the Romantics held very specific views about nature and the individual. The Romantics believed in a <u>union</u> of people with nature. This idea was the direct opposite of the <u>impudence</u> that many great thinkers of the time felt about nature. These thinkers did not have respect for nature and believed that nature had an evil power over humankind.

The Romantics believed that the main <u>trouble</u> in their society could be found in the fact that the individual was not appreciated. They felt that this was a problem because a person's personality deserved to be examined. Some Romantics worked to develop <u>schemes</u> to help others appreciate people's individuality. They believed that these plans would make many problems in society disappear. This view was simple and easy to understand for many people who lived during this time. As a result, Romanticism quickly became popular.

Furthermore, Romanticism rejected the use of formal rules, especially as they applied to the arts. This rejection is evident in the many new artistic styles that flourished during this period.

As a movement, Romanticism had no <u>companion</u> or peer in its variety and impact on the world. It quickly reached all corners of the globe because its emphasis on the individual appealed to common people everywhere. In fact, its influence is still felt in the arts.

1. Underline the words that explain why Romanticism was not a fleeting <u>notion</u>. Tell what *notion* means.

2. Circle the words that tell what were typical <u>social</u> ideas of that time. If a young man has a boring *social* life, what might he do to make it better?

3. Underline the phrase that tells what can be seen when Romantic works are <u>compared</u>. Tell what *compared* means.

4. Circle the phrase that tells the type of <u>union</u> in which Romantics believed. For what purpose might students in your school form a *union*?

5. Underline the phrase that tells what <u>impudence</u> means. Use *impudence* in a sentence.

6. Circle the word in a nearby sentence that means about the same as <u>trouble</u>. Give an example of one kind of *trouble* some modern societies have.

7. Underline the word in a nearby sentence that means about the same as <u>schemes</u>. What is an example of a career that involves coming up with *schemes*?

8. Circle the word that means about the same as <u>companion</u>. Use *companion* in a sentence.

To a Mouse • To a Louse
Robert Burns

Woo'd and Married and A'
Joanna Baillie

Summaries In Robert Burns's poems, the speaker addresses small animals. In **"To a Mouse,"** the speaker sympathizes with the mouse whose home he has plowed up. He concludes that the plans of both "mice and men" often go wrong. In **"To a Louse,"** Burns talks to a louse he sees on a finely dressed lady. (*Louse* is the singular form of *lice*.) The lady's ignorance of the louse shows her foolish pride. In Joanna Baillie's **"Woo'd and Married and A',"** a bride is upset because she is poor. Her parents tell her she should not be upset, but that does not help. Then, her husband-to-be flatters her and comforts her.

Note-Taking Guide

Use this chart to record details about each poem.

	How the Speaker Finds His Topic	Whom/What the Speaker Addresses	Speaker's Main Message
"To a Mouse"	The speaker is plowing a field and plows up the mouse's home.		
"To a Louse"			
"Woo'd and Married and A'"			

To a Mouse • To a Louse • Woo'd and Married and A'

1. **Literary Analysis:** What does the use of **dialect** in the poems by Burns suggest about the speaker's social standing?

_____

_____

2. **Literary Analysis:** Use the chart below to analyze the poems.

Poem	Subject	Message
To a Mouse		
To a Louse		
Woo'd and Married A'		

3. **Reading Strategy:** How do **text features,** such as footnotes, help you understand the three poems in this section?

_____

_____

 Writing About the Essential Question

How does literature shape or reflect society? What are the poets' attitudes toward the behaviors described in the poems?

_____

_____

_____

The Lamb • The Tyger • The Chimney Sweeper • Infant Sorrow

Literary Analysis

William Blake's poetry presents both an **archetypal perspective** and a **political or historical perspective.** To understand these critical perspectives, you need to know about archetypes and the issues of Blake's time.

An **archetype** is a symbolic image, detail, or type of character that appears often in the literature or myth of different peoples. Archetypes have universal meanings with which readers have strong emotional connections. Consequently, readers see a similar meaning in an archetype each time it appears in a work. For example, William Blake's poetry contains archetypal images of an ideal world and a world that is flawed.

Readers can find **political** and **historical perspectives** in Blake's poetry, too. Blake sympathized with the people who experienced poverty during the Industrial Revolution. Blake's sympathy is reflected in poems such as "The Chimney Sweeper" and "Infant Sorrow." An archetypal perspective might show images that readers associate with a flawed world. A political perspective shows that economic oppression is one aspect of a flawed world.

Reading Strategy

Applying critical perspectives will help you find meaning in a literary work. Look for images, details, or patterns that seem to have strong emotional connections and universal meanings. Then, look for details that suggest political or economic oppression. Use the graphic organizer below to list the images and details you find that help you analyze the critical perspectives in Blake's poetry.

Archetypal Perspective	
Political and Historical Perspectives	

Word List A

Study these words from the selections. Then, complete the activities that follow.

aspire [uh SPYR] *v.* to have a great ambition or goal; desire strongly
I hope my child will aspire to attend college.

bound [BOWND] *v.* confined by limits; tied
The medic bound the soldier's broken arm with a bandage.

mead [MEED] *n.* a meadow
We had our picnic on the mead behind our house.

mild [MYLD] *adj.* gentle or kind in behavior; pleasant
Janet is such a mild person that she smiles at everyone she meets.

rejoice [rih JOYS] *v.* celebrate
My friends and I will rejoice when we graduate from high school.

seize [SEEZ] *v.* grab; take possession of something forcefully
Li did not make her loan payments, so the bank will soon seize her car.

struggling [STRUG ling] *v.* striving; to make a strenuous effort
Martha is struggling to learn how to swim.

wept [WEPT] *v.* shed tears; cried
We wept during the sad part of the movie.

Exercise A

Fill in each blank below using the appropriate word from Word List A.

The weather was [1] _____ and sunny. There was a gentle breeze blowing over the waving grass of the [2] _____ and onto the hills beyond it. We were [3] _____ to carry our camping equipment into the meadow. The equipment was [4] _____ with heavy rope so that it would stay in place in our packs. The rope binding made it easier to [5] _____ and carry the heavy packs. When we reached the meadow, Jane [6] _____ from the pain that her blisters caused her. Our hope was to camp in the meadow for three days, but a change in the weather suddenly brought flood conditions that forced us to change our minds. We had to climb into the hills to reach safety. I knew we would both [7] _____ when we escaped the dangerously rising water. For our next trip, we will [8] _____ to complete a much easier activity.

Read the following passage. Pay special attention to the underlined words. Then, read it again, and complete the activities. Use a separate sheet of paper for your written answers.

1. Underline the words that tell what people should <u>seize</u>. What is a word that means about the same as *seize*?

2. Underline the phrase that tells what some people want to <u>aspire</u> to. What is something you *aspire* to?

3. Circle the words that hint at what <u>struggling</u> means. Use *struggling* in a sentence.

4. Circle that word that hints at what <u>wept</u> means. What is a happy occasion at which you have seen someone who *wept* for joy?

5. Circle the word in a nearby sentence that indicates what <u>rejoice</u> means. What is an example of something about which someone might *rejoice*?

6. Underline the words that tell what a <u>mead</u> is. What is something children might do in a *mead*?

6. Circle the word that means about the same as <u>mild</u>. What is a word that means the opposite of *mild*?

7. Underline the phrase that tells by what the metal strips of the sculpture were <u>bound</u>. Tell what *bound* means.

Jeff believes that people should have the ability to nurture any special abilities that they have. He thinks people should <u>seize</u> opportunities to explore their potential. If people want to <u>aspire</u> to achieve their creative goals, Jeff is willing to help them.

To help those people who are <u>struggling</u> with difficulty to survive as artists on their own, Jeff used part of his vast fortune to open a school that supports them in their goals. Many of the first artists to be admitted to this school were so grateful that they <u>wept</u> with tears of joy. They could <u>rejoice</u> because they would no longer have to strive on their own and face the difficulties of poverty and loneliness.

Jeff's school focuses on providing these artists with an education that would aid them in the creative process. To do this, the school provides the artists with housing. Even though the living quarters are not fancy, the artists decorate them and make each one unique. In exchange for their education and housing, the artists are simply required to present Jeff with an example of their best work at the end of their stay.

The artists are free to create what they choose, and they produce many different pieces of art. One woman painted a landscape scene that pictured a <u>mead</u>, wildflowers, and a clear blue sky. This <u>mild</u> and gentle image of a peaceful meadow is contrasted by an abstract sculpture made of metal strips that are <u>bound</u> by heavy chains.

Jeff is satisfied that he is doing his part to help artists and encourage artistic expression in his community. He hopes that other people who are more fortunate will also find a cause they would be willing to support in order to improve society.

The Lamb • The Tyger • The Chimney Sweeper • Infant Sorrow

William Blake

Summaries In **"The Lamb,"** the speaker of the poem is a child. The child asks questions of a lamb. The speaker explains that the Creator made them both. An adult speaker in **"The Tyger"** wonders who could have made such a frightening creature. In **"The Chimney Sweeper,"** a child named Tom has a dream that gives him a new attitude toward life. In **"Infant Sorrow"** the speaker is a baby who describes life as a kind of trap.

Note-taking Guide

Use this chart to record the important words and ideas in each poem.

Poem	Key Words	Key Ideas
The Lamb		
The Tyger		
The Chimney Sweeper		
Infant Sorrow		

The Lamb • The Tyger • The Chimney Sweeper • Infant Sorrow

1. **Infer:** Reread lines 15–18 of "The Lamb." What do the speaker and the lamb have in common with the lamb's creator?

_____

_____

2. **Literary Analysis: Archetypes** can be symbolic images or details that have universal meanings. In "The Lamb," the lamb reminds the reader of purity, goodness, and gentleness. What might the lamb symbolize?

_____

_____

3. **Reading Strategy:** "The Chimney Sweeper" is partly about suffering caused by political and economic oppression. Use the chart below to **analyze the critical perspective** of the poem.

Who Suffers?	Why?	Is Suffering Fair?	Suggested Solution	Is the Solution Fair?

Writing About the Essential Question

How does literature shape or reflect society? How do these poems prompt you to rethink assumptions about society?

_____

_____

_____

Introduction to *Frankenstein*

Literary Analysis

Gothic literature is concerned with the supernatural. Gothic writers use their imaginations to create worlds that are beyond the everyday world of reason. This type of writing became popular in the late eighteenth and early nineteenth centuries. Gothic stories were set in scary places, such as dark, mysterious castles, towers, and underground passages. *Frankenstein* is an example of Gothic literature because it takes the reader out of the world of reason into an imaginary world of horror.

The Gothic novel became popular in the late 1700s and was part of the new **Romantic Movement** in literature. The Romantics rejected the idea that reason could explain everything. Instead, they believed in the powers of nature and the imagination.

Reading Strategy

One way to be an active reader is to **predict,** or make guesses about what will happen next. Making predictions is similar to drawing inferences. Good readers revise, or change, their predictions as they learn more about characters and events. Use the chart below to make predictions, check them, and change them as you read.

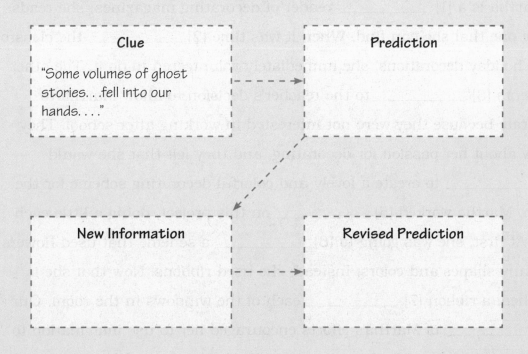

Clue	Prediction
"Some volumes of ghost stories. . .fell into our hands. . . ."	

New Information	Revised Prediction

Word List A

Study these words from the selection. Then, complete the activities that follow.

acceded [ak SEED ed] *v.* yielded (to); agreed
  We acceded to the judge's final decision.

adorns [uh DORNZ] *v.* gives beauty; decorates
  A ribbon adorns each dress.

contrive [kuhn TRYV] *v.* plan; devise
  A clown must contrive ways to entertain the children.

devout [duh VOWT] *adj.* sincere; earnest
  Never missing a performance, Judy is a devout opera fan.

endeavor [en DEV uhr] *n.* a purposeful, industrious activity
  Levi puts great energy into each and every endeavor.

furnish [FUR nish] *v.* supply; give
  The company should furnish instructions on how to use the dishwasher.

incitement [in SYT muhnt] *n.* act of urging; encouragement
  With the coach's incitement, the team let out a roar of determination.

successively [suk SES iv lee] *adv.* in proper order or sequence
  For three years, Dorothy took classes successively.

Exercise A

Fill in each blank below using the appropriate word from Word List A.

Martha is a [1] _____ reader of decorating magazines; she reads every one that she can find. When it was time [2] _____ the classroom with holiday decorations, she immediately volunteered to do it. The other students [3] _____ to the teacher's decision to allow Martha to decorate because they were not interested in working after school. They knew about her passion for decorating, and they felt that she would [4] _____ to create a lovely and colorful decorating scheme for the room. Martha worked [5] _____ on this project, doing a little each day. At first, she was going to [6] _____ a scheme that used flowers of many shapes and colors. Instead, she used ribbons. Now that she is finished, a ribbon [7] _____ each of the windows in the room. Our [8] _____ of Martha's efforts encouraged her to use imagination to create a colorful and festive atmosphere for our winter celebration.

Read the following passage. Pay special attention to the underlined words. Then, read it again, and complete the activities. Use a separate sheet of paper for your written answers.

Mary Wollstonecraft Shelley lived and wrote primarily during the nineteenth century. Her sincere and <u>devout</u> interest in literature arose out of the family and society in which she grew up. She was the only child of Mary Wollstonecraft, a famous feminist, and William Godwin, who was a philosopher and novelist.

From the time that she was born, Mary's father tried to <u>furnish</u> her with the belief that she would realize the great potential that her father believed she had. Thus, it was through her father's <u>incitement</u> and encouragement that Mary got an education and developed an understanding of literary and philosophical matters at a young age.

Mary wrote *Frankenstein,* or *The Modern Prometheus*, in 1818, when she was nineteen years old. She undertook this <u>endeavor</u> because her husband, the poet Percy Bysshe Shelley, suggested the task. During one rainy evening when Mary, Percy, and their friends had gathered at the fireside to read a book, Percy suggested that they should each <u>contrive</u> to write a horror story. The rest is history. Since that time, Frankenstein has been acclaimed as one of the most famous novels ever published. It <u>adorns</u> the bookshelves of countless literature fans all over the world, who admire it as an exceptional example of Gothic literature.

Nearly two hundred years later, this famous novel still inspires people to write plays and create films, and many scholars have <u>acceded</u> to the judgment it is a great work. The monster, which is the main character in the book, is a being that works <u>successively</u>, in a series of steps, to bring about the destruction of the young scientist who created him. Through her story, Mary warns against the dangers of relying heavily on scientific technology.

1. Circle the word that means about the same as <u>devout</u>. Use *devout* in a sentence.

2. Underline the words that tell what Mary's father tried to <u>furnish</u> for her. What is a synonym for *furnish*?

3. Circle the word that means about the same as <u>incitement</u>. Tell what *incitement* means.

4. Circle the word that means about the same as <u>endeavor</u>. What is an *endeavor* you might like to try some day?

5. Underline the phrase that tells why Mary and her friends decided to <u>contrive</u> to write horror stories. Tell what *contrive* means.

6. Underline the sentence that tells what judgment many scholars have <u>acceded</u> to. If a teacher *acceded* to his students' request for more time on an assignment, what would this mean?

7. Underline the phrase that tells what <u>successively</u> means. What is an example of something people do *successively*?

8. Underline the words that tell why Frankenstein <u>adorns</u> the bookshelves of Gothic literature fans. What is an example of something that often *adorns* the hair of little girls?

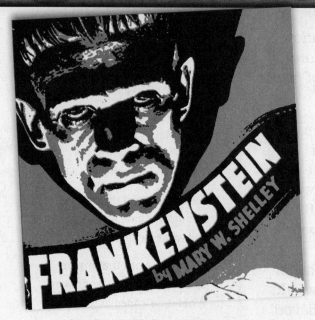

Introduction to
Frankenstein
Mary Wollstonecraft Shelley

Summary In this introduction, Mary Shelley tells how she got the idea for *Frankenstein*. While visiting Lord Byron, a group of friends told ghost stories. At first, Shelley couldn't think of one. One night, the friends discussed experiments that involved creating life. Later that night, Shelley began to imagine an awful sight. She pictured someone kneeling over a thing he had put together, a thing that showed signs of life. Once created, the living creation could not be stopped. Shelley knew she had her story. All she had to do was describe the terror she felt in her imagination.

Note-taking Guide

Use this chart to record details about the Introduction to *Frankenstein*.

Who Is Involved:
When It Takes Place:
Where It Takes Place:
What Happens:
How It Happens:

Introduction to *Frankenstein*

1. **Connect:** Shelley gets the idea for *Frankenstein* from a discussion about the possibility of creating life. After hearing this discussion, she has a strange vision. What does this vision suggest about her reaction to Dr. Darwin's experiments?

   _____

   _____

2. **Literary Analysis: Gothic literature** contains supernatural elements. In her third paragraph, Shelley recalls reading ghost stories. Which characteristics of **Gothic literature** do these ghost stories share? List examples in the chart.

Gothic Characteristic	Example in Shelley

3. **Reading Strategy:** When you **predict,** you use clues in the text to guess what will happen next. Were you able to predict how Shelley would react to the discussion of Darwin's experiments? Explain.

   _____

   _____

Writing About the Essential Question

What is the relationship of the writer to tradition? Why does Shelley's use of a dream to write her novel confirm Romantic beliefs about the imagination?

_____

_____

_____

_____

Lines Composed a Few Miles Above Tintern Abbey • *from* The Prelude • The World Is Too Much With Us • London, 1802

Literary Analysis

Romanticism was a literary movement that took place in late-eighteenth-century Europe. Earlier writers, such as Pope and Jonson, used fancy language to discuss themes that had little to do with everyday life and feelings. Unlike those earlier writers, the works of many Romantic poets include these elements:

- Simple or direct language
- The expression of strong, personal feelings
- Deeply felt and thoughtful responses to nature

English Romanticism began with William Wordsworth. His poetic form was the **lyric,** a poem in which a single speaker expresses personal emotions and observations.

Diction, or word choice, was simpler in Romantic poetry. Although, Wordsworth used simple words, also he relied on abstract terms such as *a sense sublime* to convey ideas.

Reading Strategy

As you read a literary work, you should **evaluate the influence of the historical period** on that work. The **historical period** is defined by the philosophical ideas, politics, and other issues of the era that influenced the author. Use the chart to record examples from his poems that support Wordsworth's belief in the topics listed in the left column.

Philosophical and Political Influences	
Celebration of Common Folk	
Love of Nature	
Admiration for French Revolution	
Loss of Faith in Reason	

Word List A

Study these words from the selection. Then, complete the activities that follow.

assist [uh SIST] *v.* to aid
We will underline{assist} *our mother with the housework.*

duties [DOO teez] *n.* obligations; an act required by custom, law, position, or religion
One of the secretary's underline{duties} *is to keep a record of attendance at meetings.*

gentle [JEN tuhl] *adj.* not harsh or severe; mild
The underline{gentle} *breeze made us feel cool during the hot afternoon.*

glimpses [GLIMP siz] *n.* quick, imcomplete views or looks
We could only catch underline{glimpses} *of the movie stars as they entered the theatre.*

inward [IN wuhrd] *adj.* located inside; inner
The hurricane moved underline{inward} *toward the center of the state.*

orchard [OHR churhd] *n.* land used for growing fruit or nut trees
We went to the underline{orchard} *to pick apples.*

region [REE juhn] *n.* area
The northern underline{region} *of the country has many mountains.*

uncertain [uhn SER tuhn] *adj.* not known; doubtful
Jack was underline{uncertain} *of the answer to the teacher's question.*

Exercise A

Fill in the blank, using each word from Word List A only once.

We came to this [1] _____ of the country because of its famous scenic beauty. At first, we were [2] _____ about where to go to see the beautiful views we had read about. We found some local people to [3] _____ us, and they helped us by taking us to the top of a large hill. We looked down from there, and we saw farmland that included an apple [4] _____ and wheat fields. Although some trees partially blocked our view, we occasionally had [5] _____ of a lake in the distance. We saw this lake whenever the [6] _____ breezes blew through the trees and moved the branches. Turning [7] _____ and looking toward the hill directly above us, we saw a small village nestled there. Excitedly, we climbed toward it, knowing that all too soon this adventure would end, and we would have to return to work and the [8] _____ that awaited us there.

1. Circle the word that tells in what type of orchard John and the narrator walked. Tell what *orchard* means.

2. Circle the word that tells what *region* means. Use *region* in a sentence.

3. Underline the phrase that tells what the gentle breezes did. Tell what *gentle* means.

4. Underline the phrase that describes John's duties at work. Tell what *duties* means.

5. Underline the phrase that tells what uncertain means. Use *uncertain* in a sentence.

6. Circle the word that tells what assist means. Use *assist* in a sentence.

7. Underline the phrase that tells what John and the narrator caught glimpses of. Tell what *glimpses* means.

8. Underline the phrase that tells what John and the narrator saw when they turned inward and away from the view. Tell what *inward* means.

Read the following passage. Pay special attention to the underlined words. Then, read it again, and complete the activities. Use a separate sheet of paper for your written answers.

As my husband, John, and I walked through the apple orchard, we looked around us and took stock of our environment. We were far away from the fast pace of city life, vacationing in a region of the country known for its small-town lifestyle and striking countryside. We rented a place that was located next to a small farm, and we enjoyed walking through the fields while the gentle breezes kept us cool in the summer sun.

This was a very different lifestyle from what John and I were accustomed to. As the vice president of a small company, John's work duties included supervising a large staff and reporting important issues directly to the company's president. As a newspaper reporter, I was always out in the field, covering the stories that occurred within the bustling city. Neither of us had much free time to enjoy the outdoors.

The pace of our lives left us both exhausted, and John and I both decided that we needed a break. We were uncertain about the type of vacation we wanted. Because we were not sure about this, a friend advised us to visit this small town in the north of the country. As soon as we arrived there, we were glad that we had asked her to assist us in selecting a vacation destination. She helped us to plan the best vacation we ever had.

Aside from walking around the farm, we have also taken long hikes in the hills above it. On clear days, we caught glimpses of faraway cities where we imagined people just like us were toiling away. Turning inward and away from this view, we saw a small lake populated by many varieties of birds. This was a quiet, secluded place where we were finally able to relax. We wished our vacation could go on forever.

Lines Composed a Few Miles Above Tintern Abbey

William Wordsworth

Summary The poet revisits a country place near Tintern Abbey in Wales after five years. He addresses this poem to his sister, Dorothy. He explains that the memory of this place had a soothing effect on him during his absence. He recalls his childhood relationship to nature. By contrast, the adult poet now feels a great spirit in nature. He calls upon his sister to share his feelings for this place and to remember his devotion to nature.

Note-Taking Guide

Use this chart to record main ideas about the poem.

Who	
When	
Where	
What	
Why	

Reading Check

In the bracketed passage, circle two features of the scene that the speaker notices with his senses of hearing and vision.

Stop to Reflect

Reread lines 12–15 and underline the answers to these questions.

1. Where was the speaker located when he felt "sensations sweet"?

2. In what parts of his body did he have these feelings?

Lines Composed a Few Miles Above Tintern Abbey

William Wordsworth

Five years have passed since Wordsworth last visited the valley of the River Wye and the ruins of Tintern Abbey in Wales. On a second visit, he has brought his sister Dorothy with him to share the experience.

◆ ◆ ◆

Five years have passed; five summers, with
   the length
Of five long winters! and again I hear
These waters, rolling from their mountain
   springs
With a soft inland murmur. Once again
5 Do I <u>behold</u> these steep and lofty cliffs,
That on a wild <u>secluded</u> scene impress
Thoughts of more deep seclusion; and
   connect
The landscape with the quiet of the sky.

◆ ◆ ◆

The poet lies under a sycamore tree. He observes the silent, peaceful orchards and farms around him.

◆ ◆ ◆

               These beauteous[1] forms,
10 Through a long absence, have not been to me
As is a landscape to a blind man's eye:
But oft,[2] in lonely rooms, and 'mid the <u>din</u>
Of towns and cities, I have owed to them
In hours of weariness, sensations sweet,
15 Felt in the blood, and felt along the heart. . . .

Vocabulary Development

behold (bee HOHLD) *v.* see

secluded (suh KLOOD id) *adj.* isolated

din (DIN) *n.* loud noise

---

1. **beauteous** (BYOO tee uhs) *adj.* beautiful.
2. **oft** *adv.* often.

Memories of peaceful nature are precious to the poet. They make him a kinder, better person. They also inspire his soul. In moments of distress, memories of the Wye valley have consoled his spirit.

◆ ◆ ◆

And now, with gleams of half-extinguished[3]
   thought,
With many recognitions dim and faint,
And somewhat[4] of a sad <u>perplexity</u>,
The picture of the mind revives again;
20 While here I stand, not only with the sense
Of present pleasure, but with pleasing
   thoughts
That in this moment there is life and food
For future years.

◆ ◆ ◆

The speaker remembers how he felt about nature on his first visit five years ago. Then, he was younger and more passionate. Now, he is more mature and reflective.

◆ ◆ ◆

               For I have learned
To look on nature, not as in the hour
25 Of thoughtless youth; but hearing
   oftentimes
The still, sad music of humanity,
Nor harsh nor <u>grating</u>, though of ample
   power
To chasten[5] and subdue. And I have felt
A presence that disturbs me with the joy

Read Fluently

Read the bracketed passage aloud. How does the speaker relate the present to the future in this passage?

_____

_____

_____

Reading Check 📖

What has caused the speaker to look differently at nature?

_____

_____

_____

_____

Vocabulary Development

perplexity (puhr PLEK suh tee) *n.* confusion; bewilderment
grating (GRAYT ing) *adj.* annoying; irritating

3. **half-extinguished** *adj.* half-destroyed.
4. **somewhat** *adv.* something.
5. **chasten** (CHAY suhn) *v.* punish in order to correct.

© Pearson Education

Lines Composed a Few Miles Above Tintern Abbey 219

TAKE NOTES

Literary Analysis

In **Romanticism**, a deeply felt response to nature is an important theme. In the underlined passage, what feeling about all creation does nature inspire in the speaker?

_____

_____

_____

Reading Strategy

The ideas in a **historical period** influence a writer's beliefs. What do the bracketed lines reveal about Wordsworth's beliefs?

_____

_____

_____

30 Of <u>elevated</u> thoughts; a sense <u>sublime</u>
   Of something far more deeply <u>interfused</u>,[6]
   Whose dwelling is the light of setting suns,
   And the round ocean and the living air,
   And the blue sky, and in the mind of man;
35 A motion and a spirit, that <u>impels</u>
   <u>All thinking things, all objects of all
     thought,</u>
   <u>And rolls through all things.</u> Therefore am I
     <u>still</u>
   A lover of the meadows and the woods
   And mountains; and of all that we behold
40 From this green earth; of all the mighty
     world
   Of eye, and ear—both what they half create
   And what perceive; well pleased to
     recognize
   In nature and the language of the sense,
   The anchor of my purest thoughts, the
     nurse,
45 The guide, the guardian of my heart, and
     soul
   Of all my moral being.

◆ ◆ ◆

The speaker prays that his sister will also experience the joy that nature offers. The quietness and beauty of nature have the power to comfort us in all the troubles of life. The poet predicts that his sister will cherish precious memories of their visit together.

Vocabulary Development

elevated (EL uh vay tuhd) *adj.* noble; inspiring
sublime (suh BLYM) *adj.* noble and thrilling; majestic
impels (im PELZ) *v.* pushes; moves forward

6. **interfused** (in tuhr FYOOZD) *adj.* closely linked together.

◆ ◆ ◆

Nor, perchance—
If I should be where I no more can hear
Thy voice, nor catch from thy wild eyes
   these gleams
50 Of past existence—wilt thou then forget
That on the banks of this delightful stream
We stood together; and that I, so long
A worshipper of Nature, hither came
Unwearied in that service: rather say
55 With warmer love—oh! with far deeper zeal
Of holier love. Nor wilt thou then forget,
That after many wanderings, many years
Of absence, these steep woods and lofty cliffs,
60 And this green pastoral landscape, were to
   me
More dear, both for themselves and for thy
   sake!

Reading Check

According to the speaker, what are the two reasons that the woods and cliffs have become "more dear" to him?

Reason 1:

_____

_____

Reason 2:

_____

_____

Vocabulary Development

pastoral (PAS tuh ruhl) *adj.* rural

from The Prelude
• The World Is Too Much
With Us • London, 1802

William Wordsworth

Summaries In ***The Prelude,*** the speaker contrasts the promise of freedom at the start of the French Revolution with the terrible reality that followed. In **"The World Is Too Much With Us,"** the speaker says people waste their lives by going after material things instead of appreciating Nature. In **"London, 1802,"** the speaker expresses worry about the present time. He calls on the great poet Milton to return England to its former values of passion and freedom.

Note-Taking Guide

Use this chart to record the main message of each poem.

from The Prelude	
The World is Too Much With Us	
London, 1802	

Lines Composed a Few Miles Above Tintern Abbey • *from* The Prelude • The World Is Too Much With Us • London, 1802

1. **Infer:** Explain the difference in the poet's attitude from his first to his second visit to Tintern Abbey.

_____

2. **Literary Analysis:** Find examples in the poems of **diction** that is specific and simple, abstract but simple, or abstract and difficult. List one example for each heading in the chart below.

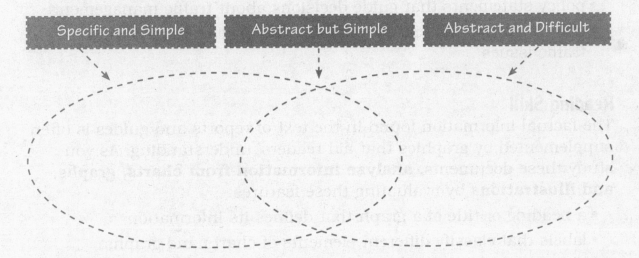

Specific and Simple	Abstract but Simple	Abstract and Difficult

3. **Reading Strategy:** What do the hopes described in *The Prelude* tell you about the **historical period** during the Romantic movement?

_____

_____

_____

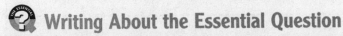 **Writing About the Essential Question**

What is the relationship of the writer to tradition? What qualities did you find in Wordsworth's poems that make him a poetic rebel?

Traffic Reports

About Traffic Reports

Traffic reports describe the movement of cars, buses, and trucks in a particular area, such as a city center or a national park. Information from traffic reports helps local leaders and citizens make decisions about an area's quality of life. Traffic reports also can be used as travel references. Tourists can use the information in the reports to plan trips and vacations. Traffic reports often include the following features to help people understand the road and travel conditions in an area:

- a general description of the area
- a history of traffic in the area
- a list of problems caused by traffic
- policy statements that guide decisions about traffic management
- charts, graphs, and illustrations that help readers understand traffic issues

Reading Skill

The factual information found in the text of reports and guides is often supplemented by graphics that aid readers' understanding. As you study these documents, **analyze information from charts, graphs, and illustrations** by evaluating these features:

- a heading or title of a graph that defines its information
- labels that classify different elements of charts and graphs
- captions explaining symbols and images

Use a checklist like the one shown to assess graphics in these texts.

Features	Yes/No	Content
Graph and chart titles	❏ / ❏	
Graph and chart labels	❏ / ❏	
Photos or images	❏ / ❏	
Captions	❏ / ❏	
Explanations of symbols	❏ / ❏	

LAKE DISTRICT
National Park Authority

Education Service Traffic Management

The Lake District National Park is an area of outstandingly beautiful and varied landscape and the scenery is the reason most people give for visiting the Lake District (62%, 1994 All Parks Visitor Survey).

The Lake District remained relatively isolated until the 19th century when new railways allowed the large urban populations of Northwest England to visit the area easily. Both trade and early tourism flourished. In the 1940s, it was recognised that areas such as the Lake District would benefit from some kind of special protection. The Lake District was designated a National Park in 1951 to conserve and enhance its special landscape while providing opportunities for the public to enjoy that landscape. At this time, it was expected that "walkers, cyclists, riders and students of nature" would be the main users of the National Park rather than motorists, although National Parks were intended for all to enjoy.

Since then, car ownership has increased and now the vast majority of visitors come by car. Today, over 12 million people visit the National Park annually (staying for 22 million days) while 42,000 people live in the National Park. 89% of visitors come to the National Park by private motor vehicle.

The Lake District National Park Authority (LDNPA) and Cumbria County Council (CCC) have a number of automatic traffic counters around the National Park to help understand traffic movements. Traffic is greatest during the summer months when most visitors come to the National Park and mid-mornings and late afternoons can be exceptionally busy. In recent years, the rate of increase of traffic has slowed down, with recorded increases being largely confined to main roads such as the A591.

The heading "Lake District" and the words "Traffic Management" in the report's heading reveal the focus and purpose of the report.

This paragraph establishes the focus of the report on the issue of car traffic in the park.

Traffic Issues

Large volumes of traffic can lead to a number of issues, especially in an area like the Lake District where roads are often narrow.

- **Pollution:** Motor vehicles emit various pollutants which may reach high levels in certain weather conditions, especially within towns.

- **Noise:** 'Peace and Quiet' is often given as a reason for visiting, so this is an issue, especially when considering development.

- **Visual intrusion:** Lines of parked cars can detract from the natural beauty of the National Park.

- **Congestion:** Congestion can be a problem in certain areas and towns at peak times of day and the year.

- **Reducing visitor traffic:** Traffic Management aims to minimize the impact of traffic and encourage visitors to use public transport rather than private cars.

- **Parking:** A balance needs to be found between provision of parking for visitors and locals and impact on the landscape.

- **Hazards to vulnerable road users:** Walkers, cyclists and horse riders should be at ease on the roads in the Lake District. Actual and perceived hazards to these road users should be minimized.

The traffic problems are clearly described in this bulleted list.

The graph's clear title, different colors, and sidebar labels make information easy to interpret.

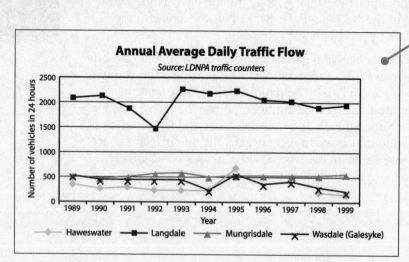

Annual Average Daily Traffic Flow

Source: LDNPA traffic counters

Traffic Management in the National Park

The guiding principle underpinning the policies of the LDNPA towards transport and traffic is that demand should be managed in order to:

- Minimize its impact on the landscape
- Improve the quality of life for local residents
- Improve the quality of enjoyment for visitors
- Encourage use of sustainable means of travel

The policies of the LDNPA are set out in the Lake District National Park Management Plan. These clearly state that increasing road capacity is not an appropriate solution to traffic management in the National Park. Instead, traffic management policy is to tailor traffic to existing roads.

A balance of interests is needed between the purposes of the National Park, local people and visitors to ensure the special qualities of the National Park are not compromised. For example, in 1966 the Lake District Special Planning Board published a "Report on Traffic in the Lake District National Park" suggesting that in the future it might become necessary to restrict all except local traffic along secondary routes. Objections were raised by local residents of Langdale and Borrowdale concerning the impact of these closures on the tourism trade.

> This paragraph addresses the different groups the traffic problem and proposed solutions affect.

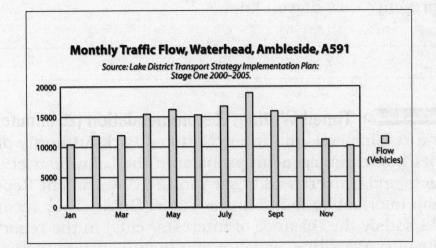

Monthly Traffic Flow, Waterhead, Ambleside, A591

Source: Lake District Transport Strategy Implementation Plan: Stage One 2000–2005.

Thinking About the Traffic Report

1. How do most tourists reach the Lake District National Park?

_____

2. Why must decision-makers balance the needs of the National Park, local citizens, and tourists?

_____

_____

_____

(TALK)(ABOUT IT) **Reading Skill**

3. In the Annual Average Daily Traffic Flow chart, what do the labels along the side and bottom of the chart show?

_____

_____

4. In the Monthly Traffic Flow chart, what do the vertical bars represent? How do you know?

_____

_____

WRITE ABOUT IT ▷ **Timed Writing: Recommendation (25 minutes)**

Make a recommendation to the National Park Authority on how to deal with its traffic management problem in the Lake District. Draw on the facts and concerns addressed in the Government Report and the tourism information found in the Travel Guide. Your recommendation should satisfy the "balance of interests" cited in the report. Allow five minutes for prewriting, which might include listing the needs of all parties affected by policy decisions. Use about 15 minutes for drafting, and save five minutes for reviewing and revising.

The Rime of the Ancient Mariner • Kubla Khan

Literary Analysis

Romantic poetry uses **poetic sound devices** to create music, beauty, and emotion. These devices including the following:

- **Alliteration** is the repetition of a consonant sound at the beginnings of words: "The fair breeze blew, the white foam flew..."
- **Consonance** is the repetition of consonant sounds at the end of stressed syllables that have different vowel sounds: "A frightful fiend / Doth close behind ..."
- **Assonance** is the repetition of a vowel sound in stressed syllables that have different consonant sounds: "The western wave was all aflame."
- **Internal Rhyme** is the use of rhymes within a line of poetry: "With heavy thump, a lifeless lump ..."
- **Slant rhyme** is the use of words that end with very similar sounds but do not rhyme: "(And I heard nor sigh nor groan) / They dropped down one by one."

"The Rime of the Ancient Mariner" and "Kubla Khan" are **narrative poems,** or poems that tell stories. In both poems, Coleridge uses the **language of fantasy** to describe imaginary places and creatures.

Reading Strategy

Comparing and contrasting elements, such as those discussed above, will help you appreciate poetry. As you read each poem use a chart like the one shown. Find examples of sound devices, and note how these devices affect the poems.

Poetic Sound Device	"The Rime of the Ancient Mariner"	"Kubla Khan"	Effects of sounds on images in the two poems
Alliteration	The silence of the sea!	Five miles meandering with a mazy motion	The two s sounds highlight the lack of sound, and the m sounds accent the long distance.

Word List A

Study these words from the selections. Then, complete the activities that follow.

ancient [AYN chuhnt] *adj.* very old
   The ancient statue was more than one thousand years old.

blossomed [BLAH suhmd] *v.* bloomed; flourished
   The bud blossomed into a beautiful flower.

burst [BERST] *v.* came apart suddenly
   The balloon burst when Jack pricked it with a pin.

glorious [GLOHR ee uhs] *adj.* marked by great beauty; magnificent
   The glorious day was sunny and warm.

harbor [HAHR buhr] *n.* a sheltered part of a body of water deep enough to anchor ships
   The boat pulled into the harbor, and the sailors unloaded its cargo.

merry [MEHR ee] *adj.* delightful; jolly
   The merry man sang many happy songs.

pleasure [PLE zhuhr] *n.* delight
   Listening to classical music gives me great pleasure.

sheen [SHEEN] *n.* sparkling brightness; shininess
   The sheen on the water was caused by the reflection of the sun.

Exercise A

Fill in the blank, using each word from Word List A only once.

The [1] _____ city has existed for thousands of years. It is located

next to the great [2] _____, where many ships from around the world

stop to receive new supplies. This city is [3] _____ and beautiful

because of its location and its architecture. The [4] _____ on the

water makes the whole area bright. It is a [5] _____ to walk the cool,

tree-lined streets and to look at the beautiful buildings and gardens. It is

especially nice to visit in the spring, when all of the colorful flowers have

[6] _____ and filled the gardens with color. The people who live here

are a [7] _____ group, and they are happy because they know that

they live in a beautiful place. Thus, they were greatly saddened by the

destruction that was caused when a tower filled with water [8] _____

and flooded most of the city.

Read the following passage. Pay special attention to the underlined words. Then, read it again, and complete the activities. Use a separate sheet of paper for your written answers.

The passengers alighted from the airplane and into a <u>glorious</u> day on the tropical island. Beauty was everywhere. To their right, they saw a <u>harbor</u> filled with crystal blue water and cruise ships that were anchored there. To their left, they viewed endless gardens in which colorful flowers <u>blossomed</u> and filled the air with their exotic fragrance. Many of the airplane passengers were tourists who were visiting this place because of its famous beaches, beautiful scenery, and hospitality. Looking around, they felt like they had truly entered a paradise.

Throughout the island, visitors had the opportunity to relax on sandy, white beaches or to tour <u>ancient</u> cities that have existed for hundreds of years. Friendly native islanders catered to their needs and wants. No one was dissatisfied with the service or attention that was given.

What these tourists did not see behind the <u>sheen</u> of happy faces and lush scenery was the poverty in which many of the islanders lived. Many residents had no electricity or running water in their own homes, even though all of the areas that served the tourists did. Government officials made sure that this part of island life was well hidden from tourists, because they were afraid that it would discourage people from visiting. After all, they reasoned, people traveled to the island for purposes of <u>pleasure</u>, not social justice. Knowing about these problems would interfere with their enjoyment of their trip. This other life on the island was located far away from the hotels and beaches, and no visitors ever found it.

Thus, if the passing visitor dared to look into the eyes of the <u>merry</u> tour guide who showed her the sights of the island, perhaps she would see the suffering that existed there. Then, her views about the island would have <u>burst</u>, once she realized the truth about how the islanders really lived.

1. Circle the word that tells what *glorious* means. Use *glorious* in a sentence.

2. Underline the phrase that tells with what the *harbor* was filled. Tell what *harbor* means.

3. Underline the phrase that tells what occurred after the flowers had *blossomed*. Tell what *blossomed* means.

4. Underline the phrase that supports the idea that the cities on the island were *ancient*. Tell what *ancient* means.

5. Underline the phrase that tells what was behind the *sheen*. Tell what *sheen* means.

6. Circle the word that tells what *pleasure* means. Use *pleasure* in a sentence.

7. Underline the phrase that tells what a visitor would have found if she looked into the eyes of a *merry* islander. Tell what *merry* means.

8. Underline the phrase that tells what would have *burst* if the truth about the islanders' situation was known. Tell what *burst* means.

The Rime of the Ancient Mariner • Kubla Khan

Samuel Taylor Coleridge

Summaries In **"The Rime of the Ancient Mariner,"** an old sailor, or mariner, stops a guest on his way to a wedding. The Mariner tells the guest of a voyage through strange seas during which he killed a bird called an albatross. The albatross is a symbol of good luck. A curse falls on the ship, and all die except the Ancient Mariner. When the Mariner finds love for nature in his heart, the curse is partially lifted. The dead crew begins to steer the ship. Still, the Mariner is doomed to retell the tale.

"Kubla Khan" is an unfinished poem. The first part describes a "pleasure dome" built by Kubla Khan. Near the pleasure dome is a deep pit from which negative things arise. The second part of the poem describes a dream vision of a "damsel," or young woman, with a musical instrument called a dulcimer. The speaker says he would build the dome in the air if he could bring back her song. Yet those who heard the song would cry "Beware!" and close their eyes.

Note-Taking Guide

Use this chart to record details of the setting—the time and place of the action—in each poem.

Poem	Details of the Setting
The Rime of the Ancient Mariner	
Kubla Khan	

The Rime of the Ancient Mariner
Samuel Taylor Coleridge

It is an ancient Mariner,
And he stoppeth one of three.
"By thy long gray beard and glittering eye,
Now wherefore stopp'st thou me?"

5 "The Bridegroom's doors are opened wide,
And I am next of kin;
The guests are met, the feast is set:
May'st hear the merry din."

He holds him with his skinny hand,
10 "There was a ship," quoth[1] he.
"Hold off! unhand[2] me, graybeard loon!"
Eftsoons[3] his hand dropped he.

He holds him with his glittering eye—
The Wedding Guest stood still,
15 And listens like a three years' child:
The Mariner hath his will.

◆   ◆   ◆

The mariner tells how his ship sails
south until it crosses the equator. A storm
then drives the ship to the South Pole.

◆   ◆   ◆

"The ice was here, the ice was there,
The ice was all around;
It cracked and growled, and roared and
howled,
20 Like noises in a swound![4]

Vocabulary Development

mariner (MAR uh nuhr) *n.* sailor
wherefore (HWAHR fawr) *adv.* why
din (DIN) *n.* loud noise

1. **quoth** (KWOHTH) *v.* said.
2. **unhand** *v.* release.
3. **Eftsoons** *adv.* immediately.
4. **swound** *n.* swoon; fainting spell.

TAKE NOTES

Reading Check

Circle two phrases in the first stanza that describe the mariner.

Stop to Reflect

Mark the line in the bracketed stanza that explains how the mariner is able to make the wedding guest listen to his story.

Literary Analysis

This is a **narrative poem,** so it tells a story. What elements do lines 1–16 in this poem contain that make it similar to a story?

_____

_____

_____

_____

_____

Stop to Reflect

In the bracketed lines, which events are connected to the presence of the albatross around the ship?

_____

_____

_____

Literary Analysis

Which lines in the underlined stanza contain an example of **slant rhyme?** Circle the rhyming words.

Reading Check

There are two speakers in the underlined stanza. Who speaks which lines?

First speaker

_____

Second speaker

_____

"At length did cross an Albatross,
Thorough[5] the fog it came;
As if it had been a Christian soul,
We hailed it in God's name.

25 "It ate the food it ne'er had eat,[6]
And round and round it flew.
The ice did split with a thunder-fit;
The helmsman steered us through!

"And a good south wind sprung up behind;
30 The Albatross did follow,
And every day, for food or play,
Came to the mariner's hollo!

"In mist or cloud, on mast or shroud,[7]
It perched for vespers[8] nine;
35 Whiles all the night, through fog-smoke
    white,
Glimmered the white Moonshine."

"God save thee, ancient Mariner!
From the fiends, that plague thee thus!—
Why look'st thou so?"[9] "With my crossbow
40 I shot the Albatross!"

◆   ◆   ◆

The breeze drops and the ship is becalmed. The crew runs out of water. The mariner's shipmates condemn him for killing the albatross.

◆   ◆   ◆

Vocabulary Development

helmsman (HELMZ muhn) *n.* person who steers a ship
fiends (FEENDZ) *n.* devils

5. **thorough** *prep.* through.
6. **eat** (ET) old form of *eaten.*
7. **shroud** (SHROWD) *n.* ropes stretching from the ship's side to the masthead.
8. **vespers** *n.* evenings.
9. **God . . . so** spoken by the Wedding Guest.

"Ah, well a-day! What evil looks
Had I from old and young!
Instead of the cross, the Albatross
About my neck was hung!"

◆ ◆ ◆

    A mysterious, ghostly ship approaches.
Aboard the ship are Death and his mate, the
lady Life-in-Death. The mariner's shipmates
die, one by one.

◆ ◆ ◆

45 "One after one, by the star-dogged Moon,[10]
Too quick for groan or sigh,
Each turned his face with a <u>ghastly</u> pang,
And cursed me with his eye.

"Four times fifty living men,
50 (And I heard nor sigh nor groan)
With heavy thump, a lifeless lump,
<u>They dropped down one by one.</u>

"The souls did from their bodies fly—
They fled to <u>bliss</u> or woe!
55 And every soul, it passed me by,
Like the whizz of my crossbow!"

◆ ◆ ◆

    The mariner realizes he is cursed. He
suffers spiritual torture. He is the only one
alive on the ship. He tries to pray, but he
cannot.

Vocabulary Development

ghastly (GAST lee) *adj.* horrible
bliss (BLIS) *n.* great joy or happiness

10. **star-dogged Moon** omen of impending evil to sailors.

Reading Check

What did the mariner's
shipmates hang around his neck?

_____

_____

_____

Reading Strategy

Read the following lines from
"Kubla Khan."
  In Xanadu did Kubla Khan
  A stately pleasure dome decree:

Which **poetic sound device** do
these lines share with lines 51–52
of "The Rime of the Ancient
Mariner"?

_____

_____

_____

Stop to Reflect

At the moment of the crewmen's
death, how does the speaker
remind us of the albatross?

_____

_____

_____

Literary Analysis

1. Which words in the underlined section illustrate **assonance?**

_____

_____

2. Which words illustrate **alliteration?**

_____

_____

Read Fluently

Read the bracketed stanza aloud. What do you think is the symbolic significance of the albatross finally dropping from the mariner's neck into the sea? (*Hint:* What does the mariner do just before that happens?)

_____

_____

_____

"Beyond the shadow of the ship,
I watched the water snakes:
They moved in tracks of shining white,
60 And when they reared, the elfish[11] light
Fell off in hoary[12] flakes.

"Within the shadow of the ship
I watched their rich attire:
Blue, glossy green, and velvet black,
65 They coiled and swam; and every track
Was a flash of golden fire.

"O happy living things! no tongue
Their beauty might declare:
A spring of love gushed from my heart,
70 And I blessed them unaware;
Sure my kind saint took pity on me,
And I blessed them unaware.

"The selfsame moment I could pray;
And from my neck so free
75 The Albatross fell off, and sank
Like lead into the sea."

◆ ◆ ◆

The spirits of angels guide the ship onward. Two spirits discuss the mariner's crime of killing the harmless albatross. The mariner's suffering and prayers break the spell of the curse. He returns to his native country. A saintly hermit absolves the mariner from sin. Ever since his journey, the mariner must tell his tale to listeners like the wedding guest. He bids the guest farewell.

◆ ◆ ◆

Vocabulary Development

attire (uh TYR) *n.* fine clothing

11. **elfish** *adj.* like an elf, or mischievous spirit.

12. **hoary** *adj.* white.

"Farewell, farewell! but this I tell
To thee, thou Wedding Guest!
He prayeth well, who loveth well
80 Both man and bird and beast.

"He prayeth best, who loveth best
All things both great and small:
For the dear God who loveth us,
He made and loveth all."

85 The Mariner, whose eye is bright,
Whose beard with age is hoar,
Is gone; and now the Wedding Guest
Turned from the bridegroom's door.

He went like one that hath been stunned
90 And is of sense forlorn;
A sadder and a wiser man,
He rose the morrow morn.

Reading Check

According to the mariner, what kind of person prays well? Circle the words in this stanza that give the answer.

Stop to Reflect

1. Why do you think the wedding guest is sadder?

_____

_____

_____

2. Why is he wiser?

_____

_____

_____

Literary Analysis 🔍

Coleridge uses the **language of fantasy** to describe imaginary places and creatures. Write two examples of how Coleridge uses the language of fantasy.

_____

_____

_____

_____

The Rime of the Ancient Mariner • Kubla Khan

1. **Literary Analysis:** What **sound device** does Coleridge use in the line "It cracked and growled, and roared and howled . . ."?

   _____

   _____

2. **Literary Analysis:** Coleridge includes the **language of fantasy** in both poems. Identify an example in each poem and record it in the chart. Then, tell the effects created by this language.

Poem	Language	Effect
"The Rime of the Ancient Mariner"		
"Kubla Khan"		

3. **Reading Strategy:** In "Kubla Khan," how do poetic devices, such as repetition, contribute to the **poetic effect** of lines 45-54?

   _____

   _____

Writing About the Essential Question
What is the relationship between place and literature? In what ways do the settings of these poems demonstrate the Romantics' rejection of the dreariness of everyday places and activities?

   _____

   _____

   _____

   _____

She Walks in Beauty • Apostrophe to the Ocean • *from* Don Juan

Literary Analysis

Poetry usually contains **figurative language.** This is language that is meant to be understood imaginatively, rather than literally. Poets use figurative language to help readers see things in new ways. Here are some common types of figurative language:

- **Similes**—direct comparisons of things that are not alike using the words *like* or *as*

- **Metaphors**—comparisons of different things in which something is described as though it were something else.

- **Personifications**—language in which a nonhuman subject is given human characteristics

In these three poems, Byron uses figurative language to express the sense of power in nature that escapes human understanding. Compare the observations that Byron makes about the power of nature, human beauty, and aging.

Reading Strategy

Occasionally as you read, your understanding of the text may break down. **Asking questions** as you read is one way of repairing and monitoring your comprehension. Begin with *who, what, where, when,* and *why* questions. Use the chart below to record and answer your questions as you read.

Passage	Questions	Answers

Word List A

Study these words from the selections. Then, complete the activities that follow.

ambition [am BISH uhn] *n.* the object or goal desired
   Joe's ambition is to become an actor.

conceal [kuhn SEEL] *v.* to hide
   Sam tried to conceal the present under his jacket.

express [ek SPRES] *v.* to convey; to communicate
   We are encouraged to express our opinions in class.

impaired [im PAYRD] *v.* lessened in strength or quality
   Because he was exposed to loud noises, Pat's hearing was impaired.

innocent [IN noh sent] *adj.* not guilty; blameless
   The jury concluded that the defendant was innocent of the charges brought against him.

praise [PRAYZ] *n.* a compliment; an expression of approval
   The artist earned praise for his skilled portrait of the woman.

squandered [SKWAHN duhrd] *v.* wasted
   Jeff squandered his money on candy and toys.

treasure [TREZH uhr] *n.* valuable or priceless possessions
   The pirate buried his treasure on the beach.

Exercise A

Fill the blanks, using each word from Word List A only once.

Ever since he was a young boy, Robert's greatest [1] _____ was to become an opera singer. His most valuable [2] _____ was an old recording of the famous opera, "The Magic Flute." He loved to [3] _____ ideas through music. Robert never [4] _____ an opportunity to attend a live performance. Whenever someone gave him tickets to the opera, he made sure nothing [5] _____ his ability to attend it. He was also unable to [6] _____ his excitement, and he would shout for joy when he was given the tickets. Robert also took singing lessons and prac¬ticed regularly; the [7] _____ sound of his voice earned him a role as young boy in a local operatic production. He won great [8] _____ from music critics for his performance, and this led to future roles in other operas.

Read the following passage. Pay special attention to the underlined words. Then, read it again, and complete the activities. Use a separate sheet of paper for your written answers.

George Gordon, Lord Byron, was a Romantic poet who owed much of his success to the circumstances of his life. As an innocent boy, Byron and his mother struggled to make ends meet. His father had squandered the family's money, and young Byron grew up in poverty. However, at the age of ten, Byron inherited wealth and title from an uncle, and from then on, his life became more comfortable. He went on to attend Cambridge University, where he published his first volume of poetry, *Hours of Idleness*. This book received no praise; in fact, it received almost universally bad reviews. Byron achieved real success with the publication of his second volume of poetry, *Childe Harold's Pilgrimage*, which was widely acclaimed.

Because he had the title of "lord," Byron was required to sit in the English Parliament, in the House of Lords. There, he was known for his ability to express his ideas well. Unfortunately, Byron's ability to communicate did not serve him well. His left-wing political beliefs impaired his success in Parliament, as many people there disagreed with his views. Because he could not conceal his political beliefs, and because he was in debt, Byron left England permanently and settled in Switzerland and later Italy. He would never set foot in England again.

Byron's time in Italy was a period of great creativity. He produced many famous works, including the literary treasure *Don Juan*.

Byron's real ambition, aside from writing poetry, was to help the underdog. This goal led him to Greece, where he had planned to fight with the Greeks and against the Turks, who controlled Greece at that time. Byron never attained this objective because he died of fever. He was buried in England, and is regarded as one of most important Romantic poets of that period.

1. Underline the phrase that tells what Byron and his mother had to struggle with while he was growing up as an innocent boy. Tell what **innocent** means.

2. Underline the phrase that tells the result that occurred after Byron's father squandered the family's money. Tell what **squandered** means.

3. Underline the phrase that supports the idea that Byron's first book received no praise. Tell what **praise** means.

4. Circle the word that tells what express means. Use **express** in a sentence.

5. Underline the phrase that explains how Byron's left-wing political views impaired his success in Parliament. Tell what **impaired** means.

6. Underline the phrase that tells what Byron had to do because he could not conceal his political beliefs. Tell what **conceal** means.

7. Circle the title of the literary treasure that Byron composed while he lived in Italy. Tell what **treasure** means.

8. Circle the word that tells what ambition means. Use **ambition** in a sentence.

She Walks in Beauty •
Apostrophe to the Ocean •
from Don Juan
George Gordon, Lord Byron

Summaries In these poems, Lord Byron expresses the Romantic spirit. The speaker of **"She Walks in Beauty"** declares his admiration for the outer and inner beauty of a woman. In **"Apostrophe to the Ocean,"** the speaker celebrates the power and beauty of nature. In **Don Juan,** the title character thinks about his youth. Although he regrets missed opportunities, he reaches at an interesting conclusion about life and death.

Note-taking Guide

Use the chart below to help you understand the poems. For each poem, write the poem's subject—who or what the poem is about. Then write lines from the poem that describe the subject. Finally, think about the way the speakers describe each subject. Based on the descriptions, decide how each speaker feels about the subject of the poem.

	Subject of Poem	Description in Poem	Speaker's Feelings
She Walks in Beauty			
Apostrophe to the Ocean			
Don Juan			

She Walks in Beauty • Apostrophe to the Ocean • *from* Don Juan

1. **Analyze:** In "Don Juan," the speaker thinks about his age and how much of his life has passed by. How would you describe his mood?

_____

_____

2. **Literary Analysis:** These poems use **figurative language** to help make meaning clear. Find at least one example each of **simile, metaphor,** and **personification** in these poems by Lord Byron. Use the chart below to show how each example suggests the poet's idea.

Figurative Language	What Is Being Described	Associations Suggested
Simile		
Metaphor		
Personification		

3. **Reading Strategy:** When you **question** a text, you ask questions about *who, what, where, when,* and *why,* and answer these as you read. Did questioning help you understand the poems? Explain.

_____

_____

Writing About the Essential Question

What is the relationship between place and literature? Which poems express a sense of the sublime, a feeling of fear and wonder inspired by nature?

Ozymandias • Ode to the West Wind • To a Skylark

Literary Analysis

Imagery is descriptive language. Poetic imagery has certain characteristics:

- It appeals to any or all of the five senses: sight, hearing, smell, taste, and touch.
- It often creates patterns supporting a poem's theme.

By creating powerful images of the West Wind or of a skylark, Shelley links these natural beings to the desires of his own spirit. In the **Romantic philosophy** of the imagination, an image connects what is "outside" the mind with what is "inside" the mind, linking nature and spirit. Identify the specific ideas Shelley expresses through images. Then, judge how well his images capture both the thing being described and the needs of his spirit.

Reading Strategy

To help you **respond to imagery,** you can **draw on your background to make connections.** Use details from the poems and your own knowledge to find meaning in each image. Note the sensory "texture"—dark or light, rough or smooth—of each image. What feelings and ideas, or associations, does each image bring to mind? Use the chart below to note the sensory "texture" and associations of the given image.

Sensory "Texture"		Associations
massive	"Two vast and trunkless legs of stone"	surprise; may be horror

© Pearson Education

Word List A

Study these words from the selections. Then, complete the activities that follow.

antique [an TEEK] *adj.* belonging to ancient times
The antique platter was made during the Civil War.

decay [dee KAY] *n.* deterioration
Many bacteria cause decay on the surfaces they touch.

hues [HYOOZ] *n.* colors
A rainbow is made of many different hues.

keen [KEEN] *adj.* sharp; vivid
Dogs have a keen sense of smell.

prophecy [PRAH feh see] *n.* a revelation; a prediction
The oracle made a prophecy that the town would prosper.

scattering [SKAT uhr ing] *v.* dispersing; causing to break up and go in many places
The wind blew in through the open window, scattering the papers on my desk.

solid [SAH lid] *adj.* not hollow; substantial
That table is made of solid oak.

surpass [ser PAS] *v.* to outdo; to exceed
We hoped that the trip would surpass our expectations.

Exercise A

Fill in each blank using each word from Word List A only once.

Though the [1] _____ quilt was probably over one hundred years old, it was unfaded. You could appreciate the bright [2] _____ of the individual squares today because of the way it had been stored. The trunk that held the quilt for all these years was made of [3] _____ maple, so no light or dust had penetrated. The quilt experts who examined it used their [4] _____ knowledge of fabrics and textiles quilt to determine its value. They were very pleased that the original owner had kept the quilt intact instead of [5] _____ pieces to flea markets across the country. They also found no evidence of [6] _____ on either side. Many of these experts thought that the price it would bring at auction would [7] _____ quilts sold recently. One expert was so enthusiastic about the quilt's condition that he made a [8] _____ that a museum, not an individual collector, would be the buyer.

1. What did Shelley consider an antique holdover from earlier times? Then, write a sentence using the word *antique*.

2. Underline the phrase that tells what prophecy one could make about Shelley. What would your *prophecy* about Shelley be?

3. Underline the phrase that explains where Shelley's keen objections can be found. Define what *keen* means.

4. Underline the sentence that reveals how Shelley received his solid foundation in radical politics. How might a person without a *solid* political foundation act?

5. Underline the phrase that explains where Shelley and his wife were scattering pamphlets. Can politicians be found *scattering* pamphlets? Explain.

6. Circle the word that tells what decay means. Use *decay* in a sentence.

7. Underline Shelley's belief about people of all social hues. Define *hues*.

8. Underline the phrase that explains what Shelley's work would surpass. Describe a goal that an athlete might like to *surpass*?

Read the following passage. Pay special attention to the underlined words. Then, read it again, and complete the activities. Use a separate sheet of paper for your written answers.

Percy Bysshe Shelley considered the politically conservative climate of the England in which he was raised an antique holdover from earlier times. He believed it was this political conservatism that was directly responsible for inequality among the classes. These views are expressed in his poetry and in his many essays and articles.

As a young boy, Shelley had few friends, and he was taunted by other students. Perhaps, because of these experiences, it wouldn't be hard to make the prophecy that Shelley would develop a strong dislike of tyranny. His keen objections to it are reflected in his writing.

Shelley met influential politicians and read about important issues. This gave him a solid foundation in politics. He was expelled from college when it was discovered that he wrote a pamphlet about atheism. After this, Shelley married Harriet Westbrook, and they traveled throughout England and Ireland, speaking against political injustice and scattering pamphlets about the subject wherever they went.

He also wrote many articles regarding his views about the decay and deterioration of English society.

After his first marriage ended, Shelley met and married Mary Wollstonecraft Godwin, a fellow writer. Their travels and life abroad together inspired him to write some of his most famous works. While in Italy, Shelley published the political magazine *The Liberal* with his friends, Lord Byron and Leigh Hunt.

One of Shelley's beliefs was that people of all social hues should be permitted to participate in political life—in other words, everyone should have a voice. He wrote an article suggesting a national discussion on reforming the election process and improving the educational system for the working class.

Although Shelley drowned when he was only twenty-five, it was clear that he had already developed a body of work that would surpass many of his writer contemporaries for its beauty, style, and content.

Ozymandias • Ode to the West Wind • To a Skylark
Percy Bysshe Shelley

Summaries "Ozymandias" is about human pride and ambition. In the poem, a traveler describes the ruins of an ancient statue. On the base is writing that says, "Look on my works, ye Mighty, and despair!" However, what is left of the statue stands in an empty desert. The works of Ozymandias have been destroyed by time and nature.

The speaker in **"Ode to the West Wind"** describes the force of the West wind as it blows dead leaves, stirs up the ocean, destroys plants, and tells of winter's arrival. The speaker is amazed by the wind's strength. The poet wants the wind to make him new again.

"To a Skylark" is addressed to a bird. The poem describes its soaring music. The speaker wishes he could express himself as delightfully as the skylark does so that the world would listen to him.

Note-taking Guide

In the chart below, record words used to describe the subjects of each of the poems.

Poem	Words used to describe it
Ozymandias	
Ode to the West Wind	
To a Skylark	

Ozymandias • Ode to the West Wind • To a Skylark

1. **Infer:** The expression on the face of Ozymandias includes a frown, a wrinkled lip, and a sneer. What does his expression suggest about the kind of ruler he was?

_____

2. **Literary Analysis:** In **Romantic philosophy,** the imagination connects nature and spirit. Choose two images from Shelley's poems that connect the speaker and nature. Note the details of the image and its associations in the chart below.

Image	How Vivid?	Associated Ideas	Link: Nature and Spirit

3. **Reading Strategy:** Select a passage from one of the poems that contains images that you find striking or memorable. **Draw on your background** to explain your response to the passage.

_____

_____

 **Writing About the Essential Question**

How does literature shape or reflect society? In what ways does the sculpture in "Ozymandias" represent tyranny and the wind in "Ode to the West Wind" rebellion?

_____

_____

_____

Poetry of John Keats

Literary Analysis

An **ode** is a lyric poem that is very emotional. Odes pay respect to a person or thing. The speaker of the poem addresses that person or thing directly. There are three types of odes.

- The **Pindaric ode** contains groups of three stanzas. Within each group, one stanza differs in form from the other two.
- The **Horatian ode** contains only one type of stanza.
- An **irregular ode** has no set pattern.

John Keats created his own type of ode, using ten-line stanzas. Each line in Keats's odes contains ten beats with a repeated pattern of weak syllable/strong syllable, known as iambic pentameter. Often those stanzas begin with four lines rhymed *abab* followed by six rhymed lines.

In his odes, Keats follows the tradition of paying respect to something. Yet his odes tell as much about him as they do about his topics. In "Ode to a Nightingale," for instance, Keats longs for an ideal beauty he cannot find in real life. As you read, compare how each work describes a conflict in the speaker.

Reading Strategy

One way to **determine the main idea or essential message** of a literary work is to **paraphrase** the work. Paraphrasing is restating text in your own words. Use the chart below to paraphrase Keats's poems and to help you determine the main idea or essential message of each poem.

Original Words	Paraphrase
"When I have fears that I may cease to be . . ."	When I fear death . . .

Word List A

Study these words from the selections. Then, complete the activities that follow.

brim [BRIM] *n.* the rim of a vessel; edge
 The brim that man's hat is a small one.

dissolve [diz ZAHLV] *v.* melt; disintegrate
 Those tablets will dissolve in water.

fame [FAYM] *n.* great renown
 The artist's fame made him well-known to everyone.

immortal [im MOHR tuhl] *adj.* lasting forever; not subject to death
 In ancient mythology, the gods were described as immortal.

passion [PASH uhn] *n.* boundless enthusiasm; zeal
 John's great passion for cooking led to his career as a chef.

pursuit [per SOOT] *n.* an activity, such as a hobby or vocation
 My favorite pursuit is reading.

realms [RELMZ] *n.* areas; domains
 The social sciences cover many different realms of study.

rhyme [RIME] *n.* the correspondence of sounds at the ends of words
 Jack composed a rhyme with very common words.

Exercise A

Fill in the blanks, using each word from Word List A only once.

A poet deals with more than just rhythm and [1] _____ when she

writes poetry. She is in [2] _____ of much more than that. A poet also

deals with various [3] _____ of fiction and reality when she decides

on the content of the poem. She works to make the lines between those

two worlds [4] _____ so that all that remains is the picture that she

paints with her words. A good poem is filled to the [5] _____ with

rich language, sounds, and images. It is the product of a writer who has

a [6] _____ for words and how to use them to create beauty. A good

poem can also bring the poet [7] _____ because everyone will want

to read it. However, a truly great poem can make the poet [8] _____

because it will endure the test of time.

Read the following passage. Pay special attention to the underlined words. Then, read it again, and complete the activities. Use a separate sheet of paper for your written answers.

John Keats did not gain <u>fame</u> from his poetry until after his death. Keats's talent was not recognized because he did not have the advantages of social position, wealth, or education. In fact, Keats grew up and lived in poverty and hardship for most of his life. However, Keats did not allow these problems to destroy his <u>passion</u> for poetry. He engaged in this lifelong <u>pursuit</u> in the face of these difficulties.

Both of Keats's parents were dead by the time he was ten years old, and he and his siblings were faced with a life of poverty. Pursuing a literary life was outside the <u>realms</u> of possibility for young Keats, and he decided to train to become a surgeon. This decision did not cause his love for literature to <u>dissolve</u>; he read widely while he was in school, and he wrote his first poem, "Lines in Imitation of Spenser," in 1814, while he was training in surgery in London.

Keats published his first book of poems in 1817. At around this time, he was forced to care for his brother, Tom, who was very ill with tuberculosis. Eventually, Keats's brother died, and Keats was greatly saddened by this loss.

Keats published his second volume of poetry in 1820, and he received great acclaim for it. However, he soon discovered that he was not <u>immortal</u>; he was ill with the same disease that <u>killed</u> his brother, Tom.

Keats moved to Italy, where he hoped that the milder climate would improve his health. He died in 1821, at the age of twenty-five. His poetry, filled to the <u>brim</u> with beautiful images, is still enjoyed by many people. These poetic images and the <u>rhyme</u> in which he conveys them gave him the renown he never had while he was alive.

1. Underline the phrase that tells when Keats gained <u>fame</u> from his poetry. What is a synonym for *fame*?

2. Underline the sentence that supports the idea that poverty and hardship did not destroy Keats's <u>passion</u> for poetry. Tell what *passion* means.

3. Underline the phrase that tells how Keats engaged in his lifelong <u>pursuit</u> of writing poetry. Tell what *pursuit* means.

4. Underline the phrase that tells what Keats decided to pursue, since having a literary career was outside of the <u>realms</u> of possibility for him. Tell what *realms* means.

5. Underline the phrase that supports the idea that Keats's decision to train as a surgeon did not cause his love for literature to <u>dissolve</u>. What is a synonym for *dissolve*?

6. Underline the phrase that tells how Keats knew that he was not <u>immortal</u>. Tell what *immortal* means.

7. With what was Keats's poetry filled to the <u>brim</u>? Tell what *brim* means.

8. Underline the phrase that tells what the images and the <u>rhyme</u> in which Keats conveys them gave Keats. Tell what *rhyme* means.

On First Looking into Chapman's Homer • When I Have Fears That I May Cease to Be • Ode to a Nightingale

John Keats

Summaries In these poems, the poet looks across time, into both the past and the future. In **"On First Looking into Chapman's Homer,"** the speaker shows his delight in discovering the works of the ancient Greek poet Homer. In **"When I Have Fears That I May Cease to Be,"** the poet writes about his fear of dying young. Ultimately, he learns that neither love nor fame is important. In **"Ode to a Nightingale,"** the speaker writes about his desire to join with the bird in its world of beauty, joy, and imagination.

Note-taking Guide

Use the chart below to list the subjects, major points, and speaker's attitudes in each poem.

Poem	Subject	What the Poem Shows	Speaker's Attitude
"Homer"	Classical poetry	Admiration for the past	
"Fears"			
"Nightingale"			

Ode on a Grecian Urn

John Keats

Summary Keats's poem is addressed to an ancient Grecian urn and contains thoughts about beauty and truth inspired by the urn. The urn is decorated with the following scenes and details: men or gods chasing young women, a musician, trees, a priest leading a young cow to be sacrificed, and the empty town from which the priest and others have come. Keats reflects that those who are depicted pursuing the women will never catch them. However, they will also never grow old. Keats uses the urn to draw a conclusion about the human experience.

Note-taking Guide

Use the chart below to analyze the images and meaning of each stanza.

Images	Speaker's Observation
Men, women, and gods playing musical instruments and chasing one another	

Stop to Reflect

Personification gives human qualities to something nonhuman. Circle three words or phrases that the speaker uses to personify the urn.

Reading Check

The **setting** is the time and place of an event or a work.

1. In what region of the world does the scene on the urn take place?

_____

_____

_____

2. At what period in history does this scene occur?

_____

_____

_____

Ode on a Grecian Urn
John Keats

Thou still unravished[1] bride of quietness
Thou foster child of silence and slow time,
Sylvan[2] historian, who canst thus express
A flowery tale more sweetly than our rhyme:
5 What leaf-fringed legend haunts about thy shape
Of deities or mortals, or of both,
In Tempe[3] or the dales of Arcady?[4]
What men or gods are these? What maidens loath?[5]
What mad pursuit? What struggle to escape?
10 What pipes and timbrels?[6] What wild ecstasy?

◆ ◆ ◆

On the urn there is a picture of a young man. He seems to be singing of his love for a young woman. Unlike love in the real world, their love will last forever. Another picture on the urn shows a procession and a sacrifice in an ancient little town. The speaker wonders about the occasion for the ceremony. But the urn will not reveal the secret.

◆ ◆ ◆

Vocabulary Development
deities (DEE uh teez) *n.* gods
dales (DAYLZ) *n.* valleys
ecstasy (EK stuh see) *n.* great joy

1. **unravished** *adj.* pure.
2. **Sylvan** (SIL vuhn) *adj.* rustic; representing the woods or forest.
3. **Tempe** (TEM pee) valley in Greece that has become a symbol of supreme rural beauty.
4. **Arcady** (AR kuh dee) region in Greece that has come to represent the peace and contentment of countryside surroundings.
5. **loath** (LOHTH) *adj.* unwilling.
6. **timbrels** (TIM bruhlz) *n.* tambourines.

O Attic[7] shape! Fair attitude! with brede[8]
Of marble men and maidens overwrought,[9]
With forest branches and the trodden[10] weed;
Thou, silent form, dost tease us out of
  thought
15 As doth eternity: Cold Pastoral![11]
When old age shall this generation waste,
Thou shalt remain, in midst of other woe
Than ours, a friend to man, to whom thou
  say'st
"Beauty is truth, truth beauty,"—that is all
20 Ye know on earth, and all ye need to know.

7. **Attic** Attica was the region of Greece in which Athens was located; the art of the region was characterized by grace and simplicity.

8. **brede** *n.* interwoven pattern.

9. **overwrought** *adj.* adorned with.

10. **trodden** *v.* trampled.

11. **Cold Pastoral** unchanging rural scene.

TAKE NOTES

Reading Strategy

In a paraphrase, you use your own words to restate a passage. Paraphrase the bracketed lines to help you **determine their main idea or essential message.**

_____

_____

_____

_____

_____

Literary Analysis

An **ode** honors a person or thing. Why do you think the speaker calls the urn a "friend to man" in the final lines?

_____

_____

_____

Poetry of John Keats

1. **Compare and Contrast:** In "Ode to a Nightingale," the speaker wishes to leave the world behind and join the nightingale. What differences does he see between the bird's life and his own that cause him to wish this?

_____

_____

2. **Literary Analysis:** An **ode** is a lyric poem that pays respect to a person or thing. In what ways does Keats honor his subjects? Explain, using examples from the poems.

_____

3. **Reading Strategy:** To help you **determine the main idea or essential meaning** of a literary work, put lines or passages into your own words. Using the chart shown, paraphrase the following lines.

Poem	Lines	Paraphrase
Homer	9–10	
Nightingale	71–72	
Grecian Urn	3–4	

Writing About the Essential Question

What is the relationship of the writer to tradition? In what ways are these poems traditional odes? In what ways has Keats personalized them?

_____

_____

On Making an Agreeable Marriage • *from* A Vindication of the Rights of Woman

Literary Analysis

Social commentary is writing or speech that offers criticisms about society. Social commentary can be *unconscious* or *conscious*. In *unconscious* social commentary, a writer reveals a problem caused by social customs without directly challenging those customs. The commentary is *conscious* when a writer points out a direct link between a problem and a social custom. As you read these selections, pay attention to the assumptions about women that they reveal, consciously or unconsciously.

Both authors use **persuasive techniques** such as the following:

- appeals to logic based on sound reasoning
- appeals to readers' sense of morality or ethics
- appeals to emotion, addressing readers' feelings

Reading Strategy

When reading, **analyze how the author's purpose affects the meaning** of the work. First, determine the author's purpose by using background knowledge and other clues from the text. Then, complete the chart shown by giving examples of how the author's purpose affects the work's meaning.

Selection	Background	Other Clues From the Text	Writer's Purpose	How Purpose Affects Meaning
On Making an Agreeable Marriage	The author writes about the manners and morals of society during the early 1800s.			
A Vindication of the Rights of Woman	The author supported rights for women.			

Word List A

Study these words from the selections. Then, complete the activities that follow.

amiable [AY mee uh buhl] *adj.* friendly and agreeable
With an amiable smile, Mr. Diaz greets his new students.

attribute [uh TRIB yoot] *v.* relate to a particular cause or source
Dan can attribute his fine tennis game to months of practice at the club.

comprehension [kahm pree HEN shuhn] *n.* understanding
Elizabeth has no comprehension of what happened in the story.

conscientiously [kahn shee EN shus lee] *adv.* with extreme care
Always acting conscientiously, Amanda picks up the trash in the park.

conviction [kuhn VIK shuhn] *n.* an unshakable belief in something
Her kind nature further fuels John's conviction of her innocence.

deficiencies [dee FISH uhn seez] *n.* shortages; insufficient amounts
Vitamin deficiencies cause many health problems.

partial [PAR shuhl] *adj.* favoring one side over others; biased
If the referees are partial, they are not doing their job properly.

uniformly [yoo ni FORM lee] *adv.* in a consistent manner
Each morning, Eliza makes all the beds uniformly.

Exercise A

Fill in the blanks, using each word from World List A only once.

Janet has a firm [1] _____ that no one should live in poverty. She puts her belief into practice by volunteering at the local soup kitchen, where she [2] _____ tries to make sure that everyone gets enough to eat. She performs this work with an [3] _____ smile because she believes that the people who come for help deserve friendly service. She treats everyone who comes there fairly and [4] _____ so that they do not feel neglected. She prevents other volunteers from showing [5] _____ treatment toward anyone because she thinks that showing such bias would discourage people from coming to the soup kitchen. Janet works closely with local supermarkets to make sure that food is delivered regularly and that there are no [6] _____ in the supply of food to the soup kitchen. Janet gives presentations to local organizations in order to increase [7] _____ and awareness of poverty and the ways to eliminate it. She hopes that one day she will be able to [8] _____ the end of poverty in her community to these efforts.

Read the following passage. Pay special attention to the underlined words. Then, read it again, and complete the activities. Use a separate sheet of paper for your written answers.

Pat is the first woman in her family to go to college. She can attribute much of her success to her parents' support of her efforts. They raised her with the conviction that she could do anything if she put her mind to it. They are very proud of their daughter's accomplishments. Since they never had the opportunity to pursue higher education, they made sure that Pat would get the chance to undergo the challenge of a university education.

Pat made many sacrifices in order to get a college education, including studying conscientiously in high school, carefully reading her texts. She also read outside of class in order to increase her reading comprehension. As a result, Pat was able to read at the college level while she was still in high school.

Pat's dedication to studying meant that she missed many social events and activities. Although Pat was partial to dancing, preferring it over sports, she seldom attended the school dances because of her intense study schedule. Pat promised herself that when she reached college, she would make up for these deficiencies by balancing her schoolwork with her social life.

The best day of Pat's life was graduation day. She was chosen as class valedictorian, since her grades were uniformly and consistently the best in the class. Pat was honored by this selection, and gave her thanks in a speech that she made during the ceremony.

Pat realized that she had to make many difficult decisions in order to reach her goal. While some students were having lighthearted fun, she was expanding her intellect. Throughout this experience, Pat never forgot to be true to herself. Pat is extremely friendly and one of the most amiable people you would ever want to meet.

1. Underline the phrase that tells to what Pat can attribute much of her success. Tell what *attribute* means.

2. Underline the phrase that tells what conviction Pat was raised with. Tell what *conviction* means.

3. Underline the word that means about the same as conscientiously. What is an antonym of *conscientiously*?

4. Underline the phrase that tells what Pat did in order to increase her reading comprehension. Use *comprehension* in a sentence about school.

5. Circle the word that means about the same as partial. Describe what school activity you are *partial* to.

6. Underline the phrase that tells what deficiencies Pat plans to make up for. Use *deficiencies* in a sentence.

7. Circle the word that means about the same as uniformly. What is an antonym of *uniformly*?

8. Circle the word that tells what amiable means. Use *amiable* in a sentence.

On Making an Agreeable Marriage
Jane Austen

Summary In a letter, Jane Austen responds to her niece's doubts about marriage. The author provides advice to the young woman, Fanny Knight. She also offers a glimpse into what society considered a desirable marriage in one social class during the early 1800s.

Note-taking Guide

As you read Jane Austen's letter, consider the persuasive techniques she uses. Use the chart shown to record examples of each kind of appeal that the author uses.

Appeals to Logic	Appeals to Morality	Appeals to Emotions

from A Vindication of the Rights of Woman

Mary Wollstonecraft

Summary In her essay, Wollstonecraft explains that women's education has been neglected. Because women are brought up to be admired, they are silly and vain rather than strong and useful. The only way for a woman to advance in the world is through marriage. Wollstonecraft attacks society for the limits it places on women, who in some cases clearly show more sense than their male relatives.

Note-taking Guide

As you read Mary Wollstonecraft's essay, consider the persuasive techniques she uses. Use the chart below to record examples of each kind of persuasive appeal.

Appeals to Logic	Appeals to Morality	Appeals to Emotions

from A Vindication of the Rights of Woman

Mary Wollstonecraft

Reading Strategy

How do the words *misery* and *deplore* give clues to the **author's purpose?**

_____

_____

_____

Read Fluently

Read the bracketed passage aloud. What unfortunate fact about the position of women does the author's comparison help to express?

_____

_____

_____

Wollstonecraft has studied history and the world. She concludes that either people are very different from one another or civilization has been unfair.

◆ ◆ ◆

I have turned over various books written on the subject of education, and patiently observed the conduct of parents and the management of schools; but what has been the result?—a profound conviction that the neglected education of my fellow creatures is the grand source of the misery I deplore, and that women, in particular, are rendered weak and wretched by a variety of concurring[1] causes, originating from one hasty conclusion. The conduct and manners of women, in fact, evidently prove that their minds are not in a healthy state; for, like the flowers which are planted in too rich a soil, strength and usefulness are sacrificed to beauty; and the flaunting leaves, after having pleased a fastidious eye, fade, disregarded on the stalk, long before the season when they ought to have arrived at maturity.

◆ ◆ ◆

Women are the victims of poor education and of false social expectations. They should have nobler ambitions. They should demand respect.

◆ ◆ ◆

Vocabulary Development

vindication (vin duh KAY shun) *n.* act of providing justification or support for

fastidious (fas TID ee uhs) *adj.* particular; difficult to please

1. **concurring** *adj.* joining together.

Indeed the word masculine is only a bugbear;[2] there is little reason to fear that women will acquire too much courage or fortitude, for their apparent inferiority with respect to bodily strength must render them in some degree dependent on men in the various relations of life; but why should it be increased by prejudices that give a sex to virtue, and confound[3] simple truths with sensual reveries?

◆　◆　◆

Mistaken ideas about women deprive them of a good education and of equality. These ideas also cause some women to act slyly and childishly. Many individual women, however, have more sense than their male relatives and husbands.

TAKE NOTES

Literary Analysis ✏

Besides their dependence on men, what additional problems do women face, according to the author's **social commentary** here? Circle the words that give the answer.

Vocabulary Development

fortitude (FORT uh tood) *n.* courage; strength to endure

reveries (REV uh reez) *n.* daydreams

2. **bugbear** *n.* frightening imaginary creature, especially one that frightens children.

3. **confound** *v.* confuse by mixing together.

© Pearson Education

On Making an Agreeable Marriage
• *from* A Vindication of the Rights of Woman

1. **Literary Analysis:** According to Wollstonecraft's **social commentary,** how are women's personalities affected by society's notions of the ideal woman?

_____

_____

2. **Literary Analysis:** Reread Austen's letter. Then, use a chart like the one shown to analyze the importance Austen's society placed on the elements of marriage.

	Love	Suitability for Each Other	Money	Respectability
Examples				
Importance				

3. **Reading Strategy:** Compare Wollstonecraft's and Austen's purposes in writing. Explain how the meaning of their works is affected by their purposes and whether the meanings are similar or different.

_____

_____

 Writing About the Essential Question

How does literature shape or reflect society? Which author expresses a more radical view of women for her day? In your response, use at least two of these Essential Question words: *independence, values, rebellious.*

_____

_____

from In Memoriam, A.H.H. • The Lady of Shalott • *from* The Princess: Tears, Idle Tears • Ulysses

Literary Analysis

The **speaker** is the person who says the words of a poem. The poet is not necessarily the same person as the speaker. In a narrative poem, or one that tells a story, the speaker is sometimes a character in the story and sometimes a narrator who stands outside the story. In either case, the speaker provides details about events, characters, and settings as well as his or her feelings about them.

The speakers in Tennyson's poems show different experiences of time. Typical in these poems are:

- a present in which nothing changes
- a future that is unknown
- a past that is lost

Compare the views of time in each poem you read.

Reading Strategy

Often, the ideas or emotions of a poem's speaker help convey the author's philosophical assumptions and beliefs. When you read a poem, you should examine the motivations, beliefs, and conflicts of the speaker to **analyze the author's philosophical assumptions and beliefs**. As you read Tennyson's poems, use a chart like the one shown to help you analyze philosophical assumptions or beliefs.

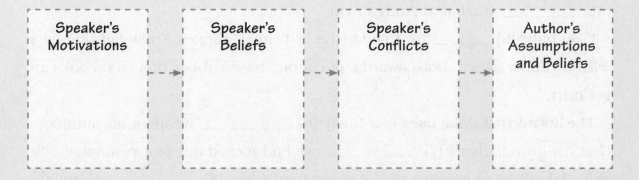

Speaker's Motivations	Speaker's Beliefs	Speaker's Conflicts	Author's Assumptions and Beliefs

Word List A

Study these words from the selections. Then, complete the activities.

discerning [di SERN ing] *v.* perceiving or recognizing clearly
   As the year goes on, Mark is discerning his new job as quite satisfying.

feigned [FAYND] *adj.* not real; imagined
   Helen's feigned interest in Hector was meant to make Sam jealous.

idle [EYE duhl] *adj.* not busy
   My father is never idle, even though we urge him to slow down and relax.

remote [ri MOHT] *adj.* distant
   Carly is visiting a remote island for her vacation this year.

smite [SMYT] *v.* to strike or hit very hard
   Don used a heavy hammer to smite the nails that held the bench in place.

vexed [VEXT] *v.* irritated or annoyed
   The misbehaving child vexed the babysitter.

wanes [WAYNZ] *v.* grows progressively smaller in size or brightness
   The moon wanes for a few weeks and then slowly appears larger.

wrought [RAWT] *v.* formed or fashioned
   Years of wind and waves wrought changes on the shoreline.

Exercise A

Fill in each blank below with the appropriate word from Word List A.

   Jake and Andy play a game they call "Knights." Their interest in it waxes and
[1] _____. Some weeks, they play it a lot; other weeks, they don't. Lately,
they have been playing it often. It keeps them from being [2] _____.

   "I'll [3] _____ you with this sword!" declares Jake with a
[4] _____ thrust at Andy's arm.

   "You have [5] _____ me for the last time!" replies Andy, fighting back
with a rubber sword. Both swords, of course, have rubber tips so no one can
get hurt.

   The sword that Jake uses is a finely [6] _____ weapon, an antique
that his grandfather's [7] _____ eye had picked out at a rummage
sale. Jake likes to imagine that it came from some [8] _____ country
long ago.

Read the following passage. Pay special attention to the underlined words. Then, read it again, and complete the activities. Use a separate sheet of paper for your written answers.

Ulysses had been away from home for twenty years, traveling in <u>remote</u>, faraway lands fighting in the Trojan War and battling various monsters. Sometimes, he had thought he would never get home, especially when he and his men were trapped in the cave of the Cyclops, the one-eyed giant. Quick thinking and courage enabled Ulysses to <u>smite</u> the monster, blinding him with one hard blow and allowing his men to escape. Now, at last, he was back home and looking forward to relaxing with his wife, Penelope, and enjoying some <u>idle</u> hours doing nothing but resting.

However, it would not be as easy as he thought. While Ulysses was gone, Penelope had been <u>vexed</u> by various suitors who annoyed her daily. They insisted that her husband was dead and she should remarry. They refused to leave until she made a choice. With <u>feigned</u> sincerity, Penelope pretended she was interested in marrying one of them. She told them, "My hope for my husband's return <u>wanes</u>, growing weaker the longer he is gone. I will choose a new husband after I finish weaving a funeral robe for Laertes, my father-in-law."

Each day, she wove beautifully fashioned cloth at her loom. Each night, she undid the finely <u>wrought</u> designs she had made that day. You would think that even the least <u>discerning</u> eye would have recognized what was happening, but the suitors never caught on. Perhaps they were having too much fun living at Penelope's expense to say anything that might end the party.

Ulysses knew that he had to get rid of the suitors. His life would be in danger if they found out he had returned. In a mad frenzy, he and three friends managed to kill every last suitor. Finally, Ulysses was able to enjoy his own home.

1. Underline the word that means nearly the same as <u>remote</u>. Use *remote* in a sentence of your own.

2. Circle the words that give a clue to the meaning of <u>smite</u>. Write a definition for *smite*.

3. Underline the words that give a clue to the meaning of idle. What is an antonym for *idle*?

4. Circle the word that means nearly the same as <u>vexed</u>. Use *vexed* in an original sentence.

5. Circle the word that means nearly the same as <u>feigned</u>. Write a sentence of your own using *feigned*.

6. Underline the words that give a clue to the meaning of <u>wanes</u>. What is an antonym for *wanes*?

7. Circle the words that give a clue to the meaning of <u>wrought</u>. Describe a finely *wrought* tool or other item you own or would like to own.

8. Underline the words that give a clue to the meaning of <u>discerning</u>. Describe a piece of art or furniture that a *discerning* person might enjoy.

from In Memoriam, A.H.H. • *from* The Princess: Tears, Idle Tears • Ulysses

Alfred, Lord Tennyson

Summaries In *In Memoriam, A.H.H.*, Tennyson is both the poet and the speaker. In this poem he is mourning the death of his friend, Arthur Henry Hallam. Hallam died at the age of twenty-two. Tennyson is angry because his friend is no longer in a place where they can sit and talk and be together. Tennyson comes to accept the death of his friend. His sense of loss is softened by his memories of his friend.

"Tears, Idle Tears" and **"Ulysses"** have different speakers. The speaker in "Tears, Idle Tears" cries when he thinks of friends who have died and love that was lost a long time ago. The speaker in the poem "Ulysses" is the hero named in the title—Ulysses. The poem takes place after Ulysses has returned home from being away at war. He is the king, but no one knows him anymore. He is facing old age, and he is tired of staying at home. He thinks about another journey to exotic lands.

Note-taking Guide

In each poem, the speaker deals with feelings of loss. Use this chart to record details about each speaker's feelings.

In Memoriam	Tears, Idle Tears	Ulysses

The Lady of Shalott

Alfred, Lord Tennyson

Summary The Lady of Shalott lives on an island in a river. This river flows down to Camelot, the town where King Arthur has his court. She is a weaver and has heard that she will be cursed if she looks "down to Camelot." She views the world through the mirror hung before her loom, or weaving machine. Often she likes to weave into her cloth the scenes from outdoors that she sees reflected in the mirror. One day she sees in her mirror Sir Lancelot, King Arthur's greatest knight, as he rides by on the way to Camelot. She is disturbed by the sight, the mirror cracks, and she realizes that the curse is taking effect. She leaves her home, finds a boat, and paints on it *The Lady of Shalott*. Then, she gets in the boat and begins drifting toward Camelot. Singing, she dies before the boat reaches the town. The residents of Camelot come out and wonder who the dead woman is. Lancelot says to himself, "She has a lovely face; . . ."

Note-taking Guide

Use this chart to record the events of the poem.

Part I	Part II	Part III	Part IV
The Lady of Shalott lives on an island in a river flowing toward Camelot.	The Lady weaves a magic web.	Sir Lancelot comes riding by.	The Lady finds a boat.

Literary Analysis

1. What impression does the **speaker** give of the setting? Circle the letter of the best answer below.
   a. dreamy and attractive
   b. ugly and polluted
   c. poor and shabby
   d. dark and gloomy
2. Now circle images in the bracketed stanza that help convey this impression.
3. Besides the images you circled, what else helps convey this impression? (*Hint:* Read the stanza aloud before answering.)

_____

_____

_____

Reading Check

1. What does the Lady of Shalott do all the time? Circle the answer in the underlined stanza, and label it *What*?
2. Why does she never look directly at Camelot? Circle the answer and label it *Why*?

The Lady of Shalott
Alfred, Lord Tennyson

According to legend, King Arthur ruled England from a place called Camelot (KAM uh lot). There he invited all the great knights of the day. The Shalott (shuh LOT) of this poem is an island in the river that flows to Camelot.

◆ ◆ ◆

On either side the river lie
Long fields of barley and of rye,
That clothe the wold[1] and meet the sky;
And through the field the road runs by
   To many-towered Camelot,
And up and down the people go,
Gazing where the lilies blow
Round an island there below,
   The island of Shalott.

◆ ◆ ◆

The Lady of Shalott lives in a gray-towered castle on the island. No one ever sees her. They do hear her singing. She sits at a loom, a device for weaving yarn into fabric. The loom has a mirror over it.

◆ ◆ ◆

There she weaves by night and day
A magic web with colors gay.
She has heard a whisper say,
A curse is on her if she stay
   To look down to Camelot.
She knows not what the curse may be,
And so she weaveth steadily,
And little other care hath she,
   The Lady of Shalott.

1. **wold** *n.* rolling land.

And moving through a mirror clear
That hangs before her all the year,
Shadows of the world appear.
There she sees the highway near
    Winding down to Camelot:

◆ ◆ ◆

The Lady of Shalott sees all of life, from
weddings to funerals, in her mirror.

◆ ◆ ◆

And sometimes through the mirror blue
The knights come riding two and two:
She hath no loyal knight and true,
    The Lady of Shalott.

◆ ◆ ◆

The Lady of Shalott grows tired of
looking at a shadow world. One day she sees
the knight Sir Lancelot in her mirror.

◆ ◆ ◆

His broad clear brow in sunlight glowed;
On burnish'd[2] hooves his war horse trode;[3]
From underneath his helmet flowed
His coal-black curls as on he rode,
    As he rode down to Camelot.
From the bank and from the river
He flashed into the crystal mirror,
"Tirra lirra,"[4] by the river
    Sang Sir Lancelot.

She left the web, she left the loom,
She made three paces through the room,
She saw the waterlily bloom,
She saw the helmet and the plume,[5]
    She looked down to Camelot.

© Pearson Education

Vocabulary Development

paces (PAY suhz) *n.* steps made walking back and forth

2. **burnish'd** *adj.* polished; shining.

3. **trode** *v.* trod; walked.

4. **Tirra lirra** a meaningless sound for singing, like "Tra-la-la."

5. **plume** *n.* the feather on Lancelot's helmet.

TAKE NOTES

Literary Analysis

Complete the sentence below to explain how the Lady of Shalott sees the world. Then circle the details in the underlined section that help you answer.
She sees the world _____

_____

_____

Literary Analysis ✏

What impression does the **speaker** give of Sir Lancelot? Circle the letter of the best answer below.

a. young and foolish
b. handsome and cheerful
c. strange and mysterious
d. dark and gloomy

Now circle details in the bracketed stanza that help convey this impression.

Reading Strategy

1. Why do you think the Lady of Shalott risks the curse and does what is forbidden?

_____

_____

2. Based on the Lady's behavior, what do you think the **author's assumptions and beliefs** are?

_____

_____

3. Do you agree with the message? Why, or why not?

_____

_____

_____

Literary Analysis

Is the **speaker** of this poem a character in the story? Explain how you know.

_____

_____

_____

Out flew the web and floated wide;
The mirror cracked from side to side;
"The curse is come upon me," cried
   The Lady of Shalott.

◆ ◆ ◆

   The Lady of Shalott goes down to the river. She finds a boat, unties it, and lies down in it. The river carries the boat downstream.

◆ ◆ ◆

Lying, robed in snowy white
That loosely flew to left and right—
The leaves upon her falling light—
Through the noises of the night
   She floated down to Camelot:
And as the boathead[6] wound along
The willowy hills and fields among,
They heard her singing her last song,
   The Lady of Shalott.

Heard a carol, mournful, holy,
Chanted loudly, chanted lowly,
Till her blood was frozen slowly,
And her eyes were darkened wholly,
   Turned to towered Camelot.
For ere[7] she reached upon the tide
The first house by the waterside,
Singing in her song she died,
   The Lady of Shalott.

◆ ◆ ◆

6. **boathead** *n.* the front of the boat.
7. **ere** (AYR) *adv.* before.

As the boat drifts into Camelot, the knights and ladies come to see who is inside. On the prow, or front, of the boat, they read the name, *The Lady of Shalott*.

◆ ◆ ◆

Who is this? and what is here?
And in the lighted palace near
Died the sound of royal cheer;
And they crossed themselves for fear,
  All the knights at Camelot:
But Lancelot mused a little space;[8]
He said, "She has a lovely face;
God in his mercy lend her grace,[9]
  The Lady of Shalott."

Reading Check

What happens to the Lady of Shalott?

_____

_____

_____

Literary Analysis

Read Sir Lancelot's words aloud. What tone will you use? Circle the letter of the best answer below.

a. passionate and angry
b. cool and uninterested
c. sympathetic and thoughtful
d. grief-stricken and sobbing

Vocabulary Development

mused (MYOOZD) *v.* thought about; considered

8. **a little space** some; a bit.
9. **grace** *n.* divine love and protection.

from In Memoriam, A.H.H. • The Lady of Shalott • from The Princess: Tears, Idle Tears • Ulysses

1. **Literary Analysis:** How does the loss of the **speaker's** friend affect the scene in *In Memoriam?*

   _____

   _____

2. **Literary Analysis:** What inner conflict does the speaker face in the poem "Ulysses"?

   _____

   _____

3. **Literary Analysis:** Use this chart to compare Ulysses' view of time with the Lady of Shalott's view.

	Past	Present	Future
Ulysses			
The Lady of Shalott			

4. **Reading Strategy:** Choose one poem and **analyze the author's assumptions and beliefs**.

   _____

   _____

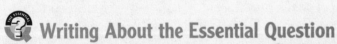 **Writing About the Essential Question**

How does literature shape or reflect society? What values do you think Tennyson celebrates in his poetry? Explain.

   _____

   _____

My Last Duchess • Life in a Love •
Porphyria's Lover • Sonnet 43

Literary Analysis

A **dramatic monologue** is a long speech by one character. Though dramatic monologues are often parts of plays or other longer works, they are characteristic of the Victorian period. Robert Browning specialized in short poems that are dramatic monologues all on their own. Browning's dramatic monologues have these elements:

- A speaker whose remarks reveal his or her situation and character
- A silent listener whom the speaker talks to

Browning's monologues also capture the rhythm of everyday speech by using **run-on lines** and **end-stop lines.** Run-on lines occur when the flow of words forces you to read on without a pause. End-stop lines end at points where the speaker would normally pause. Look for these elements as you read "My Last Duchess."

Reading Strategy

Readers can gain a deeper understanding of a literary work by comparing and contrasting it with another work. For example, you might compare the scornful complaints expressed by the speaker of one poem with the deep, abiding love expressed by the speaker of another poem. As you read poems by the Brownings, **compare and contrast the elements** in the poems. Use a Venn diagram to record the similarities and the differences.

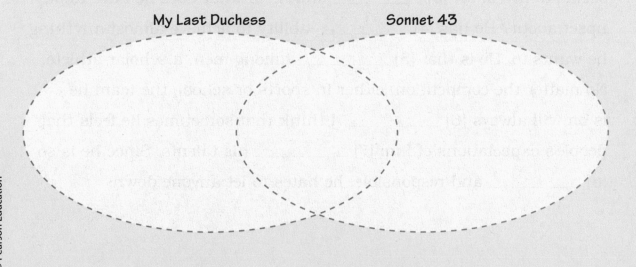

My Last Duchess   Sonnet 43

Word List A

Study these words from the selections. Then, complete the activities.

ample [AM puhl] *adj.* abundant; liberal
This huge room has ample *space for two beds and two dressers.*

baffled [BAF uhld] *v.* puzzled; confused; bewildered
Paulo, baffled *by the difficult math problem, turned to Anar for help.*

earnest [ER nist] *adj.* very serious; determined; sincere
Edwin made an earnest *plea for mercy, but the judge was not sympathetic.*

exceed [ek SEED] *v.* to go beyond the limits of
When fishing in this lake, you cannot exceed *the limit of four fish.*

ideal [y DEE uhl] *adj.* perfect; excellent
The house was built in an ideal *location, overlooking the ocean.*

prevail [pree VAYLE] *v.* to win or succeed; to be most common
Superior free-throw shooting helped the team prevail *against its rival.*

rarity [RAIR uh tee] *n.* the condition of being uncommon or infrequent
This large and perfect diamond is truly a rarity *among gems.*

sullen [SUL uhn] *adj.* showing bad humor or resentment; gloomy
Not even the promise of ice cream could shake Ivan's sullen *mood.*

Exercise A

Fill in the blanks, using each word from Word List A only once.

Whenever I see my brother with that glum and [1] _____ expression on his face, I am completely [2] _____. After all, he seems to live in an [3] _____ world, so what does he have to be upset about? He has [4] _____ ability to achieve almost anything he wants to. He is that [5] _____ among men, a scholar-athlete. No matter the competition, either in sports or school, the team he is on will always [6] _____. I think that sometimes he feels that people's expectations of him [7] _____ his talents. Since he is so [8] _____ and responsible, he hates to let anyone down.

Read the following passage. Then, complete the activities.

Many modern readers are quick to say they are baffled by poetry. They consider poetry a confusing and frustrating way to express an idea. Readers worry that they won't comprehend the figurative language that a poet uses, or that the structure of the phrases will exceed their ability to understand, leaving them bewildered.

At its origins, poetry is simply a way to pass down stories. In the earliest poems, the rhyming phrases and rhythmic patterns helped people memorize the words. Thus, it made it easier to take the information from village to village. In this way, epics such as *The Odyssey* were passed across miles and down through generations.

It is unfortunate that so many people avoid poetry. In fact, poetry can be the ideal art form to express emotions. For many poets, poetry is not only the best but the only way to bring a thought to life.

Understanding poetry may not come easily at first. It takes an earnest effort, not just a quick, insincere first reading. To really discover the layers of meaning in a poem may take time and thought. But it is worth the struggle to prevail and finally understand a poem.

Many people insist that they have never read poetry that they enjoy, and it is a rarity for them to find a poem that evokes a response. If people would abandon their sullen and negative attitude that poetry is a waste of time, they would surely be happily surprised to find an ample number of poets whose work impresses and inspires them.

1. Circle the words that give a clue to the meaning of baffled. Then write a sentence using the word *baffled*.

2. Underline the phrase that tells what readers are worried that poetry will exceed. Then give a word or phrase that means the same as *exceed*.

3. Circle the word that gives a clue to the meaning of ideal. Then underline the phrases that tell what poets think poetry is *ideal* for.

4. Underline the word that means the opposite of earnest. Then give a word or phrase that is a synonym for *earnest*.

5. Underline the phrase that tells what it will take to prevail. Then write a new sentence using the word *prevail*.

6. Underline the phrase that tells what some people think is a rarity. Give a word or phrase that means the same as *rarity*.

7. Circle the word that gives a clue to the meaning of sullen. Then circle the word that is an antonym for *sullen*.

8. Underline the phrase that tells what people will find an ample number of. Then give a word or phrase that means the opposite of *ample*.

My Last Dutchess
Robert Browning

Summary As the poem begins, the Duke is showing a man a painting of the Duke's first wife, who is now dead. The man is an agent representing the father of the woman the Duke hopes to marry. The Duke tells the man that his first wife was "Too easily impressed" by whatever she saw or by whatever anyone did for her. He did not like the way she seemed to rank his "gift" of a great family "name" as equal to "anybody's gift." The Duke "gave commands;/Then all smiles stopped together." The two men begin to leave. The Duke tells the agent that he knows his demands for an adequate dowry, property due to him as the groom, will be met by the new bride's father.

Note-taking Guide

Use the chart shown to determine the meaning and inferences of the speaker's words and actions.

Words/Actions of Speaker	Meaning	Inferences
"That's my last Duchess painted on the wall, . . ."		

My Last Duchess
Robert Browning

The Duke of Ferrara is an Italian
nobleman in the 1500s. He has lost his first
wife after just three years of marriage. Now
he hopes to wed the daughter of another
nobleman, a Count. He is speaking to the
Count's representative about the planned
marriage.

♦ ♦ ♦

That's my last Duchess painted on the wall,
Looking as if she were alive. I call
That piece a wonder, now: Frà Pandolf's[1]
    hands
Worked busily a day, and there she stands.

♦ ♦ ♦

The Duke explains that the joy on the
Duchess's face did not come only from her
husband's presence.

♦ ♦ ♦

                        She had
A heart—how shall I say?—too soon made
    glad,
Too easily impressed; she liked whate'er
She looked on, and her looks went
    everywhere.

♦ ♦ ♦

    Everything pleased her—the Duke's
love, the setting sun, a small gift, even the
mule she rode.

♦ ♦ ♦

    She thanked men—good! but thanked
Somehow—I know not how—as if she ranked
My gift of a nine-hundred-years-old name
With anybody's gift.

♦ ♦ ♦

Literary Analysis

1. Who is the speaker of this
   dramatic monologue?

   _____

2. Who is the person spoken to?

   _____

3. Explain the situation that
   brings the two together.

   _____

   _____

Reading Check

Read the underlined passage.
How did the Duchess displease
the Duke?

_____

_____

_____

---

1. **Frà Pandolf's** work of Brother Pandolf, an imaginary painter.

© Pearson Education

Stop to Reflect

Do you think the commands had anything to do with the smiles stopping? Circle yes or no, and then explain your opinion.

yes   no

_____

_____

_____

Reading Strategy

In "Life in a Love," the speaker expresses a deep and enduring love. **Contrast** the type of love expressed by the speaker of "Life in a Love" with the type of love expressed by the speaker of "My Last Duchess."

_____

_____

_____

Her attitude disgusted the Duke. But he would not lower himself to correct something so small. He is a man who never stoops.

♦ ♦ ♦

          Oh sir, she smiled, no doubt,
Whene'er I passed her; but who passed without
Much the same smile? <u>This grew; I gave commands;</u>
<u>Then all smiles stopped together.</u> There she stands
As if alive. Will 't please you rise?

♦ ♦ ♦

As they head downstairs, the Duke mentions the Count's daughter's fine dowry, or property she will bring to the marriage. He also points out a bronze statue of the Roman sea god Neptune.

♦ ♦ ♦

          Notice Neptune, though,
Taming a sea horse, thought a <u>rarity</u>,
Which Claus of Innsbruck[2] cast in bronze for me!

Vocabulary Development

rarity (RAYR uh tee) *n.* something unusual and valuable

2. **Claus of Innsbruck** an imaginary Austrian sculptor.

Life in a Love • Love Among the Ruins
Robert Browning

Sonnet 43
Elizabeth Barrett Browning

Summaries These poems look at romantic love from different angles. **"Life in a Love"** features a love-struck speaker who explains that he will follow his beloved forever. In **Porphyria's Lover,** the narrator tells the reader about an encounter he had with Porphyria one rainy evening. In **Sonnet 43,** the speaker describes her unending love for her beloved.

Note-taking Guide
Use this chart to record your ideas about how each speaker feels about love. Put a checkmark (✔) in the boxes that apply to that speaker. Categories may apply to more than one poem.

Speaker	Believes in love forever	Believes in love that will continue after death	Believes that his love is greater than even a great civilization	Believes that love hurts those who love
"Life in a Love"				
"Porphyria's Lover"				
Sonnet 43				

My Last Duchess • Life in a Love • Love Among the Ruins • Sonnet 43

1. **Literary Analysis:** Because a **dramatic monologue** reveals the thoughts and feelings of a speaker, it can tell a great deal about that speaker. Describe two details that you learn about the speaker in "My Last Duchess," based on his dramatic monologue.

_____

_____

2. **Literary Analysis:** Use this chart to analyze the places at which a speaker would naturally pause in lines 14–16 of "My Last Duchess."

Line 14	Her hus-	-band's pre-	-sence on-	-ly, called	that spot
Natural pauses					
Line 15	Of joy	into	the Duch	-ess' cheek;	perhaps
Natural pauses					
Line 16	Frá Pan	-dolf chanced	to say	"Her man-	-tle laps
Natural pauses					

3. **Reading Strategy: Compare and contrast** the love expressed by the speakers of "Life in a Love" and "Sonnet 43."

_____

_____

? Writing About the Essential Question

What is the relationship of the writer to tradition? Which speakers in these poems are most dramatic? Explain.

_____

_____

from Hard Times

Literary Analysis

A novel is a long work of fiction with a plot, or sequence of events. Many novels have multiple settings in which the events occur. Novels also express one or more themes, or general messages about life.

Although novels contain imaginary characters and events, they may include historical, settings, characters, and events. The novels written by Charles Dickens **evaluate the ethical and social influences** of Victorian society. Dickens's novels usually give clues to his philosophical assumptions. For example, the novels call attention to the problems of Victorian society, such as the tendency of schools to be run like factories and the extremes of poverty during the period. As you read the excerpt from *Hard Times*, think about how Dickens's philosophical assumptions influenced his characterization.

Reading Strategy

All forms of writing have a purpose. For example, the author may write to address the ethical and social problems of society. You should **analyze the author's purpose** to understand the meaning of a literary work. Look for clues to the author's purpose by examining the details in the work. Note the context, and consider the author's purpose for including certain details and events. Keep track of them by using a chart like the one below.

Word List A

Study these words from the selections. Then, complete the activities.

contradiction [EM fuh SYZD] *v.* stressed something as being important; made something stand out

In contradiction *to his previous answer, Tony now said he could come to the party.*

discard [dis KAHRD] *v.* to throw away, get rid of

Be sure to discard *the gum wrapper in the appropriate place.*

dismal [DIZ muhl] *adj.* cheerless, gloomy; poorly performed

The dismal *weather kept us indoors all afternoon.*

emphasized [EM fuh SYZD] *v.* stressed something as being important; made something stand out

The judge emphasized *his call for silence by banging the gavel.*

feeble [FEE buhl] *adj.* physically or mentally weak; lacking strength

Two weeks of fever left Rhonda feeble *and tired.*

immense [i MENS] *adj.* huge, extremely large

An immense *pile of snow blocked the entrance to the parking lot.*

maim [MAYM] *v.* to wound someone very seriously

Firecrackers have been known to maim *people on the Fourth of July.*

reign [RAYN] *n.* period during which a monarch, a royal power, or an authority rules a country

The American Revolution took place during the reign *of King George III.*

Exercise A

Fill in the blanks, using each word from Word List A only once.

Although we think of kings and queens as something from the distant past, monarchies still exist around the world today. In England, for example, although their political leaders are elected, a monarch continues to

[1] _____ in Buckingham Palace. When the United States broke ties with

England in 1776, the Founders thought that monarchy and democracy stood

in [2] _____ to each other. They chose to [3] _____ the monarchy,

and instead [4] _____ a system in which everyone is equal. This was an

[5] _____ change, and it had a profound impact on the French, who soon

overthrew their own royal family. Unfortunately for the French upper classes,

revolutionaries there left a [6] _____ trail of violence and death. They saw

their rulers as [7] _____ and useless, and used these views to justify

their desire to [8] _____ or execute their rulers.

Read the following passage. Then, complete the activities.

During Queen Victoria's long reign, England underwent radical changes, including changes in the field of education. Schooling, which was previously only for the wealthy, began to be available to all children. Previously, the poor grew up unable to read or write. They were sent to work as soon as they were able, in order to help provide for their families. The dismal, bleak conditions in which they worked were an expected part of life for most children.

Victorian education emphasized a specific course of study. It stressed reading, writing, and arithmetic—known as the three Rs, based on the initial sound of each word. Repetition and memorization were key factors in a Victorian student's school day.

Classroom order was kept with strict discipline. It was not unusual for students to be struck with a cane or a ruler for an infraction of the rules. Teachers would never tolerate a student who disagreed with them or offered a contradiction to anything they said. Though perhaps the students were not beaten hard enough to maim them, it is not overstating the case to say that students received painful beatings on a regular basis.

Due to the immense expense involved, Victorian students did not write on paper and then discard their assignments in the trash when they were finished. Rather, they wrote on slates that could be wiped clean and then reused. For some lessons, boys and girls learned together. However, girls were considered too feeble of mind to handle the extra mathematics and science that the boys often studied. Instead, girls studied needlework and other household skills that they would most likely need later in life.

Victorian schools certainly bear little resemblance to their modern counterparts. Nonetheless, they represent an important step in the development of a universal system of education.

1. Circle the words that tell whose reign is described. Then, explain the difference between *reign* and term.

2. Circle the word that gives a clue to the meaning of dismal. Give a word that means the opposite of *dismal*.

3. Underline the phrase that tells what Victorian education emphasized. Use the word *emphasized* in a new sentence.

4. Circle the word that gives a clue to the meaning of contradiction. Then, give another word for *contradiction*.

5. Underline the word or phrase that gives a clue to the meaning of maim. Give a synonym for *maim*.

6. Circle the word that tells what was immense. Then, use the word *immense* in a sentence.

7. Underline the phrase that tells what Victorian students did not discard. Give a word or phrase that means the opposite of *discard*.

8. Circle the word that tells who was considered feeble. Give a synonym for *feeble*.

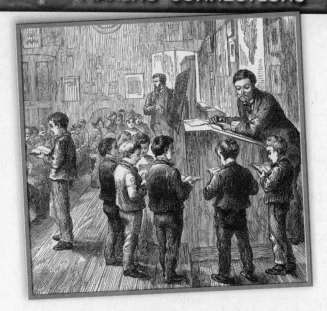

from Hard Times
Charles Dickens

Summary Mr. Gradgrind, who runs a school, lectures its students on the importance of facts. He calls on a girl named Sissy Jupe and, learning her name, tells her to change it to Cecilia. On hearing her father works with horses, he asks her to define a horse. She cannot do so. Then, a boy drily defines a horse as "Quadruped. Graminivorous. Forty teeth . . ." and wins Gradgrind's approval. A teacher named M'Choakumchild teaches the students in such a way as to discourage the exercise of imagination.

Note-taking Guide

Read the purpose in the chart below. Then, find details in the text that support that purpose. Write the details in the right-hand column.

Purpose	Details That Support Purpose
• To humorously criticize the philosophy called utilitarianism (yoo til uh TER ee un iz um), which emphasizes facts and discourages imagination	

from Hard Times
Charles Dickens

In the industrial city of Coketown, England, a rich retired businessman named Gradgrind has started a school for poor children. Gradgrind believes that facts and logic must rule all activities. He feels that everything can be weighed and measured and that material things will make people happy. He explains his ideas when he meets with a government official and the teacher he has hired, Mr. M'Choakumchild.

◆ ◆ ◆

"Now, what I want is, Facts. Teach these boys and girls nothing but Facts. Facts alone are wanted in life. Plant nothing else, and root out everything else. You can only form the minds of reasoning animals upon Facts: nothing else will ever be of any service to them. This is the principle on which I bring up my own children, and this is the principle on which I bring up these children. Stick to Facts, sir!"

The scene was a plain, bare, monotonous vault of a schoolroom.

◆ ◆ ◆

The children are seated in number order. Mr. Gradgrind thinks of them as little pitchers, waiting to have facts poured into them. Now he addresses the class.

◆ ◆ ◆

"Girl number twenty," said Mr. Gradgrind, squarely pointing with his square forefinger, "I don't know that girl. Who is that girl?"

"Sissy Jupe, sir," explained number twenty, blushing, standing up, and curtseying.

"Sissy is not a name," said Mr. Gradgrind. "Don't call yourself Sissy. Call yourself Cecilia."

"It's father as calls me Sissy, sir," returned the young girl in a trembling voice, and with another curtsey.

© Pearson Education

Literary Analysis

Coke is a coal product used as a fuel in industry or left over when other fuels burn.

1. What might Dickens want us to think a city called Coketown is like? Circle two words.

polluted   wealthy   sunny
lonely   green   ugly

2. List one **ethical or social influence** of Victorian society that Dickens might **evaluate** in a novel with this setting.

_____

_____

Reading Check

What is the one thing that Mr. Gradgrind wants his school to teach? Circle your answer in the bracketed passage.

Reading Strategy

Circle the letter of the choice below that best states the **author's purpose.**

a. to reveal Sissy's character
b. to poke fun at building styles of the day
c. to criticize millionaires who fund ugly schools but live in lovely homes
d. to show how schools like this stifle individual expression

Read Fluently

Read aloud Mr. Gradgrind's words in the underlined passage. Try to use the tone of voice he might have used. How do you think Sissy felt when she heard these words?

_____

_____

_____

Reading Strategy

Put a check in front of each choice that might be the **author's purpose** in this bracketed passage. Check at least two.

____ to introduce the character of Bitzer to readers

____ to poke fun at the facts-only method of teaching

____ to help readers understand what a horse is

____ to poke fun at Mr. Gradgrind

"Then he has no business to do it," said Mr. Gradgrind. "Tell him he mustn't. Cecilia Jupe. Let me see. What is your father?"

"He belongs to the horse-riding, if you please, sir."

◆   ◆   ◆

Sissy's father rides horses in the circus. Mr. Gradgrind does not approve of this job. He tells Sissy to say that her father trains and shoes horses and treats them when they are ill. He continues:

◆   ◆   ◆

"Give me your definition of a horse."

(Sissy Jupe thrown into the greatest alarm by this demand.)

"Girl number twenty unable to define a horse!" said Mr. Gradgrind, for the general behoof[1] of all the little pitchers. "Girl number twenty possessed of no facts, in reference to one of the commonest of animals! Some boy's definition of a horse. Bitzer, yours."

◆   ◆   ◆

Bitzer is the sort of "pitcher" Mr. Gradgrind likes. He has an excellent memory and has absorbed many facts. He is a pale, freckled boy with cold eyes.

◆   ◆   ◆

"Quadruped.[2] Graminivorous.[3] Forty teeth, namely twenty-four grinders, four eye-teeth, and twelve incisive. Sheds coat in the spring; in marshy countries, sheds hoofs, too. Hoofs hard, but requiring to be shod with iron.[4] Age known by marks in mouth." Thus (and much more) Bitzer.

"Now girl number twenty," said Mr. Gradgrind. "You know what a horse is."

◆   ◆   ◆

1. **behoof** (bi HUF) *n.* behalf; benefit.
2. **Quadruped** (KWAHD ruh ped) *n.* an animal with four legs.
3. **Graminivorous** (gram uh NIV uh ruhs) *adj.* grass-eating.
4. **shod with iron** shoed with iron horseshoes to protect the horse's feet.

The other visitor now steps forward. He is a government official who has spent his life following petty rules and dull routine.

"Now, let me ask you girls and boys. Would you paper a room with <u>representations</u> of a horse?"

After a pause, one half of the children cried in chorus, "Yes, sir!" Upon which the other half, seeing in the gentleman's face that Yes was wrong, cried out in chorus, "No, sir!"—as the custom is, in these examinations.

"Of course, No. Why wouldn't you?"

The children have no idea. The visitor points out that horses never walk up and down rooms in reality. So it makes no sense to have them do it on wallpaper. Then he asks if the students would get a carpet with pictures of flowers on it. By now, most of the children know they should answer "No." A few still say "Yes," including Sissy Jupe.

Sissy blushed, and stood up.

"So you would carpet your room—or your husband's room, if you were a grown woman, and had a husband—with representations of flowers, would you," said the gentleman. "Why would you?"

"If you please, sir, I am very fond of flowers," returned the girl.

"And is that why you would put tables and chairs upon them, and have people walking over them with heavy boots?"

Stop to Reflect

What does Dickens recognize about the way students often answer questions? Circle the letter of the correct choice.

a. They often argue with the teacher.

b. They do better if the subject is interesting to them.

c. They do better if they are taught only facts.

d. They tell the teacher what he or she wants to hear.

Reading Check

What is Sissy's reason for wanting a carpet with pictures of flowers?

_____

_____

_____

_____

Vocabulary Development

representations (rep ruh zen TAY shuhnz) *n.* pictures; illustrations

© Pearson Education

Literary Analysis

The *M'* in the teacher's name is an old way of writing Mc.

1. What does the rest of the teacher's name suggest? Explain below.

Choakumchild:

_____

_____

2. What **ethical or social influence** in Victorian society does Dickens use the character of Mr. M'Choakumchild to **evaluate?**

_____

_____

Reading Check 📖

Explain what the underlined statement means by completing the sentence below.

If Mr. M'Choakumchild only

_____

_____

he would be

_____

_____

"It wouldn't hurt them, sir. They wouldn't crush and <u>wither</u> if you please, sir. They would be the pictures of what was very pretty and pleasant, and I would fancy—"

"Ay, ay, ay! but you mustn't fancy," cried the gentleman, quite <u>elated</u> by coming so happily to his point. "That's it! You are never to fancy."

"You are not, Cecilia Jupe," Thomas Gradgrind solemnly repeated, "to do anything of that kind."

"Fact, fact, fact!" said the gentleman. And "Fact, fact, fact!" repeated Thomas Gradgrind.

♦ ♦ ♦

The official tells Sissy to forget the word *fancy,* for it is the very opposite of *fact.* Then, he asks Mr. M'Choakumchild to begin teaching the first lesson.

♦ ♦ ♦

So, Mr. M'Choakumchild began in his best manner. He and some one hundred and forty other schoolmasters had been lately turned at the same time, in the same factory, on the same principles, like so many pianoforte[5] legs.

♦ ♦ ♦

Mr. M'Choakumchild has learned the facts in a long list of subjects. He knows all about language, geography, and science.

♦ ♦ ♦

<u>If he had only learnt a little less, how infinitely better he might have taught much more!</u>

Vocabulary Development

wither (WITH uhr) *v.* shrivel up; dry out, wrinkle, and die

elated (i LAY tid) *adj.* excited

---

5. **pianoforte** (PYAN oh fawrt) *n.* an old term for a piano.

from Hard Times

1. **Literary Analysis:** In *Hard Times*, the setting is a "plain, bare, monotonous vault of a schoolroom." How does Dickens use this description to **evaluate the ethical and social influences** of Victorian society?

   _____

   _____

2. **Literary Analysis:** Choose a passage from the selection, and then complete the chart below.

Passage	Intended Effect on Reader	Intended Message

3. **Reading Strategy:** To **analyze an author's purpose,** look at details and think about why the writer chose to include them. In *Hard Times*, what is the author's purpose in naming the instructor Mr. M'Choakumchild?

   _____

   _____

Writing About the Essential Question

How does literature shape or reflect society? What values does Dickens believe a system of education should teach? Explain.

   _____

   _____

Web Sites

About Web Sites

A **Web site** is a place on the Internet with its own address, or URL (Universal Resource Locator). You can move from one page to another on a Web site by clicking your mouse on a picture, a "button," or a highlighted or underlined phrase called a *link*.

If you read *Hard Times*, you may want to learn more about its author, Charles Dickens. The Web site that follows describes a museum that celebrates Dickens. Museum Web sites provide many types of information, including:

- a description of the museum and its exhibits
- hours of operation and contact information
- virtual tours
- a museum map

Reading Skill

Home pages and brochures are designed for quick location of important information, allowing you to preview content without extensive reading. You can **predict the content and purpose** of a document by scanning these *text features*:

- simple section headings, sometimes in FAQ style, with frequently asked questions and answers
- introductions providing basic background information
- captions or explanations of graphics

Use a chart like this one to guide your review of the documents.

Checklist	Yes/No	Suggested Improvements
Was the information well organized?	☐ / ☐	
Did the headings or title explain how to use it?	☐ / ☐	
Were there photos or art?	☐ / ☐	
Was the information accurate?	☐ / ☐	
Were links or references included?	☐ / ☐	
Was the site or brochure helpful?	☐ / ☐	

URL goes here

These links to other parts of the Web site help users quickly locate the information they need.

The Dickens Museum Home Page and Virtual Tour Link *London*

The Museum	Private Views	Books & Gifts	Media
Opening Hours	Events	Events	Research
Find Us	Teachers	Hire the Museum	Links
History	Access	Exhibitions	Access
Groups	Learning	Support	

The front of 48 Doughty Street.

The Museum

The Charles Dickens Museum in London is the world's most important collection of material relating to the great Victorian novelist and social commentator. The only surviving London home of Dickens (from 1837 until 1839) was opened as a Museum in 1925 and is still welcoming visitors from all over the world in an authentic and inspiring surrounding.

On four floors, visitors can see paintings, rare editions, manuscripts, original furniture and many items relating to the life of one of the most popular and beloved personalities of the Victorian age.

Gifts and Books
Here you will find gifts for all the family as well as a wide range of books by or about Charles Dickens.

Support
Click here to find out how you can support the Museum in its many educational, conservational and curatorial activities.

Events
For our program of events and educational activities, please click here.

Hire the Museum
The Museum can be hired for private functions, performances, soirees, book launches and many other social occasions. Click here to find out more.

This introduction provides a short history of the museum and a brief description of its holdings. To the left, you can see a photograph of the museum's entrance.

URL goes here

The Charles Dickens Museum *Virtual Tour*

| Main | Museum Map | Museum Guide | Tour Tutorial |

© Adam Woolfitt/CORBIS

Basement
Library
Still room
Main Hallway
Wash House
Wine Cellar
Stairs to Ground Floor

Ground Floor
Front Hallway
Dining Room
Morning Room
Back Parlour
Stairs to First Floor

First Floor
Drawing Room
Study
Stairs to Second Floor

Second Floor
Dressing Room
Charles and Catherine
Bedroom
Mary Hogarth Room

Welcome to the Virtual Tour of the Charles Dickens Museum!

What follows is a photographic tour of the former home of Charles Dickens, located at 48 Doughty Street, London. You can explore the house much as you would in an actual visit, going between rooms and focusing on items that catch your interest. This tour is meant to provide to you a feeling of actually exploring the house, from the comfort of any computer with access to the Internet.

As you make your way about the house you may notice some glare from light fixtures and windows present in pictures. This is a result of the fact that the purpose is to provide an accurate account of what a visitor to the actual museum experiences, and glare and reflections would be present in a real-life visit. It is also important to note that since the museum is constantly acquiring new items related to Charles Dickens, not everything currently on display at the museum will be present in this virtual tour. This tour was created during March and April of 2005, and since then some items may have been added, moved or removed.

The requirements to view this tour are minimal. It relies on providing an immersive experience through the use of pictures and text. File sizes are small enough so that visitors with low speed connections should be able to view it without problems, but please be patient, especially when viewing the panoramic photos.

To the left of this main section, you will see a column of links. These links will allow you to jump to specific rooms within the museum, and will be visible no matter what page within the tour you are currently viewing. If you are unsure of where to begin, you can start in The Morning Room and then follow the links at the bottom of each room's page. If you require more help making your way through the museum, check the tutorial which is also linked at the top.

The tour was developed at no cost to the museum by four college students in an effort to help The Charles Dickens Museum comply with the Disability Discrimination Act. Enjoy your visit!

© 2005 Charles Dickens Museum

Users can take a virtual tour of the museum by clicking on the links in the left column. The text in the main column provides background on the tour.

ANDALUSIA

home of Flannery O'Connor

Milledgeville, Georgia

Andalusia is open on Monday, Tuesday and Saturday from 10:00 a.m. to 4:00 p.m. or by appointment. Guided trolly tours can be arranged by calling the Milledgeville, Baldwin County Visitors Center at 1-800-653-1804

2628 N. Columbia Street (Hwy 441 N)
Milledgeville, Georgia
www.andalusiafarm.org   478-454-4029

Where was Flannery O'Connor born?

Flannery O'Connor was born in Savannah, Georgia on March 25, 1925, the only child of Edward F. O'Connor, Jr. and Regina Cline O'Connor.

Where did Flannery O'Connor attend school and college?

O'Connor attended St. Vincent's Grammar School and Sacred Heart Parochial School in Savannah, Georgia; St. Joseph's Parochial School and North Fulton High School in Atlanta, Georgia; Peabody High School and Georgia State College for Women in Milledgeville, Georgia; and the State University of Iowa in Iowa City.

How long did Flannery O'Connor live at Andalusia?

Flannery O'Connor lived at Andalusia with her mother, Regina Cline O'Connor, from early 1951 until Flannery's death in 1964. She completed all her published books while living here.

Why is the farm called Andalusia?

In the fall of 1946, before the death of Dr. Bernard Cline, Flannery O'Connor met on a bus to Atlanta a descendant of the original Hawkins family that owned Andalusia. It was the descendant who told her the original name of the place in the 19th century was Andalusia. She wrote her mother, and when her uncle Bernard heard of it, he was pleased and liked the name. From then on the name was Andalusia.

What happened to Flannery's peacocks?

None of the descendants of O'Connor's domestic flock has survived at the farm. Regina Cline O'Connor gave two pair of peafowl to Stone Mountain Mansion, one pair to Our Lady of Perpetual Help Cancer Home in Atlanta, and another pair to the Monastery of the Holy Spirit near Conyers, Georgia.

Andalusia is the picturesque farm where American author Flannery O'Connor lived from 1951 until her death from lupus in 1964. Listed on the National Register of Historic Places, Andalusia is brought to life on many occasions in O'Connor's published letters. In the 1950s Andalusia was a dairy farm operated by O'Connor's mother, Regina Cline O'Connor. The agricultural setting of Andalusia provided for O'Connor not only a place to live and write, but also a landscape in which to set her fiction.

The farm complex consists of the 19th century Main House, Jack and Louise Hill's house (the home of farm workers), the cow barn, an equipment shed, the milk-processing shed, an additional smaller barn, a parking garage, a water tower, an old well house (storage), a horse stable, a pump house, several small tenant houses, a small pond, and nature trails.

Flannery O'Connor did not live a reclusive life at Andalusia. She traveled for various speaking engagements and made frequent visits into town for dining, social events, and to attend Mass regularly at Sacred Heart Catholic Church. She routinely wrote every morning until noon in her downstairs bedroom/study and spent her afternoons and evenings tending to her peafowl and other domestic birds or entertaining visitors.

Publications by Flannery O'Connor:

Wise Blood — 1952

A Good Man Is Hard To Find — 1955

The Violent Bear It Away — 1960

Everything That Rises Must Converge — 1965

Mystery and Manners — 1969

The Complete Stories, winner of the 1971 National Book Award for Fiction.

The Habit of Being — 1979, winner of the National Book Critics Circle Award.

Flannery O'Connor: Collected Works (Library of America) — 1988

The brochure provides background information about the house and the author.

Andalusia is located just north of the Wal-Mart shopping center on Hwy 441 North of Milledgeville

The map helps visitors planning a trip to the site.

Thinking About the Web Site

1. Which button on the first page of the Web site would you click for information about the museum's hours of operation?

_____

_____

2. On which floor of the museum would you find Dickens's study?

_____

_____

TALK ABOUT IT **Reading Skill**

3. What can you predict about the content of the Web site from its name on the home page?

_____

_____

_____

4. What is the purpose of the brochure about Andalusia?

_____

_____

_____

WRITE ABOUT IT > **Timed Writing: Persuasive Essay (25 minutes)**

Write a persuasive essay convincing a friend of the value of visiting museums and parks focused on authors' lives. Use the information you learned from the Web site home page and museum brochure to support your argument. Allow about five minutes for planning your essay. Then, use about fifteen minutes for writing and five minutes for reviewing and revising.

from Jane Eyre

Literary Analysis

Authors often make **assumptions** about the people, places, and events about which they write. An assumption is something that someone believes to be true, whether or not evidence supports that belief. People make assumptions based on their experiences, their feelings and opinions, their personal preferences, and their cultural heritage. An author's assumptions shape the way that he or she portrays a particular character, an institution or a government, or an entire society.

Reading Strategy

To understand how an author's assumptions affect his or writing, you must identify and **analyze assumptions** as you read. To analyze assumptions, look for opinions and emotions in a selection. Pause to consider whether the author has described a particular person, group of people, place, institution, or idea in a positive or negative way. Then, think about the author's background, cultural heritage, and position in society. Ask:

- How might this author's experiences have influenced his or her assumptions?
- What does the author want me to believe based on his or her assumptions?

Use the chart to record and analyze an assumption found in the selection.

Assumption	Analysis

Word List A

Study these words from the selections. Then, complete the activities.

abyss [uh BIS] *n.* a bottomless space or gulf; anything extremely deep
At the canyon's edge, Barrett looked over the railing into the abyss.

commendations [kahm en DAY shuns] *n.* praise, approval
Liz received commendations from the mayor and the police for bravery.

crevices [CREV is ez] *n.* narrow cracks or openings
During the drought, crevices appeared in the dry lawn.

gleeful [GLEE fuhl] *adj.* full of joy; delighted
Gleeful laughter could be heard from the children's room.

merit [MER it] *n.* value; excellence; worth
Although his first book was poorly written, the second had some merit.

ominous [AHM uh nuhs] *adj.* threatening; menacing
An ominous silence preceded the explosion.

punctual [PUNK choo uhl] *adj.* strictly on time; prompt
Travis knew it was important to be punctual for his job interview.

retained [ri TAYND] *v.* kept hold of; remembered; hired
Ellie retained only random facts from the lecture.

Exercise A

Fill in the blanks, using each word from Word List A only once.

As a child, Marcus approached the world with a [1] _____ smile. He was always [2] _____, arriving in class well before the bell rang. Because he took time with his papers, they usually had considerable [3] _____, and he received more than his share of [4] _____ from teachers for his good work. In high school, however, small [5] _____ began to appear in his apparent perfection. Although for the most part he [6] _____ his positive attitude, there were [7] _____ signs that could change at any moment. Fortunately, his basic optimism led him to see that adulthood was not the frightening [8] _____ that it seemed to be.

1. Circle the words that give clues to the meaning of abyss. Use the word *abyss* in a new sentence.

2. Underline the phrase that gives a clue to the meaning of gleeful. Give a word that means the opposite of *gleeful.*

3. Underline the phrase that tells where the crevices were. Give another word for *crevices.*

4. Circle the word that mean nearly the opposite of commendations. Give an example of an action that might receive *commendations.*

5. Underline the phrase that tells what held merit for Julia's parents. Give a synonym for *merit.*

6. Circle the word that tells what sound was ominous. Then, use the word *ominous* in a sentence.

7. Underline the phrase that tells what Julia retained. Give a word or phrase that means the opposite of *retained.*

8. Circle the word that gives a clue to the meaning of punctual. Give an antonym for *punctual.*

Read the following passage. Then, complete the activities.

Julia stared at the blank page in front of her. The paper seemed so vast and empty that Julia felt she was looking into an abyss. Usually writing was a gleeful experience, the high point of her day, but for the past hour Julia had been unable to bring her story to a satisfactory conclusion.

Her writing, so vital to her, was nevertheless a secret from her family. She had been compelled to hide the manuscript, stuffing its pages into the crevices in the attic's unfinished walls. So far, the fis¬sures in the wall had kept her work safe. Julia knew she would receive no commendations from her parents for her creativity. Rather, they would disapprove, and would be disappointed that their daughter shirked her household duties for such a frivolous activity. They saw no merit in a well-turned phrase or an imaginative plot twist. It was their belief, and, indeed, that of all society, that a well-raised girl should turn her fingers to needlework or piano practice, not the quill.

Suddenly Julia heard the ominous creaking of the bottom stair. Filled with dread, she had no doubt that the heavy tread belonged to her father. Julia, well practiced at hiding her hobby, quickly covered the evidence with a blotter and pulled out the tattered copy of Jane Eyre. She retained her composure, so she wouldn't look guilty and raise anyone's suspicions.

"Julia, have you forgotten the time? I expect my children to be punctual for meals," said her father in an annoyed tone.

"I was just coming down—but I just couldn't stop in the middle of the chapter," fibbed Julia. As she followed her father back downstairs, Julia breathed a quiet sigh of relief that her secret was safe for another day.

from Jane Eyre
Charlotte Brontë

Summary In this chapter of the novel, Jane is at a boarding school for orphan girls called Lowood. She describes the harsh physical conditions, the lack of sufficient food for the girls, and the cruel way in which one of the teachers, Miss Scatcherd, treats a girl named Helen Burns. Later, Jane has the opportunity to speak with Helen in private. Jane is surprised by Helen's acceptance of the wrongs done to her.

Note-taking Guide

Use the chart below to compare and contrast the characters of Jane Eyre and Helen Burns.

	Jane Eyre	Helen Burns
Similarities		
Differences		

Literary Analysis

On the list below, check the **assumptions** that the author may have about schools like Lowood. Circle the details that help make this criticism.

____ Lighting is poor.

____ Heating is poor.

____ Food portions are skimpy.

____ Clothing is falling apart.

Reading Check

Why is it impossible for the girls to wash on this morning?

_____

_____

_____

from Jane Eyre
Charlotte Brontë

After Jane Eyre's parents die, her selfish aunt sends her to a school for poor girls called Lowood. The school is a grim place with a strict routine that Jane does not like. Little money is spent on the girls' food or comfort. Though it is January, there is almost no heat. Jane, who is telling the story, has been at Lowood for two days.

◆ ◆ ◆

The next day <u>commenced</u> as before, getting up and dressing by rushlight;[1] but this morning we were <u>obliged</u> to <u>dispense</u> with the ceremony of washing: the water in the pitchers was frozen. . . . Before the long hour and a half of prayers and Bible reading was over, I felt ready to <u>perish</u> with cold. Breakfast time came at last. . . . How small my portion seemed! I wished it had been doubled.

◆ ◆ ◆

Jane is unfamiliar with the school routine. She is glad when her lessons end at three o'clock and she is given a hem to sew. But some older girls are still reading with Miss Scatcherd, the history teacher. The girls are seated with the best reader first. The best reader is a girl who spoke kindly to Jane the day before. Jane is surprised when the teacher suddenly sends this girl from first to last place for no very good reason.

◆ ◆ ◆

Vocabulary Development

commenced (kuh MENST) *v.* began

obliged (uh BLYJD) *v.* forced

dispense (dis PENS) *v.* give up

perish (PER ish) *v.* die

---

1. **rushlight** cheap, smelly, smoky lighting obtained from burning rushes, or reeds, twisted together and dipped in wax.

Miss Scatcherd continued to make her an object of constant notice: she was continually addressing to her such phrases as the following:—

"Burns" (such it seems was her name: the girls here, were all called by their surnames,[2] as boys are elsewhere), "Burns, you are standing on the side of your shoe, turn your toes out immediately." "Burns, you poke your chin most unpleasantly, draw it in." "Burns, I insist on your holding your head up: I will not have you before me in that attitude," etc. etc.

A chapter having been read through twice, the books were closed and the girls examined. . . . Every little difficulty was solved instantly when it reached Burns: her memory seemed to have retained the substance of the whole lesson, and she was ready with answers on every point. I kept expecting that Miss Scatcherd would praise her attention; but, instead of that, she suddenly cried out:—

"You dirty, disagreeable girl! you have never cleaned your nails this morning!"

Burns made no answer: I wondered at her silence.

"Why," thought I, "does she not explain that she could neither clean her nails nor wash her face, as the water was frozen?"

♦ ♦ ♦

Jane is called away by another teacher. That teacher needs help winding thread for sewing. When Jane returns to her seat, Miss Scatcherd has just sent Burns to get a bundle of twigs to be used as a punishment rod.

♦ ♦ ♦

Vocabulary Development

addressing (uh DRES ing) *v.* talking to

2. **surnames** (SUR naymz) last names; family names.

TAKE NOTES

Reading Strategy

What does the author want you to believe about Burns?

_____

_____

What does the author want you to believe about Miss Scatcherd?

_____

_____

Reading Check

Who seems to be Miss Scatcherd's brightest student? Write your answer here:

_____

Then, circle the details that tell you.

Read Fluently

Read Miss Scatcherd's words aloud in the tone you think she might use. Why do you think she is so mean to Burns?

_____

_____

_____

Stop to Reflect

Which phrase below best describes Burns? Circle the letter of the best answer. Also circle the details that support your answer.

a. an obedient, accepting child
b. an angry champion of justice
c. a timid crybaby
d. a hardened, brutal girl

Why do you think Burns behaves this way?

_____

_____

_____

Reading Strategy

What does the author **assume** when she writes that Jane is angry about the way Burns is being treated?

_____

_____

_____

. . . then she quietly, and without being told, unloosed her pinafore,[3] and the teacher instantly and sharply inflicted on her neck a dozen strokes with the bunch of twigs. Not a tear rose to Burns's eye; and, while I paused from my sewing, because my fingers quivered at this spectacle with a sentiment of unavailing and impotent anger, not a feature of her <u>pensive</u> face altered its ordinary expression.

"Hardened girl!" exclaimed Miss Scatcherd, "nothing can correct you of your <u>slatternly</u> habits: carry the rod away."

Burns obeyed: I looked at her narrowly as she emerged from the book closet; she was just putting back her handkerchief into her pocket, and the trace of a tear glistened on her thin cheek.

◆ ◆ ◆

Soon it is evening play hour. This time is Jane's favorite time at school so far. Still hungry, she is glad to have a bit of bread and coffee. She then looks for Burns and finds her reading by the fireplace.

◆ ◆ ◆

I sat down by her on the floor.

"What is your name besides Burns?"

"Helen."

"Do you come a long way from here?"

"I come from a place further north; quite on the borders of Scotland."

"Will you ever go back?"

"I hope so; but nobody can be sure of the future."

Vocabulary Development
pensive (PEN siv) *adj.* serious; thoughtful
slatternly (SLAT ern lee) *adj.* like a slob; very sloppy

3. **pinafore** (PIN uh for) *n.* an overdress of light fabric resembling an apron and bib.

"You must wish to leave Lowood?"

"No: why should I? I was sent to Lowood to get an education; and it would be of no use going away until I have attained that object."

"But that teacher, Miss Scatcherd, is so cruel to you?"

"Cruel? Not at all! She is severe: she dislikes my faults."

"And if I were in your place I should dislike her: I should resist her; if she struck me with that rod, I should get it from her hand; I should break it under her nose."

"Probably you would do nothing of the sort: but if you did, Mr. Brocklehurst[4] would expel you from the school; that would be a great grief to your relations. It is far better to endure patiently a smart[5] which nobody feels but yourself, than to commit a hasty action whose evil consequences will extend to all connected with you—and, besides, the Bible bids us return good for evil."

◆ ◆ ◆

Jane does not really understand Helen's views. She feels it makes no sense to reward mean people with kindness and good behavior, for then they will never change. Yet she deeply admires Helen for holding such noble views.

◆ ◆ ◆

"You say you have faults, Helen: what are they? To me you seem very good."

"Then learn from me, not to judge by appearances: I am, as Miss Scatcherd said, slatternly; I seldom put, and never keep, things in order; I am careless; I forget rules; I read when I should learn my lessons; I have no method; and sometimes I say, like you, I cannot *bear* to be subjected to systematic arrangements.

4. **Mr. Brocklehurst** the man who runs the school.
5. **smart** pain; sting.

TAKE NOTES

Reading Strategy

Put a check in front of any **assumption** that you think the bracketed passage supports.

____ Poor girls often put up with bad treatment to get an education.

____ Family pressure forced the girls to compete to see who was smart.

____ The girls were not treated with the religious ideals that they were taught.

____ The schools were so crowded that girls were expelled for no reason.

Reading Check

Number the seven faults that Helen says she has.

Literary Analysis 🔍

1. Why do you think the monitor is mean to Helen?

She is mean because _____

_____.

2. What **assumptions** about schools does her behavior support?

Her behavior supports the assumption that in schools

_____

_____.

This is all very <u>provoking</u> to Miss Scatcherd, who is naturally neat, punctual, and particular."

"And <u>cross</u> and cruel," I added; but Helen Burns would not admit my addition: she kept silence. . . .

She was not allowed much time for <u>meditation</u>: a monitor, a great rough girl, presently came up, exclaiming in a strong Cumberland[6] accent—

"Helen Burns, if you don't go and put your drawer in order, and fold up your work this minute, I'll tell Miss Scatcherd to come and look at it!"

Vocabulary Development

provoking (pruh VOH king) *adj*. irritating

cross (KRAWS) *adj*. easily irritated; angry

meditation (med i TAY shun) *n*. deep thought

---

6. **Cumberland** (KUM ber lind) *n*. a county in northern England.

from Jane Eyre

1. **Compare and Contrast:** How does Helen's opinion of Miss Scatcherd differ from Jane's?

   _____

   _____

2. **Literary Analysis:** Record one **assumption** that the author makes in each situation listed below.

Jane's aunt sends Jane to Lowood.	
Jane and the other girls spend an hour and a half praying and reading from the Bible.	
Miss Scatcherd uses a bundle of twigs to punish Helen.	

3. **Reading Strategy:** What does the author want you to believe about girls from poor families in England at this time?

   _____

   _____

 Writing About the Essential Question

How does literature shape or reflect society? How do you think Brontë would like to reform schools like Lowood?

_____

_____

_____

Dover Beach • The Widow at Windsor • Recessional

Literary Analysis

The thoughts and emotions in a poem create the mood. The **mood** is the feeling that a poem creates. It is closely related to the poem's central message, or **theme.** Read poetry with your feelings. Respond to the emotionally charged words, and you will find your way to the poem's theme.

Reading Strategy

The mood and theme in a poem often **relate to the historical period** in which the poem was written. During the Victorian period, the British Empire experienced great scientific progress, material wealth, and power. The mood and theme in these poems portrays not only these successes, but also the difficulties that came with them.

To determine how the mood and theme relate to a particular historical period, ask:

- What language does the poet use to describe people, places, and things?
- How does the poet's language make readers feel about people, places, and times in the poem?
- What does the poem reveal about the people, places, and ideas of the period?

Use the chart to list one way in which each poem's mood relates to the Victorian period.

Poem	Mood	How the Mood Relates to the Historical Period
"Dover Beach"		
"The Widow at Windsor"		
"Recessional"		

Word List A

Study these words from the selections. Then, complete the activities.

vast [VAST] *adj.* very large; great in size
The United States is a vast country.

widow [WID oh] *n.* woman whose husband has died
The widow had many happy memories of her departed husband.

tide [TYD] *n.* the rise and fall of ocean waters each day
The high tide washed away items left on the beach.

ebb [EB] *n.* lessening or decline
She felt an ebb in her pain after taking her medicine.

fling [FLING] *v.* throw with great force
Don't fling your litter out the car window.

valiant [VAL yuhnt] *adj.* brave
The valiant hero saved many people during the hurricane.

furled [FERLD] *adj.* rolled up tightly
The awning on the storefront was furled during the storm to keep it from flapping.

retreating [ri TREET ing] *v.* going back or going away
When the rain stopped, the flood waters began retreating into the river.

Exercise A

Fill in each blank in the paragraph below using each word from Word List A only once.

As the [1] _____ walked along the beach, she looked out into the
distance at the [2] _____ ocean, which extended as far as the eye
could see. In her hand, she carried an umbrella, [3] _____ for now,
but easy to open in case a storm blew in. Lost in thought, she watched
the ocean [4] _____ come in, and she heard it [5] _____
pebbles and shells onto the shore. As she watched, she remembered
her [6] _____ husband, who had lived and died so bravely. Then,
observing the [7] _____ of the weakening waves, she brought her
thoughts back to the present. As her memories were [8] _____, she
was appreciating the beauty of the land and sea around her.

1. Underline the words that give a hint to the meaning of the word vast. Give a synonym for *vast*.

2. Underline the words that suggest the meaning of the word furled. Tell what *furled* means.

3. Underline the comparison that helps you understand the meaning of fling. Use *fling* in a sentence.

4. Underline the words that hint at the meaning of widow. Tell what *widow* means.

5. Circle the word that is a synonym for valiant. Give an antonym for *valiant*.

6. Underline the words that hint at the meaning of the word tide. Tell what *tide* means.

7. Underline words that suggest the meaning of the word retreating. Use *retreating* in a sentence.

8. Underline the words that hint at the meaning of the word ebb. Tell what *ebb* means.

Read the following passage. Pay special attention to the underlined words. Then, read it again, and complete the activities. Use a separate sheet of paper for your written answers.

In the 1800s, many fishing families lived on the northeast coast of England. The men set off into the vast Atlantic, often sailing for several days across the great ocean to search for good fishing spots. If a storm came up, the fishermen rode it out. They had the sails of their boats tightly furled to keep them from blowing away. Mighty winds would fling the boats across the water as an angry child would throw a toy.

These people knew the sea was dangerous. Many a widow mourned a husband who had died on the job. To help save lives, communities formed rescue squads, valiant friends and neighbors who were brave enough to oppose the stormy sea. Usually, it was the women who launched the rescue boats. They waded into the water and dragged the boats out against the powerful incoming tide. The tide was often strong enough to knock them down and turn over the lifeboats.

People of the coast even rescued the passengers of steamships. One famous rescuer was Grace Darling, the daughter of a lighthouse keeper on Farne Island. When the steamship *Forfarshire* sank near the island, Grace's father rescued nine survivors. The survivors were clinging to rocks near the shore. Instead of retreating to safety further inland, Grace insisted on helping her father. Thanks to their efforts, all nine passengers were brought to safety in the lighthouse.

With the ebb of the ocean waters after the storm had passed, the grateful survivors were able to make their journeys home. They spread the story of Grace Darling, and Grace became the hero of many poems and songs.

© Pearson Education

Dover Beach
Matthew Arnold

The Widow at Windsor
Rudyard Kipling

Summaries "Dover Beach" is about the British Empire in the Victorian Period. The speaker in "Dover Beach" looks out a window from the white chalk cliffs of Dover. He describes the moonlit beach to his love. He tells her to think about the ocean. It reminds him of the sadness of the times. He decides that lovers have only each other in the modern world, which has neither faith, happiness, love, nor hope.

"The Widow at Windsor" is also about the Victorian Period. The poem describes Queen Victoria. The speaker is a soldier. The speaker is proud of the queen's wealth, power, and military strength. At the same time, he understands the suffering of the soldiers. They must fight for the queen. The speaker reminds the people of Britain that their rule over much of the world comes at a high price.

Note-taking Guide

In the chart, record images from each poem that illustrate the world the speaker describes.

Dover Beach	The Widow at Windsor

Recessional
Rudyard Kipling

Summary This poem is also about the Victorian Period. The title, "Recessional," means the end of a religious service. It also means the end of the British Empire. The speaker warns the people of England that things change over time. He tells them that today's glories can disappear. He says that the people should still be humble, and depend on God.

Note-taking Guide

Use this chart to record the main idea of each stanza in the poem. Then, write the main idea of the entire poem.

Stanza 1	Stanza 2	Stanza 3	Stanza 4	Stanza 5

Main Idea of Poem:

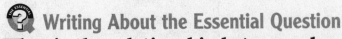

Dover Beach • The Widow at Windsor • Recessional

1. **Literary Analysis:** How does the mood in "Recessional" help you understand the poem's theme?

_____

_____

2. **Literary Analysis:** Complete the first column with images in "Dover Beach." In the second column, record where each image is in the poem. In the third column, write the **mood** that each image suggests. On the line under the chart, write the **theme** of the poem.

Image	Where It Appears	Mood It Suggests

Theme of poem: _____

3. **Reading Strategy:** What does the mood and theme in each poem indicate about the Victorian period of the British Empire?

_____

_____

Writing About the Essential Question

What is the relationship between place and literature? What comment is the speaker making about the extent and power of the British Empire?

_____

_____

Remembrance • The Darkling Thrush • "Ah, Are You Digging on My Grave?"

Literary Analysis

Stanzas are a number of lines that form a unit within a poem. Stanzas are like paragraphs in prose. Stanzas may be repeated groups of two or more verse lines that make up a pattern. Patterns can be based on length, rhythm, frequency, and rhyme. The **stanza structure** of a poem is the pattern of stanzas. Readers usually expect a regular pattern when they read a poem.

Irony occurs when what is said is different from what is meant. Writers use irony to provide humor or to show that things are not what they seem. Irony also helps evoke the reader's emotions.

Both stanza structure and irony relate to what the reader expects in the poem. For example, the first stanza may lead you to think that all the stanzas should be the same. Then, irony surprises you; the remainder of the poem may not be what you expected.

Reading Strategy

As you read a literary work, you should **analyze how patterns of organization affect clarity.** By understanding the organization of a work, you can gain a clearer understanding of the work's meaning. For example, in a poem that contains stanzas, each stanza builds on information in the stanza that comes before it. Use this chart to analyze how the organization of the first three stanzas of "Remembrance" affects the meaning of the poem.

Remembrance

Stanza 1	Stanza 2	Stanza 3
Speaker may be forgetting her true love, who died.		

VOCABULARY WARM-UP

Remembrance • The Darkling Thrush and Ah, Are You
Digging on My Grave?

Word List A

Study these words from the selections. Then, complete the activities.

pulse [PUHLS] *n.* regular or rhythmical beating; throb
The pulse of the music was created by the drumbeat.

check [CHEK] *v.* arrest the motion of; halt; restrain
You can check the flow of water in that pipe by shutting the valve.

shone [SHOHN] *v.* emitted light; glowed
Happiness shone in her eyes when she found her lost dog.

canopy [KAN uh pee] *n.* a high overarching covering, such as the sky or trees
The canopy in the forest prevents most sunlight from reaching the ground.

dreary [DRIR ee] *adj.* dismal; boring; gloomy; dull
The weather has been dreary this week with constant rain and gray skies.

bleak [BLEEK] *adj.* depressing; providing no encouragement
After months without work, the actor felt his prospects were bleak.

sternly [STURN lee] *adv.* harshly; severely; firmly
The teacher spoke to the class sternly, warning them not to misbehave.

existence [ig ZIS tens] *n.* the state of continued being; life
The existence of many plants and animals is threatened by pollution.

Exercise A

Fill in the blanks using each word from Word List A only once.

Forests are natural wonders that [1] _____ with life and countless

numbers of plants and animals. Despite the dark, [2] _____, and

frightening reputation they earn in stories, forests provide everything

needed to keep a human being alive when lost or stranded in the wilderness.

Common sense and simple skills ensure someone's [3] _____.

Conditions may look hopelessly [4] _____, but the [5] _____

of trees will provide initial shelter, and branches can be used to construct

shelter that will protect the survivor from the elements. Often people

lost in the woods were rescued when the light reflected from a mirror

[6] _____ brightly enough to be spotted by a passing plane. To avoid

becoming disoriented in thick brush, hikers should [7] _____ any

impulse they have to wander off established trails. This warning is often

repeated [8] _____, since too many have ignored it.

© Pearson Education

READING WARM-UP

Remembrance • The Darkling Thrush and
Ah, Are You Digging on My Grave?

1. Circle the words that describe the pulse of the raindrops. Then, explain what *pulse* means.

2. Circle the words that tell what Carrie wished to check. Then, describe something you'd like to *check*.

3. Rewrite the sentence using a synonym for dreary. Then, give an example of something you consider to be *dreary*.

4. Circle the words that tell what kind of canopy Carrie saw. Describe a different kind of *canopy*.

5. Rewrite the sentence using a synonym for sternly. Then, give an example of some one acting *sternly*.

6. Circle the words that tell what others thought was bleak. Name something you consider to be *bleak*.

7. Circle the words that show Carrie's existence was peaceful. Then, give a synonym for *existence*.

8. Rewrite the sentence using a synonym for shone. Then, describe something else that *shone*.

Read the following passage. Pay special attention to the underlined words. Then, read it again, and complete the activities. Use a separate sheet of paper for your written answers.

As the digital face of Carrie's clock jumped to 5 A.M., her quiet apartment was filled with blaring noise. The alarm seemed louder than ever as it disrupted the gentle pulse of raindrops rhythmically hitting her window. Carrie rolled over in bed, reached for the "off" button, and with a practiced swipe, was able to check the incessant beeping. Even though it was still dark outside, she knew she would have regrets if she didn't stick to her schedule. So she got out of bed, drank some orange juice, and got ready for her morning jog.

As Carrie stepped out the door and into the dreary, rainy day, she had a smile on her face. A thick canopy of clouds and the slick, wet sidewalk gave the whole world a cold, gray appearance. She started along her usual route, dodging puddles, dog walkers, and other determined runners who were sternly refusing to let the bad weather interfere with their daily exercise. It was these days—the gray days—that Carrie loved best. The cold weather kept most people in their homes, making the park unusually quiet. This allowed the rhythm of her footsteps to be the only sound that broke the silence. This rainy atmosphere that others considered bleak and depressing, Carrie felt made her existence peaceful, and she was filled with tranquility as she jogged undisturbed through the empty park.

By the time she headed home, a weak sun shone through the clouds. While others greeted this with relief, Carrie felt she had already enjoyed the best part of the day.

Remembrance
Emily Brontë

The Darkling Thrush •
"Ah, Are You Digging on My Grave?"
Thomas Hardy

Summaries The speaker in **"Remembrance"** is a woman addressing her love, who died fifteen years before. She asks him to forgive her if she forgets him. Although her joy died with him, her mind is now on other desires and hopes. In **"The Darkling Thrush,"** the speaker describes a bleak winter day that is suddenly brightened by a bird called a thrush. The bird's song gives the speaker hope. The speaker in **"Ah, Are You Digging on My Grave?"** is a dead woman wondering who is digging on her grave. Is it her loved one, her family, or an enemy?

Note-taking Guide
Use this chart to record feelings of sadness and hope that are described in each poem. Record the stanzas in which you find each emotion.

Poem	Sadness	Stanza	Hope	Stanza
"Remembrance"				
"The Darkling Thrush"				
"Ah, Are You Digging on My Grave?"				

Remembrance • The Darkling Thrush • "Ah, Are You Digging on My Grave?"

1. **Literary Analysis:** Use this chart to compare the first and last **stanzas** of each poem.

Number of lines	Number of lines	Rhyme scheme	Meter
Remembrance	First Stanza:		
	Last Stanza:		
The Darkling Thrush	First Stanza:		
	Last Stanza:		
"Ah, Are You Digging on My Grave?"	First Stanza:		
	Last Stanza:		

2. **Literary Analysis:** What is **ironic** about the last stanza of "'Ah, Are You Digging on My Grave?'"

_____

_____

3. **Reading Strategy: Analyze how the organization of stanzas affects clarity** in "Remembrance." How does the speaker gradually work out an answer to the question in the first stanza?

_____

_____

 Writing About the Essential Question

What is the relationship between place and literature? How do the places in which Hardy's speakers find themselves limit their knowledge?

_____

_____

God's Grandeur • Spring and Fall: To a Young Child • To an Athlete Dying Young • When I Was One-and-Twenty

Literary Analysis

Rhythm is the pattern of stressed and unstressed syllables. Poetry with regular rhythm is called **metrical verse**. Metrical verse is made up of different groups of syllables called **feet**. Following are some samples of feet and the pattern of stressed (´) and unstressed (˘) syllables in them:

- **Iambic:** unstressed, stressed, as in *the time*
- **Trochaic:** stressed, unstressed, as in *grandeur*
- **Anapestic:** unstressed, unstressed, stressed, as in *to the low*

Lines with three feet are called **trimeter**. Lines with four feet are called **tetrameter**. Lines with five feet are called **pentameter**. Iambic pentameter is a five-foot line with iambic feet. Trochaic tetrameter is a four-foot line with trochaic feet. Housman uses iambic and trochaic tetrameter. Hopkins created other rhythms:

- **Counterpoint rhythm**—two different rhythms are used, such as two trochaic feet in an iambic line.
- **Sprung rhythm**—all feet begin with a stressed syllable (sometimes marked with an accent); they have a different number of unstressed syllables.

Reading Strategy

Analyzing the author's beliefs helps you understand the ideas and images in a poem. As you read, use details from the poem, the author's biography, and other works by the author to help you examine the author's beliefs. Use a diagram like the one shown to help you analyze those beliefs as you read each poem.

Biographical Details	+	Details in Author's Work	=	Author's Beliefs

Word List A

Study these words from the above selections. Then, complete the activities.

seared [SEERD] *v.* charred, scorched, or burned the surface
   The chef seared the steak to seal in the juice.

flame [FLAYM] *v.* burn; ignite
   The lighter fluid made it easy to flame the charcoal.

smudge [SMUHJ] *n.* a blotch or smear, often made by dirt
   After eating the candy, the child had a smudge of chocolate on her chin.

fleet [FLEET] *adj.* swift; rapid or nimble
   The fleet rabbit ran faster than the dog.

trod [TRAHD] *v.* walked on, over, or along; trampled
   The hikers made a path when they trod through the meadow's tall grass.

smeared [SMEERD] *v.* spread or daubed on a surface, sometimes messily
   The hunter smeared insect repellent on his face and arms.

shod [SHAHD] *v.* furnished with shoes
   Horses have to be shod to protect their hooves.

toil [TOYL] *n.* exhausting labor or effort; hard work
   The farm laborers were paid for their toil with cash and produce.

Exercise A

Fill in the blanks using each word from Word List A only once.

When a fire begins mysteriously, inspectors examine the site for

[1] _____ objects and clues that might show what made the

building [2] _____. If arson is suspected, they will check out any

[3] _____ that could be a fingerprint or a footprint. Although not as

reliable as fingerprints, patterns that reveal how a foot was [4] _____

can sometimes lead police to a guilty party. An arsonist might not have

worried about where he or she [5] _____, thinking any footprints

would have burned away. Inspectors will also test any flammable substance

that seems to have been [6] _____ on a surface. Hopefully, all this

[7] _____ will provide answers before a rainstorm arrives and, with

one [8] _____ cloudburst, destroys needed evidence.

Read the following passage. Pay special attention to the underlined words. Then, read it again, and complete the activities. Use a separate sheet of paper for your written answers.

Before candles were invented, Egyptians used torches that were made of reeds smeared or thickly coated with melted tallow. When lit, the torches created a large flame that sometimes seared the hands of those who held them. Lighted pieces of reed and sparks also fell off the torches, burning the feet of those who weren't properly shod.

Candlewicks were developed by the Romans to make lighting safer. They put wicks in the rendered animal fat to create a means to slowly burn the suet. These first candles were used to light homes and places of worship. They also aided those who trod on foot at night.

Tallow was used in all candles until the Middle Ages when sweet- smelling beeswax was introduced. Beeswax candles did not produce dirty smoke that would cause a smudge on nearby walls or ceilings. Instead, when lighted, beeswax would flame pure and clean. However, these candles were expensive, and only the wealthy could afford them.

America's colonial women contributed to candle making when they discovered that boiling the grayish green berries of bayberry bushes produced a sweet-smelling wax that burned clean. However, extracting the wax from the bayberries was a tedious process that required a lot of toil. As a result, the bayberry candle quickly went out of fashion after a fleet period of popularity. It was quickly replaced in the late eighteenth century by the wax candle created from sperm whale oil. Harder than beeswax or tallow, this candle was in demand since it did not soften in the summer heat.

1. Circle the words that tell what smeared means. Name something that you might see being *smeared*.

2. Circle the words that tell what seared people's hands. Explain was *seared* means.

3. Circle the words that tell what happened when sparks fell on someone who wasn't properly shod. Then, tell what *shod* means.

4. Circle the words that tell how the people who used the candles trod. Then, name a place where you *trod*.

5. Circle the words that tell what produced the smudge. Tell where might you find a *smudge*.

6. Circle the words that tell when the beeswax would flame pure and clean. Then, describe something you've seen *flame*.

7. Circle the words that show that making bayberry candles required a lot of toil. Describe something you think requires a lot of *toil*.

8. Circle the words that tell that the bayberry candle had a fleet period of popularity. Then, tell what *fleet* means.

God's Grandeur • Spring and Fall: To a Young Child
Gerard Manley Hopkins

Summaries Both of these poems talk about nature. In **"God's Grandeur,"** the speaker asks why people hurt nature. He says that nature always shows the grandeur, or greatness, of God. Nature remains fresh no matter what people do to it. In **"Spring and Fall: To a Young Child,"** the speaker talks about a girl's sadness. The girl is sad because the autumn leaves are falling. The speaker says that everything dies. He says the girl is really sad over her own mortality, or the knowledge that she too will one day die.

Note-taking Guide

Use this chart to record lines from each poem that talk about beauty or about the fact that things die.

Poem	Beauty	Line	Mortality	Line
"God's Grandeur"				
"Spring and Fall: To a Young Child"				

To an Athlete Dying Young • When I Was One-and-Twenty

A. E. Housman

Summaries The speaker in **"To an Athlete Dying Young"** watches as people carry home the body of a young athlete. The speaker says that the glories of youth do not last. He also says that disappointment comes with age and experience. The speaker thinks that perhaps the athlete was lucky to have died young. That way, he did not have to live past his glory.

In **"When I Was One-and-Twenty,"** the speaker talks about advice he received when he was a young man. The advice was to give young women gifts, but not his heart. The theme of this poem is similar to that of "To an Athlete Dying Young." The theme is that the glories of youth do not last, and that disappointment comes with age and experience.

Note-taking Guide

Use this chart to record the words and phrases that support the poet's theme.

Poem	Words/Phrases	Line Number
"To an Athlete Dying Young"		
"When I was One-and-Twenty"		

God's Grandeur • Spring and Fall: To a Young Child • To an Athlete Dying Young • When I Was One-and-Twenty

1. **Literary Analysis:** Use this chart to record the **scansion symbols** (˘) that show the pattern of stressed and unstressed syllables in line 5 of "God's Grandeur."

   > Generations have trod, have trod, have trod, . . .
   >
   > _____   _____

2. **Literary Analysis:** In lines 1-8 of "To an Athlete," the **meter** includes five **iambic tetrameter** lines and three **trochaic tetrameter** lines. How do the trochaic lines strengthen the idea of a "stiller town"?

   _____

   _____

   _____

3. **Reading Strategy:** Use Hopkins's biography and details from "God's Grandeur" to **analyze the author's beliefs** regarding nature.

   _____

   _____

Writing About the Essential Question

What is the relationship of the writer to tradition? Which are more effective, Hopkins's inventive rhythms or Housman's more traditional ones? Explain.

_____

_____

When You Are Old • The Lake Isle of Innisfree • The Wild Swans at Coole • The Second Coming • Sailing to Byzantium

Literary Analysis

William Butler Yeats had his own **philosophy,** or set of principles, that he used in the writing of his poetry. This philosophy was based largely on the use of symbols. In literature, a **symbol** is an image, character, object, or action that serves the following purposes:

- It stands for something beyond itself.
- It triggers a number of related thoughts, or associations.
- It makes readers' feelings stronger and adds deeper meaning.

The swans in "The Wild Swans at Coole" combine associations of beauty (they are graceful and attractive), pureness (they are white), freedom (they are wild), and the eternal (they return year after year). Like other strong symbols, the swans have multiple meanings: They can stand for the cycle of nature and the speaker's earlier life.

Yeats's system of symbols is most visible in "The Second Coming" and "Sailing to Byzantium." In each poem, symbols are used to create multiple meanings. By using vivid images and language, Yeats makes his philosophy real and emotionally persuasive to the reader.

Reading Strategy

A writer's philosophy shapes his or her works. As you read, **analyze the author's philosophical assumptions.** Find examples of symbols in each poem, and explain how each symbol supports Yeats's philosophy. Use the chart below.

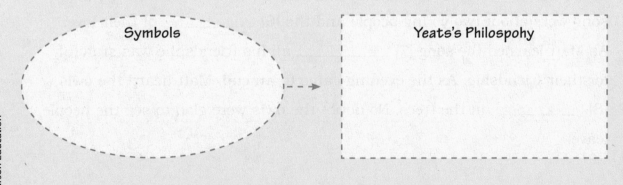

Symbols → Yeats's Philospohy

Word List A

Study these words from the selections. Then, complete the activities that follow.

amid [uh MID] *prep.* in the midst of; among
    The one red rose stood out underlined{amid} all the white ones in the bouquet.

consume [kuhn SOOM] *v.* to use up or waste, as money or time
    Jennifer's part-time jobs consume all her free time.

core [KAWR] *n.* the central or innermost part of anything
    A burning desire to help others is at the core of Anna's heart.

glade [GLAYD] *n.* an open place in a forest
    Walter and Maria had a picnic in the glade.

innocence [IN uh suhns] *n.* freedom from guilt, blame, or sin
    The accused person declared his innocence in a loud voice.

murmur [MER muhr] *v.* to make a low, unclear, steady sound
    The two friends murmur between themselves in the shade of the oak.

sensual [SEN shoo uhl] *adj.* having to do with the body or the senses
    The aroma of the flowers was quite a sensual treat for all of us.

twilight [TWY lyt] *n.* the light of the sky just before sunrise or after sunset
    Having missed the sunset, Janet and Carl met at twilight.

Exercise A

Fill in each blank below with the appropriate word from Word List A.

Every Friday, at [1] _____, Matt and a group of his friends met in

the forest. There, in a [2] _____ not far from the forest's edge, they

enjoyed a [3] _____ celebration of the season. Included in the

celebration were all kinds of gourmet foods to [4] _____. The

[5] _____ of the evening's entertainment was the learning of a

new song, which everyone enjoyed singing together. The lyrics of tonight's

song were about two young people and the [6] _____ of their love.

As Matt learned the song [7] _____ all his friends, he was grateful

for their friendship. As the evening came to an end, Matt heard the owls

[8] _____ in the trees. No doubt the owls were glad to see the people

leave.

Read the following passage. Pay special attention to the underlined words. Then, read it again, and complete the activities. Use a separate sheet of paper for your written answers.

Trumpeter swans are the largest swans in the world, growing to a length of 58 to 72 inches with a wingspan of eight feet. Trumpeter swans, like all swans, are graceful birds whose lovely appearance has a <u>sensual</u> appeal to all bird-lovers. Their long, <u>bendable</u> necks, interestingly, have more bones than a giraffe's neck.

Trumpeter swans live on lakes and rivers in the grasslands and forests of the northwestern United States and western Canada. If you happen to be walking through the center, the <u>core</u>, of a forest some lovely day, strolling <u>amid</u> the tall trees, and come to a <u>glade</u> near a body of water, you might have the good fortune to see one or more of them. Listen closely! You might even hear the low sounds they make as they <u>murmur</u> to each other.

Because mature swans are covered in white feathers, they can be seen as symbols of <u>innocence</u>. They have dark brown eyes and long black legs and feet. Cygnets (juvenile swans) are mostly gray. They slowly turn whiter in their first year of life. It's hard to imagine a lovelier sight than a family of swans at sunset, just before <u>twilight</u>, with the colorful sky reflected in their watery surroundings.

When swans are three years old, they mate for life. Unlike other birds, swans do not build nests in trees. They are too heavy for that. The female lays three to nine eggs, which are guarded diligently by the male until they can safely hatch. The cygnets stay close to their parents as they learn to find food and to fly. Swans <u>consume</u> a diet of aquatic insects and mollusks. The cygnets can fly at about 14 weeks of age. However, they stay with their parents for about a year. At age three, they start families of their own.

1. Underline the words in this sentence and a nearby sentence that hint at the <u>sensual</u> appeal swans have. What does *sensual* mean?

2. Circle the word that means about the same as <u>core</u>. What do you find in the *core* of an apple?

3. Underline the words that tell what you might stroll <u>amid</u> in a forest. Use *amid* in a sentence.

4. Circle the word that tells where you would find a <u>glade</u>. Describe what you might see in a *glade*.

5. Underline the words that describe what you might hear as swans <u>murmur</u> to each other. If you were to *murmur* something to your best friend, what might it be?

6. Circle the words that tell why swans might be seen as symbols of <u>innocence</u>. What do you consider a symbol of *innocence*?

7. Underline the word that describes a time just before <u>twilight</u>. What activity are you usually doing when it is *twilight*?

8. Circle the words that tell what swans <u>consume</u>. What do you normally *consume* at lunchtime?

When You Are Old •
The Lake Isle of Innisfree •
The Wild Swans at Coole •
The Second Coming •
Sailing to Byzantium

William Butler Yeats

Summaries Yeats uses themes of aging, loss, and change in these poems. **"When You Are Old"** is written to a woman the speaker loved. He tells her that of all the men who loved her, only he loved her for her soul. In **"The Lake Isle of Innisfree,"** a poet in the city wishes for the simple country life. In **"The Wild Swans at Coole,"** the speaker thinks about his past and compares himself to the swans. Swans do not change, but he has had to make many changes in his life. In **"The Second Coming,"** Yeats gives his view of history. In **"Sailing to Byzantium,"** Yeats says that though humans will die, art lives on.

Note-taking Guide

Use this chart to record which of the general themes of aging, loss, and change are used in each poem. Check each box that applies. Each poem may have more than one checkmark (✔).

Poem	Aging	Loss	Change
When You Are Old			
The Lake Isle of Innisfree			
The Wild Swans at Coole			
The Second Coming			
Sailing to Byzantium			

Poetry of William Butler Yeats

1. **Make a Judgment:** Do you agree that in the modern world "things fall apart," as Yeats writes in "The Second Coming"? Explain.

_____

_____

2. **Literary Analysis:** Use this chart to compare the effect and meaning of the swans in "The Wild Swans at Coole" with those of the Sphinx in "The Second Coming."

Symbol	Personal/ Traditional	Vivid/Flat in Effect	Rich/Poor in Associations	Easy/Hard to Interpret
swans				
Sphinx				

3. **Reading Strategy:** Consider Yeats's **philosophy** when analyzing the meaning of "The Second Coming." How do the symbols used in "The Second Coming" reveal Yeats's philosophy that society is decaying?

_____

_____

_____

Writing About the Essential Question

What is the relationship between place and literature? How is Yeats's poetry affected by both real and imagined places?

_____

_____

_____

Preludes • Journey of the Magi • The Hollow Men

Literary Analysis

Modernism was a trend in poetry that took place in the early twentieth century. A Modernist poem has the following features:

- It emphasizes images, or words and phrases that appeal to one or more of the five senses.
- It relies on the use of the symbol—an image, character, object, or action that stands for something beyond itself.
- It contains allusions, or indirect references to people, places, events, or works of literature.
- It focuses on the spiritual troubles of modern life.

Reading Strategy

One method of interpreting literature is to **relate literary works to the historical period** in which they were written. Modernist writers were troubled by the circumstances of the time. Find patterns in Eliot's works that suggest these problems.

- Life in crowded cities left people isolated.
- The rise of technology and the need for material goods left people without spiritual purpose.
- Factory work was dehumanizing.

Follow these steps to create a historical analysis of one of Eliot's poems.

1. Look carefully at important passages.
2. Identify elements that illustrate Modernist features.
3. Think about what you know about the historical period in which the poem was written.
4. Come to a conclusion about how the elements of the poem relate to the historical period. Then, record your analysis in the chart.

Modernist Elements	Information About Historical Period	Conclusion

Word List A

Study these words from the selections. Then, complete the activities that follow.

consciousness [KAHN shuhs nuhs] *n.* awareness; a conscious condition
After being in a coma for a week, Marvin regained consciousness.

constituted [KAHN stuh toot id] *v.* made up; composed
Four quarts have always constituted a gallon.

deliberate [duh LIB uhr it] *adj.* done on purpose; thought about; intended
Linda's deliberate attempt to annoy me just made me laugh.

gesture [JES chuhr] *n.* a motion of the head, hands, or other part of the body expressing some idea or feeling
Orlando's gesture indicated that we should come in and sit down.

grimy [GRY mee] *adj.* full of or covered with dirt
The mother sent her grimy child directly to the bathtub.

regretted [ri GRET id] *v.* felt sorrow or grief about something
Alma forever regretted ending her friendship with Tameka.

satisfactory [sat is FAK tuhr ee] *adj.* good enough to meet expectations
Steve's job performance was satisfactory but not outstanding.

temperate [TEM puhr it] *adj.* moderate in temperature; mild
San Diego has a pleasant, temperate climate all year long.

Exercise A

Fill in each blank below with the appropriate word from Word List A.

Patricia thought that Calvin had made a [1] _____ effort to get extra dirty that afternoon. She thought she might lose [2] _____ because he smelled so bad. As she looked at his [3] _____ clothes, she wondered with annoyance why he did it. Didn't he understand what [4] _____ careful behavior as opposed to careless behavior? With a [5] _____ of anger, she sent him to his room. Immediately, she [6] _____ being so hard on the little boy. After all, they lived in a lovely, [7] _____ climate. It was normal for a young boy to play outside and get dirty on such a beautiful day. Patricia apologized to Calvin, and he smiled to show that her apology was [8] _____ and acceptable.

1. What <u>constituted</u> the longest trip the three magi had ever taken? Define *constituted*.

2. Underline the word that means about the opposite of temperate. Name a city that enjoys *temperate* weather.

3. Circle the words that tell what the wise men might have <u>regretted</u>. Tell about something a movie character did that he or she *regretted*.

4. Circle the word that means about the same as <u>grimy</u>. If you were *grimy*, what is the first thing you would do?

5. Underline the words that tell what <u>deliberate</u> decision the men might have made. What does *deliberate* mean?

6. Underline the word that means about the same as <u>consciousness</u>. Use *consciousness* in a sentence.

7. Circle the words that describe the <u>gesture</u> made by the magi when they found the baby king. Describe a *gesture* that can indicate confusion.

8. Underline the word that means about the same as <u>satisfactory</u>. How do you know if an assignment you turn in is *satisfactory*?

Read the following passage. Pay special attention to the underlined words. Then, read it again, and complete the activities. Use a separate sheet of paper for your written answers.

The journey of the Magi, also called the Three Wise Men or the Three Kings, to see the newborn baby Jesus is a popular story from the Christian tradition. It is interesting to imagine the journey these three men might have taken. According to the story, they set out from Persia, or present-day Iran. The distance from there to Jerusalem is between 1,000 and 1,200 miles and would have taken three to twelve months by camel. This perhaps <u>constituted</u> the longest trip they had ever taken.

As they traveled across the land, through weather that must have ranged from <u>temperate</u> to cold, we can imagine that they <u>regretted</u> their decision to make the trip. They must have been tired, hungry, and dirty to the point of looking <u>grimy</u> as they traveled between rest points. Still, they must have made a <u>deliberate</u> decision to keep going. Uppermost in their <u>consciousness</u> would have been an awareness of how important it was to find the newborn king and pay their respects.

When they finally arrived, so the story goes, they took turns kneeling in a <u>gesture</u> of respect and adoration. The youngest magi, Caspar of Tarsus, was a European. He knelt first and presented his gift of gold, which symbolized Christ's immortality and purity. In exchange, Caspar received the gifts of charity and spiritual wealth. Melchior, a middle-aged Persian, knelt next, offering myrrh, a fragrant resin, which was believed to make children stronger. In exchange, he received the gifts of humility and truth. Finally, Balthasar, an elderly Ethiopian, offered a gift of frankincense, a resin that symbolizes prayer and sacrifice. In exchange, he received the gift of faith. The gifts of the magi must have been <u>satisfactory</u> and acceptable to the tiny king, for they received priceless gifts in return.

Preludes
T. S. Eliot

Summary This poem presents a bleak vision of a world in which suffering, grime, and dreariness are the main features. Eliot may not just have been reveling in despair, however; he may have seen it as a necessary "prelude" to spiritual awakening. Each segment, or prelude, describes a different depressing urban scene. In Prelude IV, however, a new note is sounded—that of something "infinitely gentle / Infinitely suffering."

Note-taking Guide

Use this chart to record a description of each scene. Then, put a checkmark (✔) in either the "hopefulness" column or the "despair" column.

Segments	Description of Scene	Hopefulness	Despair
I			
II			
III			
IV			

Journey of the Magi
T. S. Eliot

Summary In this poem, the speaker is one of the three Magi (MAY jy), or wise men, who traveled to Bethlehem to honor the baby Jesus. Now he is an old man, and he reflects on the meaning of the journey he made many years ago. He tells about the various difficulties that he and his companions encountered. Finally, he confesses that the scene he witnessed was like a death, because it was "hard and bitter" for him and his companions. Having seen the baby Jesus, they returned to their own kingdoms. However, they no longer felt at ease among people who worshiped many gods rather than one.

Note-taking Guide
Use the following chart to record information from the poem.

Character:
Goal:
Difficulties Encountered:
Result:
Resolution ⟶ Years Later, Continuing Problems: or Lack of Resolution

Journey of the Magi
T.S. Eliot

"A cold coming we[1] had of it,
Just the worst time of the year
For a journey, and such a long journey:
The ways deep and the weather sharp,
The very dead of winter."[2]

◆ ◆ ◆

The travelers have difficulty with the camels. The animals are stubborn and sore and don't want to move.

The speaker says the travelers miss the warm weather and the serving girls at home. Instead they meet cursing camel drivers, have trouble finding shelter, and visit unfriendly and expensive towns.

The travelers finally decide to travel at night. They have little sleep and begin to wonder if their journey is wise.

◆ ◆ ◆

TAKE NOTES

Reading Check

Read the bracketed part of the poem. Circle two difficulties the wise men encountered on their journey.

Read Fluently

Read the bracketed paragraph aloud. What tone of voice did you use as you read?

_____

_____

_____

1. The speaker is one of the three wise men, or magi, who traveled to Bethlehem to visit the baby Jesus. In this poem, the speaker reflects upon the meaning of the journey.

2. **"A . . . winter":** Adapted from a part of a sermon delivered by 17th-century Bishop Lancelot Andrews: "A cold coming they had of it at this time of year, just the worst time of the year to take a journey, and specially a long journey in. The ways deep, the weather sharp, the days short, the sun farthest off . . . the very dead of winter."

Literary Analysis

Which characteristic of **Modernist** poetry does Eliot use in this poem? Circle the letter of the correct answer.

a. symbol   c. image

b. allusion   d. all of these

Stop to Reflect

Is the speaker's journey positive or negative? Why do you think so?

_____

_____

_____

Then at dawn we came down to a <u>temperate</u>
  valley,
Wet, below the snow line,[3] smelling of
  <u>vegetation</u>;
With a running stream and a water-mill
  beating the darkness,
And three trees[4] on the low sky.

◆ ◆ ◆

The travelers arrive at a tavern but can get no information. They continue and find the place they are looking for that evening.

The speaker says that this journey took place a long time ago. He's not sure whether the event was a birth or a death. The miraculous birth of Jesus caused the death of his old world, his old life, and his old beliefs.

Vocabulary Development

temperate (TEM per it) *adj*. neither hot nor cold

vegetation (vej i TAY shun) *n*. the plants of an area or region

---

3. **snow line** the boundary where a snow-covered area begins.

4. **three trees** a Biblical allusion to the three crosses of Calvary, the hill outside ancient Jerusalem where Jesus and two other men were crucified.

The Hollow Men

T.S. Eliot

Summary **"The Hollow Men"** describes a world in which people have no faith, no courage, no spirit, and no awareness. Spoken by the hollow men themselves, the poem is a self-portrait of the typical modern person.

Note-Taking Guide

Use this cluster diagram to identify and record the images in the five parts of "The Hollow Men."

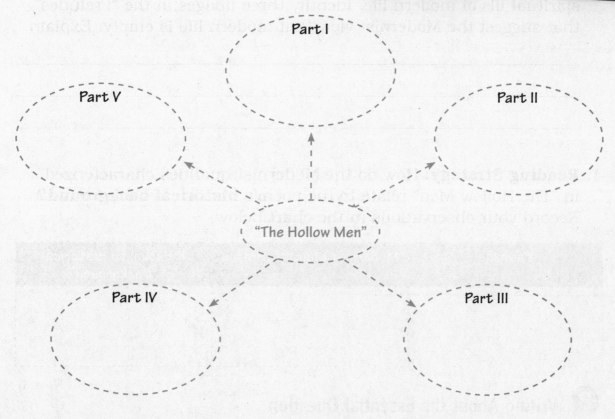

Part I

Part V

Part II

"The Hollow Men"

Part IV

Part III

Preludes • Journey of the Magi • The Hollow Men

1. **Interpret:** It is winter at 6:00 p.m. at the beginning of Prelude I. What cycle of time takes place from Prelude I to Prelude IV?

_____

_____

2. **Compare and Contrast:** The speaker in "Journey of the Magi" has gone on a journey to witness a miraculous event. How do the descriptions of the journey compare to the descriptions of the event?

_____

_____

3. **Literary Analysis: Modernism** often emphasizes a concern with the spiritual ills of modern life. Identify three images in the "Preludes" that suggest the Modernist view that modern life is empty. Explain.

_____

_____

_____

4. **Reading Strategy:** How do the Modernist qualities characterized in "The Hollow Men" relate to the poem's **historical background?** Record your observations in the chart below.

Passage	Modernist Characteristics	Relation to Historical Background

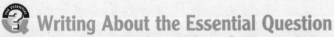 **Writing About the Essential Question**

What is the relationship of the writer to tradition? In what ways do Eliot's poems both break with tradition and connect to tradition?

In Memory of W. B. Yeats •
Musée des Beaux Arts • Carrick Revisited
• Not Palaces

Literary Analysis

Some literary genres can be placed in **subgenres,** or smaller groups within a larger genre. Two such subgenres are allegory and pastoral.

- An **allegory** is a narrative in which symbols are used to create a meaning beyond what is explicitly portrayed in the narrative. For example, lines 36–41 of Auden's "In Memory of W. B. Yeats" are essentially a short allegory. Similarly, the landscape described in "Musée des Beaux Arts" is an allegorical, symbolic landscape. This landscape is designed to teach the reader a moral, or lesson—a common feature of allegory.

- A **pastoral** is literature that idealizes life in a rural setting. The landscape of Carrick in "Carrick Revisited" is described as an idealized version of MacNeice's childhood. In "Not Palaces," Spender embraces a life of energy and social equality over a more conventional life celebrated in pastorals.

Reading Strategy

A useful way to aid your reading of literature is to **compare and contrast elements** in the text. While reading the two Auden poems, compare and contrast the way in which allegory is used. Likewise, while reading the MacNeice and Spender poems, compare and contrast the way in which pastoral is used. Use the following chart to record your conclusions.

Allegory		Pastoral	
In Memory of W.B. Yeats	Musée des Beaux Arts	Carrick Revisited	Not Palaces

Word List A

Study these words from the selections. Then, complete the activities that follow.

concealment [kuhn SEEL muhnt] *n.* the act of hiding
  The concealment of the moon behind clouds made the night quite dark.

emphasis [EM fuh sis] *n.* a stressing by the voice of a particular syllable, word, or phrase
  His mother's emphasis on the word no meant Raj would not get his way.

interlude [IN ter lood] *n.* a short interval of time that interrupts something
  Kevin enjoyed his interlude at the park between work sessions.

intolerant [in TAHL uhr uhnt] *adj.* unsympathetic
  Mr. Larson is intolerant of students who do not do their homework.

isolation [eye suh LAY shuhn] *n.* the state of being alone
  Mimi endured weeks of isolation in the cabin during the harsh winter.

leisurely [LEE zher lee] *adv.* in a slow, relaxed manner
  Carlos and Maria leisurely enjoyed their iced teas on the porch.

miraculous [muh RAK yuh luhs] *adj.* seeming to be impossible
  The friendship between the lion and the lamb was miraculous.

rapture [RAP chuhr] *n.* very great or complete pleasure or delight
  In a rapture, Marla danced gracefully in Pedro's arms.

Exercise A

Fill in each blank below with the appropriate word from Word List A.

Joyce was getting tired of the [1] _____ attitude of her friends and family, who just would not understand or respect her desire to be alone. She thought she would enjoy the [2] _____ of her family's mountain cabin. In no hurry, she [3] _____ packed up and left. When she got there, she went into a [4] _____ over the beauty of the surroundings. Sunset over the lake was so beautiful that first night that it seemed like a [5] _____ event. She was determined to put the [6] _____ on relaxing, for she felt that she needed a good rest. She enjoyed watching the squirrels as they worked hard on the [7] _____ of their winter food supply. Joyce enjoyed every moment of her one-week [8] _____ among the pines.

Read the following passage. Pay special attention to the underlined words. Then, read it again, and complete the activities. Use a separate sheet of paper for your written answers.

According to Greek mythology, Daedalus was a talented architect, inventor, and master craftsman from Athens. He moved to Crete and started to work for King Minos and his wife, Queen Pasiphae.

Daedalus soon angered King Minos, who was intolerant of even the slightest disrespect—he simply would not allow it. Minos sent Daedalus and his son Icarus away to the Labyrinth, a giant maze, where their isolation from society would be their punishment. Minos knew that being alone all the time would be a terrible fate for the father and son.

Daedalus had built the Labyrinth many years before for the imprisonment and concealment of the Minotaur, a half-man, half-bull that had been born on the island. Because Daedalus had been the architect of the Labyrinth, he knew his way out of it, but escape by land or sea was not a possibility. Since Minos controlled the sea around the island, Daedalus knew that the only way out was by air.

Daedalus constructed wings for himself and his son. He made them with feathers held together by wax. Daedalus put the emphasis on safety, stressing that his son not fly too close to the sun, for it would melt the wax. Soon, father and son were ready to attempt the seemingly impossible. It was truly a miraculous accomplishment when they took off and flew like birds.

As the two began to fly leisurely and slowly away from Crete, Icarus forgot his father's warning. In a rapture of delight with his new-found freedom, he flew higher and higher, until the wax holding his wings together melted. His happy interlude in the air over, Icarus plunged quickly to the sea. His father, unable to save him, could only watch helplessly as his son disappeared beneath the surface.

1. Circle the words that tell what intolerant means. Then, explain how King Minos showed that he was intolerant.

2. Circle the words that mean about the same as isolation. Tell about a time you found yourself in isolation.

3. Underline the word that tells what was meant for the concealment of the Minotaur. What might be a good place for the concealment of a small treasure?

4. Circle the word that means about the same as emphasis. What is one safety rule that you think deserves great emphasis?

5. Circle the words in a nearby sentence that mean about the same as miraculous. Use miraculous in a sentence.

6. Underline the word that means about the same as leisurely. What is one activity of yours that you do in a leisurely fashion?

7. Underline the word that means about the same as rapture. Use rapture in a sentence.

8. Circle the words that tell what Icarus did during his interlude in the air. What is an interlude you might enjoy?

In Memory of W. B. Yeats
• Musée des Beaux Arts
W. H. Auden

Carrick Revisited
Louis MacNeice

Not Palaces
Stephen Spender

Summaries These poems are about looking—looking back, looking away, and looking ahead. **"In Memory of W. B. Yeats"** memorializes Yeats's death and explores the nature of poetry. **"Musée des Beaux Arts"** describes scenes from paintings showing tragic events, such as the fall to death of Icarus, that happen while people go about their daily lives. **"Carrick Revisited"** explores how the poet feels about his childhood home. **"Not Palaces"** urges readers to leave behind the palaces of the past and take in the energy of social change in the present.

Note-taking Guide

Record the topic of or inspiration for each poem in column 2. Write the theme of the poem in column 3. This will help you understand how these poems are alike and how they differ.

Poem	Topic/Inspiration	Theme
In Memory of W. B. Yeats		
Musée des Beaux Arts		
Carrick Revisited		
Not Palaces		

In Memory of W. B. Yeats • Musée des Beaux Arts • Carrick Revisited • Not Palaces

1. **Summarize:** Summarize what the poem "In Memory of W. B. Yeats" says about poetry.

   _____

   _____

2. **Literary Analysis:** Use the chart below to identify one example or element of either **allegory** or **pastoral** in each of the poems.

Poem	Subgenre	Example or Element of Subgenre
In Memory of W.B. Yeats		
Musée des Beaux Arts		
Carrick Revisited		
Not Palaces		

3. **Reading Strategy: Compare and contrast** the way in which pastoral is used in "Carrick Revisited" and "Not Palaces."

   _____

   _____

? Writing About the Essential Question

What is the relationship between place and literature? Do these poems reflect a sense of a particular place or time?

   _____

   _____

   _____

The Lady in the Looking Glass: A Reflection • from Mrs. Dalloway • from A Room of One's Own: from Shakespeare's Sister

Literary Analysis

Writers often experiment with **point of view,** the perspective from which a story is told.

- **Stream-of-consciousness** narration follows the flowing, branching thoughts inside a character's mind.
- **First-person narration** tells the story through the thoughts of one character. The reader is limited to the perspective of that one character.
- **Third-person narration** comes from a narrator who is not a character in the story. Third-person **limited** narration follows only one character's experiences throughout the story. A third-person **omniscient** narrator knows all that happens in a story.

Reading Strategy

Experimental works offer great rewards but also place great demands on readers. Should your understanding of the reading break down, a useful skill can be to **repair comprehension by questioning.** Ask questions as you read to help you find your way through the story. Use the chart below to help you.

Detail	Question	Answer
"There she perched, never seeing him, waiting to cross, very upright."	To whom is the narrator referring?	

Word List A

Study these words from the selections. Then, complete the activities.

abundantly [uh BUN duhnt lee] *adv.* plentifully; bountifully
   It was abundantly clear that the meeting would never happen.

dislodge [dis LAHJ] *v.* to remove; to force out of a place
   If you dislodge that cup, the whole pile will come crashing down.

distinguished [di STIN gwisht] *adj.* standing out for excellence or dignity
   The judge looked so distinguished in his formal robes.

futility [fyoo TIL uh tee] *n.* uselessness
   Karen tried to call the manager, but it was an exercise in futility.

heiress [AIR is] *n.* a woman who has inherited wealth
   She was an heiress to a manufacturing fortune.

perpetual [per PECH yoo uhl] *adj.* continuing forever
   The three children seemed to be in perpetual motion.

profound [proh FOWND] *adj.* very deep; having great meaning
   Sometimes profound ideas are expressed in simple words.

substantial [sub STAN shuhl] *adj.* of solid quality; of real value
   The Smiths were substantial members of the community.

Exercise A

Fill in the blanks, using each word from Word List A only once.

We have heard that the woman who lives in that estate near the park

is a wealthy [1] _____ whose grandfather invented something

important. Her garden is lovely, its pond [2] _____ stocked

with carp and other fish. She always appears so handsome and

[3] _____ as she strolls around town with her two little

dogs, wearing a [4] _____ expression of self-satisfaction on her

face. Who knows what kinds of [5] _____ thoughts are going

on in her mind? It is rumored that she is planning to add on to her property

and is likely to [6] _____ several of the residents of Fourth

Street from their homes. They have tried to protest, but they have a sense of

[7] _____, since they know in the end she will get her way. As

a [8] _____ citizen of this little town, what she says carries a

lot of weight.

1. Underline the words that tell what was abundantly praised. Name a synonym for *abundantly*.

2. Underline the nearby words that have a similar meaning to *futility*. Define *futility* in your own words.

3. Circle the words that explain the meaning of *heiress*. What is required for someone to be an *heiress*?

4. Give a word that could substitute for *substantial* in this sentence. What clues are there that Woolf was a *substantial* writer?

5. Underline the words that explain the meaning of *dislodge*. Use *dislodge* in a new sentence.

6. Underline the word that gives a clue to the meaning of *profound*. Give an antonym for *profound*.

7. What words give a clue to the meaning of *distinguished*? Describe a person who appears *distinguished*.

8. Underline the words in the paragraph that give a clue to the meaning of *perpetual*. Give a synonym for *perpetual*.

Read the following passage. Then, complete the activities.

Virginia Woolf is well known for her abundantly praised novels and stories. This bountiful praise is well deserved. Through her writing, Woolf became an important figure in the history of feminism. In 1929, she wrote an essay entitled "A Room of One's Own." It is about the futility of a woman's trying to live as a creative person. It also talks about the near-impossibility of becoming an individual apart from one's family.

Woolf felt that for a woman to be able to become a writer, she must first have money. She knew that inheriting wealth was not possible for everyone. But even if every woman could not be an heiress, she must still be financially secure enough to be able to think beyond the basics of life.

Woolf's essay does not say that every woman who wants to write must have a large office. But she does insist that a woman who wants to become a substantial writer needs a space made for doing only that. She must be able to separate herself from the cares of the household to focus on her own work.

Woolf wrote her essay to shake loose some of the fixed thinking of her day. She wanted to dislodge old beliefs that writing was a man's job because men were naturally better at expressing profound and important ideas.

Though Woolf is thought of as a distinguished writer of great talent, she faced serious depression throughout her life. She was able to overcome many barriers, but her perpetual, unending struggle with mood swings eventually ended her writing career and her life.

The Lady in the Looking Glass: A Reflection

Virginia Woolf

Summary Isabella Tyson is a wealthy woman who lives alone. The narrator looks at the objects in Isabella's home and at Isabella's reflection in a mirror. The descriptions of her home and of her reflection show that she is happy and successful. While she picks flowers from her garden, a mailman delivers letters. Isabella returns from the garden and looks at herself in the mirror. At that moment, we see Isabella's true nature.

Note-taking Guide

Use this chart to record information from the story about how the narrator describes Isabella.

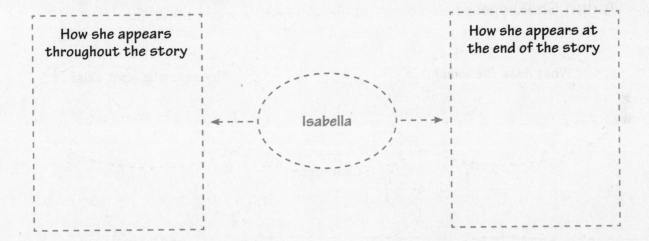

How she appears throughout the story

Isabella

How she appears at the end of the story

from Mrs. Dalloway •
from A Room of One's Own:
from Shakespeare's Sister
Virginia Woolf

Summaries *Mrs. Dalloway* is the story of a day in the life of Clarissa Dalloway. In this short selection, the opening lines of the novel, Clarissa has ventured out on the morning of a party that she is planning. She muses about the party, about her past, and about her life in London. In the essay *from* Shakespeare's Sister, Woolf describes the life of Shakespeare's equally gifted but nonexistent sister, Judith. The vastly different paths that Shakespeare and his sister follow illuminate the disparity between the ways in which men and women were treated in both Shakespeare's time and Woolf's.

Note-taking Guide
Use this chart to list information about either Clarissa Dalloway or Judith Shakespeare.

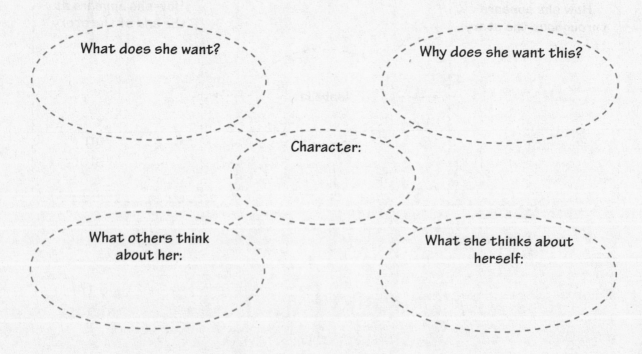

What does she want?

Why does she want this?

Character:

What others think about her:

What she thinks about herself:

The Lady in the Looking Glass: A Reflection • *from* Mrs. Dalloway • *from* A Room of One's Own: *from* Shakespeare's Sister

1. **Interpret:** In "The Lady in the Looking Glass: A Reflection," Isabella is seen through a looking glass, or mirror. How does the looking glass "guide" the narrator to an understanding of Isabella?

   _____

   _____

   _____

2. **Literary Analysis:** Use the chart below to compare the narrative techniques in "The Lady in the Looking Glass: A Reflection," and the selection from *Mrs. Dalloway*.

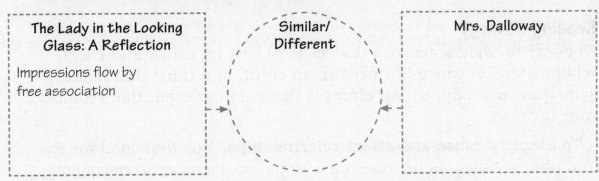

The Lady in the Looking Glass: A Reflection	Similar/ Different	Mrs. Dalloway
Impressions flow by free association		

3. **Reading Strategy:** In *Mrs. Dalloway*, what **questions** did you ask while reading in order to repair your comprehension of the story?

   _____

   _____

   _____

Writing About the Essential Question

What is the relationship of the writer to tradition? How do the selections by Woolf reveal her to be a writer interested in changing tradition?

_____

_____

_____

The Lagoon • Araby

Literary Analysis

A **plot device** is a particular technique used to build a story. Plot devices help you identify and understand the theme, or main idea, of a story. An epiphany and a story within a story are examples of plot devices.

An **epiphany** is a character's sudden insight. An epiphany

- reveals an important truth.
- occurs during an ordinary event or situation.
- forms the climax, or high point of interest, of the story.

A **story within a story** refers to a story that is told during the action of another story. A story within a story

- entertains or serves as an example for the characters.
- reveals an important truth about the events or characters of the main story.

Reading Strategy

One way to understand plot devices is to look for cause-and-effect relationships. A **cause** is a person, an event, or a thing that makes something else happen. An **effect** is the action or event that results from a cause.

To **identify cause-and-effect relationships,** look for signal words and phrases such as *because, as a result, so, therefore, consequently,* and *led to.* These signals provide clues to stated causes and effects. If a cause and its effect are not clearly stated, ask yourself these questions:

- What happened in the story or passage? (This is the effect.)
- Why did this happen? (This is the cause.)

Use the chart to explain a cause-and-effect relationship in each story.

	Cause	Effect
The Lagoon	Arsat and his brother take Diamelen from the Rajah. →	
Araby		→ The narrator is late getting to the bazaar.

Word List A

Study these words from the selections. Then, complete the activities that follow.

discreetly [dis KREET lee] *adv.* in a tactful, cautious, and wise manner
  Very discreetly, Franklin asked questions about Ryan's character.

enchantment [in CHANT muhnt] *n.* the use or effect of charms or spells
  As if under enchantment, Gregory stared at Isabella without blinking.

fascination [fas uh NAY shuhn] *n.* great interest
  Our fascination with the magician's tricks kept us interested for hours.

fringing [FRINJ ing] *adj.* bordered with or as if with an ornamental trim
  The fringing flowers surrounded the scene like a frame.

noiselessly [NOYZ lis lee] *adv.* quietly; silently
  The little spider noiselessly crept up the wall.

offensive [uh FEN siv] *adj.* unpleasant or disagreeable
  An offensive odor hung over the swamp.

somber [SAHM buhr] *adj.* having little light or color; dark
  For some reason, Rachel always wears dark, somber colors.

withstand [with STAND] *v.* to oppose; to resist
  This well-made broom can withstand hard use.

Exercise A

Fill in each blank below with the appropriate word from Word List A.

Nathan had always felt a great [1] _____ for magic. He watched every magic show he could, [2] _____ keeping his eyes on the magician's hands at all times. Most of the time, he could not figure out the trick. Once, trying not to make any sound, he [3] _____ crept behind the stage to see what he could see, but the annoyed magician's assistant noticed this [4] _____ behavior and shooed him away. Another time he dressed in especially [5] _____ clothing, hoping to avoid being noticed in the dark. At intermission, he sneaked past the curtains [6] _____ the stage, hoping to get some insight. No one bothered to [7] _____ this intrusion—perhaps the magician understood what Nathan was going through. He actually did find out how one trick was done. After that, all the [8] _____ seemed to be over for him.

1. Underline the word that means about the same as fascination. What holds great *fascination* for you?

2. Circle what made Polly seem like she was under an enchantment. Tell about a story you have read that includes *enchantment*.

3. Underline the words that describe the fringing border on the scarf.

4. Circle the word that is close to somber. When would you wear a *somber* outfit?

5. Circle the words that describe an example of the abuse the jade sculpture might be able to withstand. What is the worst weather your town has had to *withstand*?

6. Underline the words that explain what Polly thought was so offensive. How do people usually react when something is *offensive*?

7. Underline the word that means the same as noiselessly. Where would it be important to move *noiselessly*?

8. Circle the word in a nearby sentence that means about the same as discreetly. Tell about a time you had to act *discreetly*.

Read the following passage. Pay special attention to the underlined words. Then, read it again, and complete the activities. Use a separate sheet of paper for your written answers.

The bazaar in Chinatown had always been a source of great fascination and interest for Polly, luring her with its charm. She tried to get over there every Saturday so she could browse among the stalls and shops along the main street. She would stroll along in a daze, as if under some mysterious enchantment, and marvel at the interesting toys, gadgets, foods, tablecloths, scarves, bangles, soaps, incense, and such.

Once she found a scarf with a fringing border of strung beads. She just had to have it. She knew it would brighten up any dark, somber outfit that she or her mother might wear. It would make a perfect gift for her mother—one that Polly could borrow anytime.

Another time she saw a small jade sculpture of an elephant. The owner of the shop told her it would withstand any kind of abuse. Even if Polly dropped it on a hard tile floor, she said, it would not break. Polly didn't believe the owner. In fact, she thought it rather offensive that she would tell such an obvious lie to make a sale. Even so, Polly wanted to buy the jade elephant. She just couldn't afford it right now.

One particular Saturday, as Polly was noiselessly poking her way along the street, she noticed another girl about her age, also silently examining every trinket that caught her eye. Then she saw the girl pick up the jade elephant. Polly held her breath for what seemed like a full five minutes until the girl put it back down. That evening, Polly vowed, she would have to discreetly approach her mother and ask for a loan. If she asked tactfully, promising to pay it back soon, perhaps she could come back tomorrow and buy the elephant.

The Lagoon
Joseph Conrad

Summary In this story, a white man visits Arsat, a Malay who lives by a jungle lagoon. Arsat's wife is dying, and the visitor learns her history. She and Arsat had run away from a Malaysian ruler with the help of Arsat's brother. They were pursued, and Arsat abandoned his brother to save the woman. While Arsat tells the story, his wife dies, and Arsat decides to return to face his former pursuers.

Note-taking Guide

Use this chart to record the action of the story that Arsat tells his friend.

Climax Action:

_____

_____

_____

_____

Beginning Action

Ending Action

Araby
James Joyce

Summary The narrator tells about an experience he had as a boy growing up in Dublin, Ireland, in the late nineteenth century. He had a crush on another boy's sister. The first time she spoke to him, she asked whether he was going to a fair called Araby. She herself could not go. The narrator offered to bring her something from Araby. He asked his uncle—he lived with his uncle and aunt—for the money to go to the fair. The night of the fair, his uncle came home late, and it was after nine when he gave the narrator the money. By the time the narrator arrived at the fair, it was nearly over. The big hall in which the fair was being held was already dark. At one stall, a young woman with an English accent was talking and laughing with two young men. The narrator refused her offer to serve him. He suddenly realized that he had been foolish about everything, and he felt both grief and anger.

Note-taking Guide
Use the chart to examine the plot of Araby.

Exposition	Rising Action	Climax	Falling Action	Resolution

Araby

James Joyce

The narrator, or storyteller, lives on a quiet, dead-end street. He enjoys playing on the street with his friends. They explore the dark alleys, gardens, and stables behind the houses. In the winter, the boys stay out until dark. From the shadows they watch the narrator's uncle come home. They also watch the sister of a boy whose last name is Mangan. The narrator has a serious crush on Mangan's sister. Every morning he watches her door until she comes out. Then, he follows her when she goes to school. He even thinks about her when he helps his aunt with her shopping in the busy, dirty markets in Dublin. Although the narrator has strong feelings for Mangan's sister, he has never said a single word to her.

◆ ◆ ◆

At last she spoke to me. When she addressed the first words to me I was so confused that I did not know what to answer. She asked me was I going to *Araby*. I forget whether I answered yes or no. It would be a splendid bazaar,[1] she said; she would love to go.

"And why can't you?" I asked.

While she spoke she turned a silver bracelet round and round her wrist. She could not go, she said, because there would be a retreat[2]

© Pearson Education

Vocabulary Development

addressed (uh DREST) *v.* directed to

---

1. **bazaar** (buh ZAHR) *n.* a market or fair where various goods are sold in stalls.
2. **retreat** (ri TREET) *n.* a period of retirement or seclusion for prayer, religious study, and meditation.

Background

This story takes place in Dublin, Ireland, in the early 1900s. The main character is a boy who lives on North Richmond Street and goes to a bazaar. Like the narrator in "Araby," James Joyce, the story's author, once lived with his family on North Richmond Street. When Joyce was twelve years old, he went to the Araby bazaar held in Dublin in May 1894. Look at a library book, a social studies textbook, or the Internet to find a map of Dublin. Use the map to answer the following questions:

• What river flows through the city?

_____

• What is the name of one park in Dublin?

_____

• In what part of Dublin does the narrator live with his aunt and uncle?

_____

Reading Strategy

Why does the narrator follow Mangan's sister when she goes to school? Underline the sentence that tells you.

Read Fluently

Read aloud the bracketed paragraph. Identify difficult and unfamiliar words. Look in a dictionary to find out what these words mean and how to pronounce them. Then, read the bracketed passage again.

Reading Strategy

Why does the narrator have to wait to go to the bazaar?

_____

_____

_____

Reading Check

In the second bracketed paragraph, the narrator hears his uncle coming in. Circle the details that tell him what his uncle is doing.

that week in her convent.[3] Her brother and two other boys were fighting for their caps and I was alone at the railings. She held one of the spikes, bowing her head towards me. The light from the lamp opposite our door caught the white curve of her neck, lit up her hair that rested there and, falling, lit up the hand upon the railing. It fell over one side of her dress and caught the white border of a petticoat,[4] just visible as she stood at ease.

♦ ♦ ♦

Mangan's sister is happy for the narrator. He promises to bring her something from the bazaar.

The narrator cannot stop thinking about Mangan's sister. He is excited about going to the bazaar. He has trouble doing his schoolwork, and he daydreams in class. On Saturday morning the narrator reminds his uncle that he wants to go to the bazaar that night. His uncle leaves for the day. While the narrator eagerly waits for his uncle to return and give him money, he stares at the clock. He stands at the window for an hour and watches his friends play outside. He pictures Mangan's sister in his mind.

♦ ♦ ♦

At nine o'clock I heard my uncle's latchkey in the hall door. I heard him talking to himself and heard the hallstand rocking when it had received the weight of his overcoat. I could interpret these signs. When he was midway through his dinner I asked him to give me the money to go to the bazaar. He had forgotten.

"The people are in bed and after their first sleep now," he said.

3. **convent** (KAHN vent) _n._ a school run by an order of nuns.
4. **petticoat** (PET ee koht) _n._ a woman's slip that is sometimes full and trimmed with lace or ruffles.

I did not smile. My aunt said to him energetically:

"Can't you give him the money and let him go? You've kept him late enough as it is."

My uncle said he was very sorry he had forgotten. He said he believed in the old saying: *All work and no play makes Jack a dull boy.* He asked me where I was going and, when I had told him a second time he asked me did I know *The Arab's Farewell to His Steed.*[5] When I left the kitchen he was about to recite the opening lines of the piece to my aunt.

◆ ◆ ◆

> The narrator leaves the house with money his uncle gives him. He rides an empty train to the bazaar. The train arrives just before ten o'clock. The narrator pays the fee and enters a large, dark hall. Because it is late, most of the stalls are closed. The bazaar is as quiet as a church.

◆ ◆ ◆

Remembering with difficulty why I had come I went over to one of the stalls and examined porcelain[6] vases and flowered tea sets. At the door of the stall a young lady was talking and laughing with two young gentlemen. I remarked their English accents and listened vaguely to their conversation.

"O, I never said such a thing!"

"O, but you did!"

"O, but I didn't!"

"Didn't she say that?"

"Yes. I heard her."

Vocabulary Development

remarked (ri MARKT) *v.* noticed

5. **The Arab's . . . His Steed** *n.* popular nineteenth-century poem.

6. **porcelain** (POR suh lin) *n.* a hard, white type of clay pottery also known as china.

Read Fluently

Read the bracketed paragraph aloud. Write three words you would use to describe the narrator's uncle.

1. _____

2. _____

3. _____

Stop to Reflect

Does this description of the bazaar fit with your expectations of it?

_____

Why, or why not? _____

_____

_____

_____

Stop to Reflect

Is the narrator's trip to Araby a success? Why or why not?

_____

_____

_____

Literary Analysis

The bracketed passage is the narrator's **epiphany**. Tell in your own words what the narrator realizes about himself in the epiphany.

_____

_____

_____

◆   ◆   ◆

The young lady offers to help the narrator. He answers that he doesn't need help, and she doesn't encourage him. She watches him as she returns to the conversation with the two young gentlemen.

The narrator lingers and pretends to be interested in the items in the stall. Then, he leaves, jingling the coins in his pocket.

◆   ◆   ◆

I heard a voice call from one end of the gallery that the light was out. The upper part of the hall was now completely dark.

Gazing up into the darkness I saw myself as a creature driven and derided by vanity; and my eyes burned with anguish and anger.

Vocabulary Development

derided (dee RYD id) *v.* made fun of
vanity (VAN uh tee) *n.* excessive pride

The Lagoon • Araby

1. **Literary Analysis:** In "The Lagoon," Conrad uses the **plot device** of a **story within a story.** What information would you lack if all of "The Lagoon" had been narrated in the first person by Arsat?

   _____

   _____

2. **Literary Analysis:** Write a paragraph describing the narrator's feelings when he experiences his **epiphany** in "Araby."

   _____

   _____

   _____

   _____

3. **Reading Strategy:** Complete the **cause-and-effect** chain below by explaining what causes Arsat to tell his story within a story and what effect results from the telling of his story.

Cause	Effect/Cause	Effect
	Arsat tells Tuan the story of how he and his brother took Diamelen.	

Writing About the Essential Question

What is the relationship of the writer to tradition? Do the plot devices these writers use, story-within-a-story and epiphany, help convey the pain of wanting something very much and then failing to get it?

_____

_____

_____

The Rocking-Horse Winner
• A Shocking Accident

Literary Analysis

Most short stories have a **theme.** A theme is a central idea or question that the writer explores. Writers often show the theme through a **symbol.** This is a person, thing, or action that brings to mind a deeper meaning. Look for symbols as you read.

Each of these stories is told from a **third-person point of view.** This means that the narrator does not take part in the action. As you read, compare the ways in which both authors use this point of view to show their themes. Note that each author tells what the characters are thinking and uses symbols to suggest meanings. Ask yourself how the third-person point of view is different in each story.

Reading Strategy

As you read a literary work, **make and confirm predictions** about the outcome of the work. A prediction is a reasoned guess about what will happen next. Use your own background knowledge and details from the text to make a prediction. Then, determine whether your prediction is correct as you read the work. Use the graphic organizer below to help you make and confirm predictions about the selections by Lawrence and Greene.

Background Knowledge		Predictions		Confirm Predictions
Details from Text				

Word List A

Study these words from the selections. Then, complete the activities that follow.

colleagues [KAHL eegz] *n.* fellow workers in a profession or organization
  Jerry's colleagues all advised him not to ask for a raise.

commiseration [kuh miz uh RAY shuhn] *n.* expression of sympathy
  After Bonnie's words of commiseration, Jane felt better.

distinguished [dis TING wisht] *adj.* dignified
  In his tuxedo, Harry looked quite distinguished.

extraordinarily [eks truh AWR duh ner uh lee] *adv.* remarkably
  Jesse is extraordinarily strong for a boy his age.

furnishings [FER nish ingz] *n.* furniture or appliances, as for a room
  Sam's new furnishings were all very modern and sleek.

inevitably [in EV uh tuh blee] *adv.* unavoidably; certainly
  If Tammy keeps spending so recklessly, she will inevitably go into debt.

moderately [MAHD uhr it lee] *adv.* not extremely or excessively
  If you eat moderately and exercise regularly, you can control your weight.

noiselessly [NOYZ lis lee] *adv.* silently; quietly
  The cat noiselessly stalked the mouse.

Exercise A

Fill in each blank in the paragraph below using each word from Word List A only once.

Jo was looking for new [1] _____ for her office. She tried to tiptoe
through the furniture store as [2] _____ as possible, because she didn't
want to attract the salesperson's attention. Her budget was tight and so she
was interested only in [3] _____ priced pieces, but she knew that,
without fail, the salesperson would [4] _____ try to steer her toward
more expensive items. She wished she could find a desk that would impress
her [5] _____ at work when they passed her office. She kept looking at
elegant, [6] _____ pieces, which of course were all too costly for her.
Then she spotted exactly what she wanted—an [7] _____ well-designed
desk, both beautiful and practical, on sale, just within her price range. She
couldn't believe her eyes. When the salesperson came over, however, she noticed
the kind expression of [8] _____ on his face. "I'm sorry, miss," he said
sympathetically. "That piece has already been sold."

1. Circle some examples of furnishings. Define *furnishings*.

2. Underline the phrase that is a sign that Mr. Appleby looks distinguished. Then, use *distinguished* in a sentence.

3. Circle the phrase that tells what Mr. Appleby thinks his extraordinarily gifted grandson deserves. Name an animal that jumps *extraordinarily* high.

4. Underline the words that tell what the saleswoman's colleagues were doing.

5. Circle the words in these sentences that reinforce the meaning of the word inevitably. Name one thing that will *inevitably* happen today.

6. Underline the words that explain what moderately realistic means. Where do you buy *moderately* priced clothing?

7. Circle the words that suggest the reason for the woman's commiseration. Describe a time that *commiseration* with a friend comforted you.

8. Circle the words that contrast with noiselessly. Describe something that you do *noiselessly*.

Read the following passage. Pay special attention to the underlined words. Then, read it again, and complete the activities. Use a separate sheet of paper for your written answers.

Mr. Appleby, better known as "Grandpa" to young William Appleby, was on a mission. He had already provided most of the <u>furnishings</u> for William's bedroom, such as a "big boy" bed and a dresser. Now, he was looking for the perfect rocking horse. A well-groomed, <u>distinguished</u> gentleman of eighty, Mr. Appleby remembered fondly the beautifully carved rocking horse he had had as a child. He hoped to find something like it for William, an <u>extraordinarily</u> gifted young boy who deserved only the best.

As Mr. Appleby entered the finest children's store in town, he was approached by a young saleswoman. She had just broken away from a few of her <u>colleagues</u> who appeared to be having a meeting in the center of the floor. "How may I help you?" she asked.

"I'm looking for a very special rocking horse," Mr. Appleby said. "It's a gift for my grandson. That's why it has to be wonderful. I want a traditional wooden horse. None of those plastic things."

"Well, follow me, sir," she said. They walked into an area filled with rocking horses. <u>Inevitably</u>, each was plastic. All were battery-powered, and every one had a gimmick of some kind. Some were able to make noises that sounded <u>moderately</u> realistic, as if an actual horse's neigh had been badly recorded. Mr. Appleby sighed, and the salesperson smiled in <u>commiseration</u>. She sympathized with the difficulty of finding a traditional horse. Then, a gorgeous wooden horse caught Mr. Appleby's eye. It had no batteries. It did not snort or neigh. It rocked <u>noiselessly</u> and naturally when he pushed it. Best of all, it looked very much like the one Mr. Appleby had had as a child. "I'll take it," he said. Then he added, "Actually, I'd like two." The saleswoman smiled.

The Rocking-Horse Winner

D. H. Lawrence

Summary This story explores the cost of greed. An unhappy, greedy woman feels little for her children and complains about a lack of money. She tells her son, Paul, that luck is the only thing that brings money. Paul wants to make his mother happy, so he tries to become lucky. He discovers that when he sits on his rocking horse, he suddenly knows which horses will win at the races. He wins a small fortune by betting. He secretly gives money to his mother, but she is not satisfied. Paul drives himself nearly crazy trying to please her.

Note-taking Guide

Use this chart to record the main events in the story.

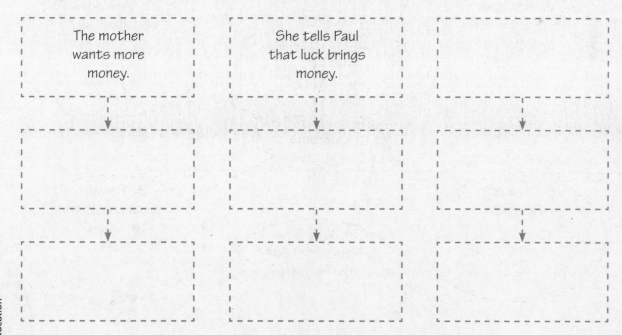

The mother wants more money.

She tells Paul that luck brings money.

A Shocking Accident
Graham Greene

Summary In this story, Jerome learns that his beloved father has been killed in a freak accident. A pig fell on him from a balcony as the man walked down the street. It is difficult for Jerome to share this story because he hates to see people try not to laugh. He worries about telling his fiancée the story. He fears that if he sees her trying not to laugh, he will not be able to marry her.

Note-taking Guide

Fill in the chart to help you to understand Jerome.

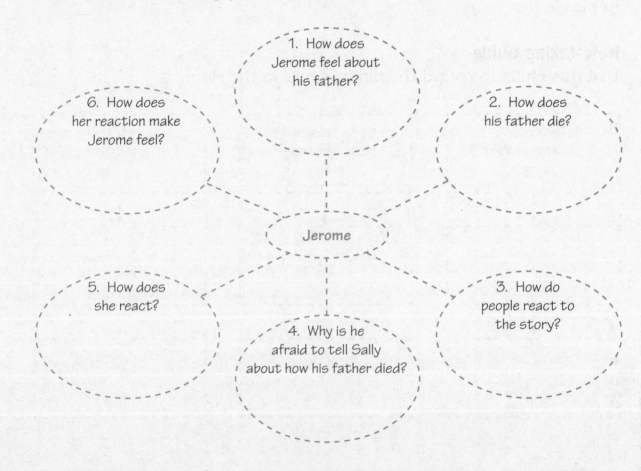

1. How does Jerome feel about his father?

2. How does his father die?

3. How do people react to the story?

4. Why is he afraid to tell Sally about how his father died?

5. How does she react?

6. How does her reaction make Jerome feel?

Jerome

The Rocking-Horse Winner • A Shocking Accident

1. **Literary Analysis:** Complete the chart below by noting passages that show the **symbolic** meanings of the rocking horse. Explain how these meanings connect to the overall **theme** of the story.

Symbolic Meanings	Passages That Illustrate	Links to Overall Theme
Effort to satisfy a need that cannot be satisfied		
Frightening power of desire and wishes		

2. **Literary Analysis:** How is the use of the **third-person point of view** similar in both "The Rocking-Horse Winner" and "A Shocking Accident"?

_____

_____

3. **Reading Strategy:** List the background knowledge and details that you used to **make a prediction** about one of the selections. Then, **confirm** the accuracy of your prediction. Explain why your prediction was accurate or inaccurate.

_____

_____

_____

_____

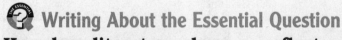 **Writing About the Essential Question**

How does literature shape or reflect society? Does the uniqueness of the main character in either or both of the stories suggest a message about society? Explain.

_____

_____

The Soldier • Wirers • Anthem for Doomed Youth

Literary Analysis

The **tone** of a literary work is the writer's attitude toward the readers and toward the subject. The words and details the writer uses set the tone of a work. For example, in these lines from Rupert Brooke's "The Soldier," the underlined words set a tone of happy memories and loyalty toward England.

> Her sights and sounds; dreams happy as her day:
> And laughter, learnt of friends; and gentleness,
> In hearts at peace, under an English heaven.

In a way, these selections are like letters sent home by soldiers during World War I. Each "letter" contains a **theme** about the war for those in England who are not fighting. The theme is an insight or message about life. You can use tone as a key to **determining the theme** of the work. Identify words and phrases that reveal each writer's attitude toward the war and toward civilian readers. Then, think about what the tone reveals about the author's insight or message about the war.

Reading Strategy

Writers often suggest themes rather than state them directly. Therefore, readers must use relevant details from the text to **infer the essential message** of the work. Use the chart below to infer the essential message in these works.

Passage	Relevant Details	Essential Message
The Soldier		
Wirers		
Anthem for Doomed Youth		

Word List A

Study these words from the selections. Then, complete the activities.

bore [BAWR] *v.* gave birth to; produced; endured; carried
Our dog bore three litters of puppies, all of them adorable.

concealed [kuhn SEELD] *v.* kept from being seen; hidden
The birthday gifts were concealed behind the dresser.

eternal [ee TER nuhl] *adj.* without a beginning or end; lasting forever
President Kennedy's grave is marked by an eternal flame.

mended [MEND ed] *v.* repaired; fixed
It was only a small tear, and he mended it with a couple of stitches.

muffled [MUF uhld] *adj.* wrapped up; deadened or quieted (a sound)
Although she covered the phone, I could hear muffled laughter on her end.

shrill [SHRIL] *adj.* high-pitched; piercing
The shrill whistle told the factory workers that lunch break was over.

stride [STRYD] *v.* walk with long steps
The graduates stride proudly across the stage to receive their diplomas.

toil [TOYL] *v.* work hard
The brothers will toil all day building the tree house.

Exercise A

Fill in the blanks, using each word from Word List A only once.

We can hear the [1] _____ screech of the siren as it announces the arrival of an approaching ambulance. The ambulance pulls up to the entrance, and there are [2] _____ sounds coming from inside the closed doors. Although the driver calls ahead to warn us, we rarely really know what is [3] _____ behind those doors. That's part of what makes our work exciting. Night after night, we [4] _____ here at the hospital. Some nights fly by quickly, while others feel almost [5] _____. The best nights are those on which each patient is healed or [6] _____ and sent home. That doesn't happen often, but when it does, we [7] _____ out to our cars in the morning with a good feeling. The job gives us plenty of stories to tell, like the night a woman [8] _____ triplets in an elevator. Who knows what could happen next?

1. Circle the word that gives a clue to the meaning of muffled. What might make a noise sound *muffled*?

2. Circle the word that tells what was shrill. Write a sentence using the word *shrill*.

3. Underline the phrase that tells what the soldiers toil to do. Give a word that means the same as *toil*.

4. Circle the word that gives a clue to the meaning of eternal. Give a word or phrase that means the opposite of *eternal*.

5. Underline the phrase that tells what the top brass concealed. Now give a synonym for *concealed*.

6. Give a word that could substitute for stride in the sentence. Now write a new sentence using the word *stride*.

7. Circle the word that tells what bore the idea. Give a word or phrase that means the same as *bore*.

8. Underline the phrase that tells what the soldier mended. Use *mended* in a new sentence.

Read the following passage. Then, complete the activities.

Dear Father and Mum,

As I write, I can hear off in the distance the muffled sounds of artillery fire. I am glad they are faint now. Yet, even when the sounds of battle are farther away, the shrill cries of the explosives continue to echo in my head loudly, leaving me with vicious headaches.

Some of us continue to toil digging the trenches, the hard labor wearing some of us down. For others, sitting day after day in those dreary ditches is much worse. The physical effort is draining, but the eternal waiting, the endless boredom, takes its own toll.

The top brass certainly concealed this part of the war from us recruits. If we had known what it is like to sit and wait for an attack to come at any time, from any quarter, I feel sure we would not have been quite so quick to stride confidently forward to sign our names on the line.

Not that I wish the long-awaited attack to come, by any means. We have heard enough rumors about gas attacks to interfere with sleep for years to come. What warped mind bore that idea of warfare? How could anyone conceive of such a weapon? Bullets and bombs are bad enough without adding this new poison gas in the bargain.

But enough of my complaining. Mum, you'll be happy to hear I have mended my socks all on my own. They don't look as nice as when you used to fix them for me. But when it's not raining, they're good enough to keep my toes warm during these long nights. They'll do until I get home—here's hoping that will be very soon.

Your loving son,

Jeremy

The Soldier
Rupert Brooke

Wirers
Siegfried Sassoon

Anthem for Doomed Youth
Wilfred Owen

"If ye break faith — we shall not sleep"

BUY VICTORY BONDS

Summaries These poems arose from the battlefields of World War I. The patriotic speaker in **"The Soldier"** imagines that his grave will be a patch of rich English dust in foreign soil. There, his soul will reflect the gentleness of England. **"Wirers"** describes a night among soldiers who repair the barbed wire around the trenches. **"Anthem for Doomed Youth"** describes the shows of emotion that must take the place of funeral rites in times of war.

Note-taking Guide

Each of these poems offers a different point of view on the topic of war. Use this chart to record the central image or idea of each poem.

Poem	Central Image/Idea
The Soldier	
Wirers	
Anthem for Doomed Youth	

The Soldier • Wirers • Anthem for Doomed Youth

1. **Evaluate:** Which of the two poems, "Wirers" or "Anthem for a Doomed Youth," does a better job of showing the horrors of war? Explain.

   _____

   _____

2. **Literary Analysis:** Use the chart to briefly describe the **tone** in a key passage from one of these works.

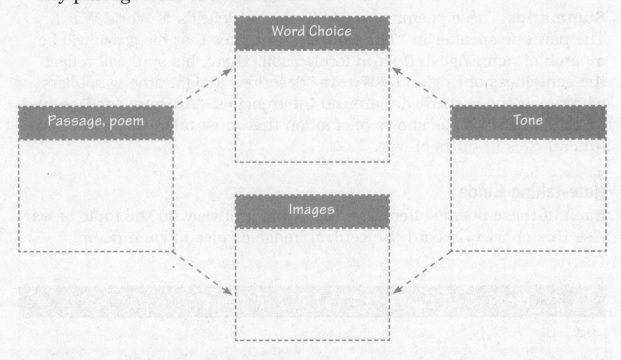

3. **Reading Strategy:** Use relevant details from lines 9–14 of "Anthem for Doomed Youth" to **infer the essential message** expressed in those lines.

   _____

   _____

 Writing About the Essential Question

How does literature shape or reflect society? Do you think Sassoon's poem affected the attitude of British readers toward the war?

The Demon Lover

Literary Analysis

A **ghost story** is a tale in which part of the past—typically, a dead person—seems to appear in the present. Ghost stories include

- a strange or mysterious setting.
- the suggestion that something unexplained is at work.

A ghost story may include a **flashback.** Flashback is a scene that interrupts a story to tell about events that occurred in the past. A flashback in a ghost story can add to the sense that the past is still alive.

Ghost stories blur the familiar and the unfamiliar to create **ambiguity**—the effect of two or more different possible explanations. Ambiguity creates uncertainty.

Reading Strategy

"The Demon Lover" allows you to **relate a literary work to a primary source document.** Bowen's fiction takes place in the real world described by Winston Churchill in his "Wartime Speech." Churchill describes the fighting in France and encourages Britons to persevere. As you read Bowen's story, use a graphic organizer like one shown to relate Mrs. Drover's private battle to the public battle in Churchill's **primary source document.**

	Literary Work: Demon Lover	Primary Source: Wartime Speech
Source of Fear	ghostly lover	German army
Atmosphere		
Weapons		
Tactics		
Main Goal		
End Result		

Word List A

Study these words from the selection. Then, complete the activities that follow.

alight [uh LYT] *adj.* lit up
   The room was alight with the glow of ten candles.

apprehension [ap ree HEN shuhn] *n.* a worried expectation
   With great apprehension, Nora crept into the cobweb-covered crawl space.

assent [uh SENT] *n.* consent or agreement
   We cannot go ahead with the plan without the manager's assent.

caretaker [KAIR tay kuhr] *n.* a person hired to look after a place
   The morning after the big party, the caretaker tidied up the yard and the pool area.

dependability [di pen duh BIL uh tee] *n.* the quality of being reliable
   Maureen's dependability is her greatest qualification for this job.

heightening [HYT uhn ing] *adj.* increasing or intensifying
   The ticking clock added to the heightening terror Charles felt.

knowledgeably [NAHL uh jib lee] *adv.* in an informed way
   Paul spoke knowledgeably about baseball history at the sports dinner.

perplexed [puhr PLEXT] *adj.* doubtful; confused; bewildered
   Angela was perplexed about how to use the new software for her computer.

Exercise A

Fill in each blank in the paragraph below using each word from Word List A only once.

Noticing that all the rooms in the corner apartment were [1] _____,
Carol wondered who could be inside. She had had the job of [2] _____ for
a few months, but she had never seen anyone occupying that unit. Very sensible
and known for her [3] _____, Carol was also very concerned about
conserving energy. She was [4] _____ about who might be wasting
so much electricity. She was sure she had met all the tenants before and she
[5] _____ matched their names and apartments in her mind, continuing
to wonder about the corner apartment. She began to feel some [6] _____
as the day went on, for the lights remained on, even during daylight hours.
With rapidly [7] _____ concern, she walked to the apartment and
knocked on the door. A tiny old woman answered. When Carol asked her about
the lights, the woman said, "I thought I could turn on my own lights without
your [8] _____!"

Read the following passage. Pay special attention to the underlined words. Then, read it again, and complete the activities. Use a separate sheet of paper for your written answers.

If you are confused, <u>perplexed</u>, or simply wondering about how you might be able to support yourself in the future, one job you might want to consider is that of a <u>caretaker</u> of an estate or hotel grounds.

The job of a caretaker is to make sure the property is kept clean, tidy, and in good repair. If you have any <u>apprehension</u>—any worry at all—that you might not be up to the task, here is a list of questions; if you can answer *yes* to all of them, then you could probably do the job well.

- Do you know how to use basic tools, such as hammers, screwdrivers, and drills?
- If someone asked you a question about basic landscaping and maintenance, do you know enough to answer <u>knowledgeably</u>?
- Do you have excellent communication skills?
- Can your employer count on your <u>dependability</u> as a worker? Can someone else vouch for your reliability?
- Do you have a current driver's license?
- Are you physically fit, able to bend and lift, and willing to work hard?
- Can you work odd hours, including some evenings and weekends?
- Would you be able to deal with rapidly <u>heightening</u> demands from increasing numbers of people during possible emergencies?
- Would you be able to check that, at night, common areas are properly <u>alight</u> and therefore more secure? If need be, can you replace any burned-out bulbs in lamps?

If you are interested in being a caretaker, fill out an application for the job; as a qualified candidate, you can look forward to a job offer. All that would be needed is your <u>assent</u>, and once you communicate your agreement to work in this position, you can start immediately.

1. Underline two words that mean about the same as <u>perplexed</u>. Tell about something that once caused you to feel *perplexed*.

2. Circle the words that describe the job of a <u>caretaker</u>. What is something you would want a *caretaker* to do at your home?

3. Underline the word that means about the same as <u>apprehension</u>. Name one thing that gives you some *apprehension*.

4. Circle the words that indicate that a person is answering a question <u>knowledgeably</u>. Use *knowledgeably* in a sentence.

5. Underline the word that is close in meaning to <u>dependability</u>. Name one area in which you demonstrate *dependability*.

6. Circle the word that is close in meaning to <u>heightening</u>. How do you usually react to *heightening* demands on your time and patience?

7. Circle the word that is described as <u>alight</u>. What does *alight* mean?

8. Underline the word that means about the same as <u>assent</u>. To what job offer would you eagerly give your *assent*?

The Demon Lover
Elizabeth Bowen

Summary During World War II, Mrs. Drover returns to her shut-up London house to pick up some items. A mysterious unstamped letter has appeared on her table, but there is no clue as to how it arrived. Mrs. Drover is horrified at the realization that it appears to be from her ex-fiancé, whom she believes to have died in World War I. Referring to a vow that the engaged couple had made to each other, he now promises to return, most likely on that day, at the "hour arranged." A haunted Mrs. Drover seeks a place of safety and escapes into a taxi, only to discover that its driver is her ex-fiancé.

Note-taking Guide
Use this chart to describe the events in "The Demon Lover."

Characters:	
Setting:	
Problem:	
Event 1:	
Event 2:	
Event 3:	
Event 4:	
Event 5:	
Event 6:	
Conclusion:	

The Demon Lover

1. **Infer:** The appearance of the letter in Mrs. Drover's house is unexpected because the Post Office has been delivering the mail to their country house. Why is she so upset by this letter?

   _____

2. **Literary Analysis:** Find examples in the tale of the following characteristics of a **ghost story**: _intrusion of the past_ and _the suggestion of supernatural explanations for events._

   _____

   _____

3. **Literary Analysis:** Identify two examples of **ambiguity** in phrases in the story's opening paragraph. Then, explain how they hint at the strange events to come. Record you responses in the chart.

Ambiguity	What Does it Reveal?

4. **Reading Strategy: Relate a literary work to a primary source** by writing two ways in which "The Demon Lover" with Churchill's "Wartime Speech" are similar.

   _____

   _____

Writing About the Essential Question

What is the relationship between place and literature? Beyond the _physical_ effects of war on the home front, what _emotional_ effects of the war does Bowen's story suggest?

   _____

   _____

   _____

Vergissmeinicht • Postscript: For Gweno • Naming of Parts

Literary Analysis

Theme refers to the central idea of a work. Sometimes writers focus on **universal themes,** or ideas that are meaningful to most readers, regardless of their individual backgrounds. Universal themes

- feature concepts to which most people can relate.
- include topics such as love, war, death, and honor.

The poems in this group focus on the connection between love and war. Their **irony** comes from the idea that these two contradictory elements are inseparable. As you read, look for ways in which the poets set images of love against the violence of war.

Reading Strategy

When you **analyze the author's purpose,** you examine his or her reason for writing. Ask yourself: *What is the poet's overall message or theme?* As you read, consider what the poets are saying by putting together images of love and war. Use the chart below to compare images within each poem.

	Images of Love or Tenderness	Images of War or Violence
"Vergissmeinicht"		
"Postscript: For Gweno"		
"Naming of Parts"		

Word List A

Study these words from the selections. Then, complete the activities.

beloved [bi LUV id] *n.* a person who is dearly loved
His beloved smiled back at him with joy in her eyes.

decayed [dee KAYD] *v.* wasted away; rotted
The bananas sat in the dish so long that they decayed.

fumbling [FUM bling] *n.* clumsily grasping at something
Lisa was fumbling the ball and could not quite catch it.

gestures [JES cherz] *n.* nonverbal movements or acts that convey ideas or emotions to the observer
The teacher's friendly gestures punctuated her welcoming speech.

gothic [GAHTH ik] *adj.* using an elaborate, ornate style of lettering
On his diploma, words were hand-written in fancy, angular gothic letters.

mingled [MING guhld] *v.* mixed together
Red, purple, and green mingled on the canvas of Stefan's painting.

mocked [MAHKT] *v.* ridiculed; scorned
Arjun mocked our attempts to build a robot as powerful as his.

tormented [tawr MENT ed] *adj.* physically or mentally tortured; anguished
After the wind pounded it, the tormented tree looked twisted and bare.

Exercise A

Fill in the blanks, using each word from Word List A only once.

When Amanda caught sight of the beige envelope in her mailbox, she assumed it must be from her [1] _____. Each week, Thomas faithfully sent a postcard or letter, professing his love. These messages were only some of his many sweet [2] _____, like sending her flowers on her birthday. Every happy emotion [3] _____ together in Amanda's brain when she recognized the [4] _____ script, which Thomas had taught himself when he took up hand-lettered calligraphy as a hobby. Amanda was so excited that she could not help [5] _____ as she grasped for the envelope. However, as it slipped through her trembling fingers, she noticed this was not one of his regular letters. No, it looked more like an invitation. What if Thomas's love for her had suddenly [6] _____ and died, and he had become engaged to someone else? Would he have ridiculed and [7] _____ her love so cruelly by sending her an invitation to his marriage? Suddenly, Amanda felt [8] _____ by doubts.

1. Circle the words that tells who is Maria's beloved. Write your own definition for the noun *beloved*.

2. Circle a word that has the same meaning as <u>tormented</u>. Underline the reasons that Maria felt *tormented*.

3. Underline the words that explain where Maria's thoughts <u>mingled</u>. Write a synonym for the word *mingled*.

4. Circle the words that tell what kind of <u>gestures</u> Maria saw in the cacti. Write a sentence describing *gestures* you could imagine seeing in nature.

5. Underline the words that tell how the aloe <u>mocked</u> Maria's return. Then write a synonym for the word *mocked*.

6. Circle the words that tell what <u>decayed</u>. Write a sentence using the word *decayed*.

7. Underline the words that tell what Diego was <u>fumbling</u> for. Write a sentence describing why you think he might have been *fumbling* at that particular moment.

8. Underline the words that describe the word <u>gothic</u>. Where else might you find *gothic* script?

Read the following passage. Then, complete the activities.

It was difficult, at moments, to be a soldier at the same time you were a mother, Maria thought, as she waited for her husband, her <u>beloved</u>, to meet her at the house on the first day she returned home from the war. She felt <u>tormented</u> by the thought of having left behind her comrades, who were still in so much danger. Yet she was equally anguished because of the reason she had been allowed to return home: her daughter had needed an operation. Thank goodness it had gone well, and now she, Maria, had been granted a special leave of absence to visit her little Isabel.

Maria paced the path through the rocky front garden of her home. Her garden <u>mingled</u> different plants, with aloe plants blended among the blooming cacti. The large white waxy flowers of the saguaro cacti seemed to be making <u>gestures</u> of welcome by opening their blooms for her arrival.

On the other hand, the aloe plant she had nurtured for a decade seemed to have <u>mocked</u> her return by dying while she was gone. Its green spikes had shriveled and <u>decayed</u> to brown, leathery lumps.

Her thoughts were interrupted when her husband Diego drove up and wrapped her in his arms. For a few moments, they said nothing. Then he began <u>fumbling</u> for something in his jacket, reaching clumsily to grasp a document with strange, <u>gothic</u> writing on it. The fancy, angular lettering turned out to be part of an award Isabel had received at school for her excellent grades the entire year. Isabel was recovering well, Diego said. In fact, she had insisted her mother see the award before going to the hospital. Together, Maria and Diego laughed and cried and blessed their good fortune.

Vergissmeinicht
Kith Douglas

Postscript: For Gweno
Alun Lewis

Naming of Parts
Henry Reed

Summary The subjects of these poems connect to World War II. In **"Vergissmeinicht"** a soldier returns to a battlefield and studies the dead body of a German soldier. **"For Gweno"** is a message from a soldier to his wife, reminding her that they will be together forever. Finally, **"Naming of Parts"** details an English drill sergeant giving his soldiers instruction on their rifles while the flowers from nearby gardens watch.

Note-taking Guide
Use this chart to identify the speaker, what is happening to the speaker, and how he feels in each poem.

	Speaker	What the Speaker Is Experiencing	How the Speaker Feels
"Vergissmeinicht"			
"Postscript: For Gweno"			
"Naming of Parts"			

Vergissmeinicht • Postscript: For Gweno • Naming of Parts

1. **Infer:** Consider the speaker's thoughts in "Naming of Parts." What can you infer about the speaker?

   _____

   _____

2. **Literary Analysis:** These poems explore **universal themes** by combining images of love and tenderness with the brutality and violence of war. Use the chart below to identify the poets' overall statements about love and war.

	Statement About Love and War
"Vergissmeinicht"	
"Postscript: For Gweno"	
"Naming of Parts"	

3. **Reading Strategy:** Why do these poets combine love and war, two seemingly opposite human experiences?

   _____

   _____

Writing About the Essential Question

How does literature shape or reflect society? In these three poems, how are vital social bonds affected, or annihilated, by war? Explain.

_____

_____

_____

Shooting an Elephant • No Witchcraft for Sale

Literary Analysis

Cultural conflict is the struggle between different social, economic, and historical attitudes and beliefs. For example, a cultural conflict may occur if one group of people wants to build a town on land that another group of people considers sacred to its ancestors. Cultural conflict appears in both fiction and nonfiction. As you read, pay attention to the ways in which the thoughts and emotions of people from two different cultures differ.

Stories of cultural conflict often contain **irony. Verbal irony** is the difference between what a character says and what a character thinks. In a cultural conflict, verbal irony may be used for self-protection. **Situational irony** occurs when something happens that contradicts the expectations of the characters or audience. In a cultural conflict, situations may become ironic when a group's actions do not coincide with its attitudes or beliefs.

Reading Strategy

Both "Shooting an Elephant"—a work of nonfiction—and "No Witchcraft for Sale"—a work of fiction—involve themes of cultural conflict. As you read the selections, use a graphic organizer like the one shown to **analyze and evaluate the similar themes.**

	Shooting an Elephant	No Witchcraft for Sale
Aspect of Theme: Cultural Conflict		
Source of Conflict		
Details of Conflict		
Result of Conflict		

© Pearson Education

Word List A

Study these words from the selections. Then, complete the activities.

comparable [KAHM puh ruh buhl] *adj.* having features that are similar or can be compared
   This is not the brand of yogurt I like, but it tastes comparable.

inevitable [in EV ih tuh buhl] *adj.* sure to happen; not avoidable
   After it rains in the desert come the inevitable flash floods.

inflicted [in FLIK ted] *v.* imposed something unpleasant
   The fire inflicted great damage on the nearby grassland.

invariably [in VER ee uh blee] *adv.* the same every time; constantly
   You can count on it — Carla is invariably late.

petty [PET ee] *adj.* small-minded; mean; ungenerous
   He made petty remarks in an attempt to hurt her feelings.

scorching [SKAWR ching] *adj.* extremely hot
   It was a scorching afternoon, too hot even to go swimming.

tyranny [TEER uh nee] *n.* very cruel, oppressive, unjust use of power or authority
   Stalin's tyranny in Russia left millions dead or in prison.

writhing [RY thing] *v.* squirming or twisting as if in pain
   The quarterback lay writhing on the field after the play.

Exercise A

Fill in the blanks, using each word from Word List A only once.

It was a hot August day, and the sidewalk was so [1] _____ that it almost melted our shoes. If you stepped on it with your bare feet, you'd soon be [2] _____ in pain. Every time we have weather like that, Mr. Johnson [3] _____ tells the story of the summer of 1940. Because we know it is [4] _____, we're ready for it. We always have to ask him, "Mr. Johnson, was the heat that summer [5] _____ to what we have today?" Of course, we know the answer. "Oh, my, no," he always says. "The [6] _____ of the sun that year was so cruel, I will never forget it. For starters, that sun [7] _____ such damage on the crops that we ate nothing but canned food all summer. It was so hot, we put aside our [8] _____ disagreements because it was too exhausting to argue." We knew the rest, of course, but we listened politely. It was, after all, a good story.

Read the following passage. Then, complete the activities.

It was said that the sun never set on the British Empire because the amount of land under British control at the height of its power was so great. There is no comparable nation today. None comes close to matching the expansionism of England that began in the fifteenth century.

Of course, opposition to the British Empire was an inevitable result of its colonial behavior. The nations that were being swallowed by the British Empire invariably tried to resist English domination, constantly offering various forms of resistance. Over time, some successfully gained their freedom.

In the eighteenth century, the thirteen colonies were successful in overthrowing the tyranny and oppression of British rule. Freed from the petty, mean-spirited British laws, they established themselves as the independent United States of America.

It took much longer for the colonies in Africa and Asia to gain their independence. Though they, too, were writhing under the painful yoke of imperialism, they were under tighter control, making rebellion harder.

The destruction inflicted by World War II was the key factor in the independence of the rest of the British colonies. Physically, bombing raids and scorching fires damaged Britain. But the war also imposed unpleasant political and economic strains. English financial power, greatly diminished by the war, could no longer be stretched across the globe. Thus began the end of the British Empire. Though the British Empire is now gone, its legacy can still found today in the prevalence of the English language around the globe.

1. Circle the words that suggest the meaning of comparable. Describe two things that are *comparable*.

2. Underline the words that hint at the meaning of inevitable. Define *inevitable* in your own words.

3. Circle the word that gives a clue to the meaning of invariably. Give a word or phrase that means the opposite of *invariably*.

4. Underline the words that tell what tyranny refers to. Give another historical example of a *tyranny*.

5. Circle the word that means nearly the same as petty. Give an example of a *petty* action.

6. Circle the word that gives a clue to the meaning of writhing. Use the word *writhing* in a new sentence.

7. Underline the word that tells what the war inflicted. Use *inflicted* in a new sentence.

8. Explain the word that gives a clue to the meaning of scorching. Give a synonym for *scorching*.

Shooting an Elephant
George Orwell

Summary Orwell describes his experience as a British police officer in Burma. Burma was then a British colony. Orwell secretly feels that the British should leave Burma. He is also angry with the Burmese people who insult him every day. One day, he hears that an elephant has gone wild. Orwell sends for a gun and goes looking for the beast. A large crowd follows him. The elephant has damaged property and killed a man. The animal is now peaceful. Orwell decides that he must kill it so that he does not look foolish in front of the Burmese.

Note-taking Guide
Use this chart to record important details from the essay.

Details about . . .			
Where it takes place	The problems Orwell faces	The actions he takes	His feelings and thoughts

Shooting an Elephant
George Orwell

The author, George Orwell, is a police officer in Burma. He is hated in this anti-European area. The feelings of the Burmese aren't strong enough for crowds to cause a riot, but he is an individual target.

◆ ◆ ◆

When a <u>nimble</u> Burman tripped me up on the football field and the referee (another Burman) looked the other way, the crowd yelled with hideous laughter. This happened more than once. In the end the sneering yellow faces of young men that met me everywhere, the insults hooted after me when I was at a safe distance, got badly on my nerves. The young Buddhist priests were the worst of all. There were several thousands of them in the town and none of them seemed to have anything to do except stand on street corners and jeer at Europeans.

◆ ◆ ◆

Orwell is confused and upset by the behavior of the Burmese. He decides that the reason for the problem is imperialism, or the fact that Burma is a colony of Great Britain. Orwell confesses that he sides with the Burmese and opposes British rule. He hates

Reading Strategy

One aspect of this selection's **theme** is the cultural conflict between the Burmese and Orwell's presence in their country. Cite one detail from this page that supports this claim.

_____

_____

_____

_____

Reading Check

How do the Burmese view the English? Give examples to support your answer.

_____

_____

_____

Vocabulary Development

nimble (NIM buhl) *adj.* quick or light in movement

© Pearson Education

Reading Check 📖

What problem does the subinspector call Orwell about?

_____

_____

_____

_____

Stop to Reflect 📖

If Orwell doesn't know what he can do, why does he take his rifle with him?

_____

_____

_____

his job because he feels guilty about how poorly Burmese prisoners are treated by the British and because he dislikes how the Burmese treat him.

◆ ◆ ◆

One day something happened which in a roundabout way was enlightening. It was a tiny incident in itself, but it gave me a better glimpse than I had had before of the real nature of imperialism—the real motives for which despotic governments act.

◆ ◆ ◆

One morning a subinspector calls Orwell. An escaped elephant is destroying the market. The subinspector asks Orwell to do something about the problem.

◆ ◆ ◆

I did not know what I could do, but I wanted to see what was happening and I got onto a pony and started out. I took my rifle, an old .44 Winchester and much too small to kill an elephant, but I thought the noise might be useful. . . .

◆ ◆ ◆

Orwell learns that the elephant is tame. But the elephant is in a temporary, dangerous state of frenzy known as "must." The elephant had escaped from its chains, destroyed a bamboo hut, killed a cow, eaten fruit at some fruit stands, and knocked over a garbage truck. Orwell joins Burmese and

Vocabulary Development

enlightening (en LYT en ing) *adj.* giving insight or understanding to
imperialism (im PEE ree uh lizm) *n.* policy of forming an empire and securing economic power by conquest and colonization
despotic (de SPOT ik) *adj.* harsh, cruel, unjust

Indian police officers who question residents of a poor neighborhood to find out where the elephant has gone. The men hear a woman yelling at a group of children. Orwell investigates and finds the body of a dead Indian laborer lying in the mud. The man had been killed by the elephant. After finding the man's body, Orwell sends for his elephant rifle. Some Burmese tell Orwell that the elephant is in nearby rice fields. They are excited by the idea that he is going to shoot the elephant. A crowd gathers and follows him. Orwell spots the elephant eating grass by the side of the road.

◆ ◆ ◆

I had halted on the road. As soon as I saw the elephant I knew with perfect certainty that I ought not to shoot him. It is a serious matter to shoot a working elephant—it is comparable to destroying a huge and costly piece of machinery—and obviously one ought not to do it if it can possibly be avoided.

◆ ◆ ◆

At that moment, the elephant seems harmless. Orwell feels that the elephant's frenzy is over, and he won't be dangerous. Orwell really doesn't want to shoot him. He decides to watch the elephant for a while before going home.

◆ ◆ ◆

But at that moment I glanced round at the crowd that had followed me. It was an immense crowd, two thousand at the least and growing every minute. It blocked the road for a long distance on either side. I looked at the sea

Literary Analysis

Which type of **irony** does Orwell use in the sentence underlined in blue? Circle the letter of the correct answer.
a. situational   b. verbal

Reading Check

Does Orwell think the elephant is dangerous? Why or why not?

_____

_____

_____

© Pearson Education

Read the first bracketed section. What makes Orwell know that he will have to shoot the elephant?

_____

_____

_____

Literary Analysis

Read the second bracketed passage. What **cultural conflict** does the passage describe?

_____

_____

_____

Literary Analysis

What type of **irony**—verbal or situational—lies in Orwell's comments underlined in blue?

_____

_____

_____

of yellow faces above the garish clothes—faces all happy and excited over this bit of fun, all certain that the elephant was going to be shot. They were watching me as they would watch a conjurer[1] about to perform a trick. They did not like me, but with the magical rifle in my hands I was momentarily worth watching. And suddenly I realized that I should have to shoot the elephant after all. The people expected it of me and I had got to do it; I could feel their two thousand wills pressing me forward, irresistibly.

◆ ◆ ◆

Despite his position of authority, Orwell senses that he must do what the people expect him to do. He does not wish to harm the elephant, especially because the creature is worth more alive. However, he feels he has no choice. He thinks about what might happen if something goes wrong. He believes that the crowd would run him down and trample him to death if he fails to kill the animal. Orwell prepares to shoot the elephant.

◆ ◆ ◆

The crowd grew very still, and a deep, low, happy sigh, as of people who see the theater curtain go up at last, breathed from innumerable throats. They were going to have their bit of fun, after all.

◆ ◆ ◆

Orwell really doesn't know how to shoot an elephant. He should aim at the ear hole.

Vocabulary Development
garish (GAR ish) *adj.* loud and flashy
innumerable (i NYOO muhr uh bul) *adj.* too many to be counted

1. **conjurer** (KAHN juhr uhr) *n.* a magician.

Instead, he aims in front of the ear hole, because he thinks that is where the brain is.

♦ ♦ ♦

When I pulled the trigger I did not hear the bang or feel the kick—one never does when a shot goes home—but I heard the devilish roar of glee that went up from the crowd.

♦ ♦ ♦

The elephant changes immediately. He doesn't fall, but finally he slobbers and falls on his knees. He seems to deteriorate.

♦ ♦ ♦

One could have imagined him thousands of years old. I fired again into the same spot. At the second shot he did not collapse but climbed with desperate slowness to his feet and stood weakly upright, with legs sagging and head drooping. I fired a third time. That was the shot that did for him. You could see the agony of it jolt his whole body and knock the last remnant of strength from his legs.

♦ ♦ ♦

The elephant appears to rise. His trunk reaches skyward as he trumpets, but his hind legs collapse.

♦ ♦ ♦

And then down he came, his belly toward me,

Reading Check

Read the bracketed passage. Then, circle the words and phrases that help you form a mental picture of the dying elephant.

Reading Check

What happens to the elephant after Orwell's first shot?

_____

_____

_____

Vocabulary Development

remnant (REM nuhnt) *n.* what is left over

1. Why does Orwell go away?

_____

_____

2. How long does it take the elephant to die?

_____

_____

What is Orwell's real reason for shooting the elephant?

_____

_____

_____

with a crash that seemed to shake the ground even where I lay.

◆ ◆ ◆

The elephant is clearly dying, but he is not yet dead. Orwell fires more shots, but the elephant still breathes.

◆ ◆ ◆

In the end I could not stand it any longer and went away. I heard later that it took him half an hour to die. Burmans were bringing dahs[2] and baskets even before I left, and I was told they had stripped his body almost to the bones by the afternoon.

Afterward, of course, there were endless discussions about the shooting of the elephant. The owner was furious, but he was only an Indian and could do nothing.

◆ ◆ ◆

In Burma, the law states that a mad elephant must be killed. Orwell feels he did the right thing. The Europeans do not agree.

◆ ◆ ◆

And afterward I was very glad that the coolie had been killed; it put me legally in the right and it gave me a sufficient <u>pretext</u> for shooting the elephant. I often wondered whether any of the others grasped that I had done it solely to avoid looking a fool.

Vocabulary Development

pretext (PREE tekst) *n.* excuse

2. **dahs** (daz) *n.* knives.

© Pearson Education

No Witchcraft for Sale
Doris Lessing

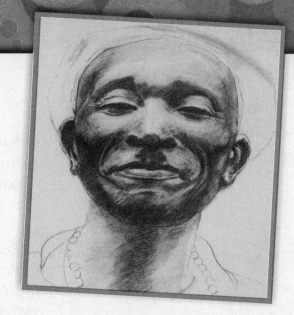

Summary The Farquars are a white couple who own a farm in southern Africa. They have a young son named Teddy. An African man named Gideon works for the family as a cook. Gideon is very fond of Teddy. One day, a snake spits poison into Teddy's eyes. Gideon saves Teddy's sight with medicine from the root of a plant. The Farquars are grateful to Gideon and reward him with gifts and a raise in pay. A scientist calls on the Farquars to find out what plant Gideon used in his cure. The Farquars never expect that Gideon will refuse to share this information.

Note-taking Guide

Use this chart to record key events from the story. Write at least one detail about each event.

Teddy is born.	→	Event:	→	Event:	→	Event:	→	Event:
Detail:	→	Detail:	→	Detail:	→	Detail:	→	Detail:

No Witchcraft for Sale

Doris Lessing

No Witchcraft for Sale

The Farquars, a white couple in southern Africa, who had been childless for years, finally have their first child. Their servants bring gifts, and they love the baby's blonde hair and blue eyes.

◆　◆　◆

They congratulated Mrs. Farquar as if she had achieved a very great thing, and she felt that she had—her smile for the lingering, admiring natives was warm and grateful.

◆　◆　◆

Gideon, the Farquars' cook, affectionately nicknames Teddy "Little Yellow Head." Gideon plays with the little boy and helps him learn how to walk. Mrs. Farquar recognizes Gideon's love for her son and rewards him with a raise in pay. Gideon and Mrs. Farquar notice what happens when a native child and Teddy meet. The children curiously stare at one another's skin, eye, and hair color.

◆　◆　◆

Gideon, who was watching, shook his head wonderingly, and said: "Ah, missus, these are both children, and one will grow up to be a baas,[1] and one will be a servant"; and Mrs. Farquar smiled and said sadly, "Yes, Gideon, I was thinking the same."

◆　◆　◆

Gideon knows that this is God's will. Gideon and the Farquars share the common bond of being very religious.

◆　◆　◆

1. **baas** (BAHS) *n.* boss.

Reading Check

What is one reason why the Farquars are particularly happy when Teddy is born?

_____

_____

_____

_____

Reading Check

Underline two words or phrases that reveal **cultural values** the Farquars and Gideon share.

Teddy was about six years old when he was given a scooter, and discovered the <u>intoxications</u> of speed.

◆　◆　◆

Teddy races around the farm and into the kitchen. He scares the farm animals and family pets. Gideon laughs as he watches this activity.

◆　◆　◆

Gideon's youngest son, who was now a herdsboy, came especially up from the compound to see the scooter. He was afraid to come near it, but Teddy showed off in front of him. "Piccanin,"[2] shouted Teddy, "get out of my way!" And he raced in circles around the black child until he was frightened, and fled back to the bush.

◆　◆　◆

Gideon blames Teddy for frightening his son. Teddy rudely replies that Gideon's son is only a black boy.

Gideon's feelings toward Teddy change. He realizes that Teddy will soon grow up and go away to school. Gideon treats Teddy kindly but acts much less friendly. Teddy, in turn, begins to treat Gideon more like a servant.

◆　◆　◆

But on the day that Teddy came staggering into the kitchen with his fists to his eyes, shrieking with pain, Gideon dropped the pot full of hot soup that he was holding, rushed to

Stop to Reflect

Teddy and Gideon's son are the same age, but their futures will be very different. What is the difference?

_____

_____

_____

Reading Strategy

Describe one detail from this page that helps you **analyze and evaluate the similar themes** in this selection and "Shooting an Elephant."

_____

_____

_____

Reading Check

How does Teddy get hurt?

_____

_____

_____

Vocabulary Development

intoxications (in TAHKS i KAY shunz) *n.* great excitement

2. **piccanin** (PIK uh nin) *n.* an offensive term for a native child.

© Pearson Education

the child, and forced aside his fingers. "A snake!" he exclaimed.

◆ ◆ ◆

As Teddy rested on his scooter, a tree-snake spat right into his eyes. Mrs. Farquar sees that Teddy's eyes are already swollen. She is terrified that Teddy will go blind.

◆ ◆ ◆

Literary Analysis

Mrs. Farquar and Gideon react differently to Teddy's injury. Underline two words, phrases, or sentences in the bracketed passage that reveal their **cultural differences**.

Reading Check

What does Mrs. Farquar remember about natives she's seen that really frightens her?

_____

_____

_____

Gideon said: "Wait a minute, missus, I'll get some medicine." He ran off into the bush.

Mrs. Farquar lifted the child into the house and bathed his eyes with permanganate.[3] She had scarcely heard Gideon's words; but when she saw that her remedies had no effect at all, and remembered how she had seen natives with no sight in their eyes, because of the spitting of a snake, she began to look for the return of her cook, remembering what she heard of the efficacy of native herbs.

◆ ◆ ◆

Terrified, she holds her son and waits for Gideon to return. He soon appears with a plant. He shows her the root and assures her that it will provide a cure for Teddy's eyes.

◆ ◆ ◆

Without even washing it, he put the root in his mouth, chewed it vigorously, and then held the spittle there while he took the child forcibly

---

Vocabulary Development

remedies (REM i deez) *n.* medicines or therapies that take away pain or cure diseases

efficacy (EF i kuh see) *n.* power to produce intended effects

vigorously (VIG uhr uhs lee) *adv.* forcefully; energetically

---

3. **permanganate** (per MANG guh nayt) *n.* salt of permanganic acid used as a remedy for snake poison.

from Mrs. Farquar. He gripped Teddy down between his knees, and pressed the balls of his thumbs into the swollen eyes, so that the child screamed and Mrs. Farquar cried out in protest: "Gideon, Gideon!"

◆　◆　◆

Gideon ignores her and opens Teddy's eyes to spit into them. When Gideon is finished, he promises Mrs. Farquar that Teddy will be fine. But she finds this hard to believe.

◆　◆　◆

In a couple of hours the swellings were gone: the eyes were <u>inflamed</u> and tender but Teddy could see. Mr. and Mrs. Farquar went to Gideon in the kitchen and thanked him over and over again.

◆　◆　◆

They do not know how to express their gratitude. They give Gideon gifts and a raise, but nothing can really pay for Teddy's cured eyes.

◆　◆　◆

Mrs. Farquar said: "Gideon, God chose you as an instrument for His goodness," and Gideon said: "Yes, missus, God is very good."

◆　◆　◆

The story of how Gideon saved Teddy's eyesight spreads throughout the area. The whites are frustrated because they do not know what plant Gideon used. The natives will not tell them. A doctor in town hears the story but does not really believe it.

One day, a scientist from the nearby laboratory arrives. He brings a lot of equipment.

◆　◆　◆

Vocabulary Development
inflamed (in FLAYMD) *adj.* reddened

TAKE NOTES

Literary Analysis

What is the cause of the **cultural conflict** in this passage? Circle the letter of the correct answer.
a. Teddy's feelings of superiority
b. Gideon's knowledge of native medicine
c. Mrs. Farquar's religious beliefs

Reading Check

1. What is the result of Gideon's medicine?

_____

_____

2. What do the Farquars do to reward Gideon?

_____

_____

_____

_____

Reading Check

Read the bracketed paragraphs.
What three words or phrases
suggest the Farquars' mixed
feelings about the scientist's
visit?

1. _____

2. _____

3. _____

Reading Check

How does Gideon respond when
he hears the reason for the
scientist's visit?

_____

_____

_____

_____

Mr. and Mrs. Farquar were flustered and
pleased and flattered. They asked the scientist to
lunch, and they told the story all over again, for
the hundredth time. Little Teddy was there too,
his blue eyes sparkling with health, to prove the
truth of it.

◆ ◆ ◆

The scientist explains that people
everywhere would benefit if the drug that
helped Teddy could be available to them.
The Farquars are pleased at the idea of being
able to help.

◆ ◆ ◆

But when the scientist began talking of the
money that might result, their manner showed
discomfort.

◆ ◆ ◆

They do not want to think of money
in connection with the miracle that has
happened. The scientist realizes how they
feel and reminds them that they can help
others.

After eating their meal, the Farquars
tell Gideon why the scientist came to
visit. Gideon seems surprised and angry.
Mr. Farquar tells Gideon that thousands
of people could be cured by the medicine
he used to save Teddy. Gideon listens but
stubbornly refuses to reveal what root he
used. The Farquars realize Gideon will
not tell them what they want to know. To
Gideon, the Africans' traditional knowledge
of plant medicine, which is passed on from
generation to generation, represents power
and wisdom. Suddenly, however, Gideon
agrees to show the root to the Farquars and
the scientist. On an extremely hot afternoon,
the group silently walks for two hours.
Gideon appears to search for the root.

◆ ◆ ◆

At last, six miles from the house, Gideon suddenly decided they had had enough; or perhaps his anger evaporated at that moment.

◆ ◆ ◆

Gideon finally picks up flowers just like the ones they have seen all along their journey. He hands them to the scientist and leaves the group to go home.

When the scientist stops in the kitchen to thank Gideon, he is gone. He's back to prepare dinner, but it is days before he and the Farquars are friends again.

◆ ◆ ◆

The Farquars made inquiries about the root from their laborers. Sometimes they were answered with distrustful stares. Sometimes the natives said: "We do not know. We have never heard of the root."

◆ ◆ ◆

A cattle boy who has worked for the family for a long time tells them to ask Gideon. He says that Gideon is the son of a famous medicine man and can cure anything, although he is not as good as a white doctor.

◆ ◆ ◆

After some time, when the soreness had gone from between the Farquars and Gideon, they began to joke: "When are you going to show us the snake-root, Gideon?" And he would laugh

TAKE NOTES

Literary Analysis 🔍

What does Gideon finally do in response to requests that he identify the plant?

_____

_____

_____

Is Gideon's action an example of **verbal irony** or **situational irony?** Explain.

_____

_____

_____

Stop to Reflect 📖

What do the Farquars find out about Gideon from the cattle boy?

_____

_____

_____

_____

Vocabulary Development

evaporated (ee VAP uh ray tid) *v.* disappeared

Literary Analysis 🔍

Is the **cultural conflict** resolved? Why or why not?

_____

_____

_____

Stop to Reflect 📖

What do you think Gideon's last words to Teddy mean?

_____

_____

_____

and shake his head, saying, a little uncomfortably: "But I did show you, missus, have you forgotten?"

◆ ◆ ◆

Later, Teddy even teases Gideon about tricking everyone about the cure for the snake bite.

◆ ◆ ◆

And Gideon would double up with polite laughter. After much laughing, he would suddenly straighten himself up, wipe his old eyes, and look sadly at Teddy, who was grinning mischievously at him across the kitchen: "Ah, Little Yellow Head, how you have grown! Soon you will be grown up with a farm of your own. . . ."

Vocabulary Development

mischievously (MIS chuh vuhs lee) *adv.* playfully

Shooting an Elephant • No Witchcraft for Sale

1. **Literary Analysis:** Explain why Orwell's feeling that the Burmese rule him is **ironic.**

   _____

   _____

2. **Literary Analysis:** Use the chart below to examine how three events in "No Witchcraft for Sale" show a **cultural conflict.** Write down the event in the middle column. Write down how the Farquars and Gideon feel about the event in the other columns.

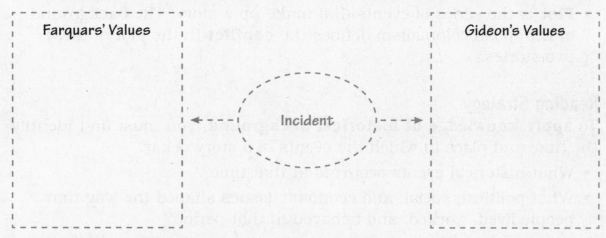

Farquars' Values

Incident

Gideon's Values

3. **Reading Strategy: Analyze and evaluate** how the **themes** of "Shooting an Elephant" and "No Witchcraft for Sale" are **similar.** Give an example from each story.

   _____

   _____

 Writing About the Essential Question

How does literature shape or reflect society? What insights do Orwell's essay and Lessing's story provide into how people deal with cultural differences?

   _____

   _____

The Train from Rhodesia • B. Wordsworth

Literary Analysis

The historical period in which a story takes place is often critical to the elements of the story. Historical events provide context. **Context** refers to the situation, events, or information that relate to something and help you understand it. The historical context of "The Train from Rhodesia" and "B. Wordsworth" shapes the setting, characterization, and plot of both works.

- **Setting** is the time and place in which the action of a story occurs.
- **Characterization** is the way in which a writer develops his or her characters to make them seem like real people.
- **Plot** is the series of events that make up a story. The background of European colonialism defines the **conflict** in the plot of these two stories.

Reading Strategy

To **apply knowledge of historical background,** you must first identify the time and place in which the events of a story occur.

- What historical events occurred at that time?
- What political, social, and economic issues shaped the way that people lived, worked, and behaved in that period?

As you read, look for clues that reflect the effects of the historical period. Ask yourself how each character reflects the culture and ideas of the period. Then, ask yourself how the plot—and especially the main conflict—relates to specific political, social, and economic issues.

Use the chart to record how the historical period affects the story.

Historical Period: Inequality of Apartheid	Effects on Setting, Character, or Conflict
	1. Native vendors squat in the dust, selling wooden carvings.
	2.
	3.

Word List A

Study these words from the selections. Then, complete the activities.

compartments [kuhm PART muhnts] *n.* separate sections
   The suitcase has three handy compartments for shoes.

encouragingly [en KER ij ing lee] *adv.* giving hope and confidence
   The teacher nodded encouragingly as Nella told her story.

majestic [muh JES tik] *adj.* grand; suggesting royalty
   The giant redwood trees looked majestic against the blue sky.

rite [RYT] *n.* a regular observance; a formal ceremony
   Baptism is a rite observed in Christian religions.

uninvited [un in VY ted] *adj.* unwelcome; not invited
   Ants are uninvited guests at many picnics.

untidy [un TY dee] *adj.* messy; not neat
   The bedroom was so untidy Vern could not find his socks.

vendors [VEN ders] *n.* people who sell things
   Arts and crafts vendors lined the streets during the festival.

wryly [RY lee] *adv.* in a dryly humorous way
   Charles said wryly that he had aged ten years while waiting.

Exercise A

Fill in the blanks, using each word from Word List A only once.

In the town of Punxsutawney, Pennsylvania, it is almost a religious

[1] _____ to observe Groundhog Day. The groundhog, not a grand nor

[2] _____ creature, nevertheless rules the city every year on February

second. The animal has even been given a name, Punxsutawney Phil. The

legend is that if Phil sees his shadow on that date, there will be six more

weeks of winter. So while the officials call [3] _____ to get Phil to

come out, they consider the sun to be an [4] _____ guest. Although

many laugh [5] _____ at the antics of their fellow humans, the

[6] _____ of T-shirts and other groundhog gear always profit from

the event. The town center may look a little [7] _____ after the holiday,

but it is soon cleaned, and preparations can get underway for the next year.

All the banners and signs can be stored in their [8] _____ until they

are needed again.

1. Circle the words that suggest the meaning of majestic. What other natural sight might be *majestic*?

2. Underline the words that hint at the meaning of rite. Define *rite* in your own words.

3. Circle the word that tells who was uninvited. Which word in the sentence gives a clue to the meaning of *uninvited*?

4. Underline the phrase that tells the condition of the other compartments. Where else might you find *compartments*?

5. Underline the words that give a clue to the meaning of encouragingly. Use the word *encouragingly* in a new sentence.

6. Circle the words that mean nearly the same as untidy. Give an antonym for *untidy*.

7. Underline what made the man grin wryly. Write a new sentence using the word *wryly*.

8. Underline the words that give a clue to the meaning of vendors. Where else would you find *vendors*?

Read the following passage. Then, complete the activities.

As the train carried her swiftly, yet noisily, toward her destination, Angela looked out her window. Even through the smudged pane, the <u>majestic</u> mountains were awe-inspiring, their rocky slopes rising out of sight into the heavy-hanging clouds. As was her custom, she took out her journal and began to put her impressions into writing. This was a <u>rite</u> that Angela had practiced religiously, especially when she traveled, ever since she could grasp a pen.

As she wrote, immersed in her thoughts, an <u>uninvited</u> visitor intruded upon Angela's concentration.

"Excuse me, but all the other <u>compartments</u> are completely full," said the man, sitting down in the seat opposite Angela. "I hope I'm not disturbing you by sharing your section of the train with you."

Always one to take an interest in strangers, as they made great fodder for her writing, Angela smiled <u>encouragingly</u> at her fellow passenger.

"It's no bother," she answered, observing the man's rumpled coat and <u>untidy</u> knapsack in a quick glance. "Have you been traveling long?"

Grinning <u>wryly</u> at his disheveled appearance, the man said, "I can understand why you say that."

Angela smiled at his dry humor.

"But no, I just ran to catch this train as it was pulling away. I was so enticed by the <u>vendors</u> selling their wares in the station that I didn't notice the time until I heard the last whistle!"

Angela laughed in recognition.

"I know how you feel—I've often been tempted myself. But I've always believed that the best souvenirs are the ones I create for myself in these pages," she said, holding up her journal.

"Well, don't let me interrupt you," said her seatmate.

"On the contrary," Angela replied, returning to her task. "You've given me a wonderful new souvenir to add to my collection!"

The Train from Rhodesia

Nadine Gordimer

Summary In this story, a train from Rhodesia pulls into a station in a poor section of South Africa. Native people try to sell wooden carvings to the passengers. A newly married young woman wants to buy a carved lion. She decides it is too expensive. Later, her husband convinces an old man to sell the lion for very little money. When the husband gives his wife the lion, she does not accept it the way he thought she would.

Note-taking Guide

Use the chart below to write down details about this story.

```
┌──────────────────────────┐          ╭─────────────────────╮
│     Setting (Place)      │          │       Details       │
│                          │ - - →    │                     │
│                          │          │                     │
└──────────────────────────┘          ╰─────────────────────╯

┌──────────────────────────┐          ╭─────────────────────╮
│       Characters         │          │       Details       │
│                          │ - - →    │                     │
│                          │          │                     │
└──────────────────────────┘          ╰─────────────────────╯

┌──────────────────────────┐          ╭─────────────────────╮
│        Problems          │          │       Details       │
│                          │ - - →    │                     │
│                          │          │                     │
└──────────────────────────┘          ╰─────────────────────╯
```

B. Wordsworth
V. S. Naipaul

Summary This story is told by a young boy who lives in Trinidad. One day, a poet comes to the boy's house. He asks to watch the bees. The poet calls himself B. Wordsworth. The man talks strangely. When he leaves, the boy wants to see him again. The two become friends. B. Wordsworth teaches the boy to appreciate beauty. He helps the boy escape the pain in his life. One day, the boy visits the poet and thinks that he looks old and weak. B. Wordsworth reveals something that makes the boy question everything he knows.

Note-taking Guide
Use the chart below to record what you learn about B. Wordsworth.

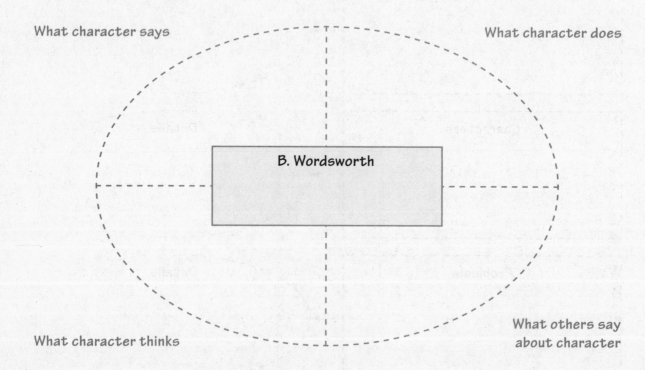

What character says

What character does

B. Wordsworth

What character thinks

What others say about character

The Train from Rhodesia • B. Wordsworth

1. **Literary Analysis:** A **conflict** is a struggle. The woman has a conflict with her husband. Describe one conflict that she has with herself.

   _____

2. **Literary Analysis:** Fill in the chart below by recording details about the elements of "B. Wordsworth."

	Setting	Characterization	Conflicts
"B. Wordsworth"			

3. **Reading Strategy:** How does the **historical background** of Trinidad shape the conflicts in "B. Wordsworth"?

   _____

   _____

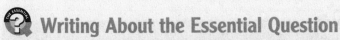 **Writing About the Essential Question**

What is the relationship between place and literature? Does B. Wordsworth's name reflect the harmful effects of colonialism on the identity of colonized peoples? Explain.

_____

_____

from Midsummer, XXIII • *from* Omeros, *from* Chapter XXVIII

Literary Analysis

Derek Walcott employs political critique and allusion to give readers clues to his themes. The **theme** is the main message of a poem.

- **Political critique of art** explores how a piece of art might affect a particular people, government, or society. Political critique often explores the issue of who "owns" art by asking questions like these: *Who can produce art? Who can judge art? Who can understand and enjoy art?*

- **Allusions** are references to other literary works, people, or historical events. Allusions form connections between a poet and a reader by suggesting that they share a common culture or background.

Reading Strategy

Literary allusions refer to characters, ideas, and events in other literary works. Historical allusions refer to people and events from history. Popular allusions refer to well-known people, places, and things in one's culture. To **understand allusions,** look for references to people, places, events, and things that relate to other works of literature, to history, or to a particular culture. Then, think about how those things relate to what you are reading. Ask: *How does this allusion affect my understanding of the poem? What does the allusion tell me about the speaker of the poem?*

Use this chart to record an allusion from *Midsummer* and an allusion from *Omeros*.

Poem	Allusion	How Does It Affect Your Understanding of the Poem?
from Midsummer, XXIII		
from Omeros, *from* Chapter XXVIII		

Word List A

Study these words from the selections. Then, complete the activities that follow.

ashen [ASH uhn] *adj.* of, like, or pale as ashes; gray
  Andrea's ashen appearance made us think she was ill.

fronds [FRAHNDZ] *n.* large, leaflike parts, as of a palm tree or fern
  The palm fronds were all over the ground after the storm.

horizon [huh RY zuhn] *n.* the line where the earth and sky seem to meet
  The shipwrecked sailor scanned the horizon for signs of a rescue ship.

quips [KWIPS] *n.* clever or witty, and sometimes sarcastic, remarks
  Dave was a good talk show host because his quips were entertaining.

scurry [SKER ee] *n.* the act of running quickly or hastily
  With a sudden scurry, the mice were gone.

thatched [THACHT] *adj.* covered with reeds, straw, or similar material
  The lovely, rose-covered cottage had a thatched roof.

triangular [try ANG yuh luhr] *adj.* shaped like a three-sided figure
  They threw the ball in a triangular pattern from Mel to Jack to Bobbie.

withered [WITH uhrd] *v.* became limp, dry, or lifeless
  Months without rain withered the crops.

Exercise A

Fill in each blank below using the appropriate word from Word List A.

Belle stood on the beach and looked out at the [1] _____, a hazy line in the distance. Would anyone ever find her on this remote island? From inside the [2] _____ hut she had constructed, her pet monkey peeked out. All along the beach, palm [3] _____ littered the sand. They had been [4] _____ by the heat of the sun. Belle searched a [5] _____ area, from her hut to the sea and back to the rainforest behind her. She saw nothing unusual, until she noticed the [6] _____ of twenty or so monkeys from one tree to another. "What are they up to?" she wondered. Being alone on this beach, Belle hadn't heard any good [7] _____ from a human being for about a year—she missed her best friend's clever jokes. All the conversation she ever heard was the chattering of the monkeys. She looked into the sliver of a mirror she had managed to save. Her face had lost its [8] _____ appearance as she had tanned under the tropical sun.

1. Underline the words that mean about the same as <u>quips</u>. Use *quips* in a sentence.

2. Circle the word in a nearby sentence that tells how children move when they <u>scurry</u>. What does *scurry* mean?

3. Underline the words that tell what a plant that <u>withered</u> might look like. What can be done to help a plant that has *withered*?

4. Circle the words in a nearby sentence that tell what a hut might be <u>thatched</u> with. In what type of environment would you be very unlikely to find a *thatched* hut?

5. Circle the words that tell where the <u>fronds</u> came from. Use *fronds* in a sentence.

6. Underline the words in a nearby sentence that tell what the <u>triangular</u> shape might have been. What is an example of something that is *triangular*?

7. Circle the word that tells in what direction the <u>horizon</u> is, if you are watching the sunset. What is the *horizon*?

8. Underline the words in a nearby sentence that mean about the same as <u>ashen</u>. What kind of experience might give you an *ashen* face?

Read the following passage. Pay special attention to the underlined words. Then, read it again, and complete the activities. Use a separate sheet of paper for your written answers.

Darryl and his sister Charlene were getting tired of hearing the <u>quips</u>, witty remarks, and jokes exchanged by their parents as they relaxed in the restaurant of the fancy hotel. "Please, can we go to the beach instead?" they whined.

Their parents gave them permission, and with a quick <u>scurry</u>, the kids were off. They ran past the plants in the lobby that had <u>withered</u> slightly in the heat, thinking that somebody should give those plants a misting so they wouldn't look so dry and lifeless.

They went up to the room to change into their bathing suits and then ran down to the beach. They ordered lemonades at a little <u>thatched hut</u> that served as a snack bar. <u>Fronds</u> of palm trees decorated the roof of the hut, with some hanging over to provide a little shade. The kids drank their lemonades on the beach and thought about going in for a little dip. Before they managed to get up off their beach towels, they noticed some sort of commotion down at the shore. "What could be the problem?" they wondered.

As they looked out to the water, they noticed a <u>triangular</u> shape swimming back and forth just beyond the waves. Then it turned around and headed west, toward the <u>horizon</u>. Could it have been the fin of a shark? Their question was answered when a man with an <u>ashen</u> face approached them. They learned later that his pale gray appearance was caused by fear. He had been in the water when he saw the shark approach. Luckily, he had been able to get out. No one had been hurt, but it looked as if the water would be off limits for a while.

from Midsummer, XXIII
Derek Walcott

Summary This poem reflects the author's West Indian background and experience. The poem shows the speaker's responses to the Brixton riots. It tells his mixed feelings about British culture and power. The speaker also talks about his own racial background. He considers his position as a black Caribbean poet in white British society.

Note-taking Guide
Use this chart to list context details from the poem that directly relate to the conflict in the poet's mind.

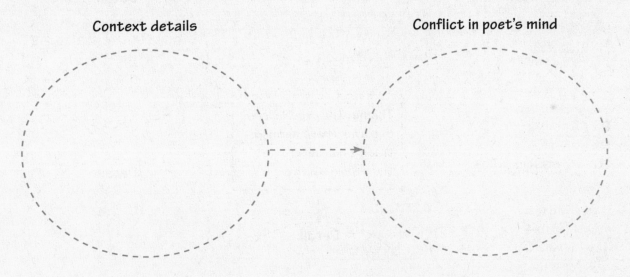

from Omeros, from Chapter XXVIII
Derek Walcott

Summary This part of the poem looks at the painful past of how Africans were brought to America and the Caribbean and forced to work as slaves. An African storyteller, called a griot, tells the story in song. The story he tells is about the horrible experiences on the slave ships. Another speaker talks about how slavery still affects the people today.

Note-taking Guide

In the chart, list details that support the theme.

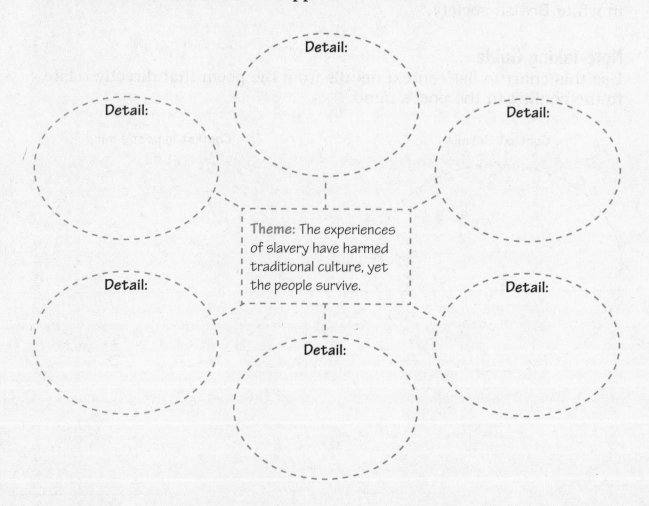

Detail:

Detail:

Detail:

Detail:

Detail:

Detail:

Theme: The experiences of slavery have harmed traditional culture, yet the people survive.

from Midsummer, XXIII •
from Omeros, from Chapter XXVIII

1. **Interpret:** Reread lines 31–33 in *Omeros*. What does Walcott mean when he says, "Now each man was a nation / in himself"?

_____

_____

_____

2. **Literary Analysis:** Derek Walcott makes a **political critique** in *Midsummer*. How does his critique relate to the theme of understanding the West Indian's place in British society?

_____

_____

3. **Reading Strategy:** Use this chart to identify Walcott's use of **allusion** in *Midsummer* or in *Omeros*.

Allusions	Literary	Historical	Popular
"our skulls on the scorching decks"		inhumane treatment on slave ships	

Writing About the Essential Question

What is the relationship of the writer to tradition? Does Walcott effectively use traditions to address current controversies? Explain.

_____

_____

_____

Follower • Two Lorries • Outside History

Literary Analysis

A writer must make choices about diction and other elements of style:

- **Diction** refers to the words that a writer uses. The words may be formal or informal, conversational or scholarly.
- **Style** refers to the way in which a writer expresses ideas. Style includes word choice, use of forms and rhythms, and themes and imagery.

The message of a poem is important. However, the style and diction used by the poet are just as important to what a poem is and how it affects you. As you read, think about the diction and styles that the writers use.

Reading Strategy

Summarizing a poem means rewriting its key points using fewer words. The process of summarizing helps you **determine the main idea or message** of a poem. Use a chart like the one below to summarize the poems. Then, write the main idea of each poem. You may find it helpful to summarize each stanza before summarizing the entire poem.

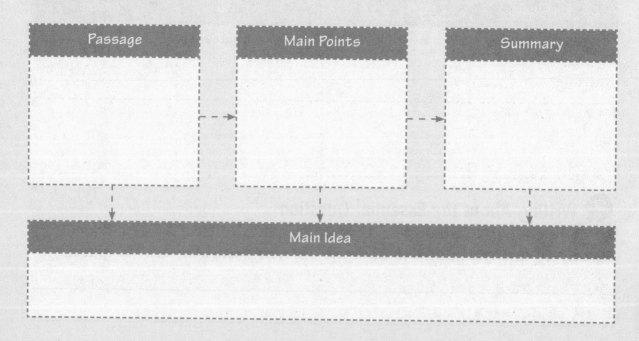

Word List A

Study these words from the selections. Then, complete the activities that follow.

angled [ANG uhld] *v.* moved or turned at a slant
The football player angled his way down the field.

conceit [kuhn SEET] *n.* too high an opinion of oneself
Paula's conceit about her intelligence is almost comical.

expert [EK spert] *n.* a person who has special skill or knowledge
Tiffany is such an expert at knitting that she should give lessons.

heft [HEFT] *v.* to lift up; heave
Two strong men will heft the heavy container onto the loading dock.

ordeal [awr DEEL] *n.* a very difficult or trying experience
The long ordeal left Jeffrey exhausted.

pluck [PLUK] *n.* a quick or sudden pull
With a pluck on the cord, Michelle signaled to the bus driver to stop.

reins [RAYNZ] *n.* straps used to control a horse being ridden or driven
Latonya pulled back on the reins to get the horse to stop.

strained [STRAYND] *v.* made a great effort
Bruno strained against the current but made no progress in the canoe.

Exercise A

Fill in each blank below using the appropriate word from Word List A.

Tyler wished he had brought an [1] _____ with him to pick out equipmentfor his new horse. He thought he knew everything, so his own foolish [2] _____ had prevented him from realizing he needed help. He knew he needed [3] _____, but what else? If he got the wrong things, he knew it would be such an [4] _____ to return them. With a gentle [5] _____ at the salesperson's sleeve, Tyler got his attention. Soon they had selected all the necessary equipment, and they [6] _____ to get it all in Tyler's truck. It took the two of them to [7] _____ the bigger pieces into the truck. Some of the equipment barely fit, so they [8] _____ it in sideways.

1. Underline the words that tell what an expert is. In what field do you think you might like to become an *expert*?

2. Circle the word that tells what might cause a person to feel conceit. Use *conceit* in a sentence.

3. Underline the words that explain why a ride might be an ordeal for a horse. What does *ordeal* mean?

4. Circle the words that explain the result of a quick pluck at any dirt clods on the horse. Why might a rider give a *pluck* to a horse's reins?

5. Circle the word that means about the same as angled. What is one reason a person might have *angled* a car while driving?

6. Underline the words that tell why a rider would need reins. What might happen if a rider lost the *reins* while riding?

7. Underline the word in a nearby sentence that means about the same as heft. Use *heft* in a sentence.

8. Circle the words in a nearby sentence that mean about the same as strained. Tell about a time you *strained* yourself when performing a task.

Read the following passage. Pay special attention to the underlined words. Then, read it again, and complete the activities. Use a separate sheet of paper for your written answers.

You don't have to be an expert to saddle a horse correctly, but it might help if you took a lesson from a person who knows. And don't let one little lesson cause you to feel conceit about your skill—you'll likely need a demonstration, too.

The first thing to do is groom the horse. The reason for this is to remove dirt and mud from the horse's body in order to prevent sores; if a horse gets sores, every time you ride, it will be an ordeal for the animal.

Put a clean saddle blanket on the horse's back. A quick pluck at any dirt clods should pull them off easily. Put the blanket forward on the horse's withers (the highest part of its back), and then slide it back, placing the front edge four to six inches in front of the withers. This assures that the hairs will be running in the correct direction. If the hairs are angled, or slanted, incorrectly, the horse will be uncomfortable. Also, make sure that the reins don't get caught under the blanket—you'll need them later to control the horse!

Lift the saddle and bring it to the left side of the horse. Gently heft it onto the horse's back, leaving four inches of blanket in front. Move to the right side of the horse and secure the cinches properly—not too tight and not too loose. If you have strained yourself too much while tightening the cinches, they will no doubt be hurting the horse. It doesn't take too much effort to do this properly. You will probably need an actual demonstration of the entire process in order to do it properly yourself.

Follower • Two Lorries
Seamus Heaney

Outside History
Eavan Boland

Summaries In **"Follower,"** the speaker recalls stumbling and tripping behind his father as he plowed the fields. Now, he says, his father stumbles behind him. In **"Two Lorries,"** the speaker remembers two trucks. One truck was driven by a coal man who flirted with his mother. The other truck carried explosives that blew up the bus station. In **"Outside History,"** the speaker says she will not be like the stars which are outside history. She will be a part of her country's own history, even though she is too late to help those who have already died.

Note-taking Guide

Use this chart to record the images that you see in each poem. Then, record the central image, or the main concept, of each.

Poem	Images	Central Image
Follower		
Two Lorries		
Outside History		

Follower • Two Lorries • Outside History

1. **Literary Analysis:** Which words in "Follower" support the idea that Heaney's **diction** is homespun, or simple and ordinary?

   _____

   _____

2. **Literary Analysis:** Complete this chart to analyze Boland's **style** in "Outside History." Then, summarize the distinctive elements of her style.

	Diction	Imagery	Rhythm/ Rhyme	Form
Examples				
Conclusion				

3. **Reading Strategy:** Write a **summary** of "Two Lorries," including a comparison of the two incidents the poet recalls. Then, write the poem's main idea, or message.

   _____

   _____

Writing About the Essential Question

How does literature shape or reflect society? How might an author justify remaining uninvolved in a conflict?

_____

_____

_____

_____

Come and Go • That's All

Literary Analysis

Writers are often influenced by earlier works of literature even as they seek to create new ways to express their ideas. **Drama of the absurd** combines the traditional and the new by

- commenting on social issues through characters and situations that seem hopeless and meaningless.
- featuring elements of tragedy and comedy, similar to classical Greek or Shakespearean plays.
- avoiding the traditional structures such as clearly defined scenes and acts.
- using language and dialogue in unique ways.

The playwrights deliberately avoid making explicit statements about the situations or characters; instead, readers must draw their own conclusions.

Reading Strategy

Both plays have traditional elements such as characters, dialogue, and situations. However, the ways in which the playwrights use these elements differs from their use in classic dramas. Use the chart to **compare and contrast** these elements in order to better understand the characteristics of drama of the absurd.

	Come and Go	That's All
Characters		
Dialogue		
Situation		

Word List A

Study these words from the selection. Then, complete the activities.

appalled [uh PAWLD] *v.* horrified, shocked, and dismayed
Students were appalled to learn that the hurricane had blown the roof off their school.

clasped [KLASPT] *adj.* held together or grasped by something or someone
His clasped hands lay neatly in his lap.

erect [ee REKT] *adj.* standing straight up
The soldiers stood erect, at attention, awaiting their orders.

nondescript [nahn di SKRIPT] *adj.* so dull that it is hard to describe; drab
Jack worked at a desk in a nondescript cubicle.

pose [POHZ] *n.* a positioning of the body for the purpose of creating an effect
She put her hands on her hips and thrust out her chin in an arrogant pose.

realize [REE uh lyz] *v.* understand completely
Raul does realize that the coach's decision is final.

Exercise A

Fill in the blanks, using each word from Word List A only once.

Jenna stared at the blank walls of the [1] _____ waiting room. She knew she was nervous about this interview, but she was [2] _____ to find that her hands were shaking in her lap. Her mother had tried to help her prepare, saying, "Try to strike a confident [3] _____ to give your interviewer the impression that you believe in yourself. Smile, look the interviewer in the eye, and stand [4] _____ until you are invited to sit down."

The door to the inner office opened. "You must be Jenna Jones," the interviewer said warmly. "I should apologize since I [5] _____ I kept you waiting."

The interviewer reached out to take Jenna's hand in both of hers. At the sight of their momentarily [6] _____ hands, Jenna got the feeling this must be a nice place to work.

Read the following passage. Then, complete the activities.

Jonathan wrote and directed a one-act play called *Let's Eat* to fulfill a requirement for his theater class. At the time of the auditions, he had not finished revising his script. So he asked people to try out for parts by reading lines from *Waiting for Godot,* the play by Samuel Beckett.

Jonathan stood erect on the stage before his would-be cast, like a man about to give a formal speech. "I realize this may sound odd and slightly pompous," he announced, "but my play is a lot like Beckett's. Thus, I believe I can cast *Let's Eat* from listening to you read his work." Jonathan looked around and suddenly understood that perhaps he sounded more pompous than he thought. He was appalled to see people respond to him with smirks and snickers.

Jonathan was so dismayed by his poorly received introduction that he tried to make amends by assuming as humble a pose as possible. He sat with slumped shoulders at the edge of the stage, his legs dangling over the side. He put his clasped hands in his lap, holding them together tightly to hide his sweating palms.

Of all the students present, only Trinh had seen one of Beckett's plays performed. "I think what Jonathan means is that *Let's Eat* might use language that does not always sound logical, but still manages to be about big abstract ideas, am I right?" She turned to Jonathan, who nodded gratefully.

Trinh continued, "The action probably occurs in a nondescript location—some dull, undefined place that the audience will see as a bare stage with a few props."

"You explained it better than I could," Jonathan said. He turned to the actors. "I'm going to stick to writing things down and leave the speaking to you."

1. Circle the simile that illustrates the meaning of erect. Write a sentence giving another example of a time when a person might want to stand in an *erect* position.

2. Underline the words that answer the question: What does Jonathan realize? Use *realize* in a sentence.

3. Circle a word in a nearby sentence that has a meaning similar to appalled. What did Jonathan do after he felt *appalled*?

4. Underline the phrases that describe Jonathan's pose. Write a sentence describing what an angry *pose* might look like.

5. Circle the word that tells what was clasped. Give at least one other example of a thing you might see *clasped*.

6. Underline the words that give a clue to the meaning of nondescript. Write a synonym for *nondescript*.

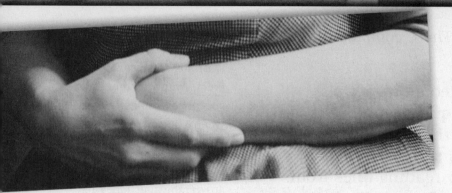

Come and Go
Samuel Beckett

That's All
Harold Pinter

Summaries *Come and Go* features three women who were childhood friends and schoolmates. The women find themselves reunited. Through a series of movements and whispered statements, each learns something about another character. The audience never hears the women's secrets. *That's All* consists of a discussion between two women. The dialogue focuses on a third woman who seems to be avoiding one of the characters.

Note-taking Guide
Characters are central to both plays. Use the charts below to record your observations about the characters.

Come and Go		
Ru	Vi	Flo

That's All		
Mrs. A	Mrs. B	Third Woman

Come and Go • That's All

1. **Literary Analysis:** Both plays are based almost entirely on dialogue. Why do you think the playwrights chose this approach?

   _____

   _____

2. **Literary Analysis: Drama of the absurd** is related to classical drama, but displays a unique approach to plot and action, dialogue, and staging. Use the chart below to describe how these elements are used in both plays.

	Plot and Action	Dialogue	Staging
Come and Go			
That's All			

3. **Reading Strategy:** In what ways are the plays similar? How are they different?

   _____

   _____

Writing About the Essential Question

What is the relationship of the writer to tradition? In *That's All*, Pinter reduces setting, plot, and characterization to the barest minimum. What effect do you think this has on the audience?

_____

_____

_____

_____

Do Not Go Gentle into That Good Night •
Fern Hill • The Horses

Literary Analysis

Poets have different styles of writing. **Style** refers to the way in which a writer uses language. A poet's style is based on literary elements such as word choice, tone, line length, stanza form, pace, and sound devices. Thomas's style is marked by a rushed tumbling of words. Hughes's style is marked by short bursts of images.

Thomas: *All the sun long it was running, it was lovely. . . .*

Hughes: *Not a leaf, not a bird . . .*

Thomas shapes his tumbled words into strict patterns. For example, "Do Not Go Gentle into That Good Night" is a villanelle. A **villanelle** has nineteen lines in which the rhymed first and third lines repeat regularly. This repetition forms the rhyme scheme *aba aba aba aba aba abaa.* In contrast, Ted Hughes writes "The Horses" in free verse. **Free-verse poetry** has no fixed pattern.

Reading Strategy

Different poems can express similar themes in different ways. A poem's **theme** is its message. To **evaluate the expression of a theme,** follow these steps:

• Identify the theme of a poem.

• Note details from the poem that support the theme.

• Ask: *How well do the details of the poem support the theme? Does the poem reveal its theme in an interesting and effective way?*

Use a chart like the one shown to evaluate the themes of the poems.

Theme	How Elements Communicate Theme	How Details Communicate Theme	Effectiveness of Elements and Details
People must fight against death; It is human nature to resist death.			

Word List A

Study these words from the selections. Then, complete the activities.

bearing [BER ing] *v.* carrying
Bearing bags full of gifts, Grandmother arrived at our house.

cast [KAST] *v.* formed in a shape
The little statues were cast in the shape of the Eiffel Tower.

carefree [KER free] *adj.* without worries or troubles
Now that I had to work, gone were the carefree days of summer.

deeds [DEEDZ] *n.* things that are done or accomplished
Mr. Ming was honored for his good deeds in the community.

flung [FLUNG] *v.* thrown with force
Graydon was so angry, he flung his book across the room.

frail [FRAYL] *adj.* fragile; weak; delicate
The tiny woman looked frail, but she was surprisingly strong.

lilting [LIL ting] *adj.* having a graceful, light rhythm
To cheer herself up, she whistled a lilting tune.

stillness [STIL nes] *n.* the state of being quiet and calm
One loud crow broke the stillness of the dawn.

Exercise A

Fill in each blank using each word from Word List A only once.

Mrs. Winters had finished her work for the day. She

[1] _____ her apron aside and sat on the front porch,

enjoying the [2] _____ of the fields in the late afternoon.

This [3] _____ feeling would not last, she knew. There was

always work to do, there were always [4] _____ to accomplish.

She watched a pair of oxen [5] _____ a heavy load of stones in

a cart. Next to the sturdy beasts, the boy who guided them looked almost

[6] _____. His easy, [7] _____ step looked

as cheerful as Mrs. Winters felt. If only this moment could be

[8] _____ in stone so that she could hold onto it forever.

1. Circle the word that suggests the meaning of stillness. Name an antonym for *stillness*.

2. Circle the word that is a synonym for carefree. Define *carefree* in your own words.

3. Underline the words that tell where the jacket was flung. Give a word that could substitute for *flung* in this sentence.

4. Underline the words that hint at the meaning of lilting. Use the word *lilting* in a new sentence.

5. Underline the words that hint at the meaning of cast. What else could be *cast* in bronze?

6. Underline the words that tell what the horse is bearing. Name a synonym for *bearing*.

7. Circle the word that gives a clue to the meaning of deeds. Use *deeds* in a sentence of your own.

8. Circle the word that means nearly the opposite of frail. What else might be described as *frail*?

Read the following passage. Then, complete the activities.

What is the ideal way to convey the beauty of a natural scene or express a mood or tell a story? People have looked for ways to express ideas and feelings since they started living together in groups. Paintings and engravings have been found that are more than 32,000 years old. Even before there was writing, there were songs, legends, and poetry.

Of course, there is no single answer to this question. Is a photograph the best way to show a swan making a silent trail in the calm stillness of a pond? Is a painting able to communicate the carefree feeling of a person on the beach, jacket flung over her shoulder, untroubled at that moment by the problems of daily life?

Then there's poetry to consider. Can a poem make us see the lilting strides of a horse as it trots gracefully across a field? Picture the same horse cast in bronze as part of a statue in a fountain. Perhaps it is bearing a rider on its back, a king or general returning from battle. The long list of his deeds and endeavors may be found in a book, but in the statue we see him as a solid human being. The artist most likely captured him at the peak of his strength, before he became frail with age. That is how he now remains, in his prime forever thanks to the statue.

The arts in all their forms offer humans so many ways to capture moments in time and to give these moments as gifts to the generations that follow.

Do Not Go Gentle into That Good Night • Fern Hill
Dylan Thomas

The Horses
Ted Hughes

Summaries These three poems provide different views of nature. In **"Do Not Go Gentle into That Good Night,"** the speaker advises readers to resist death with all of their strength, not to yield quietly to it. In **"Fern Hill,"** the speaker recalls his childhood on a farm, when he was innocent of the knowledge that he was growing older. **"The Horses"** describes an early morning encounter with a herd of wild horses.

Note-taking Guide
Use this chart to record the major theme of each work.

Poem	Theme
"Do Not Go Gentle"	
"Fern Hill"	
"The Horses"	

Do Not Go Gentle into That Good Night • Fern Hill • The Horses

1. **Literary Analysis:** A writer's style is the way that he or she writes and communicates. Style includes word choice, sound devices, phrasing, pace, and tone. Fill in this chart to record aspects of Thomas's style.

Style	Examples
Words tumble out in a rush	
Shows an attitude of wonder about life	
Uses complex poetic forms	

2. **Reading Strategy:** How does Thomas's style help communicate **theme** in "Fern Hill?"

_____

_____

4. **Reading Strategy:** What is one effective way that Hughes reveals **theme** in "The Horses"?

_____

_____

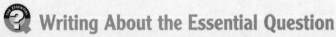 **Writing About the Essential Question**

What is the relationship between place and literature? Which details of the setting convey Thomas's and Hughes's ideas?

_____

_____

_____

An Arundel Tomb • The Explosion • On the Patio • Not Waving but Drowning

Literary Analysis

A poem's **meter** is its pattern of rhythm. Each meter is made up of lines and feet. A **foot** is a group of one or more stressed (´) and unstressed (˘) syllables.

- An **iamb** is one unstressed syllable followed by one stressed syllable (˘ ´).
- A **trochee** is one stressed syllable followed by one unstressed syllable (´ ˘).

Each line of metered poetry contains a certain number of feet. A line with four feet is called **tetrameter.** "An Arundel Tomb" uses **iambic tetrameter,** a meter with four iambs per line.

In the twentieth century, many poets began writing **free verse,** which is poetry without a regular pattern of rhythm or rhyme. Peter Redgrove uses free verse in "The Patio."

A poem's rhythm contributes to its dramatic structure. **Dramatic structure** uses contrasts to build toward a climax, the most exciting or important part of the poem.

Reading Strategy

The best way to understand a poem is to **read it in sentences.** Listen to yourself or others read the poem aloud, and try to hear the meaning. Focus on the units of thought, not on the rhythm or line breaks. Poetic sentences do not always end at line breaks. Look for punctuation marks to know when to pause or make a full stop.

Poem	Sentence	Meaning

© Pearson Education

Word List A

Study these words from the selections. Then, complete the activities that
follow.

blurred [BLERD] *adj.* made less clear or distinct in form or outline
   Ana's vision seemed blurred, but then she noticed her glasses were dirty.

comfort [KUM fuhrt] *n.* a pleasant condition, free from pain or worry
   Les was happily living a life of comfort, but then his troubles began.

lodged [LAHJD] *v.* placed or left somewhere
   Kimi lodged her special treasures in a tiny space beneath her floorboards.

moaning [MOHN ing] *v.* making a low, sad sound, as if from pain or grief
   After twisting her ankle, Sharon lay on the ground, moaning in pain.

persisted [puhr SIS tid] *v.* continued stubbornly in spite of difficulty
   Roland found math hard, but he persisted until he understood it.

prolong [proh LONG] *v.* to make longer in time or space; continue
   Having a good time, they decided to prolong their visit another hour.

trough [TRAWF] *n.* a long, narrow depression, as between ridges
   Water collected in the trough formed by wheel ruts in the mud.

vaguely [VAYG lee] *adv.* not precisely, clearly, or distinctly
   Chad vaguely remembered his mom telling him to be home early.

Exercise A

Fill in each blank below with the appropriate word from Word List A.

   Running forward to catch the softball, Carol tripped in a small

[1] _____ in the ground and twisted her ankle. As she lay

[2] _____ on the ground, her friend Lucy tried to offer some

[3] _____. Carol looked up at Lucy but could not see her clearly, as

her vision was slightly [4] _____. Carol [5] _____ remembered

questioning the wisdom of playing in the old, abandoned field. Now, as her

pain [6] _____, she knew it had been a bad idea. Not only had she

twisted her ankle, but she could tell that a small pebble was [7] _____

firmly in her knee. She did not want to [8] _____ her pain, so she

asked Carol to call emergency services so that she could get help quickly.

Read the following passage. Pay special attention to the underlined words. Then, read it again, and complete the activities. Use a separate sheet of paper for your written answers.

Abby enjoyed bike riding, and she did it often to keep in shape. She rode a minimum of four times per week. It was an activity that she persisted in, refusing to give it up. She particularly enjoyed riding though the country near her home. Today was a particularly beautiful day, sunny and clear but not too hot. Looking forward to her ride, she set out eagerly.

As she rode along, Abby enjoyed the sights and sounds around her. An abundance of wildflowers grew in the trough of the ditch beside the road, and she saw birds flitting between the trees. Occasionally, she heard the distant moaning sound of large farm equipment operating in the fields. But otherwise, it was so quiet that she could hear the pebbles lodged in the treads of her wheels making a soft crunching noise on the roughly paved country road.

Enjoying her ride immensely, Abby was only vaguely aware of the passing miles. She suddenly realized that it was getting late, and she did not want to prolong her ride past dark. It was time to turn around. Unfortunately, she had taken several turns and was no longer sure where she was. She looked for a road sign to point her in the right direction, but the only one she could find was too blurred from age and weather for her to read. She realized that nothing around her looked familiar, and she began to get slightly worried. She took comfort in knowing that she had a cell phone in her pocket and could call for help if she needed to.

Abby knew her house was to the west, so she followed the direction of the setting sun. Soon enough, she began to recognize landmarks and knew she was going the right direction.

1. Underline the words that prove that Abby persisted in her favorite activity. What is one activity in which you have *persisted*?

2. Circle the words that tell where the trough was located. What is a *trough*?

3. Underline the words that **tell** what was making a moaning sound. Describe what *moaning* sounds like.

4. Circle the word that tells **what** was lodged in Abby's wheels. Use *lodged* in a sentence.

5. Underline the words that **tell** what Abby was vaguely aware of. What is a word or phrase that means about the same as *vaguely*?

6. Circle the words that tell what Abby did not want to prolong. What is an example of something that people usually want to *prolong*?

7. Underline the words that **tell** what caused the road sign to be blurred. Tell what might cause a photograph to be *blurred*.

8. Underline the words that tell what gave Abby comfort. What other things might give a lost person *comfort*?

An Arundel Tomb •
The Explosion
Philip Larkin

On the Patio
Peter Redgrove

Not Waving but Drowning
Stevie Smith

Summaries The two poems by Philip Larkin describe the effects of death on those who are still living. **"An Arundel Tomb"** describes the statues of an earl and a countess on their ancient tomb. **"The Explosion"** recounts the events on the day of an explosion in a coal mine. **"On the Patio"** uses the image of the poet draining a glass and allowing the thunderstorm to refill it as a symbol of a person willing to be open to nature. **"Not Waving but Drowning"** uses the water that drowned a man as a symbol of the coldness and isolation that he felt his whole life and that finally led to his death.

Note-taking Guide
Use this chart to compare and contrast the poems.

Poem	Important Symbols and Their Meanings	Theme
An Arundel Tomb		
The Explosion		
On the Patio		
Not Waving but Drowning		

An Arundel Tomb • The Explosion • On the Patio • Not Waving but Drowning

1. **Connect:** How do the images in "On the Patio" link what occurs in the sky with what occurs below the earth?

   _____

   _____

2. **Draw Conclusions:** In the poem "Not Waving but Drowning," what might the "dead man" mean when he moans, "I was much too far out all my life"?

   _____

3. **Literary Analysis:** Use this chart to analyze Larkin's use of **iambic** and **trochaic tetrameter** in his two poems. Note the pattern of stresses in each line, using (´) to indicate stressed syllables and (˘) to indicate unstressed ones.

"An Arundel Tomb"	"The Explosion"
Their proper habits vaguely shown	It was said, and for a second
As jointed armor, stiffened pleat, . . .	Wives saw men of the explosion . . .

4. **Reading Strategy:** When you **read in sentences,** where do you pause at the end of the lines in "The Explosion" and where do you stop?

   _____

   _____

 Writing About the Essential Question

What is the relationship of the writer to tradition? How is the subject matter of these poems like and unlike that of traditional poetry from earlier centuries?

In the Kitchen • Prayer

Literary Analysis

In poetry, **form** refers to structure or organization.

- A **fixed-form** poem has a set number of lines or stanzas. It often follows a set pattern of rhyme or meter.

- A **Shakespearean** or **English sonnet** is a fixed form. It has fourteen lines: three sets of four lines, or quatrains, and a final couplet. The sonnet has a specific rhyme scheme: *abab cdcd efef gg.*

- **Free-form** poems follow no set rules. Poets may establish their own patterns, or they may write in free verse, with no pattern at all.

Sometimes poems are defined by content rather than by form. For example, an **elegy** is a poem that expresses loss or mourning. It can take any form.

Reading Strategy

One of the best ways to enjoy poetry is to hear it. **Recognizing parallel structure,** or the repetition of certain words, phrases, and patterns, can help you focus on important details as you read poetry aloud. Read each poem aloud, and use the chart to identify elements that are repeated in the poems.

	"In the Kitchen"	"Prayer"
Elements of Parallel Structure		

Word List A

Study these words from the selections. Then, complete the activities.

forgetfulness [fawr GET ful nes] *n.* poor memory; absent-minded
Due to her forgetfulness, she missed the appointment.

identifiable [y den tuh FY uh buhl] *adj.* able to be recognized
Jared's red hair was identifiable in any crowd.

normal [NAWR muhl] *n.* the usual way of things; regular
After exams are finished, the daily schedule will return to normal.

recites [ri SYTS] *v.* says out loud from memory
My teacher recites poetry at the start of each class.

secured [si KYORD] *v.* attached firmly; tightly fixed to
The wheels were secured to the axel with bolts.

steadfastly [STED fast lee] *adv.* unwaveringly; constantly; firmly
She steadfastly believed in her goal, pursuing it with all her focus.

Exercise A

Fill in the blanks, using each word from Word List A only once.

Maxine [1] _____ believes that keeping her mind sharp is an important element of aging gracefully. To prevent [2] _____, she memorizes poems or passages of prose from her favorite books and then [3] _____ them every morning. After that, she does the daily crossword puzzle in her newspaper. In the afternoons, when school is over, she spends an hour exercising. Three days a week she swims, and the other four days she uses a rowing machine and lifts weights. She spends so much time at the local gym that she has become [4] _____ to the staff. The rower is her favorite piece of equipment. The oars are [5] _____ to the machine, so that while she rows it can record her speed and the amount of energy she is using. Maxine has a lot less time for hanging out with friends now. Sometimes they ask her when her life is going to get back to [6] _____. She tells them this is her new routine, and she loves it, and they should try joining her at the gym sometime.

© Pearson Education

1. Circle the words that tell what is not identifiable. What is an *identifiable* element of a traditional sonnet?

2. Underline the words that explain recites. Write a sentence using *recites*.

3. Circle the nearby word that is a synonym for steadfastly. Underline what has *steadfastly* interested poets.

4. Underline words that give you a clue to the meaning of normal. Write a synonym for *normal*.

5. Underline why, according to the passage, writing a poem combats forgetfulness. Name another way a person could combat *forgetfulness* in order to preserve an important memory for others.

6. Underline the words that say what poetry has secured. Write a sentence using *secured*.

Read the following passage. Then, complete the activities.

Poetry of the twentieth and twenty-first centuries often appears as free verse. It provides a contrast to the recognizable structure of older poetry. Free verse may have no identifiable pattern to its line lengths or rhymes. Sometimes modern poetry is written to fit an older form, like the traditional 14-line sonnet. Even then, lines may end with rhymes that do not match exactly—or at all.

In a free verse poem that follows no obvious form or rhyme scheme, it is usually still possible to hear a rhythm in the language, either when you read the poem or when a person recites it out loud. Sometimes, it takes hearing a poem to understand its rhythm.

Modern poetry expresses the same essential concerns that have steadfastly fascinated, disturbed, and illuminated poetic imaginations since ancient times. These unchanging concerns include: a desire to make sense of the world, a search for meaning in that world, and a need to understand and communicate the range of human actions and emotions. Modern poems often express a reverence for life by finding meaning in the ordinary and the normal. They study the closely observed, everyday objects and sounds, like an ironing board, a kettle, or a train whistle in the night.

Some people might say that writing poems is an act of combating forgetfulness. This is because every poem is a record of something in words. In that way, poetry helps to keep alive memories of events, moments, ideas, and people.

These days, many messages we share about our experiences depend upon visual images. Nevertheless, poetry is a solid, lasting medium. It has secured itself permanently into the repertoire of human expression. Poetry renews its importance every time new poets pinpoint and express profound meanings through language.

In the Kitchen
Penelope Shuttle

Prayer
Carol Duffy

Summary In **"In the Kitchen,"** the narrator personifies ordinary items found in a kitchen. In **"Prayer,"** the speaker talks about how prayer can affect people differently.

Note-taking Guide

In both poems, nonhuman things are personified, or given human qualities. This approach gives ordinary objects a deeper, more personal value. As you read, note the humanlike qualities and actions displayed by various nonhuman things in the poems.

Examples of Personification	
"In the Kitchen"	"Prayer"

In the Kitchen • Prayer

1. **Interpret:** In "Prayer," the woman hears a tree sing, and a man hears Latin chanting in the sounds of a train. How do these images reflect the real sounds of trees and trains?

_____

_____

2. **Literary Analysis:** Both selections are **elegies,** or poems that deal with loss and mourning. Use the chart to record the speakers' losses and the ways in which they try to overcome their grief.

	Speaker's Loss	How the Speaker Finds Comfort
"In the Kitchen"		
"Prayer"		

3. **Reading Strategy: Parallel structure** emphasizes important ideas in a poem. Given the repetition in "In the Kitchen," what is the speaker working toward?

_____

_____

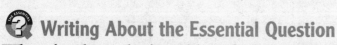 **Writing About the Essential Question**

What is the relationship of the writer to tradition? Are Duffy's sonnet and Shuttle's free-verse poem equally effective as elegies? Explain.

_____

_____

_____

A Devoted Son

Literary Analysis

Some stories feature **generational conflicts** between characters who represent older and younger generations. The way characters respond to these and other conflicts often depends on whether the characters change and grow.

- **Static characters** do not change. They may represent a social role or an attitude.
- **Dynamic characters** change. The change may be one they have chosen or one that happens to them. Writers use such characters to develop truths about life.

Writers sometimes use static characters as symbols to stand for ideas or general thoughts. When you read a story with many static characters, think about how the writer uses these characters to represent beliefs, roles, or social trends.

Reading Strategy

When you are studying character, be sure to **identify the causes of the characters' actions.** Use a chart like the one shown to record behavior and its causes for the two main characters in "A Devoted Son."

	Action	Cause
Rakesh		
Varma		

Word List A

Study these words from the selection. Then, complete the activities that follow.

amongst [uh MUNGST] *prep.* in the midst of; among
Lily saw one weed amongst the lovely irises.

colleagues [KAHL eegz] *n.* fellow workers in a profession
At lunchtime, Daisy and her colleagues ate together and talked about work.

distraught [dis TRAWT] *adj.* extremely upset; crazed
Barbara was distraught when she brought her injured dog to the vet.

humiliating [hyoo MIL ee ayt ing] *adj.* extremely embarrassing; humbling
It was humiliating for the team to lose by thirty points.

miraculously [muh RAK yoo luhs lee] *adv.* amazingly; wondrously
The cat seemed extremely sick, but, miraculously, she recovered fully.

panicky [PAN ik ee] *adj.* showing sudden, overwhelming fear
When Al yelled "Fire!" the panicky audience ran out of the theater.

thereafter [thehr AF ter] *adv.* after that time
Dee decided to save money; thereafter, she added to her account each week.

verandah [vuh RAN duh] *n.* a long, open, outdoor porch, usually with a roof
Wanda sat on the verandah, sipping lemonade and admiring the sunset.

Exercise A

Fill in each blank below with the appropriate word from Word List A.

Chad was feeling a bit depressed after his [1] _____ and

embarrassing performance at his new part-time job. He had gotten the job

only two weeks before, and he was told that he would be serving the tables

that were out on the [2] _____. He had been given a brief amount of

training; [3] _____, he had been on his own. All went well until this

afternoon when he carried a heavy tray [4] _____ the tables, chairs,

and diners. With a frightened, almost [5] _____ feeling, he realized

the tray was unbalanced. Within moments, his mood changed from slightly

nervous to [6] _____, or very upset. [7] _____, however, none

of the drinks spilled on any of the guests, and Chad still had his job. His

[8] _____ told him that they had all had similar experiences, which

was some comfort to Chad.

Read the following passage. Pay special attention to the underlined words. Then, read it again, and complete the activities. Use a separate sheet of paper for your written answers.

Ravi resided with her family in a comfortable home on†the outskirts of Calcutta, India. The oldest of three children and the only girl, Ravi had always been interested in medicine; one of her quirks as a child was to patch up her dolls with bandages whenever they got a scratch. Now, as Ravi turned eighteen, her life was about to change drastically, and Ravi's family was distraught, in turmoil, and extremely upset.

It was time for Ravi to leave home. After much planning and preparation, Ravi was ready to begin studying medicine in the United States. She was enrolled in a university in Los Angeles, more than thirteen thousand miles away from home; her passport was in order, and she was packed. As she enjoyed her last evening amongst her beloved family, Ravi felt torn: on the one hand, she wanted to go, but on the other, she knew she'd miss her family, their pleasant evenings on the verandah in front of their home, and the familiarity of their customs.

Ravi had always been an excellent student, never having had a humiliating failure when it came to her studies. She had never had the panicky, frightened feeling†that some of her friends had when they weren't prepared for a test. No, Ravi had made a resolution long ago to do her best at all times; thereafter, she had lived up to that promise to herself. Now, miraculously for someone whose family was not really wealthy, she was on her way to college, which would be followed by medical school. Ravi knew that she could look forward to a life among well-educated colleagues, the kind of co-workers who were dedicated to the idea of helping the sick get well. If only it weren't so difficult to leave home!

1. Underline two phrases that mean about the same as distraught. Tell about a situation that might make a†person feel *distraught*.

2. Underline the words that describe the people amongst whom Ravi spent the evening. What is a more common word for *amongst*?

3. Circle the words that tell where the verandah is located. Use *verandah* in a sentence.

4. Circle the word that is described as humiliating. What does *humiliating* mean?

5. Circle the word that means about the same as panicky. What might cause you to have a *panicky* feeling?

6. Ravi made a resolution. Underline the words that tell what she did thereafter. Use *thereafter* in a sentence.

7. Circle the words that tell what was miraculously happening for Ravi. What is one thing that you wish would *miraculously* happen in your life?

8. Circle the word that means about the same as colleagues. What kind of *colleagues* would you like to work with in the future?

A Devoted Son
Anita Desai

Summary This story takes place in a suburb in India. A vegetable seller and his family sacrifice to send their son, Rakesh, to medical school. Rakesh is very successful, but he dutifully returns home to his family after graduating. A devoted son, Rakesh fulfills the traditional expectations of his family. Rakesh's father is proud of his son, but as the father grows old and ill and Rakesh assumes more authority, the two come into conflict. The father comes to resent Rakesh's control of his diet and health matters and wishes to die in peace.

Note-taking Guide

Use the chart below to note whether Rakesh and Varma are static or dynamic characters. Then record details that support your choice.

Character	Static	Dynamic	Details
Rakesh			
Varma			

A Devoted Son

1. **Literary Analysis:** Are Rakesh's mother and wife **static** or **dynamic characters?** Explain your classifications.

   _____

   _____

2. **Literary Analysis:** Use a chart like this one to compare and contrast Varma's behavior in the beginning, middle, and end of the story.

	Beginning	Middle	End
Varma			

   Is Varma a **dynamic** or a **static character?**_____

3. **Reading Strategy:** Explain the **causes** of each of these actions on the part of Varma or Rakesh:

   a. Varma hosts a party for the neighbors.

   _____

   b. Varma "goes to pieces."

   _____

   c. Rakesh puts his father on a strict diet.

   _____

Writing About the Essential Question

What is the relationship of the writer to tradition? What does the story show about traditional values and changing values in India? Explain.

_____

_____

Next Term, We'll Mash You

Literary Analysis

Characters are an important element in a short story. **Characterization** is the way characters are created and developed.

- In **direct characterization,** the writer states a character's traits outright.

- With **indirect characterization,** readers must infer the character's traits.

- Dialogue, characters' reactions to situations, and others' observations about individual characters help reveal characterization. These details can support the overall theme of the story.

  As you read, look for ways in which the author provides characterization. Consider how characterization clarifies the story's theme.

Reading Strategy

Writers use their powers of observation to create stories, and they are influenced by the world around them. To fully appreciate a work, it is important to **evaluate social influences of the period.** The historical period, events of the time, social trends and ideas, and prevailing attitudes influence various story elements. Use the chart below to record social influences that impact Lively's story.

Setting:		
Characters:		
Social Class	Motivations	Reactions
What these elements reveal:		

Word List A

Study these words from the selections. Then, complete the activities.

amiable [AY mee uh buhl] *adj.* friendly; genial; good-natured
  His amiable nature was apparent in his friendly smile.

economist [i KAHN uh mist] *n.* person who specializes in the study of financial matters
  The economist predicted how much a barrel of oil might cost.

headmaster [HED mas ter] *n.* title given to the person in charge of a school, especially a private school; principal
  The headmaster is in charge of all academic decisions at our school.

inaccessible [in ak SES uh buhl] *adj.* unreachable; unobtainable
  Parents keep medicines inaccessible to young children to protect them.

prospectuses [pruh SPEK tuh sez] *n.* designs; plans
  Jamal got prospectuses from three schools to help him decide where to apply.

relentless [ri LENT lis] *adj.* persistent and unending
  The dog was relentless, refusing to stop chasing the cat.

untainted [un TAYN ted] *v.* unstained; uncorrupted; not disgraced
  Her integrity was so well known that her reputation was untainted.

unpredictable [un pree DIKT uh buhl] *adj.* unable to know or say in advance what will happen
  The unpredictable weather caused rain one minute and sunshine the next.

Exercise A

Fill in the blanks, using each word from Word List A only once.

The new [1] _____ of our school was a former [2] _____ who

had conducted research on the relationship between sleep and worker productivity.

He had written several highly regarded books on the subject, and he had an

[3] _____ reputation for scholarship and integrity. Students and staff soon

found that his [4] _____ personality was infectious in a good way; there

were a lot more people smiling on campus. He was the opposite of his predecessor,

who spent most of his time away on business trips, [5] _____ to faculty and

students. The new man's efforts to improve our school seemed [6] _____. He

changed the menu so the cafeteria served more healthy food and hired new faculty

to reverse the school's reputation for [7] _____ academic outcomes. To

attract a more diverse range of student applicants, he updated the Web site

and printed new [8] _____ containing many more photographs and

up-to-the-minute information about our school.

Read the following passage. Then, complete the activities.

1. What sometimes makes a private school seem inaccessible to some families? Give a synonym for *inaccessible*.

2. Underline the word or phrase that has a meaning similar to headmaster. Use *headmaster* in a sentence.

3. Circle the words that have a meaning similar to amiable. Give an antonym for *amiable*.

4. According to the passage, what is the reason that fundraising is relentless? Use *relentless* in a sentence.

5. Underline the words that explain the meaning of prospectuses. Pretend you are making *prospectuses* for your school, and write one or two good things you would want people to know about it.

6. Circle the phrase that describes what an economist does. Use *economist* in a sentence.

7. Underline the words that tell what untainted means. Write two antonyms for *untainted*.

8. Circle the words that say what may be unpredictable. Use *unpredictable* in a sentence.

In the United States, most children are educated in public schools, paid for with government funding. However, some families choose to pay to send their children to private schools.

The extra cost of attending private schools sometimes makes them seem inaccessible to the average family. Tuition at these institutions can be expensive. However, many private schools offer scholarships to students who otherwise might not be able to afford them.

The school's head represents the school. The head of a public school is called its principal, while the person in charge of a private school is often called the headmaster or headmistress. It is certainly an advantage for anyone in charge of a school to be amiable. A friendly, outgoing personality helps in all areas. At private schools, a head also usually participates in relentless fundraising. Private schools are persistent in their efforts to raise money in order to maintain excellent facilities.

To attract new families, private schools often invest a lot of care in their prospectuses. These documents appear on Web sites or are printed as booklets. They explain the school's mission and describe its programs to prospective students and parents.

It doesn't take an economist specializing in finance to realize that a school with an untainted reputation for excellence can raise money and attract students. In contrast, a school whose facilities may be poor and whose educational outcomes are unpredictable will have trouble. Parents don't want to take a chance on a school where their children's education may or may not be good. No matter the type of school, when it comes to education, all parents want to know that their children are receiving a great education that prepares them well for the future.

Next Term We'll Mash You

Penelope Lively

Summary In this story, a young boy and his parents tour a private school outside of London. The parents and the boy have different impressions of the school. The parents decide to send their son there without finding out if he really wants to attend.

Note-taking Guide

The things that Charles's parents find appealing about St. Edwards reveals much about them. As you read, record their comments and observations about the school.

School Grounds:

Staff:

Cost:

What Their Friends Say About the School:

Next Term We'll Mash You

1. **Summarize:** At their first meeting, Charles's mother evaluates the headmaster's wife. Summarize her observation.

_____

_____

2. **Literary Analysis:** The author uses mostly **indirect characterization** to reveal the characters in this story. Use the chart below to describe Charles and his mother.

A word that describes Charles is _____

Details that reveal this:

A word that describes Charles's mother is _____

Details that reveal this:

3. **Reading Strategy:** The boarding school setting reflects one of the author's **social influences.** Consider the positive and negative effects that attending St. Edward's might have on Charles. What is the author's message about class and education in England?

_____

_____

Writing About the Essential Question

How does literature shape or reflect society? What does the story show about class and its effects on British society? Explain.

_____

_____

from We'll Never Conquer Space

Literary Analysis

An **argumentative essay** is an essay that argues for or against a particular opinion. The opinion is often a topic of public interest or part of a public debate. It displays some or all of these features:

- a clear statement of the author's opinion
- a formal tone
- facts that support general statements
- words and phrases that readers will remember
- appeals to reason and/or emotion
- details that address reader concerns and differing opinions
- clarifications of unfamiliar ideas

Clarke uses many analogies to explain unfamiliar ideas. An **analogy** helps readers understand an idea by showing how it is like another idea we already know. As you read, notice how his analogies help you understand hard-to-picture ideas.

Reading Strategy

An **expository critique** evaluates an argument like the one presented in Clarke's essay. When you prepare a critique of an essay, you question the information in the essay. Use the following checklist to prepare an expository critique of the argument that Clarke makes.

Is an opinion clearly stated? Example:	Are there appeals to reason or emotion? Example:
Do facts support ideas? Example:	Does the author address differing opinions? Example:
Are there words and phrases that readers will remember? Example:	Are unfamiliar ideas clarified? Example:

Word List A

Study these words from the selection. Then, complete the activities that follow.

analogy [uh NAL uh jee] *n.* a likeness that exists between two things
    Barbara pointed out the analogy between our arms and fishes' fins.

conservative [kuhn SER vuh tiv] *adj.* moderate; cautious
    Tim's budget is a conservative estimate of what he actually spends.

psychological [sy kuh LAHJ uh kuhl] *adj.* having to do with the mind; mental
    Despite its physical demands, tennis is said to be largely a psychological game.

separation [sep uh RAY shuhn] *n.* the condition of being disconnected or apart
    After a two-year separation, the two friends picked up where they'd left off.

ultimate [UL tuh mit] *adj.* greatest or highest possible; maximum
    Paula mistakenly thought that the ultimate honor was to be prom queen.

vertically [VER tuh kuhl ee] *adv.* in a straight up and down manner
    Richard threw the ball vertically, straight up into the air.

virtual [VER choo uhl] *adj.* existing in effect, though not in fact or form
    Our team's victory is a virtual certainty.

voyaging [VOY uh jing] *n.* a journey, especially by sea
    Our long years of voyaging began when we bought the sailboat.

Exercise A

Fill in each blank below using the appropriate word from Word List A.

Brad's favorite video game gave the feeling of [1] _____ reality—it seemed so real, but it was not. The game required that he move his characters [2] _____, horizontally, and at various angles against a watery background. The [3] _____ goal of all their [4] _____ was to reach a peaceful place where they could rest. In his mind, Brad made the [5] _____ to coming home after a long and difficult journey, finally able to end a long [6] _____ from the family. Brad was a [7] _____ player, not taking too many chances. He believed that this gave him a [8] _____ advantage over his opponent, his friend Darla, whose personality made her more likely to take chances that would cause her to lose the game.

Read the following passage. Pay special attention to the underlined words. Then, read it again, and complete the activities. Use a separate sheet of paper for your written answers.

Some call space "the last frontier," an <u>analogy</u> that reminds us that frontiers on our own planet have, for the most part, been conquered. Not too long ago, however, most of our planet was unexplored. It's fun to imagine what it was like in, say, the time of Christopher Columbus, when the <u>ultimate</u> frontier seemed to be the wide, wild ocean, which no one had ever crossed.

The concept of a round world was not completely new in the late 1400s. What was unknown, of course, was that two huge continents separated the waters that were thought to be just one big ocean. The more cautious and <u>conservative</u> thinkers of the day, however, did not agree with this idea of a round world. That is why it was difficult for Columbus to get funding for his expedition. Persuading King Ferdinand and Queen Isabella of Spain to sponsor him must have been a great <u>psychological</u> victory for him, improving his mental state and boosting his confidence.

Ready for <u>voyaging</u>, Columbus set out on his historic ocean trip with a crew of about ninety men and three ships: the *Santa Maria,* the *Pinta,* and the *Niña.* If we could stand on the deck of one of those ships today and look up at the largest masts placed <u>vertically</u> on the decks, we would no doubt be astonished at how small they were. Compared to today's ships, Columbus's three ships were almost like toys.

Columbus's first voyage began on August 3, 1492. He arrived back in his home port on March 15, 1493. His <u>separation</u> from home lasted a little over six months, but it is a <u>virtual</u> certainty that those six months changed the world.

1. Underline two items that are compared in an *analogy.* Write an *analogy* comparing time to something else.

2. Underline the words that describe the *ultimate* frontier during the time of Columbus. Use *ultimate* in a sentence.

3. Circle the word that means about the same as *conservative.* What does *conservative* mean?

4. Circle the word that hints at the meaning of *psychological.* What might be a great *psychological* victory for a typical teenager?

5. Underline the words that mean about the same as *voyaging.* If you had time and money for *voyaging,* where would you like to go?

6. Circle the word that tells where you would have to look to see something that was placed *vertically.* Use *vertically* in a sentence.

7. Circle the words that tell what kind of *separation* Columbus had to endure. What is another word that is similar to *separation*?

8. Underline the words that tell what was a virtual *certainty.* What is one thing in your life that is a virtual *certainty*?

© Pearson Education

from We'll Never Conquer Space

Arthur C. Clarke

Summary This essay begins with the statement "Man will never conquer space." The author claims that space is too large for humanity to conquer. The speed of light limits how quickly people can communicate with one another. People living in different galaxies will be unable to have conversations. They will only be able to hear about events years later. Those who colonize space will lose their ties with Earth.

Note-Taking Guide

There are three subheadings in this excerpt from Clarke's essay. Use this chart to record the most important thought in each subheading.

Forever Too Large

"Time Barrier"

We'll Never Conquer Space

Independent "Colonies"

from We'll Never Conquer Space

1. **Evaluate:** Challenge a text by asking questions about it. Clarke writes, "Man has always accepted whatever price was necessary for his explorations. . . ." Write one question that challenges this statement.

_____

_____

2. **Literary Analysis:** Clarke makes the **analogy** that people in space will be like "ants crawling on the face of the earth." Use the chart below to interpret this analogy. In the left column, write the two things the analogy compares. In the middle column, write how the two things are the same. In the third column, write the idea this analogy helps makes clear.

Things Compared	Similarities	What Is Explained

3. **Reading Strategy:** If you were writing an **expository critique** of this essay, what support for Clarke's main point would you find most effective?

_____

_____

 Writing About the Essential Question

What is the relationship between place and literature? How does Clarke's view of space as a "place" inform the argument he makes?

_____

_____

Case Studies

About Case Studies

A **case study** explains how a real-life situation developed over time. Case studies include some types of technical articles. Technical articles explain how things work. They may also be used to predict how future situations will develop over time. For example, a technical article acts as a case study when it explains how current technology can be developed for new purposes.

A case study usually has these parts:

• an introduction that states what is being studied and why
• facts and examples
• explanations that connect examples to ideas (inductive reasoning)
• explanations that connect ideas to examples (deductive reasoning)
• conclusion and suggestions

Reading Skill

Informational writing uses *text structures* such as cause-and-effect relationships, which show how one thing brings about another. Consequently, **analyzing cause-and-effect relationships** can help you better understand an informational document. As you read, look for explanations of how a particular event or situation produced or might produce particular effects. Use a chart like the one shown to help you identify causes and effects.

Event	Causes	Effects

In this article, Clarke proposed a new form of world-wide communication based on "stationary" artificial satellites that could hover in place above a single spot on the Earth. Today, such satellite communication is common, but it was a revolutionary idea when scientist and science-fiction writer Arthur C. Clarke first proposed it in the October, 1945, issue of the journal *Wireless World.* (October, 1945, pp. 305–308).

Extra-Terrestrial Relays
Can Rocket Stations Give
World-wide Radio Coverage?

By Arthur C. Clarke

> The author is suggesting that the answer to the question in the title is yes. He is also implying that the article will reveal the cause-and-effect chain leading to such "radio coverage."

. . . A rocket which achieved a sufficiently great speed in flight outside the earth's atmosphere would never return. This "orbital" velocity is 8 km per sec (5 miles per sec), and a rocket which attained it would become an artificial satellite, circling the world for ever with no expenditure of power—a second moon, in fact. . . .

> The author makes a prediction that, if true, will make possible the kind of rocket stations he refers to in his title.

It will be possible in a few more years to build radio controlled rockets which can be steered into such orbits beyond the atmosphere and left to broadcast scientific information back to the earth. A little later, manned rockets will be able to make similar flights with sufficient excess power to break the orbit and return to earth.

There are an infinite number of possible stable orbits, circular and elliptical, in which a rocket would remain, if the initial conditions were correct. The velocity of 8 km/sec. applies only to the closest possible orbit, one just outside the atmosphere . . .

It will be observed that one orbit, with a radius of 42,000 km, has a period of exactly 24 hours. A body in such an orbit, if its plane coincided with that of the earth's equator, would revolve with the earth and would thus be stationary above the same spot on the planet. It would remain fixed in the sky of a whole hemisphere and unlike all other heavenly bodies would neither rise nor set. A body in a smaller orbit would revolve more quickly than the earth and so would rise in the west, as indeed happens with the inner moon of Mars.

> The fact the author points out in this paragraph is extremely important and lays the causal basis for his proposal.

Using material ferried up by rockets, it would be possible to construct a "space station" in such an orbit. The station could be provided with living quarters, laboratories and everything needed for the comfort of its crew, who would be relieved and provisioned by a regular rocket service. This project might be undertaken for purely scientific reasons as it would contribute enormously to our knowledge of astronomy, physics, and meteorology. . . .

Although such an undertaking may seem fantastic, it requires for its fulfillment rockets only twice as fast as those already in the design stage. Since the gravitational stresses involved in the structure are negligible, only the very lightest materials would be necessary and the station could be as large as required.

Let us now suppose that such a station were built in this orbit. It could be provided with receiving and transmitting equipment . . . and could act as a repeater to relay transmissions between any two points on the hemisphere beneath . . .

A single station could only provide coverage to half the globe, and for a world service three would be required, though more could be readily utilized. Figure 3 shows the simplest arrangement. The stations would be arranged approximately equidistantly around the earth . . .

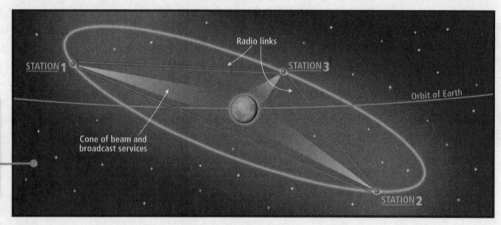

Diagrams and captions help readers to imagine what the author describes.

Figure 3. The stations in the chain would be linked by radio or optical beams and thus any conceivable beam or broadcast service could be provided. . . .

Conclusion

The author summarizes the advantages of "the space station," which can also be thought of as a series of results.

Briefly summarized, the advantages of the space station are as follows:

(1) It is the only way in which true world coverage can be achieved for all possible types of service.

(2) . . . an almost unlimited number of channels would be available.

(3) The power requirements are extremely small . . . Moreover, the cost of the power would be very low.

(4) However great the initial expense, it would only be a fraction of that required for the world networks replaced, and the running costs would be incomparably less.

Thinking About the Case Study

1. For what future purpose did Arthur C. Clarke wish rocket technology to be used?

   _____

   _____

2. What conclusion did Clarke draw about the cost of his proposal?

   _____

   _____

TALK ABOUT IT Reading Skill

3. According to Clarke, what would be the effect of a rocket reaching the "orbital" velocity of 8 km per second?

   _____

   _____

4. What events does Clarke say are required in order to construct a space station?

   _____

   _____

WRITE ABOUT IT ▷ Timed Writing: Recommendation (25 minutes)

Write an essay explaining the different uses and the benefits of satellite technology you read about in the technical article. You should use examples from the document, but you may also draw on your own knowledge of other areas in which this technology is used. Allow five minutes to prewrite and plan your essay, approximately fifteen minutes to draft, and about five minutes to review and revise.

I'm Like a Bird *from* Songbook

Literary Analysis

Poets and writers of fiction often express their beliefs indirectly. However, in a **personal essay,** the writer directly states personal observations and opinions. Most personal essays

- have a friendly, informal, and sometimes humorous tone.
- provide opinions and observations.
- reveal the author's personality and autobiographical details.
- feature comments on life in general.

   As you read Nick Hornby's personal essay, pay attention to his method of revealing his opinions on music and on life overall.

Reading Strategy

A personal essay focuses on an individual's opinions. As a result, an essayist will use **arguments and strategies** to discuss his or her ideas. These techniques are similar to those used in persuasive writing. Essayists

- anticipate and counter differing opinions.
- develop emotional appeals.
- use logic and humor to strengthen their arguments.

   Use the following chart to outline Hornby's arguments and strategies.

Thesis or Main Idea	
Differing Opinions	
Emotional, Logical, Humorous Appeals	

Word List A

Study these words from the selections. Then, complete the activities.

akin [uh KIN] *adj.* similar to
These shoes are <u>akin</u> to a pair I saw in a magazine.

cynically [SIN i kuh lee] *adv.* done in a way reflecting a belief that people are motivated only by selfishness; pessimistically
The mayor <u>cynically</u> made promises he knew he wouldn't keep.

denoting [dee NOH ting] *v.* meaning; standing for
Signs with a symbol <u>denoting</u> danger were posted along the fence.

encompass [en KUHM puhs] *v.* include
The class curriculum will <u>encompass</u> the entire history of music.

forgo [fawr GOH] *adj.* do without; give up
We were late for the theater, so we had to <u>forgo</u> dessert.

inane [in AYN] *adj.* silly; not significant
Jane found the book <u>inane</u> and the movie even more ridiculous.

mastering [MAS ter ing] *v.* becoming highly skilled or expert
Charles was finally close to <u>mastering</u> the game of chess.

repetitive [ruh PEHT uh tiv] *adj.* doing or saying the same thing over and over
The <u>repetitive</u> nature of the lesson made it stick in my mind.

Exercise A

Fill in the blanks, using each word from Word List A only once.

Russell was having difficulty [1] _____ his math homework. It seemed [2] _____ to him, the [3] _____ nature of doing problem after problem. If the decision were up to him, he would [4] _____ math entirely. The symbols [5] _____ the different mathematical functions were confusing and frustrating. He thought that someone had [6] _____ developed math just to make his life difficult. To make it worse, the class was supposed to [7] _____ both algebra and geometry. Russell's sister told him that math was actually [8] _____ to music, one of his favorite hobbies. That idea helped a little, but not much.

1. Underline the words that suggest the meaning of encompass. Use the word *encompass* in a new sentence

2. Underline the nearby words that have the same meaning as akin. Give a word or phrase that means the opposite of *akin*.

3. Circle the words that explain the meaning of mastering. What is necessary for *mastering* a skill?

4. Explain how the paragraph gives clues to the meaning of denoting. Write a new sentence using the word *denoting*.

5. Underline the words that explain the meaning of repetitive. Name something that could be described as *repetitive*.

6. Circle the word that tells what inane means. Give an antonym for *inane*.

7. Underline the words that tell what it would be a mistake to forgo. Give a word or phrase that has the same meaning as *forgo*.

8. How does the sentence give a clue to the word cynically? Does *cynically* have a positive or negative tone? Explain your answer.

Read the following passage. Then, complete the activities.

It has often been said that music is a universal language. People everywhere can enjoy the same song, whether they can talk with one another or not. Even a song with words in an unknown language can be enjoyed by anyone who appreciates tune or rhythm. Melodies and harmonies used well can encompass the full range of emotions, with or without words.

It can also be a joy to develop a deeper understanding of a musical work. Learning to recognize the elements in a beautiful piece of music is akin to noticing the brush strokes in a fine painting. It is also similar to appreciating the themes in a classic novel.

Becoming skilled as a musician can be as difficult as mastering another language, however. Learning to read a sheet of music, with the marks denoting the different tempos and notes, can be a repetitive process. At first, you make the same sounds over and over. It takes many hours of practice to become used to the new "alphabet." For a while, the page can look like an inane jumble of ridiculous symbols. Once you finish learning to read the notes, training your fingers to find the correct notes on an instrument is the next struggle to be tackled.

Though of course it is possible to enjoy music without being able to produce it yourself, it would be a mistake to forgo the study of music just because it is hard. And if you do decide to learn, you must be able to ignore those pessimists who cynically try to sell you programs that promise instant success as a musician. Unless you're Mozart, it always takes hard work.

I'm Like a Bird
from Songbook
Nick Hornby

Summary In this excerpt, Nick Hornby considers the positive and negative influence of pop music. He shows why pop music is important, and points out that the music connects him to other people.

Note-taking Guide

Hornby mentions several reasons why pop music in general and "I'm Like a Bird" in particular have value. Use the table to keep track of Hornby's reasons.

Why Pop Music Is Valuable
Reason 1:
Reason 2:
Reason 3:

I'm Like a Bird *from* Songbook

1. **Literary Analysis:** What personal view is Hornby expressing?

_____

_____

2. **Literary Analysis: Personal essays** have distinct characteristics. Use the chart below to record examples of how "I'm Like a Bird" reflects the typical qualities of a personal essay.

Informal Tone	Opinions/Observations	Information about Author's Background/Personality

3. **Reading Strategy:** Hornby uses several arguments and strategies to explain the appeal of pop music. Which argument or idea do you agree with most strongly? Why?

_____

_____

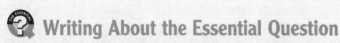 **Writing About the Essential Question**

How does literature shape or reflect society? What comment does this essay make about the cultural establishment? Explain.

_____

_____

_____

The exercises and tools presented here are designed to help you increase your vocabulary. Review the instruction and complete the exercises to build your vocabulary knowledge. Throughout the year, you can apply these skills and strategies to improve your reading, writing, speaking, and listening vocabulary.

The following list contains common word roots with meanings and examples. On the blank lines, write other words you know that have the same roots. Write the meanings of the new words.

Root	Meaning	Example and Meaning	Your Words	Meanings
Greek -chron-	time	*chronology*: arranged in order of occurrence		
Greek -top-	place; surface	*topographical*: relating to a map of the surface of a place		
Latin -cert-	sure	*certify*: to make sure		
Latin -cred-	belief	*credible*: believable		
Latin -dict-	the idea of something said	*diction*: choice of words		
Latin -duc-	to lead	*inducted*: led into a group		
Latin -fid-	faith	*fidelity*: faithfulness		
Latin -fort-	strength	*fortitude*: strength to endure pain		

Root	Meaning	Example and Meaning	Your Words	Meanings
Latin -loc-	place	*dislocation:* being out of place		
Latin -mort-	death	*immortal:* living forever; not ever dying		
Latin -puls-	push; drive	*impulse:* driving forward with sudden force		
Latin -sol-	to comfort	*solace:* an easing of grief; comfort		
Latin -spec-	to look; see	*inspector:* one who looks carefully		
Latin -spir-	breath; life	*aspire:* to yearn or seek after		
Latin -turb-	to disturb	*turbulence:* commotion or disorder		
Latin -voc-	voice	*vocalist:* one who sings		

The following list contains common prefixes with meanings and examples. On the blank lines, write other words you know that begin with the same prefixes. Write the meanings of the new words.

Prefixes	Meaning	Example and Meaning	Your Words	Meanings
Anglo-Saxon fore-	before	foreword: a short piece of writing that comes before the main part of the book		
Greek a-	without; not	amoral: without moral standards		
Greek apo-	away; separate	apothecary: druggist; one who puts away prescriptions		
Greek auto-	self	automatic: done without thought; involuntary		
Greek mono-	single; alone	monorail: a railway with a single track		
Latin circum-	around	circumscribed: limited; having a boundary around		
Latin con-	with; together	concoct: to make by combining		
Latin dis-	apart; not	dissatisfied: not satisfied		

Prefixes	Meaning	Example and Meaning	Your Words	Meanings
Latin ex-	out	*expect*: to look out for		
Latin inter-	between; among	*international*: between or among nations		
Latin mal-	bad	*malformed*: abnormally or badly formed		
Latin multi-	many; much	*multicultural*: having to do with many cultures		
Latin ob-	against; opposed to	*object*: to complain or protest against		
Latin omni-	all; every	*omnivorous*: eating all types of food		
Latin sub-	under; lower	*substandard*: lower than what is acceptable		
Latin trans-	across; through	*transplant*: to remove from one place and settle in another		

The following list contains common suffixes with meanings and examples. On the blank lines, write other words you know that have the same suffixes. Write the meanings of the new words.

Suffix	Meaning	Example and Meaning	Your Words	Meanings
Anglo-Saxon -fold	a specific number of times or ways	*manifold*: many times		
Anglo-Saxon -ful	full of	*forgetful*: apt to forget		
Anglo-Saxon -hood	state or quality of	*childhood*: the state of being a child		
Anglo-Saxon -less	without	*penniless*: without a penny; very poor		
Anglo-Saxon -ness	the state of being	*randomness*: the state of lacking purpose		
Anglo-Saxon -some	tending toward being	*worrisome*: having the tendency to worry		
Greek -ate	forms verbs	*orchestrate*: to coordinate		
Greek -itis	disease; inflammation	*appendicitis*: inflammation of the appendix		

Suffix	Meaning	Example and Meaning	Your Words	Meanings
Greek -logy	the science of study of	*sociology*: the study of human society and social relations		
Latin -able/-ible	able to	*incredible*: not able to be believed		
Latin -ade	the act of; the result of	*barricade*: the result of barring the way		
Latin -age	condition or result of	*vintage*: the wine produced in a particular place and time		
Latin -ance/-ence	quality of; state of being	*dependence*: state of being dependent or needing someone or something		
Latin -ness	the state of being	*happiness*: the state of being happy		
Latin -ous	full of	*glorious*: full of glory		
Latin -tion	the act or process of	*participation*: the process of taking part or participating		

Etymology is the history of a word. It shows where the word came from, or its **origin.** It also shows how it got its present meaning and spelling. Understanding word origins, or etymology, can help you understand and remember the meanings of words you add to your vocabulary.

A good dictionary will tell you the etymology of a word. The word's etymology usually appears in brackets, parentheses, or slashes near the beginning or the end of the dictionary entry. Part of the etymology is the language from which the word comes.

Abbreviations for Languages	
Abbreviation	Language
OE	Old English
ME	Middle English
F	French
Gr	Greek
L	Latin
ML	Medieval Latin
LL	Late Latin

You can find these abbreviations and more in a dictionary's key to abbreviations.

Words From Other Languages

The English that you speak today began in about the year 500. Tribes from Europe settled in Britain. These tribes, called the Angles, the Saxons, and the Jutes, spoke a Germanic language. Later, when the Vikings attacked Britain, their language added words from Danish and Norse. Then, when Christian missionaries came to Britain, they added words from Latin. The resulting language is called Old English, and it looks very different from modern English.

For example, to say "Listen!" in Old English, you would have said "Hwaet!"

The Normans conquered Britain in 1066. They spoke Old French, and the addition of this language changed Old English dramatically. The resulting language, called Middle English, looks much more like modern English, but the spellings of words are very different.

For example, the word *knight* in Middle English was spelled *knyght,* and the word *time* was spelled *tyme.*

During the Renaissance, interest in classical cultures added Greek and Latin words to English. At this time, English started to look more like the English you know. This language, called Modern English, is the language we still speak.

Modern English continues to add words from other languages. As immigrants have moved to the United States, they have added new words to the language.

For example, the word *boycott* comes from Ireland and the word *burrito* comes from Mexico.

Note-taking Using a dictionary, identify the language from which each of the following words came into English. Also identify the word's original and current meaning.

Word	Original Language	Original Meaning	Current Meaning
comb			
costume			
guess			
mile			
panther			

Words That Change Meaning Over Time

English is a living language. It grows by giving new meanings to existing words and by incorporating words that have changed their meaning over time and through usage.

For example, the word *dear* originally meant "expensive."

Note-taking Using a dictionary, identify the original meaning and the current meaning of each of the following words.

	original meaning	current meaning
1. havoc		
2. magazine		

Words That Have Been Invented, or *Coined,* to Serve New Purposes.

New products or discoveries need new words.

For example, the words *paperback* and *quiz* are coined words.

Note-taking Identify one word that has been coined in each of the following categories.

Category	Coined Word
sports	
technology	
transportation	
space travel	
medicine	

Words That Are Combinations of Words or Shortened Versions of Longer Words

New words can be added to the language by combining words or by shortening words.

For example, the word *greenback* is a combination of the words *green* and *back*, and the word *flu* is a shortened version of the word *influenza*.

Note-taking Generate a word to fill in the blanks in each of the following sentences correctly. Your word should be a combination of two words or a shortened version of a longer word.

Jerome served one of our favorite dinners, spaghetti and _____.

Many years ago, people might take an omnibus to work, but today they would call

that vehicle a _____.

We took the most direct route to Aunt Anna's house, which meant driving forty miles

on the _____.

We thought we could get to shelter before the storm started, but we did not quite

make it. A few _____ dampened our jackets.

A dictionary lists words in alphabetical order. Look at this sample dictionary entry. Notice the types of information about a word it gives.

Example of a Dictionary Entry

dictionary (dik′ shə ner′ ē) **n.** pl. **–aries** [ML *dictionarium* < LL *dictio*] **1** a book of alphabetically listed words in a language, with definitions, etymologies, pronunciations, and other information **2** a book of alphabetically listed words in a language with their equivalents in another language [a Spanish-English *dictionary*)

Answer the questions based on the dictionary entry.

1. What is the correct spelling? _____

2. How do you form the plural? _____

3. What language does the word come from? _____

4. How many definitions are there? _____

5 What example is given?_____

Here are some abbreviations you will find in dictionary entries.

Pronunciation Symbols	Parts of Speech	Origins of Words
′ means emphasize this syllable as you say the word	adj. = adjective	Fr = French
¯ means pronounce vowel with a long sound, such as -ay- for a and -ee- for e	adv. = adverb	Ger = German
ə means a sound like -uh-	n. = noun	L = classical Latin
o͞o means the sound of *u* in cute	v. = verb	ME = Middle English OE = Old English

As you read, look up new words in a dictionary. Enter information about the words on this chart.

My Words

New Word	Pronunciation	Part of Speech	Origin	Meanings and Sample Sentence

Academic words are words you use often in your schoolwork. Knowing what these words mean and how to use them will help you think and write better.

The following chart provides definitions and pronunciations for academic words. When you come across one of these words in your reading, write the sentence in which it appears in the middle column. In the right column, use your own words to explain what these sentences mean.

Academic Word	Example You Find	Meaning of Example
analyze (AN uh LYZ) break down into parts and explain		
apply (uh PLY) tell how you use information in a specific situation		
categorize (KAT uh gaw ryz) group similar items together		
clarify (KLA ri FY) make something more understandable		
conclude (kuhn KLOOD) use reasoning to reach a decision or opinion		
deduce (dee DOOS) figure something out by applying a general idea		
define (dee FYN) tell the qualities that make something what it is		
demonstrate (DEM uhn STRAYT) use examples to prove a point		
differentiate (dif er EN shee AYT) explain what makes two things different		

Academic Word	Example You Find	Meaning of Example
evaluate (ee VAL yoo AYT) determine the value or importance of something		
identify (y DEN ti FY) name or show you recognize something		
illustrate (IL uhs TRAYT) give examples that show you know what something means		
interpret (in TER pret) explain the underlying meaning of something		
judge (JUHJ) assess or form an opinion about something		
label (LAY bel) attach the correct name to something		
predict (pree DIKT) tell what will happen based on details you know		
recall (ri KAWL) tell details that you remember		

When you are reading, you will find many unfamiliar words. Here are some tools that you can use to help you read unfamiliar words.

Phonics

Phonics is the science or study of sound. When you learn to read, you learn to associate certain sounds with certain letters or letter combinations. You know most of the sounds that letters can represent in English. When letters are combined, however, it is not always so easy to know what sound is represented. In English, there are some rules and patterns that will help you determine how to pronounce a word. This chart shows you some of the common **vowel digraphs,** which are combinations like ea and oa. Two vowels together are called vowel digraphs. Usually, vowel digraphs represent the long sound of the first vowel.

Vowel Digraphs	Examples of Unusual Sounds	Exceptions
ee and ea	steep, each, treat, sea	head, sweat, dread
ai and ay	plain, paid, may, betray	
oa, ow, and oe	soak, slow, doe	
ie and igh	lie, night, delight, my	myth

As you read, sometimes the only way to know how to pronounce a word with an *ea* spelling is to see if the word makes sense in the sentence. Look at this example:

The water pipes were made of *lead.*

First, try out the long sound "ee." Ask yourself if it sounds right. It does not. Then, try the short sound "e." You will find that the short sound is correct in that sentence.

Now, try this example:

Where you *lead,* I will follow.

Word Patterns

Recognizing different vowel-consonant patterns will help you read longer words. In the following section, the **V** stands for "vowel" and the **C** stands for "consonant."

Single-Syllable Words

CV–go: In two-letter words with a consonant followed by a vowel, the vowel is usually long. For example, the word *go* is pronounced with a long "o" sound.

In a single-syllable word, a vowel followed only by a single consonant is usually short.

CVC–got: If you add a consonant to the word *go*, such as the *t* in *got*, the vowel sound is a short *o*. Say the words *go* and *got* aloud and notice the difference in pronunciation.

Multi-Syllable Words

In words of more than one syllable, notice the letters that follow a vowel.

VCCV–robber: A single vowel followed by two consonants is usually short.

VCV–begin: A single vowel followed by a single consonant is usually long.

VCe–beside: An extension of the VCV pattern is vowel-consonant-silent *e*. In these words, the vowel is long and the *e* is not pronounced.

When you see a word with the VCV pattern, try the long vowel sound first. If the word does not make sense, try the short sound. Pronounce the words *model*, *camel*, and *closet*. First, try the long vowel sound. That does not sound correct, so try the short vowel sound. The short vowel sound is correct in those words.

Remember that patterns help you get started on figuring out a word. You will sometimes need to try a different sound or find the word in a dictionary.

As you read and find unfamiliar words, look up the pronunciations in a dictionary. Write the words in this chart in the correct column, to help you notice patterns and remember pronunciations.

Syllables	Example	New Words	Vowel
CV	go		long
CVC	got		short
VCC	robber		short
VCV	begin		long
	open		long
VCe	beside		long

FAQs About the SAT®

What Is the SAT®?

- The SAT® is a national test intended to predict how well you will do with college-level material.

What Does the SAT® Test?

- The SAT® tests vocabulary, math, and reasoning skills in three sections:
  - Critical Reading: two 25-minute sections and one 20-minute section
  - Math: two 25-minute sections and one 20-minute section
  - Writing: one 35-minute multiple-choice section and one 25-minute essay

Why Should You Take the SAT®?

- Many colleges and universities require you to submit your SAT® scores when you apply. They use your scores, along with other information about your ability and your achievements, to evaluate you for admission.

How Can Studying Vocabulary Help Improve Your SAT® Scores?

- The Critical Reading section of the SAT® asks two types of questions that evaluate your vocabulary.
  - Sentence Completions ask you to fill in one or more blanks in a sentence with the correct word or words. To fill in the blanks correctly, you need to know the meaning of the words offered as answers.
  - Vocabulary in Context questions in Passage-based Reading ask you to determine what a word means based on its context in a reading passage.
- With a strong vocabulary and good strategies for using context clues, you will improve the likelihood that you will score well on the SAT®.

Using Context Clues on the SAT®

When you do not know the meaning of a word, nearby words or phrases can help you. These words or phrases are called context clues.

Guidelines for Using Context Clues

1. Read the sentence or paragraph, concentrating on the unfamiliar word.

2. Look for clues in the surrounding words.

3. Guess the possible meaning of the unfamiliar word.

4. Substitute your guess for the word.

5. When you are reviewing for a test, you can check the word's meaning in a dictionary.

Types of Context Clues

Here are the most common types of context clues:

- formal definitions that give the meaning of the unfamiliar word
- familiar words that you may know that give hints to the unfamiliar word's meaning
- comparisons or contrasts that present ideas or concepts either clearly similar or clearly opposite to the unfamiliar word
- synonyms, or words with the same meaning as the unfamiliar word
- antonyms, or words with a meaning opposite to that of the unfamiliar word
- key words used to clarify a word's meaning

Note-taking List several new words that you have learned recently by figuring out their meanings in context. Then, explain how you used context to decide what the word meant.

New Word	How You Used Context to Understand the Word

Sample SAT® Questions

Here are examples of the kinds of questions you will find on the SAT®. Read the samples carefully. Then, do the Practice exercises that follow.

Sample Sentence Completion Question:

Directions: The sentence that follows has one blank indicating that something has been omitted. Beneath the sentence are five words or sets of words labeled **A** through **E.** Choose the word or set of words that, when inserted in the sentence, best fits the meaning of the sentence as a whole.

1. Though he is _____, his nephew still invites him to Thanksgiving dinner every year.

   A cheerful

   B entertaining

   C misanthropic

   D agile

   E healthy

The correct answer is C. The uncle is *misanthropic.* You can use the context clues "though" and "invites him" to infer that the uncle has some negative quality. Next, you can apply your knowledge of the prefix *mis-* to determine that *misanthropic,* like *mistake* and *misfortune,* is a word indicating something negative. Eliminate the other answer choices, which indicate positive or neutral qualities in this context.

Sample Vocabulary in Context Question:

Directions: Read the following sentence. Then, read the question that follows it. Decide which is the best answer to the question.

Martin Luther King, Jr., whose methods motivated many to demand equal rights in a peaceful manner, was an inspiration to all.

1. In this sentence, the word *inspiration* means—

   A politician

   B motivation to a high level of activity

   C the process of inhaling

   D figurehead

The correct answer is *B.* Both *B* and *C* are correct definitions of the word *inspiration,* but the only meaning that applies in the context of the sentence is "motivation to a high level of activity."

Practice for SAT® Questions

Practice Read the following passage. Then, read each question that follows the passage. Decide which is the best answer to each question.

Many people are becoming Internet <u>savvy</u>, exhibiting their skills at mastering the Web. The Internet is also becoming a <u>more reliable</u> source of factual information. A <u>Web-surfer</u> can find information provided by <u>reputable</u> sources, such as government <u>organizations</u> and universities.

1. In this passage, the word *savvy* means—

   A incompetent

   B competent

   C users

   D nonusers

2. The word *reliable* in this passage means—

   A existing

   B available

   C dependable

   D relevant

3. In this passage, the term *Web-surfer* means—

A someone who uses the Internet

B a person who uses a surfboard

C a person who know a great deal about technology

D a student

4. The word *reputable* in this passage means—

A an approved Internet provider

B well-known and of good reputation

C purely academic

D costly

Practice Each sentence that follows has one or two blanks indicating that something has been omitted. Beneath the sentence are five words or sets of words labeled A through E. Choose the word or set of words that, when inserted in the sentence, best fits the meaning of the sentence as a whole.

1. "I wish I had a longer _____ between performances," complained the pianist. "My fingers need a rest."

A post-mortem   C prelude   E solo

B circumlocution   D interval

2. Instead of revolving around the sun in a circle, this asteroid has a(n)

_____ orbit.

A rapid   C interplanetary   E regular

B eccentric   D circular

3. He was the first historian to translate the _____ on the stone.

A impulsion   C excavation   E inscription

B aversion   D circumspection

4. To correct your spelling error, simply _____ the i and the e.

A translate   C transcent   E integrate

B transpose   D interpolate

5. Spilling soda all over myself just when the movie got to the good part was

a(n) _____ event.

A fortunate   C tenacious   E constructive

B premature   D infelicitous

Diction

Diction is a writer's or a speaker's word choice. The vocabulary, the vividness of the language, and the appropriateness of the words all contribute to diction, which is part of a writing or speaking **style.**

- Hey, buddy! What's up?

- Hi, how're you doing?

- Hello, how are you?

- Good morning. How are you?

These four phrases all function as greetings. You would use each one, however, in very different situations. This word choice is called *diction,* and for different situations, you use different *levels of diction.*

Note-taking Here are some examples of levels of diction. Fill in the blanks with the opposite level of diction.

Level of Diction	Formal	Informal
Example	Good afternoon. Welcome to the meeting.	

Level of Diction	Ornate	Plain
Example		I need more coffee.

Level of Diction	Abstract	Concrete
Example		The mayor has asked for volunteers to pick up litter along the river next Saturday.

Level of Diction	Technical	Ordinary
Example	My brother is employed as a computer system design manager.	

Level of Diction	Sophisticated	Down-to-Earth
Example	Thank you very much. I appreciate your help.	

Level of Diction	Old-fashioned	Modern/Slangy
Example	Yes, it is I. Shall we sample the bill of fare?	

With close friends and family, most of your conversations will probably be informal, down-to-earth, even slangy. In school or in elegant surroundings, or among people you do not know well or people who are much older than you, you will probably choose language that is more formal. Sometimes the distinctions can be subtle, so try to take your cues from others and adjust your diction accordingly.

Note-taking Complete the following activities.

1. Make a list of words and phrases that would be appropriate for you to use as you escort a visiting school board member on a tour of your school.

_____

_____

_____

_____

2. Make a second list of words and phrases that you might use as you escort your teenage cousin on a tour of your school.

_____

_____

_____

_____

3. Study the following pairs of phrases. Then, identify one phrase in each pair as formal and the other as informal.

	Phrase	Formal / Informal	Phrase	Formal / Informal
1.	Hello, it's nice to meet you.		How do you do?	
2.	What is your opinion, Professor Hughes?		What do you think, Pat?	
3.	Please accept my deepest sympathy.		That's too bad.	
4.	Sorry. I didn't hear you.		I beg your pardon. Please repeat the question.	
5.	I don't get it.		I do not quite understand.	

4. List several common phrases. Then, identify whether each phrase is formal or informal, and give its formal or informal opposite.

	Phrase	Formal / Informal	Phrase	Formal / Informal
1.				
2.				
3.				
4.				
5.				

Etiquette: Using the Vocabulary of Politeness

No matter how many words you know, the way you use those words will impact how your friends, your family, your teachers, and all the people in your life react to you. For almost every interaction you have, choosing a vocabulary of politeness will help you avoid conflicts and communicate your ideas, thoughts, and feelings effectively to others.

When in doubt, always choose the polite word or phrase.

Formal or Informal?

Polite vocabulary does not have to be formal. In fact, the definition of the word *polite* is "behaving or speaking in a way that is correct for the social situation." People often think that *etiquette*, which consists of rules for polite behavior, applies only in formal situations. All interactions with other people, though, should follow the etiquette that is appropriate for the situation.

Etiquette for Classroom Discussions

Use the following sentences starters to help you express yourself clearly and politely in classroom discussions.

Use these sentence starters to help you express yourself clearly in different classroom situations.

To Express an Opinion
I think that _____.
I believe that _____.
It seems to me that _____.
In my opinion, _____.

To Agree

I agree with _____ that _____.
I see what you mean.
That's an interesting idea.
My idea is similar to _____'s idea.
I hadn't thought of that.

To Disagree

I don't completely agree with _____ because _____.
My opinion is different from yours.
My idea is slightly different from yours.
I see it a different way.

To Report the Ideas of a Group

We agreed that _____.
We concluded that _____.
We had a similar idea.
We had a different approach.

To Predict or Infer

I predict that _____.
Based on _____, I infer that _____.
I hypothesize that _____.

To Paraphrase

So you are saying that _____.
In other words, you think _____.
What I hear you saying is _____.

To Offer a Suggestion

Maybe we could _____.
What if we _____.
Here's something we might try.

To Ask for Clarification

Could you explain that another way?
I have a question about that.
Can you give me another example of that?

To Ask for a Response

What do you think?
Do you agree?
What answer did you get?

Practice With a partner, discuss an issue about which you disagree. At the end of five minutes, list five or more polite words or phrases that you used to communicate your conflicting opinions.

_____

_____

Use this page to write down academic words you come across in other subjects, such as social studies or science. When you are reading your textbooks, you may find words that you need to learn. Following the example, write down the word, the part of speech, and an explanation of the word. You may want to write an example sentence to help you remember the word.

dissolve *verb* to make something solid become part of a liquid by putting it in a liquid and mixing it

The sugar *dissolved* in the hot tea.

_____

_____

_____

_____

_____

_____

_____

_____

_____

_____

_____

_____

_____

_____

_____

_____

Use these flash cards to study words you want to remember. The words on this page come from Unit 1. Cut along the dotted lines on pages V25 through V32 to create your own flash cards or use index cards. Write the word on the front of the card. On the back, write the word's part of speech and definition. Then, write a sentence that shows the meaning of the word.

fervent	grievous	redress
sentinel	compassionate	rapture
admonish	rancor	winsomeness

adjective having or showing great warmth of feeling There were *fervent* arguments both for and against school uniforms.	*adjective* causing sorrow; hard to bear The earthquake was a *grievous* disaster.	*noun* compensation, as for a wrong The courts provide the means of *redress* for victims of crime.
noun person or animal that guards The German shepherd sat by the door like a *sentinel*.	*adjective* sympathizing; pitying The *compassionate* man adopted the kitten that had been abandoned.	*noun* joy; great pleasure He stared in *rapture* at his baby son.
verb advise; caution The lifeguard *admonished* Hal never to swim alone.	*noun* ill will Jim and Carla ended their relationship with no *rancor*.	*noun* charm; delightfulness The young girl's smile was an example of *winsomeness*.

Use these flash cards to study words you want to remember. Cut along the dotted lines on pages V29 through V32 to create your own flash cards or use index cards. Write the word on the front of the card. On the back, write the word's part of speech and definition. Then, write a sentence that shows the meaning of the word.

The green flash cards for study words you want to remember. Cut along the dotted lines on these cards. Fold to divide each into a flash card. Write the study word's definition on the front of the card. On the back, write a sentence that shows the meaning of the word.

Use these flash cards to study words you want to remember. Cut along the dotted lines on pages V29 through V32 to create your own flash cards or use index cards. Write the word on the front of the card. On the back, write the word's part of speech and definition. Then, write a sentence that shows the meaning of the word.

Use a fold-a-list to study the definitions of words. The words on this page come from Unit 1. Write the definition for each word on the lines. Fold the paper along the dotted line to check your definition. Create your own fold-a-lists on pages V35 through V38.

reparation _____

_____

solace _____

_____

purge _____

_____

writhing _____

_____

massive _____

_____

loathsome _____

_____

innumerable _____

_____

stranded _____

_____

solicitous _____

_____

garnished _____

_____

Fold →

Write the word that matches the definition on each line.
Fold the paper along the dotted line to check your work.

something making up for
a wrong or an injury

_____

comfort; relief

_____

purify; cleanse

_____

making twisting or
turning motions

_____

big and solid; bulky

_____

disgusting

_____

too many to count

_____

forced into shallow
water or onto a beach;
left helpless

_____

showing care or concern

_____

Fold →

decorated; trimmed

_____

Write the words you want to study on this side of the page.
Write the definitions on the back. Then, test yourself. Fold
the paper along the dotted line to check your answers.

Word: _____

_____

Word: _____

_____

Word: _____

_____

Word: _____

_____

Word: _____

_____

Word: _____

_____

Word: _____

_____

Word: _____

_____

Word: _____

_____

Word: _____

_____

Fold

© Pearson Education

Write the word that matches the definition on each line.
Fold the paper along the dotted line to check your work.

Definition: _____

Definition: _____

Definition: _____

Definition: _____

Definition: _____

Definition: _____

Definition: _____

Definition: _____

Definition: _____

Definition: _____

Fold ←

Write the words you want to study on this side of the page. Write the definitions on the back. Then, test yourself. Fold the paper along the dotted line to check your answers.

Word: _____

_____

Word: _____

_____

Word: _____

_____

Word: _____

_____

Word: _____

_____

Word: _____

_____

Word: _____

_____

Word: _____

_____

Word: _____

_____

Word: _____

_____

Fold →

VOCABULARY FOLD-A-LIST

Write the word that matches the definition on each line.
Fold the paper along the dotted line to check your work.

Definition: _____

Definition: _____

Definition: _____

Definition: _____

Definition: _____

Definition: _____

Definition: _____

Definition: _____

Definition: _____

Definition: _____

Fold ←

© Pearson Education

The list on these pages presents words that cause problems for many people. Some of these words are spelled according to set rules, but others follow no specific rules. As you review this list, check to see how many of the words give you trouble in your own writing. Then, add your own commonly misspelled words on the lines that follow.

abbreviate	auxiliary	census	deficient
absence	awkward	certain	definitely
absolutely	bandage	changeable	delinquent
abundance	banquet	characteristic	dependent
accelerate	bargain	chauffeur	descendant
accidentally	barrel	chief	description
accumulate	battery	clothes	desert
accurate	beautiful	coincidence	desirable
ache	beggar	colonel	dessert
achievement	beginning	column	deteriorate
acquaintance	behavior	commercial	dining
adequate	believe	commission	disappointed
admittance	benefit	commitment	disastrous
advertisement	bicycle	committee	discipline
aerial	biscuit	competitor	dissatisfied
affect	bookkeeper	concede	distinguish
aggravate	bought	condemn	effect
aggressive	boulevard	congratulate	eighth
agreeable	brief	connoisseur	eligible
aisle	brilliant	conscience	embarrass
all right	bruise	conscientious	enthusiastic
allowance	bulletin	conscious	entrepreneur
aluminum	buoyant	contemporary	envelope
amateur	bureau	continuous	environment
analysis	bury	controversy	equipped
analyze	buses	convenience	equivalent
ancient	business	coolly	especially
anecdote	cafeteria	cooperate	exaggerate
anniversary	calendar	cordially	exceed
anonymous	campaign	correspondence	excellent
answer	canceled	counterfeit	exercise
anticipate	candidate	courageous	exhibition
anxiety	capacity	courteous	existence
apologize	capital	courtesy	experience
appall	capitol	criticism	explanation
appearance	captain	criticize	extension
appreciate	career	curiosity	extraordinary
appropriate	carriage	curious	familiar
architecture	cashier	cylinder	fascinating
argument	catastrophe	deceive	February
associate	category	decision	fiery
athletic	ceiling	deductible	financial
attendance	cemetery	defendant	fluorescent

foreign	minuscule	proceed	_____
fourth	miscellaneous	prominent	
fragile	mischievous	pronunciation	_____
gauge	misspell	psychology	
generally	mortgage	publicly	_____
genius	naturally	pursue	
genuine	necessary	questionnaire	_____
government	neighbor	realize	
grammar	neutral	really	_____
grievance	nickel	recede	
guarantee	niece	receipt	_____
guard	ninety	receive	
guidance	noticeable	recognize	_____
handkerchief	nuisance	recommend	
harass	obstacle	reference	_____
height	occasion	referred	
humorous	occasionally	rehearse	_____
hygiene	occur	relevant	
ignorant	occurred	reminiscence	_____
immediately	occurrence	renowned	
immigrant	omitted	repetition	_____
independence	opinion	restaurant	
independent	opportunity	rhythm	_____
indispensable	optimistic	ridiculous	
individual	outrageous	sandwich	_____
inflammable	pamphlet	satellite	
intelligence	parallel	schedule	_____
interfere	paralyze	scissors	
irrelevant	parentheses	secretary	_____
irritable	particularly	siege	
jewelry	patience	solely	_____
judgment	permanent	sponsor	
knowledge	permissible	subtle	_____
lawyer	perseverance	subtlety	
legible	persistent	superintendent	_____
legislature	personally	supersede	
leisure	perspiration	surveillance	_____
liable	persuade	susceptible	
library	phenomenal	tariff	_____
license	phenomenon	temperamental	
lieutenant	physician	theater	_____
lightning	pleasant	threshold	
likable	pneumonia	truly	_____
liquefy	possess	unmanageable	
literature	possession	unwieldy	_____
loneliness	possibility	usage	
magnificent	prairie	usually	_____
maintenance	precede	valuable	
marriage	preferable	various	_____
mathematics	prejudice	vegetable	
maximum	preparation	voluntary	_____
meanness	previous	weight	
mediocre	primitive	weird	_____
mileage	privilege	whale	
millionaire	probably	wield	_____
minimum	procedure	yield	

Using the Personal Thesaurus

The Personal Thesaurus provides students with the opportunity to make connections between words academic words, familiar words, and even slang words. Students can use the Personal Thesaurus to help them understand the importance of using words in the proper context and also avoid overusing words in their writing.

Use the following routine to foster frequent use of the Personal Thesaurus.

1. After students have read a selection or done some writing, have them turn to the Personal Thesaurus.

2. Encourage students to add new entries. Help them to understand the connection between their personal language, which might include familiar words and even slang, and the academic language of their reading and writing.

3. Call on volunteers to read a few entries aloud. Point out that writers have many choices of words when they write. Help students see that audience often determines word choice.

N

nice

admirable

friendly

agreeable

pleasant

cool

phat

A

B

C

D

E

© Pearson Education

F

G

H

I

J

K

L

M

N

O

P

Q

R

S

T

U

V

W

X

Y

Z

(Acknowledgments continued from page ii)

Penguin Books Ltd., London
"Prologue" from *The Canterbury Tales* by Geoffrey Chaucer, translated by Nevill Coghill (Penguin Classics 1951, Fourth revised edition 1977). Copyright 1951 by Nevill Coghill. Copyright © the Estate of Nevill Coghill, 1958, 1960, 1975, 1977.

Smithsonian Institution
"Recasting Shakespeare's Stage" by Eric Jaffe from *www.smithsonianmag.com/arts-culture/globe.html*. Copyright 2008 Smithsonian Institution.

Viking Penguin, Inc.
"Araby", from *Dubliners* by James Joyce, copyright 1916 by B. W. Heubsch. Definitive text Copyright © 1967 by The Estate of James Joyce.

Note: Every effort has been made to locate the copyright owner of material reproduced on this component. Omissions brought to our attention will be corrected in subsequent editions.

PHOTO AND ART CREDITS

© Pearson Education